Immigration, Diversity, and Education

Immigration has long been a defining force in US society, enabling its growth and prosperity. Yet, its contributions to the vitality of the nation are matched by the challenging and divisive issues it generates, particularly within the field of education. Today's debate on immigration, both legal and illegal, is closely linked to the shifting racial and ethnic profile of the US.

This edited volume presents an overview of research and policy issues pertaining to children from birth to 10 who are first- and second-generation immigrants to the US, as well as native-born children of immigrants. The contributors offer interdisciplinary perspectives on recent developments and research findings on children of immigrants. By accessibly presenting research findings and policy considerations in the field, this collection lays the foundation for changes in child and youth policies associated with the shifting ethnic, cultural, and linguistic profile of the US population.

Elena L. Grigorenko is Associate Professor of Child Studies, Epidemiology and Public Health, and Psychology at Yale University.

Ruby Takanishi is President of the Foundation for Child Development in New York City.

Immigration, Diversity, and Education

Edited by
Elena L. Grigorenko
Ruby Takanishi

NEW YORK AND LONDON

First published 2010
by Routledge
270 Madison Ave, New York, NY 10016

Simultaneously published in the UK
by Routledge
2 Park Square, Milton Park, Abingdon, Oxon OX14 4RN

Routledge is an imprint of the Taylor & Francis Group, an informa business

Typeset in Minion by Wearset Ltd, Boldon, Tyne and Wear

Library of Congress Cataloging-in-Publication Data
Immigration, diversity, and education / edited by Elena L. Grigorenko, Ruby Takanishi.

p.cm.
1. Children of immigrants–Education–United States. 2. Immigrants–United States–Social conditions. 3. Cultural pluralism–United States. I. Grigorenko, Elena L. II. Takanishi, Ruby.
LC3746.1625 2009
371.826'912–dc22 2009008562

ISBN10: 0-415-45627-4 (hbk)
ISBN10: 0-203-87286-X (ebk)

ISBN13: 978-0-415-45627-2 (hbk)
ISBN13: 978-0-203-87286-4 (ebk)

Contents

Preface

Elena L. Grigorenko

Edited volumes originate for different reasons and thus have different histories. Some are the results of conferences, some are the results of multiple convergent investigations on the same topic. This volume has its own history, reflecting, partially, the passion for working with immigrant children that emanates from the Foundation for Child Development (FCD; www.fcd-us.org), as well as the maturation of the research and careers of a group of scientists who have been supported or are supported now by the FCD's Young Scholars Program.

It is due to FCD's efforts—in particular to the vision, creativity, and persistence of the FCD's President Ruby Takanishi, FCD's Board of Directors, and FCD's staff members Annette Chin, Kimber Bogard, and Mark Bogosian—that the Foundation has had an opportunity to focus on issues of immigrant children in the US and now supports six cohorts of researchers across a variety of different fields to investigate these issues. Charissa Cheah, Dylan Conger, Robert Crosnoe, Elena Grigorenko, Ariel Kalil, Jin Li, Krista Perreira, Illiana Reyes, Selcuk Sirin, Yuuko Uchikoshi, and Jennifer Van Hook represent a larger group of scientists (www.fcd-us.org/programs/programs_show.htm?doc_id=447983) who are fortunate to have been supported by this program. However, being associated with this program does not only mean receiving financial support for one's research. It also means becoming a member of a broader network of professionals in different fields who are interested in the issue of immigration. This book is a product of such networking, triggered and stimulated by FCD. All other senior contributors to the book have worked with FCD on a variety of projects, have participated in events for FCD's young scholars, or have inspired the work of young scientists.

All in all, the volume is complete. To my knowledge, it is one of the very few (if any) comprehensive volumes on the status of immigrant children in the US. Ruby, all the authors of this book, and I sincerely hope that this volume will make a difference. And FCD's young scholars know that Ruby and FCD have already changed for the better the landscape of research and policies concerning the welfare and nurturing of immigrant children. Thank you, FCD, and thank you, Ruby!

Introduction

Ruby Takanishi

Immigration, or more accurately migration across national borders, is not a new phenomenon. For centuries, individuals and groups have intentionally, and sometimes unwillingly, left their homes to move to another place. When intentional, their goal has always been to seek a better life for themselves and their families. This remains the goal of migration today. Global migration can lead to diversity, innovation, and renewal in the receiving country, but it is too often accompanied by social conflict.

What has not changed is the fact that strangers to a new land are often not welcomed. But there are also instances in which the need for labor or social purposes—such as in the case of refugee groups—provide a welcoming policy context that can facilitate the integration of immigrants into a receiving country. Unfortunately, suspicion and discrimination against newcomers coexist with such policies.

Policy Contexts Count

As I write this introduction at the end of summer 2008, the US's official policy toward "illegal immigrants" is being expressed in raids on workplaces by the Immigration and Customs Enforcement (ICE) agency, leading to detention and deportation of immigrants. The impact of these raids on families and their children is beginning to be documented (Capps, Castañeda, Chaudry, & Santos, 2007). At the same time, anti-immigrant state and local policies have led to reports of immigrants leaving Arizona and Oklahoma, and moving to states with more hospitable policies for immigrants.

The extent of these within-US migrations and their impacts on the well-being of children and their families are also beginning to be examined. These policies are a significant context for research on the development of children of immigrants, a rapidly growing proportion of the child population. The ramifications of these policies on other children in receiving communities are beginning to be reported.

The encouraging findings of cross-national or international studies of migration is that national policies can make a difference in health, education, and labor force outcomes for immigrants and their children (Parsons & Smeeding, 2005; Smeeding, this volume). In the US, where policies regarding children, such as health and education, are largely formed at the state level, studies indicate that health outcomes for mothers and children vary by state policies regarding access to maternal and child health services (Kaushal, 2007).

In education, rigorous evaluation of the Tulsa (Oklahoma) PreKindergarten program, universally available to all children in that state, indicates that high-quality programs can make a significant difference in cognitive outcomes for second-generation immigrant children whose parents immigrated from rural Mexico (Gormley & Gayer, 2005). In contrast, studies based on a national sample of children beginning Kindergarten in 1998 indicate that Mexican-origin children are not only underrepresented in preKindergarten programs, but also start Kindergarten considerably behind their peers in mathematics (Crosnoe, 2006). Access to and participation in preKindergarten programs is related to maternal education, and access and availability of such programs (Hernandez, Denton, & Macartney, 2007). Tulsa Public Schools, because access to the preKindergarten program is open to all and free, provide an excellent test case of what high-quality preKindergarten experiences can boost the learning of children of immigrants, at least into the Kindergarten year.

A nation's public policies do matter in the lives of immigrants and their children. At this juncture in American history, however, comprehensive national immigration reform has failed. Debates at the national presidential and at the state levels have become, once again in our history, hot-button issues, often overshadowing more critical ones such as human capital investments in our nation's children. It is unlikely that comprehensive immigration reform will occur in the near future. This will constitute the context for the development of children living in immigrant families for the foreseeable future.

Child Well-Being in Immigrant Families Matters

When children of immigrants currently constitute about one-quarter of the nation's children (Hernandez et al., 2007), a proportion which is likely to grow according to the US Census, and when in states like California, one in two children born at the beginning of the 21st century are children of immigrants, young people who are second- and third-generation individuals are clearly a significant proportion of the nation's future human resources. Their well-being, particularly their health and education, and their own investments in their futures, constitute a shared responsibility between their families and the public sectors. In the very near future, they will form the prime workforce to support a large aging population (Hayes-Bautista, Schink, & Chapa, 1988), and a significant part of the nation's citizens. As a result, the people of the US have an enormous stake in their well-being.

But facts and reason do not historically prevail in the immigration debates, in the US and abroad. Every advanced economy in the world, especially those with growing older populations and declining youth populations, faces the challenge of coming to terms with the vital contributions that immigrants play in advanced economies; without immigrants and their children, countries in Europe, Asia, and the US cannot function very well. Their aging populations are already dependent on the integration of immigrants and their children into their economies.

While economic considerations are critical, they are not isolated from social relationships and forces in a society. The civic vitality of a country, how its members regard each other, and the absence of ethnic conflict are equally important. The existence of a good society rests on equality and fairness, and a sense of common purpose. History provides ample evidence of the need for constant vigilance to these values (Chua, 2004; Putnam, 2008) to foster social cohesion and order.

Research on All Children in Their Diversity is Essential

If these contextual considerations were not the only reasons for increasing our understanding of the development of children living in immigrant families, our fundamental knowledge of children's development requires attention to this growing and important group of the child population in the United States. By the year 2050 or earlier, they will be a significant part of the child population in the United States, and research must keep pace with their growth to understand what will be a majority of children of color. Anything less will compromise knowledge restricted to only a segment of all children.

Most of the chapters in this volume focus on children of immigrants in the United States. The research community has slowly focused its attention on this group, but most of the literature is primarily on older children or adolescents. This makes sense in the context of youth preparation for the workforce, and generally greater accessibility of adolescents as subjects of research.

Only within the past 10 years or so have researchers started to turn to children during their first decade of life (Birth to Age Nine). This is not a moment too soon, as education systems have discovered—how to educate children whose first language is not English is both a pedagogical and a political issue that has led to ballot initiatives in states to ban "bilingual education" in public schools.

Moreover, the challenges of conducting research on young children have always been with us, but the ante is increased when families are not conveniently found near research universities, and when anti-immigrant sentiment has intensified, especially in the aftermath of the World Trade Center attacks in September 2001. Families, particularly in specific religious and ethnic communities, have avoided contact with outside agencies, and with good reason (Sirin, this volume).

Thus, the young researchers, many of whom are represented as authors in this volume, have been bold and brave in conducting original data collection from immigrant families. Several—themselves first-generation immigrants or second-generation children from immigrant families—have second- or third-language competence that is a valuable asset in their research. Others have mined existing large datasets that include children of immigrants, such as the Early Childhood Longitudinal Study-Kindergarten Cohort (ECLS-K), noting the limitations with these existing datasets in good information about the generational status of the children.

Indeed, one of the most important contributions that future data collection can make is to have a clear definition of the generational status of the parents and children, and good methods for collecting such data (Takanishi, 2004). Without that information, knowledge about concepts such as "immigrant advantage" (also referred to as the "immigrants paradox"), the advantages that non-US-born children or children born to non-US-born/immigrant parents may have, is likely to be unresolved. When considered with a host of other variables such as poverty and parental education, does generational status matter and in what areas?

Much better data collection is needed regarding the circumstances of immigrant families (education of parents, income in country of origin, social class origins, country of origin) before they immigrated to the United States. It is not unusual still to see research reports that refer to immigrant families and their children, but do not document even the country of origin. Even on the dimension of country of origin, there can be significant differences in the life circumstances of immigrants before and after immigration. For example, Chinese immigrant families include those who are here for graduate education and those who are undocumented and those working in low-wage restaurants and garment factories (Cheah & Lee, this volume). For other groups, downward mobility despite high levels of education in their countries of origin, because of language problems and licensing requirements, creates new challenges when they enter the US economy. Whether and how these socioeconomic and educational factors affect children's well-being is not yet known.

Given the increasing diversity of the child and youth population in the United States (Hernandez et al., 2007), the formation of identity, and the intersections of ethnicity, gender, and age, remain underexamined. Is the United States moving toward what has been called "a post-racial society?" If so, how is this reflected in the child population? Given the racial and ethnic diversity of the United States, as a result of immigration, how children of today identify as part of a cultural or national group, and how that may change over time, is an important area of inquiry.

This has significant consequences for individuals, but also for social cohesion of a multiracial and ethnic society that is widely predicted by demographers. Efforts to increase respect for diversity and greater social integration must be informed by research on what is happening in classrooms and playgrounds, and in neighborhoods and informal settings. Yet most of our knowledge in this area was generated under different historical periods, and an understanding of what is happening today is urgently needed. The numbers of discriminated groups have increased, and religious intolerance has been broadened to reflect new groups that have come to the United States and European countries, traditionally characterized by the Judeo-Christian tradition, but no longer.

Overview of the Book

In editing the chapters of this volume, which constitute a first wave of studies on young children of immigrants at the beginning of the 21st century, I am impressed with how these studies are largely conducted within existing frameworks, theories, and methods of different disciplines for studying previous populations of children. The succeeding generations of studies must be shaped by a more comprehensive framework that takes into account national (and in some countries, state) policies that impact the daily lives of immigrant families and their children, and the influence of co-influential structures such as families and schools on the development of children. A greater emphasis must be placed on the phenomenology of teachers, parents, and children as they co-construct their experiences to better understand how each player sees their relationships.

By the very nature of the subject under study, the role of culture and cultural change, assimilation and accommodation, coping and adaptation, language development, and bias and discrimination are likely to be central to an emerging framework for studying the development of children living in immigrant families. Studies are likely to be bi-, if not multi-national. There is likely to be greater recognition of the countries of origin, and how experiences prior to immigration to the US influence the development of children once they are in the US. At the very least, this suggests that our existing frameworks for the study of child development are likely to be altered. Significantly, this promises that our ways of thinking about human development will be expanded.

Global migration is not new; what is new are the forces of technology and communications which now make it easier for individuals and groups to maintain contact with their home countries, and indeed, to contribute to changes in their countries of origin. A global society is a fact of life. Yet, we know very little about how two-way migration is influencing the lives of children of immigrants today and into the future as their countries, for example, China and India, gain in economic power and a reverse migration—both temporary and permanent—may occur.

The chapters in this volume document what is happening to immigrant families and their children at the beginning of the 21st century, largely in the United States. Together they constitute a good beginning, but studies that can illuminate our knowledge of human development in general, and how that knowledge can inform politics and practices specifically, remain to be generated by an emerging generation of scholars.

If I were to predict the future, these studies will be conducted by individuals who themselves are bicultural, and come from countries outside the US. They will be more likely to work both in the US and in their countries of origin, as well as others. Like the global society they are part of, they will bring to bear multiple frameworks on the study of child and adolescent development. These are exciting times for the study of diversity and human development.

New York
September 2008

References

Capps, R., Castañeda, R.M., Chaudry, A., & Santos, R. (2007). *Paying the price: The impact of immigration raids on America's children.* Washington, DC: A report by The Urban Institute for the National Council of La Raza.

Chua, A. (2004). *World on fire: How exporting free market democracy breeds ethnic hatred and global instability.* New York: Anchor Books.

Crosnoe, R. (2006). *Mexican roots, American schools. Helping children from Mexican immigrant families succeed.* Stanford, CA: Stanford University Press.

Gormley, W.T. & Gayer, T. (2005). Promoting school readiness in Oklahoma: An evaluation of Tulsa's pre-K program. *Journal of Human Resources, 40*(3), 533–558.

Hayes-Bautista, D.E., Schink, W., & Chapa, J. (1988). *The burden of support: The young Latino population in an aging American society.* Stanford, CA: Stanford University Press.

Hernandez, D.J., Denton, N.A., & Macartney, S.E. (2007). Demographic trends and the transition years. In R.C. Pianta, M.J. Cox, & K.L. Snow (Eds.), *School readiness and the transition to kindergarten in the era of accountability.* Baltimore, MD: Paul H. Brookes Publishing Co.

Hernandez, D.J., Denton, N.A., & Macartney, S.E. (in press). Early childhood education programs: Accounting for low enrollment in newcomer and native families. In M. Waters & R. Alba (Eds.), *The next generation: Immigrant youth and families in comparative perspective.* Ithaca, NY: Cornell University Press.

Kaushal, N., & Kaestner, R. (2007). Welfare reform and the health of immigrant children. *Journal of Immigrant and Minority Health, 9*(2), 699–722.

The Changing Faces of America's Children

Overall, from 1960 to 2000 the proportion of children in immigrant families tripled from 6% to 20%, and among this much larger fraction of children, those from regions of the world other than Europe and Canada expanded from only one in three (33%) to nine in ten (89%) (Hernandez & Darke, 1999). Thus, among all children, the proportion that lives in immigrant families from Latin America and the Caribbean, Asia, or Africa climbed from only 2% in 1960 to 18% in 2000.

The Rise of the New American Majority

Mainly as a result of immigration from regions other than Europe and Canada, the proportion of children aged 0–17 who are non-Hispanic White has fallen remarkably from about 78% in 1970 to 63% in 2000 (1970 calculated from Census Bureau estimates; www.census.gov/population/www/socdemo/hh-fam.html). This trend is projected by the US Census Bureau to continue, with non-Hispanic Whites accounting for only 50% of children aged 0–17 by 2030, and fewer still in the years that follow. Thus, less than 25 years from now, a new American majority will emerge among children (aged 0–17), a majority consisting of the current minorities. In fact, since younger children are the leading edge of this change, Census Bureau projections indicate for children aged 0–10 that by 2030 the proportion of non-Hispanic White will already have dipped below one-half to 49%.

Implications for All Americans

Because the shift away from a population that is predominantly non-Hispanic White is occurring at all ages, during the coming years our colleges and universities, other public and private institutions, and the economy will need to adjust accordingly. However, this demographic transformation is occurring more slowly for adults. Thus, when the baby-boom generation—born between 1946 and 1964—reaches the retirement ages of 66–84 years old, Census Bureau projections indicate that 72% of adults 65 years and older will be non-Hispanic White, compared to 56% for working-age adults, and 50% for children aged 0–17.

As a consequence, as the growing elderly population of the predominantly White baby-boom generation reaches retirement age and moves through the retirement years, it will increasingly depend for its economic support on the productive activities and civic participation (e.g., voting) of working-age adults who are members of racial and ethnic minorities. Many of these working-age adults will, as children, have grown up in immigrant families. Although the year 2030 may seem far into the future, it is important to keep in mind that children aged 0–10 in 2008 will be in the prime working ages of 22–32 in 2030. Immigrant and race-ethnic minority children of today will be providing economic resources to support the mainly non-Hispanic White baby boomers throughout their years of retirement.

Cultural Diversity Among Children of Immigrants

The cultural diversity of children of immigrants extends far beyond that reflected by their origins in the three major continental regions of Latin America and the Caribbean, Asia, and Africa, because there is enormous diversity not only across but also within continental regions. Children of immigrants have parents from an extraordinary number of countries, they speak a wide array of languages, and they vary greatly in their English-language fluency.

Immigrant Origins

The sample data from Census 2000 identify 133 distinct countries of origin for children (aged 0–17) in immigrant families. Because it is not possible within the confines of the chapter to discuss children with each of these origins separately, results presented here combine countries in the same regions that send smaller numbers of immigrant to the US to portray children with origins in a total of 30 separate country or region of origin groups. In addition, to reflect diversity that exists among children in native-born families (US-born children with only US-born parents in the home), results also are presented for nine distinct race-ethnic groups.

Attention often focuses on children with origins in Mexico, who account for 41% of children aged 0–10 in immigrant families. But the diversity of children in immigrant families is reflected in the fact that no other country/region group studied here accounts for more than 9% of the total.

Language Spoken at Home

The languages spoken in the homes of immigrants are almost as diverse as their countries/regions of origin. The sample data from Census 2000 identify 93 distinct languages spoken in the homes of children (aged 0–17) who live in immigrant families. Although the Census Bureau does not collect information about religion, it is clear that language intersects with religious and other aspects of cultural diversity in quite complex ways.

At the beginning of the 21st century, as was true a century earlier, the US is once again facing the challenges of integrating and educating children coming from homes where languages other than English are spoken and where cultural practices differ from those of the American mainstream. But the diversity of contemporary immigration is enormously greater than was true a century ago.

Immigrant Generation

Although children in immigrant families live with at least one immigrant parent and, therefore, often grow up in homes where a language other than English is spoken and with diverse cultural practices, most of these children are born in the US and are therefore American citizens.

Overall, a very large 86% of children (aged 0–10) in immigrant families are classified by demographers as second generation, because they have an immigrant parent but were themselves born in the US. The proportion is quite high for most countries/regions of origin, and falls below 75% in Census 2000 only for children with two origins discussed here. But even in these countries a majority was born in the US, at 69% for Thailand and 54% for the former Soviet Union.

In addition, nearly two-thirds of children in immigrant families (63%) have parents who have lived in the US for 10 years or more. Fewer than 60% of children in immigrant families in Census 2000 have a parent who lived in the US for less than 10 years only if they are Blacks from Africa (47%) or have origins in Japan (49%), China (58%), India (47%), Iraq (49%), Pakistan/Bangladesh (41%) or the former Soviet Union (41%).

Thus, a majority of children in immigrant families from most regions of the world have parents who have lived in the US 10 years or more, and many (one-fourth) have parents who are US citizens by virtue of being born in this country. These circumstances of children in immigrant families imply a high level of diversity beyond differences in country of origin, because most of these children and many parents have substantial exposure not only to the culture of their immigrant origins, but also to the culture of American society.

English-Language Fluency Among Children

In view of the facts that most children in immigrant families were born in the US, and that many have parents who are US-born or have lived in the US for a decade or more, it is not surprising that most children and their parents speak English, and that many report in Census 2000 that they speak English very well.

In Census 2000 only 32% of children aged 5–10 can be classified as limited-English-proficient insofar as their parents report that the children do not speak English very well. Thus, children in immigrant families are more than twice as likely to be fluent in spoken English (68%) as to be limited-English-proficient (32%). Only among the Hmong are more than half of children in immigrant families (65%) reported to be limited-English-proficient. The proportion does, however, reach one-third or more for children in immigrant families from Mexico (48%), Indochinese countries (32%–42%), China (39%), Dominican Republic (35%), Central America (34%), and the former Soviet Union (33%). However, the proportion falls below 10% only for children from Philippines (9%), and Jamaica and other English-speaking Caribbean countries (2%). Children who are limited-English-proficient may be especially likely to benefit from focused English-language training.

On the other hand, despite these noteworthy levels of limited English proficiency, larger proportions of children in immigrant families speak English fluently while also speaking another language at home, at 40% compared to 32% who are limited-English-proficient. The proportions speaking English fluently and another language at home are 43%–57% for Mexico, Central America, Cuba, Dominican Republic, Haiti, South America, China, Taiwan, Laos, India, Pakistan/Bangladesh, Afghanistan, Iran, Iraq, other West Asia, and the former Soviet Union. These children are already on a path that could lead to fluent bilingualism.

Overall, in Census 2000 between one-tenth and four-tenths of children aged 5–10 in most immigrant groups are limited-English-proficient, which can pose special challenges for the schools they attend. At the same time, between 40% and 60% of children in most immigrant groups are competent in their parents' language, but also speak English very well. If they are provided with the opportunity to maintain and develop bilingual speaking and literacy skills, children in immigrant families could become language emissaries connecting the US to nations throughout the world, including regions where the US has important economic and geopolitical interests, such as Latin America, China, and the Arabic-speaking and Persian-speaking nations of West Asia. Education policies and programs fostering bilingualism among children in immigrant families could provide a valuable competitive edge as the US seeks to position itself in the increasingly competitive global economy.

English-Language Fluency Among Parents

Parents with limited English proficiency are less likely than fluent English speakers to find well-paid full-time year-round jobs. They also may be less able to help their children study for subjects taught in English. Insofar as education, health, and social service institutions do not provide outreach in their country-of-origin language, parents may be cut off from access to programs important to their children and themselves. All together, about one-half of children in immigrant families live with a father (49%) or mother (50%) who is limited-English-proficient.

Policies to ensure outreach in country-of-origin languages by education, health, and social service organizations could help to ensure that children and families receive needed services. Moreover, expanded opportunities for English-language training for parents might not only enhance their economic opportunities and productivity in the US, but also foster the integration of parents and their children into English-speaking society. Two-generational family-literacy programs offer an especially promising vehicle for public policies to facilitate integration and foster the well-being of both children and parents in immigrant families.

Diversity in Family Living Arrangements

Most children in immigrant families live with two parents, and they often also have grandparents, other relatives, or nonrelatives in the home who can provide additional nurturance or economic resources to children and their families.

Two-Parent Families

The vast majority of children in immigrant families (86%) live with two parents, and this level is nearly this high for all immigrant groups studied here. The primary exceptions are children with origins in Dominican Republic, Haiti, Jamaica, other English-speaking Caribbean nations, and Cambodia, but even among these groups, from two-thirds to three-fourths (66%–74%) live with two parents. Among children in native-born families, about 84% of Whites live with two parents, which is less than among more than two-thirds of the immigrant groups studied here, while the proportion for other native groups is in the range of 64%–77% with the exception of Puerto Ricans born in Puerto Rico or with a parent born in Puerto Rico (52%), and Blacks in native-born families (43%).

Thus, for children in most immigrant and native-born groups, a large-to-enormous majority live with two parents. Insofar as children living with two parents tend, on average, to be somewhat advantaged in their educational success (Cherlin, 1999; McLanahan & Sandefur, 1994), many children in immigrant families benefit from this family strength.

Diversity in Parental Educational Attainments

Children in immigrant families are more diverse in their parental educational attainments across countries/regions of origin than for any other indicator discussed in this chapter. We begin by focusing on children with highly educated parents, and on those in native-born families to provide a basis for comparison, then turn to children whose parents have more limited formal education.

Parents Completing a Bachelor's Degree

The proportion of children with fathers completing a bachelor's degree is in the narrow range of 11% to 17% for most native-born groups. This jumps to the much higher levels of 32% for Whites and 45% for Asians in native-born families (results are similar for mothers, although the proportion completing college is somewhat lower than for fathers in most native-born and immigrant groups).

The proportion with a father who has completed college among children in immigrant families ranges from a low of 4% for Mexico to a high of 81% for Taiwan. Insofar as college-educated parents are well-positioned to help their children with school work, to negotiate with school teachers and administrators, and to provide guidance to their children regarding pathways to higher education, various groups of children in immigrant families differ enormously in the opportunity to benefit from these types of parental skills and knowledge.

Parents Not Graduating from High School

Children in native-born families are least likely to have a father who has not graduated from high school if they are Asian (6%), White (10%), or Hawaiian or other Pacific Islander (12%). The proportions for other native-born groups are in the much higher but narrow range of 19% to 24%, except for island-origin Puerto Ricans (35%). Among 15 of the 30 immigrant groups studied here, the proportion with a father not graduating from high school in the range of 3% to 16%, that is, similar to Asians, Whites, and Hawaiian or other Pacific Islanders in native-born families. The proportion rises to 19%–22%, that is, to the level of most native-born groups, for the five immigrant groups with origins in the Caribbean, South America, and China.

But children in the remaining 10 immigrant-origin groups are more likely, and often much more likely, to have fathers who have not graduated from high school: 27%–31% for Haiti, Thailand, and Vietnam; 36% for Iraq; 41%–46% for Dominican Republic, Cambodia, Laos, and the Hmong; and the extraordinary levels of 54% for Central America and 67% for Mexico.

Educational attainments are, however, even lower for many fathers in these 10 groups than is suggested by these results, because many have not only not graduated from high school, they also have completed no more than 8 years of school. About one in ten children in immigrant families from Haiti and Vietnam (9%–11%) have fathers who have completed no more than 8 years of school, and this rises to 16%–18% for Dominican Republic, Thailand, and Iraq, to 22%–26% for Cambodia and Laos, 29% for Central America, 35% for the Hmong, and 41% for Mexico. In fact, between 11% and 17% of children in four of these groups have fathers with no more than 4 years of schooling (Mexico, Central America, Cambodia, and Thailand), and this rises to 21% for Laos, and 32% for the Hmong.

Implications of Parental Educational Attainments

Sociological studies first found more than four decades ago that children whose parents complete fewer years of education tend, on average, to complete fewer years of school themselves, and to have lower-paying jobs when they enter the adult labor force (Blau & Duncan, 1967; Featherman & Hauser, 1978; Sewell & Hauser, 1975; Sewell, Hauser, & Wolf, 1980). Parents with educational attainments reaching only the elementary level may be especially limited in the knowledge and experience needed to help their children succeed in school. Immigrant parents often have high educational aspirations for their children (Hernandez & Charney, 1998; Kao, 1999; Rumbaut, 1999), but may know little about the US education system, particularly if they have completed only a few years of school.

Parents with little schooling may, therefore, be less comfortable with schoolwork, and less able to effectively work with teachers and education administrators on behalf of their children. It may be especially important for educators to focus attention on the needs of children in immigrant and native-born families who are most likely to have parents who have completed no more than elementary school or who have not graduated from high school.

Diversity in Parental Employment

Fathers' Employment

Children in most immigrant and native-born groups benefit from the strong work ethic reflected in high levels of fathers' employment. The proportions in Census 2000 with fathers who worked during the previous year for the immigrant and native groups as a whole were, respectively, 93% and 96%. Moreover the proportion was at least 90% for all except seven of immigrant groups, and it was as low as 80%–83% only for children with origins in Cambodia and Thailand, and the Hmong.

Despite this strong work ethic, many children live with fathers who cannot find full-time year-round work. For most groups, 15%–29% of children have fathers not working full-time year-round, but this rises to 30%–40% for children in native-born families who are Black, island-origin Puerto Rican, Hawaiian or other Pacific Islander, or Native American, and for children in immigrant families who have origins in Mexico, Central America, Dominican Republic, Haiti, Indochina (Cambodia, Laos, Thailand, and the Hmong), Pakistan/Bangladesh, Afghanistan, Iraq, the former Soviet Union, and Blacks from Africa.

Nine of these 13 immigrant groups (excluding Pakistan/Bangladesh, Afghanistan, former Soviet Union, and Blacks from Africa) are also among the groups most likely at 27% or more to have fathers who have not graduated from high school, and 11 of these 13 immigrant groups (excluding only Pakistan/Bangladesh and Blacks from Africa) are among those most likely at 43% or more to have fathers who are limited in their English proficiency.

Mothers' Employment

Although children in immigrant families are 15% less likely than those in native-born families to have mothers who work (58% vs. 73%), at least half of children in most groups have mothers who worked during the previous year. Even among the six immigrant groups with fewer working mothers, the proportions were still substantial, at 46%–49% for Japan, Afghanistan, Iraq, Israel/Palestine, and other West Asia, but somewhat lower at 34% for a single origin region, Pakistan/Bangladesh.

Diversity in Poverty Rates

Children with poverty-level incomes often lack resources for decent housing, food, clothing, books, and other educational resources, childcare/early education, and healthcare. Children from low-income families also tend to experience a variety of negative developmental outcomes, including less success in school, lower educational attainments, and earning lower incomes during adulthood (Duncan & Brooks-Gunn, 1997; McLoyd, 1998; Sewell & Hauser, 1975). Poverty rates merit considerable attention because extensive research documents that poverty has greater negative consequences than either limited mother's education or living in a one-parent family (Duncan & Brooks-Gunn, 1997; McLoyd, 1998).

It is not surprising that children in groups where many parents have limited educational attainments, work less than full-time year-around, and earn low hourly wages are also among the groups experiencing high poverty rates. The official poverty rate for children in native-born families is 8%–9% for Whites and Asians, but this doubles or triples to 18%–26% for Mexicans, Other Hispanics, Hawaiian and other Pacific Islanders, and Native Americans, and climbs still higher to 29%–36% for Blacks and Puerto Ricans.

The official poverty rate for children in immigrant families is as low or lower than the rates for Whites and Hispanics among only seven immigrant groups and are somewhat higher at 12%–16% for children with origins in Cuba, Jamaica, South America, other English-speaking Caribbean, South America, China, and Whites from Africa. Poverty climbs to the level of many native-born minority groups (17%–28%) for children with immigrant origins in Central American, Haiti, Laos, Thailand, Vietnam, Pakistan/Bangladesh, Afghanistan, Iraq, Israel/Palestine, other West Asia, former Soviet Union, and Blacks from Africa, and still higher to 31%–32% for children with origins in Mexico, Dominican Republic, and Cambodia, and to 38% for the Hmong.

Although the official poverty rate is most commonly used to assess economic need, it has come under increasing criticism because it has not been updated since 1965 for increases in the real standard of living (Citro & Michael, 1995; Hernandez, Denton, &

Macartney, 2007a). To provide a more complete picture of economic need for children, results are presented here for two alternatives that take into account the local cost of various goods and services (Bernstein, Brocht, & Spade-Aguilar, 2000; Boushey, Brocht, Gundersen, & Bernstein, 2001; Hernandez et al., 2007a).

The first alternative measure of economic need presented here is the "baseline" Basic Budget Poverty rate, which takes into account the local cost of food, housing, transportation for parents to commute to work, and "other necessities" such as clothing, personal-care items, household supplies, telephone, television, school supplies, reading materials, music, and toys. The second, more comprehensive, Basic Budget Poverty rate takes into account, in addition, the local cost of childcare/early education and healthcare, although it may somewhat overestimate the effect of the cost of childcare/early education and underestimate the effect of healthcare costs (Hernandez et al., 2007a).

The Baseline Basic Budget Poverty rate is only slightly higher than the official rate for children in native families who are White (12% vs. 9%) or Asian (14% vs. 8%), but the difference is much larger for immigrant and other native groups with official poverty rates of 15% or more. For example, the Baseline Basic Budget Poverty rate for children in immigrant families from Mexico is 48%, compared to an official poverty rate of 31%. In fact, for 10 immigrant origins the increases are at least three times greater (12% or more) than for Whites in native families, including four origins among whom the increases are at least five times greater (15%–18%) than for native Whites (Mexico, Central America, Dominican Republic, and Haiti).

The Baseline Basic Budget Poverty rates are 30% or more for children in native-born families in all race-ethnic groups except Whites and Asians, rising to a high of 40%–41% for Blacks and mainland-origin Puerto Ricans, and to 48% for Puerto Ricans who either were born in Puerto Rico or have a parent born in Puerto Rico. Baseline Basic Budget Poverty rates among children in immigrant families are 27%–38% for those with origins in Jamaica, other English-speaking Caribbean, South America, Laos, Thailand, Vietnam, Pakistan/Bangladesh, Afghanistan, Iraq, Israel/Palestine, other West Asia, former Soviet Union, and Blacks from Africa, and this rises to 41%–42% for Central America and Haiti, 48% for Mexico, and 51% for the Hmong.

But the Baseline Basic Budget Poverty measure does not take into account the cost of childcare/early childhood education, which is essential for many working parents, and which can have important beneficial consequences for educational success of children in elementary school and beyond. It also does not take into account the cost of health insurance, which can ensure timely access to preventive healthcare and to medical care for acute and chronic conditions, which in turn can affect the capacity of children to function effectively in school. A more comprehensive Basic Budget Poverty measure including these costs classifies about 3 in 10 (29%–30%) White and Asian children in native families as poor, compared to about one-half to seven-tenths (53%–70%) of children in other native race-ethnic groups. The immigrant groups with the highest levels of economic need using this measure are Jamaica, other English-speaking Caribbean, South America, Thailand, Vietnam, Pakistan/Bangladesh, Iraq, other West Asia, former Soviet Union, and Blacks from Africa (46%–56%), Central America, Haiti, Cambodia, Laos, and Afghanistan (62%–68%), Mexico and Dominican Republic (74%–76%), and the Hmong (82%).

health insurance for children in immigrant families, particularly those experiencing high poverty rates.

In addition, and importantly, while health-insurance coverage is a key determinant of access to healthcare, other circumstances of immigrant children and families can act as additional barriers to accessing and receiving needed healthcare, perhaps most notably English-language proficiency. Children and parents who are limited-English-proficient may have great difficulty communicating with healthcare providers, and various officials in health. Insofar as it is only the adolescents or children in the home who are fluent in English, the parents are not in a position to communicate with healthcare professionals on behalf of their children.

In fact, it may be the children who must act as the primary intermediary between family members and healthcare institutions, as well as educational, social service, justice, and other institutions. This role may be critical in helping immigrant families negotiate and integrate into the unfamiliar terrain of American society, but it can also lead to conflicts by undermining traditional parent–child roles and parental authority (Park, 2001, 2002; Portes & Rumbaut, 2001; Sung, 1987; Valenzuela, 1999; Zhou, 1998). Also, although children (and adolescents) may be fluent in everyday English, they may not have the technical vocabulary necessary either in English or in the father's origin-country language for effective contacts with health, social service, or legal organizations.

For this reason it may be essential that health and other organizations provide outreach and interpretive services in the home languages of children and their parents. Without these efforts, health and other organizations may be cutting themselves off from the rapidly growing client population of immigrant children and families.

Diversity in Early School Enrollment

Young children with origins in various regions and family migration circumstances experience quite different pre-K/nursery school enrollment rates (this section is drawn from Hernandez et al., 2007). The pre-K/nursery school enrollment rate for Whites in native families is 37% at age 3 and 61% at age 4. Four groups of young children in native families experience rates nearly this high or higher at ages 3 and/or 4 (Blacks, mainland-origin Puerto Ricans, Asians, and Native Hawaiian or other Pacific Islander), as do young children in immigrant families from Haiti, Jamaica, other English-speaking Caribbean islands, South America, several (mainly East) Asian countries, former Soviet Union and other Europe/Canada, and both Blacks and Whites from Africa.

But young children who experience much lower pre-K/nursery school enrollment rates include those in native families who are Mexican, island-origin Puerto Rican, or American Indian, and those in immigrant families from Mexico, Central America, Dominican Republic, Indochina, Pakistan/Bangladesh, and Iraq. The pre-K/nursery school enrollment rate gap between these groups and Whites in native families range between 4% and 21% at age 3 and these gaps (for any school) vary between 2% and 20% at age 4.

What accounts for the low enrollment rates of some groups? One possible reason sometimes cited, particularly for Hispanic immigrants, is more familistic cultural values leading parents to prefer that their children be cared for at home, rather than in formal educational settings by nonrelatives (Liang et al., 2000; Uttal, 1999). But alternative explanations include the following socioeconomic or structural factors (Takanishi, 2004; Hernandez, Denton, & Macartney, in press).

First, cost can be an insurmountable barrier for poor families. Because of limited funding, most low-income families eligible for childcare assistance do not receive such assistance (Mezey, Greenberg, & Schumacher, 2002). Second, parents with extremely limited educational attainments may not be aware that early-education programs are important and are used by most highly educated parents to foster their children's educational success. Third, in immigrant neighborhoods with many non-English speakers, there may be too few openings in early-education programs to accommodate the demand (Hill-Scott, 2005). Fourth, even if spaces are available, access may be limited for parents who are not proficient in English, because programs may not reach out to parents in their home language (Matthews & Ewen, 2006). Fifth, parents may hesitate to enroll their children in programs that are not designed and implemented in a culturally competent manner, especially if teachers lack a minimum capacity to communicate with children in the home language (Holloway et al., 1997; Shonkoff & Phillips, 2000).

Recent research indicates that socioeconomic or structural influences, especially family poverty, mother's education, and parental occupation, account for most or all of the enrollment gap separating children in immigrant and native-Mexican families and children in immigrant families from Central America and Indochina from White children in native families (Hernandez et al., in press). Depending on the age and the group, socioeconomic and structural factors account for at least half and perhaps all of the enrollment gap, while cultural influences account for no more than 14% of the gap for the Mexican groups, no more than 39% of the gap for Central Americans, and no more than 17% for the Indochinese.

These results may be surprising, especially for the Hispanics, but it is important to note that these estimates are consistent with the strong commitment to early education in contemporary Mexico, where universal enrollment at age 3 will become obligatory in 2008–2009 (OECD, 2006). In fact, in 2002–2003, 63% of children aged 4 in Mexico were enrolled in preschool, the same as the proportion for White children in native families in Census 2000 (OECD, 2006, p. 25, and Table1). Insofar as preschool is less costly in Mexico than in the US, and insofar as poverty for the Mexican immigrant group in the US is quite high, it is not surprising that the proportion enrolled in school for the immigrant Mexican group at age 4 in the US at 44% is substantially lower than the age 4 enrollment in Mexico at 63%.

In sum, familistic cultural values are sometimes cited as a plausible explanation for lower early-education enrollment rates among children in immigrant families than among White children in native families, but recent research indicates that socioeconomic and structural influences can account for at least 50% and for some groups essentially all the gap. Early-education programs have been found to promote school readiness and educational success in elementary school and beyond (Gormley et al., in press; Haskins & Rouse, 2005; Lynch, 2004). Research suggests that children with low family incomes and limited English proficiency may be most likely to benefit from early-education programs (Takanishi, 2004; Gormley & Gayer, 2005), but children in several groups challenged by these circumstances are less likely than Whites and the other groups noted above to be enrolled in early-education programs. Insofar as the socioeconomic and structural barriers can account for much or all the lower enrollment in early-education programs for these groups, public policies could be developed and implemented to ensure access to early education for these children.

Diversity in Completing High School

As children transition into adulthood, the extent of their educational success is reflected in the amount of schooling they complete. The proportion graduating from high school by ages 20–24 measures the extent to which they have successfully completed their secondary education. Because young adults are especially likely to be recent immigrants who may not have entered the US education system, it is important to distinguish between first-generation immigrants born outside the US, and the second generation born in the US.

For children who live with their parents, Census 2000 can be used to ascertain whether they are children of immigrants by looking at the parents' country of birth. But after age 17, increasingly large numbers of youth do not live with parents, and there is no separate question in Census 2000 about parents' place of birth if parents do not live in the household. Therefore, it is not possible to distinguish second-generation immigrants from those who are third generation or more. Fortunately, the Census Bureau's Current Population Survey (CPS) asks each person, including children, where both they and their parents were born. For this reason, CPS rather than Census 2000 data are presented here to compare first and second generation, to the third and later generation at ages 20–24. Because the CPS sample size is much smaller than Census 2000, CPS data for 2001–2005 are combined and report on a smaller number of race-ethnic and immigrant-origin groups than are reported for most indicators in this chapter.

Among young adults in 2005 from Mexico, 70% are first-generation immigrants, compared to only 15% among children aged 0–10 in immigrant families from Mexico. Thus, many first-generation young adults from Mexico immigrated during adolescence or early adulthood. Because 8 years of education is standard in Mexico, few first-generation immigrants (44%) have graduated from high school. These young adults should not be considered dropouts from the US education system, because many probably never entered the US system. Education policies for first-generation immigrants with little or no experience in US schools must address a very different set of issues than policies for immigrants who arrived at younger ages and obtained most or all of their education in the US.

The second generation presents a mixed picture. On one hand, 78% of second-generation Mexicans graduated from high school, much higher than the 44% graduating among the first generation. It is also encouraging that the second-generation graduation rate is similar to that of the third and later generations (80%). However, it is a concern that the high school dropout rate for the second generation and for the third and later generations is a high 20%–22%, a level more than twice the 9% dropout rate for third- and later-generation Whites, and similar to the high level experienced by Native Americans (23%) and native-born Blacks (19%).

High school graduation rates among first-generation immigrants from the Dominican Republic, Haiti, Central America, and South America are higher than among first-generation immigrants from Mexico, but much lower than among the native White group, while graduation rates of young first-generation adults from Japan, Korea, China, Philippines, Indochina, India, other West Asia, former Soviet Union, other Europe and Canada, and Blacks from Africa reach or exceed those of native Whites.

The proportion graduating from high school among the second generation with origins in Dominican Republic is similar to the level for the second generation with origins in Mexico. The graduation rate for the second generation with origins in Central America is slightly higher, but it does not reach the level of native-born Whites. The proportion completing high school among the second generation with origins in Cuba, other English-speaking Caribbean, South America, and the other countries/ regions listed above reach or exceed the overall level of third- and later-generation Whites.

Children of Immigrants are Dispersed Across the US

Children in immigrant families are dispersed widely across the US. Many immigrants live in the largest metropolitan areas, but they also live in large and growing numbers in many smaller metropolitan areas, and they represent an important component of the population in the rural portions of most states.

Immigrants are concentrated in large cities. More than one-half (54%) of children in immigrant families live in the 10 largest Consolidated Metropolitan Statistical Areas (CMSAs), compared to only one-quarter (25%) of children in native-born families. Although children in immigrant families generally account for a larger proportion of all children in the central cities of these CMSAs than in the suburbs, this is not the case in two of the 10 largest CMSAs (Washington–Baltimore and Detroit).

Children in immigrant families also account for 20% or more of all children in 76 out of 318 smaller metropolitan areas, and for 10% or more in an additional 81. Although 10%–15% may seem small, the average student–teacher ratio in public, primary, middle, and high schools across the US (excluding Massachusetts and Tennessee) is in the range of 14.8–16.0 (National Center for Education Statistics, 2002). Thus, the average classroom will include at least one child of an immigrant in places where 10%–15% live in immigrant families.

In the rural regions of many states the proportion of all children who live in immigrant families tends to be lower, but it is 5% or more in 25 states. This number is large enough that, on average, every second classroom will include a child of an immigrant, and thus the average teacher might expect to have a child from an immigrant family in class every second year. This includes many states not often viewed as immigrant destinations, including states in the west (Alaska, Idaho, Utah, Wyoming), the Midwest (Kansas, Minnesota, Nebraska), the south (Georgia, North Carolina), and the northeast (Connecticut, Delaware, New Hampshire, Rhode Island).

Conclusions

The enormous increase in the number and diversity of children in immigrant families since 1960 is leading to a demographic transformation in which non-Hispanic Whites will constitute a minority of less than half of children within 25 years. Children of immigrants have origins in more than 130 countries and their families speak more than 90 languages, and as of 2005 they account for nearly one of every four (24%) children aged 0–10. This unprecedented cultural diversity presents educational, social, and economic institutions with a historically unique array of opportunities and challenges.

New immigrants have always come with the promise of renewal. They arrive in America with the strong desire and determination to succeed, to ensure a better life for themselves and their children. Education is a key to success in America, and immigrants have high educational aspirations for their children. They also come with strong two-parent families and a vibrant work ethic, and they often put down roots in their local communities by purchasing homes for their families. The vast majority of children in immigrant families are American citizens because they were born here, yet their diverse languages and emerging bilingualism represent an extraordinary cultural resource as the US seeks to position itself in the increasingly competitive and multilingual global economy.

But there are challenges. Many children in immigrant families have highly educated parents who can earn high incomes in the US, and who are well-positioned by their own experiences and financial resources to foster the success of their children in the American education system. But many others have parents with limited English skills and educational attainments, who cannot find full-time year-round work, who earn low incomes, and who are therefore less able to help their children with school work, less able to negotiate with schools and other social and economic institutions on behalf of their children, and less able to pay for high-quality early-education programs, health insurance, and other resources that will foster their children's success.

Financial resources are essential, and children in immigrant families who are most likely to have parents with incomes too low to lift their families out of poverty include those with origins in the western hemisphere (Mexico, Central America, South America, Dominican Republic, Haiti, other Caribbean islands), Southeast Asia (Indochina), West Asia (Pakistan/Bangladesh, Afghanistan, Iraq, Israel/Palestine), the former Soviet Union, and Blacks from Africa. Taken together, children with these origins account for nearly three-fourths (72%) of children aged 0–10 in immigrant families in 200, and they account for one of every seven children (14%) in the US.

Children in immigrant families from Central America (El Salvador, Guatemala, Nicaragua), Southeast Asia (Cambodia, Laos, Thailand, Vietnam, the Hmong), and West Asia (Afghanistan, Iraq) have parents who have fled war-torn countries, and those from the former Soviet Union are often political refugees, while others come from Mexico which has long been an important source of labor for key industries, or they come from countries with extremely difficult economic or political situations (Dominican Republic, Haiti, Blacks from Africa). These children and families confront serious challenges, and they deserve access to opportunities that will allow them to succeed.

The predominantly non-Hispanic White baby-boom generation will depend increasingly, as it ages, on the political support and productive activities of the new American majority when they reach adulthood, and many of them will as children have grown up in immigrant families. America cannot afford to ignore children of immigrants, or to let them fall behind as they seek to integrate and succeed in school and in life. It is in the self-interest of all Americans that we make the public investments in education, health, and other services that the children of the new American majority require to thrive and succeed.

Acknowledgement

Adapted by permission of the publisher. Planta, R. (2007). *School readiness and the transition to kindergarten in the era of accountability* (pp. 234–235). Baltimore, MD: Paul H. Brookes Publishing Co., Inc.

References

Archibald, R.C. (2008) February 12. Arizona seeing signs of flight by immigrants. *New York Times*, Section A, p. 13.

Bernstein, J., Brocht, C., & Spade-Aguilar, M. (2000). *How much is enough? Basic family budgets for working families*, Washington, DC: Economic Policy Institute.

Blake, J. (1985). Number of siblings and educational mobility. *American Sociological Review, 50*(1), 84–94.

Blake, J. (1989). *Family size and achievement.* Berkeley, CA: University of California Press.

Blau, P.M., & Duncan, O.D. (1967). *The American occupational structure.* New York: Wiley.

Boushey, H., Brocht, C., Gundersen, B., & Bernstein, J. (2001). *Hardships in America: The real story of working families*, Washington, DC: Economic Policy Institute.

Capps, R., Kenney, G., & Fix, M. (2003). Health insurance coverage of children in mixed-status immigrant families. *Snapshots of America's children, No. 12.* Washington, DC: The Urban Institute.

Capps, R., Castañeda, R.M., Chaudry, A., & Santos, R. (2007). *Paying the price: The impact of immigration raids on America's children.* Washington, DC: National Council of La Raza.

Cherlin, A.J. (1999). Going to extremes: Family structure, children's well-being, and social sciences. *Demography, 36*(4), 421–428.

Citro, C.F., & Michael, R.T. (Eds.). (1995). *Measuring poverty: A new approach.* Washington, DC: National Academy Press.

Duncan, G.J., & Brooks-Gunn, J. (Eds.). (1997). *Consequences of growing up poor.* New York: Russell Sage Foundation.

Featherman, D.L., & Hauser, R.M. (1978). *Opportunity and change.* New York: Academic Press.

Fix, M., & Passel, J. (1999). *Trends in noncitizens' and citizens' use of public benefits following welfare reform: 1994–97.* Washington, DC: The Urban Institute.

Fix, M., & Zimmerman, W. (1995). When should immigrants receive benefits? In I.V. Sawhill (Ed.), *Welfare reform: An analysis of the issues* (pp. 69–72). Washington, DC: The Urban Institute.

Gormley, W.T., & Gayer, T. (2005). Promoting school readiness in Oklahoma: An evaluation of Tulsa's pre-k program. *Journal of Human Resources, 40*(3), 533–558.

Hernandez, D.J. (1986). Childhood in sociodemographic perspective. In R.H. Turner & J.F. Short, Jr. (Eds.), *Annual review of sociology, volume 12* (pp. 159–180). Palo Alto, CA: Annual Reviews.

Hernandez, D.J., & Charney, E. (Eds.). (1998). *From generation to generation: The health and well-being of children in immigrant families.* Washington, DC: National Academy Press.

Hernandez, D.J., & Darke, K. (1999). The well-being of immigrant children, native-born children with immigrant parents, and native-born children with native-born parents. In *Trends in the well-being of America's children and youth: 1998* (pp. 421–543). Washington, DC: US Department of Health and Human Services.

Hernandez, D.J., Denton, N.A., & Macartney, S.E. (2007a). Child poverty in the U.S.: A new family budget approach with comparison to European countries. In H. Wintersberger, L. Alanen, T. Olk, & J. Qvortrup (Eds.), *Childhood, generational order and the welfare state: Exploring children's social and economic welfare, Volume 1 of COST A19: Children's welfare* (pp. 109–140). Odense: University Press of Southern Denmark.

Hernandez, D.J., Denton, N.A., & Macartney, S.E. (2007b). Demographic trends and the transition years. In R.C. Pianta, M.J. Cox, & K.L. Snow (Eds.). *School readiness and the transition to kindergarten in the era of accountability* (pp. 217–381). Baltimore, MD: Paul H. Brookes Publishing Co.

Hernandez, D.J., Denton, N.A., & Macartney, S.E. (in press). Early childhood education programs: Accounting for low enrollment in newcomer and native families. In M. Waters & R. Alba (Eds.), *The next generation: Immigrant youth and families in comparative perspective.* Ithaca, NY: Cornell University Press.

Hill-Scott, K. (2005). *Facilities technical report.* Los Angeles: First 5 LA.

Holloway, S., & Fuller, B. (1999). *Through my own eyes: Single mothers and the cultures of poverty.* Cambridge, MA: Harvard University Press.

Kao, G. (1999). Psychological well-being and educational achievement among immigrant youth. In D.J. Hernandez (Ed.), *Children of immigrants: Health, adjustment, and public assistance* (pp. 410–477). Washington, DC: National Academy Press.

Liang, X., Fuller, B., & Singer J.D. (2000). Ethnic differences in child care selection: The influence of family structure, parental practices, and home language. *Early Childhood Research Quarterly, 15*(3), 357–384.

Matthews, H., & Ewen D. (2006). *Reaching all children? Understanding early care and education participation among immigrant families.* Washington, DC: Center for Law and Social Policy.

McLanahan, S., & Sandefur, G. (1994). *Growing up with a single parent: What hurts, what helps.* Cambridge, MA: Harvard University Press.

McLoyd, V. (1998). Socioeconomic disadvantage and child development. *American Psychologist, 53*(2), 185–204.

Mezey, J., Greenberg, M., & Schumacher R. (2002). *The vast majority of federally-eligible children did not receive child care assistance in FY2000.* Washington, DC: Center for Law and Social Policy. Retrieved March 16, 2005, from www.clasp.org/publications/1in7full.pdf.

OECD. (2006). *Early childhood education and care policy: Country note for Mexico.* OECD Directorate of Education. Retrieved March 4, 2006, from www.oecd.org/dataoecd/11/39/34429196.pdf.

Park, L. (2001). Between adulthood and childhood: The boundary work of immigrant entrepreneurial children. *Berkeley Journal of Sociology, 45,* 114–135.

Park, L. (2002). Asian immigrant entrepreneurial children. In L.T. Vo & R. Bonus (Eds.), *Contemporary Asian American communities* (pp. 161–174). Philadelphia, PA: Temple University Press.

Portes, A., & Rumbaut, R.G. (2001). *Legacies: The story of the immigrant generation.* Berkeley, CA: University of California Press.

Ruggles, S., Sobek, M., Alexander, T., Fitch, C.A., Goeken, R., Hall, P.K., et al. (2004). *Integrated public use microdata series: Version 3.0* [Machine readable database]. Minneapolis, MN: Minnesota Population Center [producer and distributor], 2004. Retrieved from www.ipums.org.

Rumbaut, R.G. (1996). A legacy of war: Refugees from Vietnam, Laos, and Cambodia. In S. Pedraza & R.G. Rumbaut (Eds.), *Origins and destinies: Immigration, race, and ethnicity in America.* Belmont: Wadsworth Publishing Company.

Rumbaut, R.G. (1999). Passages to adulthood: The adaptation of children of immigrants in Southern California. In D.J. Hernandez (Ed.), *Children of immigrants: Health, adjustment, and public assistance* (pp. 478–545). Washington, DC: National Academy Press.

Sewell, W.H., & Hauser, R.M. (1975). *Education, occupation and earnings.* New York: Academic Press.

Sewell, W.H., Hauser, R.M., & Wolf, W.C. (1980). Sex, schooling, and occupational status. *American Journal of Sociology, 83*(3), 551–583.

Shonkoff, J.P., & Phillips, D.A. (2000). *From neurons to neighborhoods: The science of early child development.* Washington, DC: National Academy Press.

Sung, B.L. (1987). *The adjustment experience of Chinese immigrant children in New York City.* New York: The Center for Migration Studies.

Takanishi, R. (2004). Leveling the playing field: Supporting immigrant children from birth to eight. *The Future of Children, Special Issue on Children of Immigrants, 14*(2), 61–79.

UNICEF. (2005). *Child poverty in rich countries, 2005.* Innocenti Report Card No. 6. Florence, Italy: UNICEF Innocenti Research Centre.

Utall, L. (1999). Using kin for child care: Embedment in the socioeconomic networks of extended families. *Journal of Marriage and the Family, 61*(4), 845–857.

Valenzuela, A., Jr. (1999). Gender role and settlement activities among children and their immigrant families. *American Behavioral Scientists, 42,* 720–742.

Zhou, M., & Bankston, C.L. (1998). *Growing up American: How Vietnamese children adapt to life in the United States.* New York: Sage.

Zimmermann, W., & Tumlin, K. (1999). *Patchwork policies: State assistance for immigrants under welfare reform.* Washington, DC: The Urban Institute, Occasional Paper No. 24.

2 Differences in Social-Transfer Support and Poverty for Immigrant Families with Children

Lessons from the Luxembourg Income Study (LIS)

Timothy Smeeding, Coady Wing, and Karen Robson

Introduction

"Immigrant" and minority economic and social outcomes are an increasingly important and controversial issue in industrialized countries. Much of the controversy is concerned with how government policy influences the composition of incoming immigrant cohorts and how it shapes the behavior and outcomes of immigrant cohorts that have already arrived. Government efforts to alleviate poverty and inequality are often at the center of debates about how to promote the integration of immigrants into a host society. Some analysts argue that the very availability of government redistribution discourages immigrant integration because it increases the number of low-skill migrants entering immigrant cohorts and reduces incentives for immigrants to invest in host-country-specific human capital after they have arrived (Borjas, 2006, 2007). Some see a race to the bottom whereby countries systematically reduce benefits so as not to attract hordes of immigrants who will become benefit dependent (Menz, 2006; Sapir, 2006; Sassen, 2008). Other analysts contend that immigrant poverty is itself a barrier to integration because it facilitates the exclusion of immigrants from various social aspects of the host country and promotes a fragmented and intolerant society (Parsons & Smeeding, 2006). In either case, the extent to which immigrants and natives receive differential benefits from government income redistribution is important to the study of immigration both across and within countries.

In this chapter, we examine poverty status and social transfer support for immigrants and their children in 12 countries. We use data from the Luxembourg Income Study (LIS) and the European Household Community Panel (ECHP) to construct relative measures of income poverty based definitions of income that both exclude and include government redistribution. In particular, our estimates of cross-nationally equivalent measures of poverty and inequality provide an opportunity to compare the design and effectiveness of the mix of immigration, social, and antipoverty policies in one nation with the experiences of other nations. Our analysis reveals considerable cross-national variation in the degree of success and failure in alleviating poverty and inequality in the presence of shared pressures related to globalization, job instability, population aging, and migration. And while there is evidence of internationalization in the design and evaluation of social policy, national social policies continue to differ substantially in ways that are important to the analysis of the social outcomes experienced by different groups (Banks, Disney, Duncan, & Van Reenen, 2005).

While all nations value low poverty, high levels of economic self-reliance, and equality of opportunity for younger persons, they differ dramatically in the extent to which they reach these goals. The "correct" course or set of policies for any one nation depends on the immigration and antipoverty policy issues which it deems to be most important. Clearly, the "right" solution depends on the institutions, culture, politics, and feasibility constraints under which it finds itself.

But still our results suggest that we take the position that country-specific policies can and do make a difference in the material living conditions faced by immigrants and majorities. We find that generous countries with strong redistributive welfare states have strong antipoverty policies that help alleviate material deprivation for both immigrant-minorities and majorities within each country. Countries that have weak redistributive welfare states have smaller effects on both majority and minority poverty. Further, our data do not yet suggest a race to the bottom in confining benefits to majority-only citizens or cutting benefits for immigrants and minorities.

The chapter unfolds in several parts. We begin by reviewing international concepts and measures of immigrant/minority status, and of relative income poverty. In doing so, we identify a number of markers that we can use to examine the success and failure of antipoverty policy in a cross-national context. We also look at the ways in which immigrants affect policy and how they are affected by policy. We conclude with a discussion of the relationship between policy differences and outcome differences among the several countries, and consider the implications of our analysis for research and for antipoverty policy.

Cross-National Comparisons of Poverty: Methodology and Measurement

There is considerable agreement on the appropriate measurement of poverty in a cross-national context. Most of the available studies and papers share many similarities that help guide our methodological strategy. Differing national experiences in social transfer and antipoverty programs provide a rich source of information for evaluating the effectiveness of alternative social policies in fighting poverty. While most rich nations share a concern over low incomes, poverty measurement began as an Anglo-American social indicator and this concern led to a wider range of countries that now measure poverty.[1]

While there is no international consensus on guidelines for measuring poverty, international bodies such as the United Nations Children's Fund (UNICEF), the United Nations Human Development Report (UNHDR), the Organization for Economic Cooperation and Development (OECD), the European Statistical Office (Eurostat), the International Labor Organization (ILO), and the Luxembourg Income Study (LIS) have published several cross-national studies of the incidence of poverty in recent years. A large subset of these studies is based on LIS data.[2]

For purposes of international comparisons, poverty is almost always a relative concept. A majority of cross-national studies define the poverty threshold as one-half of national median income. In this study, we use the 50% of median income standard to establish our national poverty lines. We could have selected 40% of national median income as our relative poverty threshold because it is closer to the ratio of the official US poverty line to median US household (pre-tax) cash income (35% in 1997 and below 30% of median since 2000),[3] but we have decided to stay with the conventional level in most of our analyses. The results we show at the 50% poverty standard can be generalized to the lower poverty standard of 40% (see Smeeding, Rainwater, & Burtless, 2001).[4]

Measurement Issues

Comparisons of poverty across nations with LIS are based on many choices. A poverty line, a measure of resources such as (market and disposable) incomes, an equivalence scale to adjust for family size, and in some cases exchange rates for conversion to real terms are all important precursors to accurate cross-national measurement of poverty status. We assess the poverty rate (percentage of persons who are poor) for all citizens and especially for minorities as follows:

- Poverty is based on the broadest income definition that still preserves comparability across nations. The best current definition is disposable cash and near-cash income (DPI) which includes all types of money income, minus direct income and payroll taxes and including all cash and near-cash transfers, such as food stamps and cash housing allowances, and refundable tax credits such as the earned income tax credit (EITC). In determining the antipoverty effects of social transfers and tax policy, we also use a measure of "before-tax-and-transfer" market income (MI), which includes earnings, income from investments, private transfers, and occupational pensions.[5]
- In tracing the effects of income transfer policy from MI to DPI poverty and from MI to DPI inequality, we determine the combined effects of two bundles of government programs: Social Insurance and Taxes (including all forms of universal and social insurance benefits, minus income and payroll taxes) and Social Assistance (which includes all forms of income-tested benefits targeted at poor people, including the EITC). Again, in making these poverty comparisons for all persons and for groups, we use poverty lines of half of median DPI anchored or fully relative, for all persons throughout.
- For international comparisons of poverty and inequality, the "household" is the only comparable income-sharing unit available for almost all nations. While the household is the unit used for aggregating income, the person is the unit of analysis. Household income is assumed to be equally shared among individuals within a household. Poverty rates are calculated as the percentage of all persons of each type who are members of households of each type with incomes below the poverty line. We focus here on the poverty-rate children (17 and under) regardless of their living arrangements, separating them according to majority- or minority-immigrant household units.
- A variety of equivalence scales has been used in cross-national comparisons in order to make comparisons of well-being between households with differing compositions. Equivalence scales are used to adjust household income for differences

> in needs related to household size. After adjusting household incomes to reflect differences in household size, we mostly compare the resulting adjusted incomes to the 50% of median poverty line. The equivalence scale used for this purpose, as in many cross-national studies, is a single parameter scale with a square-root-of-household-size scale factor.[6]

Researchers have shown that both income and family structure affect children's life chances and, thus, the real income level of children and their parents is of serious social concern (Sigle-Rushton & McLanahan, 2004; Duncan et al., 1993). The question of mobility in and out of poverty requires the use of longitudinal micro data. All of the comparisons in this chapter are based on cross-sectional data, not longitudinal data. In fact, several recent cross-national poverty studies suggest that mobility in and out of poverty is lower in the US than in almost every other rich country (Bradbury, Jenkins, & Micklewright, 2001; Goodin, Headey, Muffels, & Dirven, 1999; Duncan et al., 1993).

Definitions of Immigrants and Minorities

The definitions of "immigrant" which we find in the LIS data are termed "minorities" by the LIS staff and are not all completely consistent. These differences are crucial and reflect historical, political, social, and economic judgments made by each nation. These definitions are:

Definition one: "born outside the survey country"; United States, Canada, Italy, France
Definition two: "non-national"; Australia, Germany, Sweden
Definition three: "multiple national"; Austria, Belgium, Portugal
Definition four: "non white or minority"; United Kingdom
Definition five: "Swedish speaking"; Finland

By far, the least-satisfying definition is that used in the United Kingdom, where immigrant status is not at all identified. But we must leave the United Kingdom as is in this chapter as we have no choice given the available data.[7] Definition three is taken from the Eurostat's 1994 national samples in the ECHP which asks respondents about their current region and country relative to the one in which they were born. In contrast, the 2004 definition in the new EU Survey of Income and Living Conditions (EU-SILC) asks the following in all nations: (a) what was your country of birth (EU country of residence, other EU or other nation)? And then, if not same as country of survey, (b) Do you hold one or two(+) citizenships? This will effectively combine definitions two and three above for all EU nations from 2003 onward and will be available from LIS later in 2009. For now, we must go with what we have at hand. We also include Finland, though the vast number of "minority" status households in Finland are "Swedish speaking" and thus has little meaning in this context. We have also added two national datasets which are from the ECHP but which are not yet included in LIS: Portugal and Austria.[8] The ECHP households which come from an earlier sample frame are separated in our final analysis from other datasets with more recent immigrant samples. We find support for our basic hypotheses whether these nations are included or excluded.

Minorities in Our Sample

These differences are apparent in Table 2.1 where we present estimates of the weighted percentage of households which are minority or immigrant. While, on average, 8.2% of the populations studies are "minority or immigrant" there is considerable variation in the percentage of minorities/immigrants in these national samples, owing to several factors, including sampling frames, types of surveys and how immigrants and minorities are counted. The German panel, in contrast to the other ECHP, added a "booster" sample of immigrants in the 1990s and followed them as part of their survey. Thus immigrant counts in Portugal, Italy, and Austria are low and reflect older immigrants taken from the ECHP, while Germany is more representative of the current immigrant population. If the sampling frame is household addresses, the data will include both legal and illegal immigrants, assuming that the latter respond as much as do the former. Indeed, the US estimates of illegal immigrants, termed "undocumented aliens," are based on the CPS samples which underlie the US data employed here (Passel, 2005). Other sampling frames may include only registered immigrants.

In Australia, we estimate that minorities represent about 27% of the population.[9] This compares to about 11% in Canada (where naturalized citizens are not counted as minorities but non-naturalized are so counted), 8% in Germany, and 7% to 13% in the US, depending on whether foreign-born but naturalized immigrants are included in definition of minority. The more inclusive definition corresponds most closely to Australia, but includes undocumented immigrants in the US and perhaps also in Australia and Canada, though we are not certain of the extent of these phenomena at this time.[10]

In the US we can use two definitions with our data: pure unnaturalized immigrants or a broader definition which also includes immigrants who have been naturalized and made citizens. Both definitions provide the same result that the US has a weak welfare

Table 2.1 Prevalence of Minority Households by Country

Country	*Percent minority*
United States	7.2
United States*	12.9
Canada	10.8
Australia	27.4
Germany	8.3
Sweden	4.1
Belgium (e)	4.5
Austria (e)	7.7
Finland	5.6
United Kingdom	4.9
France	8.3
Portugal (e)	2.2
Italy	2.3
Country average	8.2

Notes
Countries marked with (e) use data from the European Community Household Panel (ECHP).
*Naturalized foreign-born heads are classified as minorities.

state for both types of immigrants as well as for majority units, and therefore strengthens our findings. The percentage of immigrant-minority therefore varies from the high (27) percentage observed in Australia all the way down to 2% in Portugal and Italy. The ECHP dataset nations within and outside LIS (Portugal, Austria, and Belgium) have estimates of minority households, from 8% in Austria to 5% in Belgium down to 2% in Portugal. The other countries range from 4% in Sweden on upwards.

The Literature and the Data

There is a fairly large and recent literature on poverty and inequality and the welfare state among European Union (EU) nations (e.g., Micklewright & Stewart, 2001; Atkinson, Cantillon, Marlier, & Nolan, 2002; Marlier, 2008) since the release of the ECHP in the mid-1990s. We cannot and do not measure "social exclusion" here (see Dennis & Guio, 2003) despite the fact that its immigrant native features might be appealing because such measures are not available outside the EU. As far as the welfare state is concerned, emergence of elder safety nets has helped this group enormously in all nations, but left families and children—both majority and minority—at risk (Marlier, 2008). Studies of the level and dynamics of poverty suggest that labor-market issues, especially high and persistent unemployment and short-term job contracts are as much of a problem as are low wages for natives (Amuedo-Dorantes & Serrano-Padial, 2005). But far less is known about immigrants and minorities and their access to welfare-state transfers in cash or in kind (health and education).

There is a vast international literature on labor markets and work by legal and illegal immigrants and natives, and that literature shows that immigrants can sometimes reduce wages and job opportunities of natives (e.g., see Borjas, 2006; Borjas, Grogger, & Hanson, 2007, for the US). But in other nations, immigration is shown to have no effect on unemployment rates (see Islam, 2007, on Canada). The comparative literature is sparser but covers the US and Canada where Canadian immigration policy leads to higher educational and better job outcomes for at least the first two generations of immigrants (Aydemir & Sweetman, 2007). In fact, high rates of undocumented immigration can have profound effects on low-wage unregulated job markets such as those of the US (Borjas et al., 2007). The European economics literature compares occupational outcomes (von Tubergen, 2006), earnings levels (Adsera & Chiswick, 2006), and other economic consequences (Brucker, Frick, & Wagner, 2006) across immigrant and non-immigrant groups. Almost all such inquiries suggest that international migrants arrive primarily seeking work and not redistributive social benefits per se. Of course, excellent higher-education systems in many nations attract high-quality foreign students, but many then return to their native lands or go elsewhere for work (Crul & Vermeulen, 2006).[11]

But, the literature on immigrant vs. non-immigrant poverty and social-program support is still in its infancy outside the US Menz (2006) and others write on welfare retrenchment in Europe in reaction to immigration, but provide no evidence of its actual effects on individual outcomes or poverty status. There is a paper that suggests higher child and family poverty among US immigrant children (Capps & Fortuny, 2006). And there is one comparative EU–United States paper by Morrissens (2006) that looks at six rich nations and finds varying outcomes for employment and unemployment-benefit generosity only. Unemployment is included in the net tax transfer benefits we use in our chapter, along with all other multiplicity of tax and transfer benefits not examined by Morrissens.

Data

The data we use for this analysis are mainly taken from the Luxembourg Income Study database, which now contains over 160 household-income data files for 30 nations covering the period 1967 to 2003 (www.lisproject.org). We can analyze both the overall level and trend in poverty for a considerable period across a wide range of nations. But, because we are computing the levels of relative poverty for nations where we can identify migrants as suggested above, we have decided to focus on 12 nations for the remainder of this chapter, each with a recent 1999–2000 LIS database, plus two other nations outside LIS where the ECHP files offers improvement over the LIS versions. The final set includes four Anglo-Saxon nations (Australia, Canada, the U.K., and the US), four continental European nations (Austria, Belgium, France, and Germany), two southern European or "Mediterranean" countries (Italy and Portugal), and two Nordic nations (Finland and Sweden). We include all of Germany, including the eastern states of the former German Democratic Republic (GDR), in most of our analyses. Thanks to the cooperation of Brian Murphy at Statistics Canada, we also have access to a special version of the Canadian data which includes all minority and immigrant units and therefore allows us to go beyond the LIS data where immigrant status is suppressed in the Canadian data for privacy purposes.

While the US is unique in both its high standard of living and its low unemployment rate, it is also unique in the small amount of its resources devoted to cash and near-cash social transfer program. In 2000, the US spent less than 3% of GDP on cash and near-cash assistance for the nonelderly (families with children and the disabled). This is less than half the amount (measured as a percentage of GDP) spent by Canada, Ireland, or Greece; less than one-third of spending in Austria, Belgium, France, Germany, or the U.K.; and less than one-quarter of the amount spent in the Netherlands, Finland, or Sweden; only Italy and Spain spends less than twice as much as the US. While there is a rough correlation between social spending and unemployment, the differences we see here are not cyclical, but are rather structural in nature (see also Garfinkel, Rainwater, & Smeeding, 2006, for more on these differences and health and education benefits in kind).

Results: Poverty Among Nations, Immigrants, and Natives

Much of the concern over social and economic vulnerability of all populations, immigrants and non-immigrants alike is centered around social programs which are mainly used to support the qualified (social insurance) and the needy (income maintenance) in all nations. Here we separately estimated poverty among households with children (under the age of 18) in both majority- and minority-immigrant groups and we examine the antipoverty effect of government policy for each of these subgroups. We conclude with a brief summary of what we have learned about how government support affects poverty and inequality for the vulnerable in a comparative perspective.

Overall: Global Relative Poverty Levels and Antipoverty Effects

Relative poverty rates using MI and DPI in the 15 nations we cover in this chapter are given in Figure 2.1 and Table 2.2. Households with children are measured by the incomes of their parents. The overall DPI poverty rate for all persons using the 50% poverty threshold varies from 5% in Austria and Finland to 16% in the US, with an average rate of about 10% across the 13 countries (Table 2.2). Earlier work (Smeeding, 2006; Munzi & Smeeding, 2008) suggests that using a lower relative poverty rate (such as the 40% of median rate) makes little difference in terms of overall poverty-rate rankings.

Higher overall DPI poverty rates (Table 2.2), focusing just on majority families for now, are found in Anglo-Saxon nations with a relatively high level of overall inequality (Australia, Canada, the U.K., and the US), and in Mediterranean countries (Portugal and Italy). Canadian and British poverty are both about 12% and are, therefore, far below the US levels. The lowest poverty rates are more common in smaller, well-developed, and high-spending welfare states (Sweden, Finland, and Austria) where they are about 5% or 6%. Middle-level rates are found in major continental European countries and in the Nordic countries where income support and unemployment compensation are more generous, where social policies provide more generous support to single mothers and working women (through paid family leave, for example), and where social assistance minimums are high. For instance, France, Belgium, and Germany have poverty rates that are in the 7% to 8% range.

On average, child-poverty rates at 11%–12% (Figure 2.1 and Table 2.2 for majorities) are a bit above those for the population at large. Single parents and their children

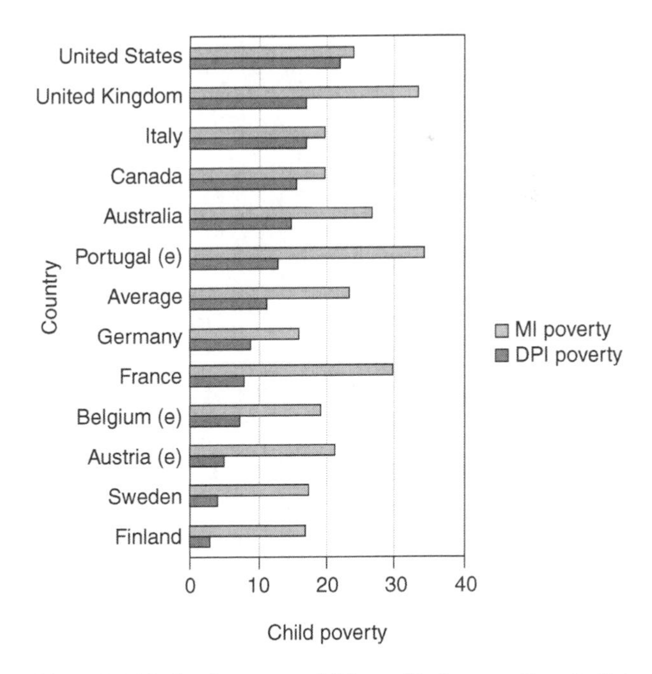

Figure 2.1 Market Income and Disposable Income Poverty Rates for All Households with Children (0–17).

Table 2.2 Household and Child Poverty by Minority Status across Countries

Country	*Household poverty*		*Child poverty*	
	Majority	*Minority*	*Majority*	*Minority*
United States	15.9	30.3	19.9	40.3
United States*	15.8	24.7	19.8	33.0
Canada	14.4	10.8	13.7	21.7
Australia	12.2	15.0	13.3	19.7
Germany	7.6	16.0	8.0	14.5
Sweden	6.1	14.2	3.6	13.6
Belgium (e)	7.4	11.8	6.6	5.2
Austria (e)	5.0	7.6	4.3	7.5
Finland	5.4	4.2	2.8	3.5
United Kingdom	11.7	22.2	15.6	28.8
France	6.3	14.8	6.1	18.5
Portugal (e)	12.5	13.1	12.8	12.5
Italy	12.8	9.9	16.6	14.7
Country Average	10.2	15.0	11.0	18.0

Notes
Countries marked with (e) use data from the ECHP outside of US.
*Naturalized foreign-born heads are classified as minorities.

generally have the highest poverty rates, while those in two-parent units experience the least poverty (not shown, but see Smeeding, 2006). Child-poverty rates are highest in countries with many single parents, low wages, and low levels of transfer support. Poverty rates for children in the richest nation, the US, are 22% in Figure 2.1, almost 90% above the average rate. There is a large gap between the US rate of 22% and the 17% found in the U.K. The other English-speaking nations as well as southern Europeans also have high disposable income child-poverty rates; between 12% and 11%. Single-digit poverty is found in central Europe (7%–9%), in Austria (5%), and in the Nordic countries (3%–4%).

Poverty rates computed using household MI for families with children do not differ among countries as much as do those calculated after-taxes-and-transfers DPI (Figure 2.1). Different levels and mixes of government spending have sizable effects on national DPI poverty rates, but not so much on MI poverty rates (Smeeding et al., 2001; Smeeding, 2006). The percentage difference between MI and DPI poverty is the smallest in the US at only 8%. The difference is largest in Sweden, Belgium, France, and Austria, where it ranges from 61% to 76%. Canada and Italy have antipoverty differences of around 18% to 25%. The remaining countries have antipoverty differences that range from 30% to 49%.

These results are not surprising given 20 years or more of LIS research. They fit well with Esping-Andersen's (1990, 1999) welfare-state typologies and earlier UNICEF results (Bradbury & Jäntti, 1999). But now the question that needs to be answered is: How do these poverty rates and social policy impacts differ for minority-immigrant groups as opposed to majority groups?

Immigrant and Minority Poverty

In all rich nations, especially in Europe, there is growing concern about the status of immigrant and other minority groups (Parsons & Smeeding, 2006). Here we briefly examine this question with respect to poverty and social assistance support. We return to Table 2.2 which summarizes overall and child DPI poverty rates by majority and minority status for each country in our sample. In most countries the DPI poverty rate for all households (first two columns) is higher in the minority population than in the majority population. On average, poverty rates for minorities and immigrants are 15% and 19% if they have children, compared to 10% and 11% for comparable majority populations. In France, Germany, Sweden, and the U.K., the overall household minority poverty rate is more than twice the majority poverty rate. In the US, the minority poverty rate is nearly twice the majority poverty rate when naturalized foreign-born household heads are included in the minority definition and is still almost 10 percentage points higher than the majority poverty rate under the less-restrictive definition of minorities where naturalized foreign-born heads are included.

This pattern of high overall minority poverty rates is reversed in some countries. In Canada and Italy minority poverty rates are actually lower than majority poverty rates. Minority and majority poverty rates for all households are close (within 2 to 3 percentage points) in Australia, Austria, Finland, and Portugal. Canada and Australia represent major immigrant destination countries. Immigrant poverty rates in Canada and to some extent Australia (where the rates are fairly close) are evidence that the skill-biased immigration policies pursued in Canada and Australia are successful in selecting/admitting immigrants who are able to succeed economically after arriving. Of course, these results would also support arguments that the immigrant settlement services and access to social benefits provided in these countries are an effective means of mitigating immigrant poverty. Germany is another popular destination country, but one where the minority rate is far below the majority rate and one like the US where skilled minority immigration is discouraged.

The third and fourth columns of Table 2.2 report child (households with children) poverty rates for the majority and minority population in each country in our sample. These results are less encouraging. In the analysis of overall minority poverty, we found that in several of the major immigrant destination countries, minority poverty rates were not higher than majority poverty rates. Minority child-poverty rates are, however, higher than majority child-poverty rates in every country except Italy and Belgium; and are close to majority rates in Finland, Portugal, and Austria. Many of these nations rely on the ECHP data and therefore have children who are liable to have been in the destination country for some time. With the possible exception of Italy, these countries are not known as key immigrant destinations at this time.

Minority child-poverty rates are considerably higher than majority child-poverty rates in the rest of the nations. The English-speaking nations have the largest differences. US immigrant child-poverty rates are 33%–40%, which are much higher than the 20% majority child rates. The U.K. has a minority child-poverty rate of 29%, which is also nearly double the majority rate. Canada has a 22% immigrant child-poverty rate and Australia is at 20%—half again as high as the majority child-poverty rates in both nations. In Germany, France, and even in Sweden, the gaps between minority and majority child-poverty rates are large. These differences are consistent with those recently published by Eurostat (Marlier, 2008) where at the 60% of median poverty standard, the poverty rates for immigrant households (heads or spouses born outside the EU) were 40.6% compared to 17.6% for households with children whose parents were both born within the country of residence. We now turn to the matter of the effect of antipoverty policy on these results.

Antipoverty Effects by Minority Status

We report MI and DPI poverty rates for majority and minority populations in each of the countries in our sample in Figures 2.2a and 2.2b. For majorities in the US (Figure 2.2a) the antipoverty effect is a 22% reduction; for minorities (Figure 2.2b) it is only a 5%–10% reduction, with a larger effect when naturalized immigrants are included. The average reduction in overall poverty is about 65% for majorities but also about 60% for minorities in this figure. Effects for both groups are larger in the high-spending welfare states (northern and central Europe) and smaller in the English-speaking nations. For minorities, starting and ending poverty rates are higher as we expect (see Table 2.2), but percentage reductions in poverty are also high for minorities, for instance in Canada, Finland, and Austria minority effects are larger than for majority units.

Further, Figure 2.3 plots the percentage difference between the MI and DPI poverty rates for minorities/immigrants against the percentage difference in MI and DPI poverty for majorities/natives. The scatter plot highlights the distribution of government

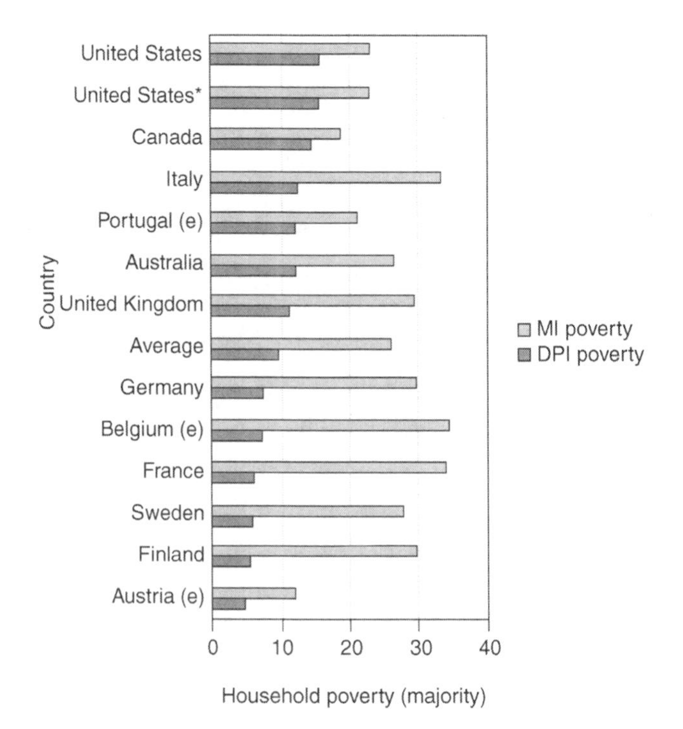

Figure 2.2a Market Income and Disposable Income Poverty for All Majority Households.

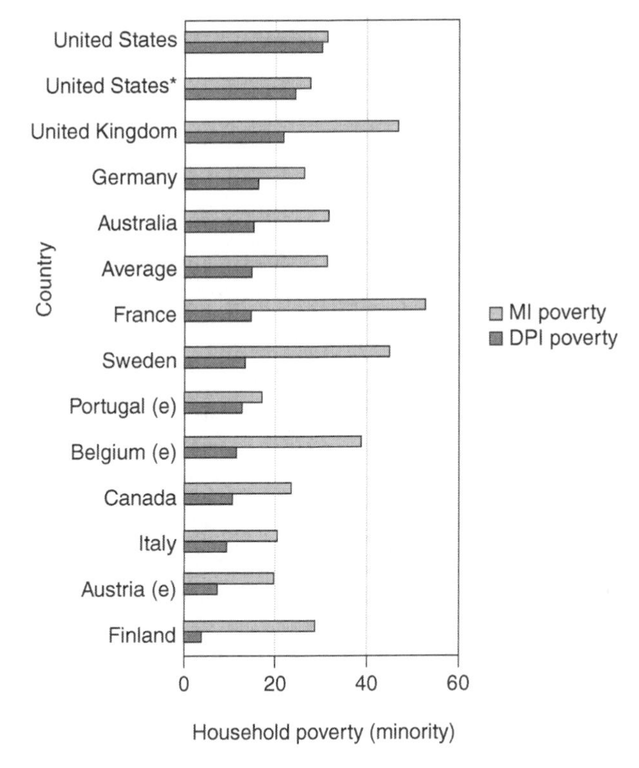

Figure 2.2b Market Income and Disposable Income Poverty for All Minority Households.

antipoverty effects with respect to minority status in each country. Note that if antipoverty effects were evenly distributed across minorities and majorities, each country's data point would fall along a 45-degree line based on the size of their antipoverty effect. Data points from countries that reduced poverty by a higher percentage for natives fall below a 45-degree line (dashed line) and data points from countries that reduced poverty by a higher percentage for immigrants fall above it. (In Figures 2.3 and 2.5, antipoverty effects are measured as the difference between MI and DPI poverty, expressed as a percentage of MI poverty.) These figures plot the simple regression line for the countries in our sample and the 45-degree line.

The regression line in Figure 2.3 shows that in most countries overall antipoverty reductions are systematically related for minorities/immigrants and for majorities/natives, but the fit is not very good. Removing the three red "ECHP" countries (Belgium, Austria, and Portugal) might marginally improve the fit, but the relationship seems clear in any case. The US stands out with a relatively small antipoverty effect, especially for minorities, but also for majorities. Canada, Finland, and Austria have larger antipoverty effect for minorities than for majority population groups. Australia and the U.K. provide similar levels of social support to immigrants and natives, achieving about 50%–70% reductions in MI poverty for both groups. Sweden, Belgium, and

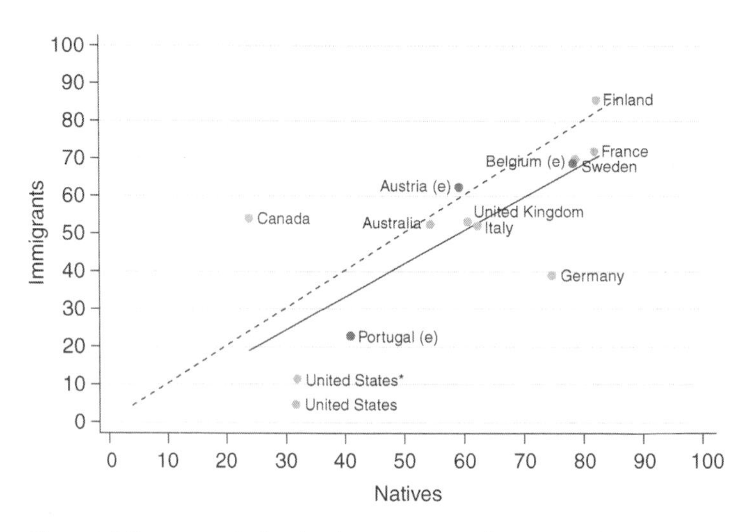

Figure 2.3 Percentage Reduction in Poverty: Immigrants vs. Natives.

France provide slightly higher support to majorities than minorities, but overall these nations are very successful in reducing MI poverty for both groups. Note also that the strange Finnish "minority" who are Swedish speakers do not greatly affect the results (though effects are large for both groups).

Figures 2.4a and 2.4b report similar statistics for child-poverty rates, and Figure 2.5 plots the anti-child-poverty effects for minorities/immigrants and majorities/natives for each country. Here the results suggest a somewhat disturbing lack of support for low-income children in several nations. The US reduces minority child MI poverty rates by less than 3% with somewhat better results for majority children, though still less than 10%, comparing Figures 2.4a and 2.4b. In Italy, the effects on the majority are larger than on the minority (though the minority rates are lower overall). But in the majority of nations antipoverty effects are about the same for minority child poverty. Belgium, Finland, Sweden, and Austria reduce child poverty in both groups by more than 70% relative to MI poverty rates. In the U.K., Australia, and Germany, we also find sizable impacts on both groups, though lesser effects for immigrant youth in Germany and Australia.

Finally, looking at Figure 2.5, the consistency of the relationship is striking. Here removing the three "red" ECHP nations would greatly improve the fit. Clearly, Italy, the US, and Canada do least for both groups; Finland, Belgium, Sweden, and France do most; and the others are in between.

Summary, Discussion, and Explanation

Comparative cross-national relative poverty rankings suggest that the 12 nations we picked suggest several distinct groupings in terms of overall poverty, with the English-speaking and southern European countries belonging to the worst half of the ranking, and the northern/continental European countries and the Nordic ones to the better

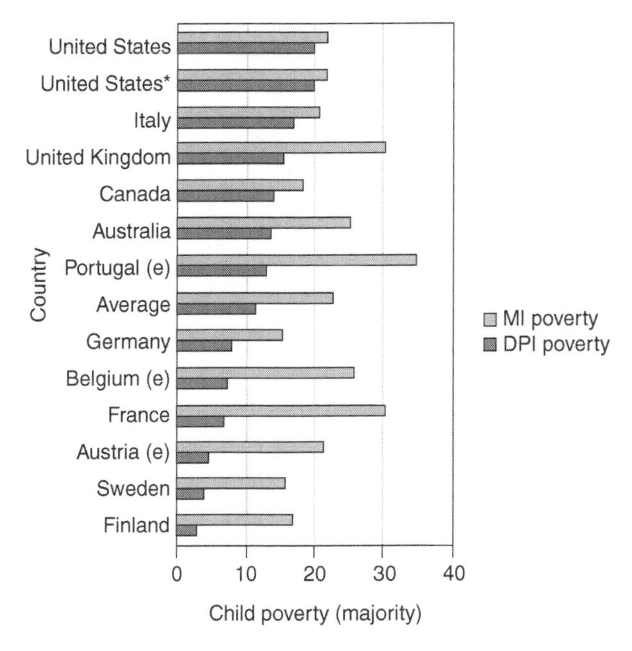

Figure 2.4a Market Income and Disposable Income Child Poverty for Majority Households with Children

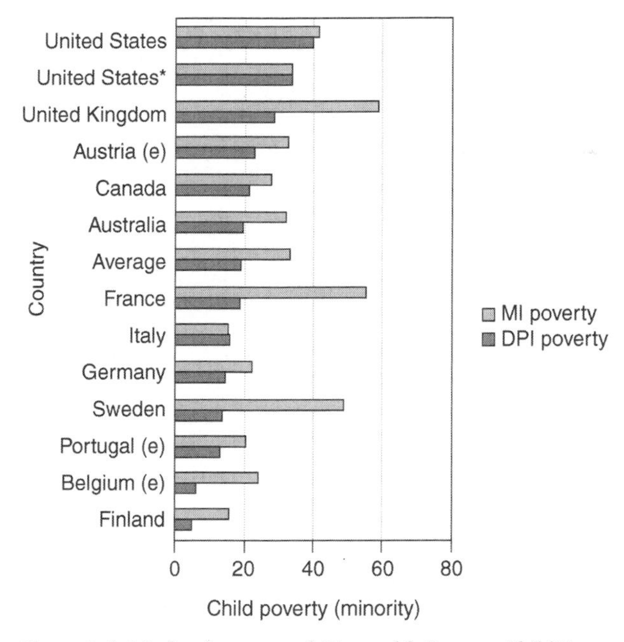

Figure 2.4b Market Income and Disposable Income Child Poverty for Minority Households with Children

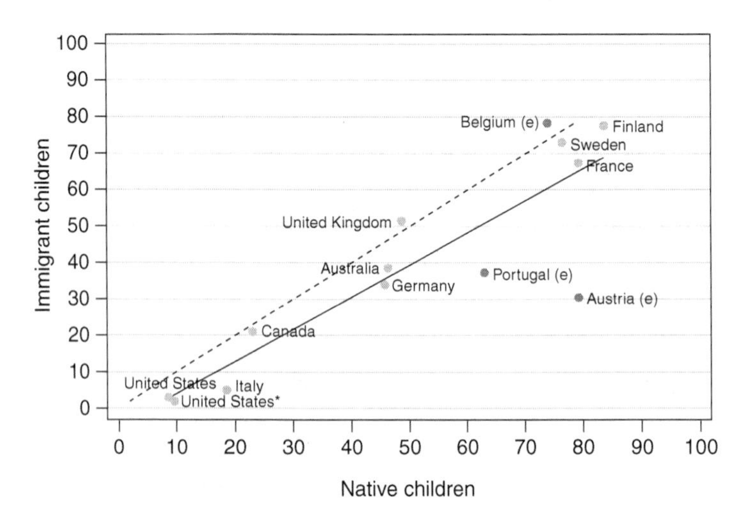

Figure 2.5 Percentage Reduction in Child Poverty: Immigrants vs. Natives.

half. We find this pattern both for the overall population and for children *and* for majorities and minorities. The US's poverty rates are at or near the top of the range for both groups of population with their relative child-poverty rates being particularly troublesome.

We also know from previous work that a substantial fraction of the variance in nonelderly cross-national poverty rates appears to be accounted for not by the variation in work or in unemployment, but by the cross-national variation in the incidence of low pay. Because the US has the highest proportion of workers in relatively poorly paid jobs, it also has the highest poverty rate, even among parents who work half-time or more (Smeeding et al., 2001; Smeeding, 2006). On the other hand, other countries that have a significantly lower incidence of low-paid employment also have significantly lower poverty rates than the US. But the prevalence of low-pay workers is, in fact, not the only reliable predictor of poverty rates. While low pay is a good predictor of poverty rates, and while poorly educated workers do not do well at keeping their families from poverty based on earnings alone, other factors, such as the antipoverty efforts of the government, are also important predictors of the poverty rate (Smeeding, 2006). Social spending reduces poverty, as we have seen above. And as a result of its low level of spending on social transfers to the non-aged, the US again has a very high overall poverty rate. But how are these results and factors influenced by immigrants and how do they influence immigrant poverty, especially among immigrant children?

The differences between immigrant and non-immigrant poverty are complex and require longer explanation than is permitted by this first pass at the data. But some findings are already clear. Immigrant children are more likely to be poor than native children and by a wide margin in some nations. However, for the most part, the effects of social tax-benefit programs on poverty for these children in Figure 2.5 (and for the population as a whole in Figure 2.3) vary much more by country of destination than by immigrant/non-immigrant status. That is, high antipoverty effects are found for both groups in the majority of generous welfare-state nations (e.g., Belgium, Sweden, France, Austria), and for somewhat less generous ones (Canada and Italy) as well. In Portugal immigrant children do worse than majority children but still have sizable poverty reductions. Small effects are found in the one nation not known for its generosity to any group (the US). In Australia and Germany all children receive substantial support though immigrant children receive less support, but not drastically less in the later two nations. Support is about the same for both groups in the U.K. Thus we conclude that policy can and does make a difference in poverty for both migrant-minority and majority children.

Conclusions and Policy Implications

Other research suggests what seems most distinctive about the American poor is that they fail to help the least-skilled in terms of education, and they work more hours than do the resident parents of most other nations where we can observe work hours (Smeeding, 2005, 2006). More generally, the US differs from most nations that achieve lower poverty rates because of its emphasis on work and self-reliance for working-age adults, regardless of the wages workers must accept or the family situation of those workers—migrants or natives. This fits well with the low-wage US labor market where many minority immigrants appear in good economic times or disappear when economic times are hard. These immigrants also receive less in transfer benefits than in other countries. Of course, these findings are in part due to the majority and minority-immigrant makeup of the US, but they are even more heavily influenced by low pay and low social spending. Indeed while overall child-poverty rates in the US are about 22%, and while minority child poverty is almost twice as high at 40%, majority US child-poverty rates alone are at 20%. Thus, high minority child poverty is not driving its incredibly high poverty rates in the U.S.—other features of the US economic and social situation are responsible for this outcome for both majority- and minority households, especially those with children.

We have a way to go here in order to more firmly establish the ways in which different types of households are affected by social programs and how they aid children and families—migrant and non-migrant, as well as minority and non-minority in these nations. The interaction between household structure, poverty status, and minority status is clearly an important element of poverty and inequality in industrialized countries. Hours worked and taxes paid vs. benefits received can be studied for all groups in each nation. Small overall effects of policy can be due to a combination of many low-wage working families who are paying large net taxes, while others are receiving high net benefits. The hours–education–earnings compositions differ greatly among the countries studied, with Australia and especially Canada having a more skill-driven immigration policy than that found in the US. New and better data from the EU-SILC will allow for a much better and more recent picture of immigrant makeup and social policy effects in those nations when these 2004 and 2005 datasets become part of LIS next year. Further, we have not been able to determine how health and education polices affect immigrant and minority vs. majority youth. But it is our understanding that healthcare is largely need-based and immigrant blind in most rich nations, except for the US where insurance is often a pre-requisite. Education systems in all nations serve the youth who reside there, though differences in school quality and outcome between immigrant and native children can also be noted.

Policy Implications

The experience of the US can give many lessons to other nations' domestic antipoverty and inequality policies for immigrants and non-immigrants alike. As long as the US relies almost exclusively on low-skill immigration and on the job market to generate incomes for working-age families, changes in the jobs and wage distributions that affect the earnings of less-skilled workers will inevitably have a big effect on poverty among children and prime-age adults. One expects that such low-skill workers are paid wages that are below those paid to even the lowest-skilled US native workers (for evidence, see Borjas, 2007, and Borjas et al., 2007). At the same time, welfare reform in the US has pushed many native-born low-income women into the labor market and they have stayed there as TANF roles continue to fall. It is hard to believe that many immigrant mothers in the US are enjoying TANF benefits both due to their rarity and due to sanctions against foreign-born mothers in state TANF programs. Even with the $25.4 billion spent on TANF today, only $11.2 billion is in the form of cash assistance; the rest is now in the form of childcare transportation assistance, training, and other services (Pear, 2003). While the switch from cash to services has undoubtedly helped account for higher earnings among low-income parents, it has not helped move many of them from poverty.

Of course, labor markets alone cannot reduce poverty because not all of the poor can be expected to "earn" their way out of poverty. Single parents with young children, disabled workers, and the unskilled will all face significant challenges earning an adequate income, no matter how much they work and no matter what is their nationality. US poverty rates among both native and immigrant children are high when compared with those in other industrialized countries. Yet US economic performance has also been outstanding compared with that in other rich countries.

The relationship between antipoverty spending and poverty rates is of course complicated, so the arguments discussed above are, at best, suggestive. But it seems to us that national antipoverty policies can make a difference in the lives of children, regardless of their minority–majority status. As the U.K. has demonstrated, carefully crafted public policy can certainly reduce poverty (Waldfogel, 2006; Hills, 2003; Bradshaw, 2002; Hills & Waldfogel, 2004; Smeeding, 2006).

Of course, the direct and indirect costs of antipoverty programs are now widely recognized (and frequently overstated) in public debate (see Lindert, 2004; Garfinkel et al., 2006). The wisdom of expanding programs targeted at children and poor families, especially those of immigrant background, depends on one's values and subjective views about the economic, political, and moral tradeoffs of poverty alleviation. For many critics of public spending on the poor, it also depends on a calculation of the potential economic efficiency losses associated with a larger government budget and targeted social programs for minority and majority families.

It is hard to argue that the US cannot afford to do more to help the poor; particularly low-skilled lowly paid workers. If the nation is to be successful in reducing child poverty, it will need to make antipoverty spending a higher priority, as did the U.K. and as do most other nations. In particular, it will have to do a better job of combining work and benefits targeted to low-wage workers in low-income families (e.g., see Danziger, Hefflin, Corcoran, Oeltmans, & Wang, 2002). There is already evidence that such programs produce better outcomes for native kids (Clark-Kauffman, Duncan, & Morris, 2003).

They could also work in the US if redistributive tax policy were broadened to serve all workers who pay taxes, including the parents of immigrant children. Expansions in the EITC, in the refundability of tax credits, and in the availability and quality of early-childhood education and health insurance could help all young children and their families, both immigrant and native. Still at least until the 2008 election, it is our guess that helping immigrant kids will be an even harder sell than helping native and majority children, especially in the US.

Acknowledgments

The authors would like to thank The Russell Sage Foundation and the Marie Curie Actions for support. We also thank Brian Murphy for his help in preparing the Canadian data for this manuscript, Emma Caspar, Dawn Duren, Mary Santy, and Katie Winograd for her help with manuscript preparation, and Sara McLanahan, Jonathan Zeitlin, and seminar participants at the Lafollette School of Public Affairs, University of Wisconsin-Madison, and at the Center for Human Potential and Public Policy at University of Chicago for helpful suggestions and support. Finally, the authors thank the Luxembourg Income Study member countries, especially, for their support. The conclusions reached are those of the authors alone and not of their sponsoring institutions.

Notes

1. In fact, "official" measures of poverty (or measures of "low income" status) exist in very few nations. Only the US (US Census Bureau, 2003b) and the UK (UK Department for Work and Pensions, 2007) have regular "official" poverty series. In Canada there is a series of Low Income Cutoffs (LICOS) which are often debated but never formally introduced as national guidelines (Statistics Canada, 2005). In northern Europe and the Nordic countries the debate centers instead on the level of income at which minimum benefits for social programs should be set and on "social exclusion" (Atkinson et al., 2002). Most recognize that their national social programs already ensure a low poverty rate under any reasonable set of measurement standards for natives at least (Björklund & Freeman, 1997). The case of immigrants is less well-known in all of these nations, though the same poverty lines are used for all residents of a country, immigrants or majority citizen.
2. For UNICEF, see UNICEF Innocenti Research Centre (2000), Bradbury and Jäntti (2005), and Chen and Corak (2005); for the United Nations, see United Nations Development Programme (1999); for the OECD, see Förster and Pellizzari (2005); for the European Union, see Eurostat (1998) and Atkinson et al. (2002); and, for LIS, see Jäntti and Danziger (2000), Smeeding (2005), Smeeding, O'Higgins, and Rainwater (1990), and Rainwater and Smeeding (2003).
3. In 1998 the ratio of the US (four-person) poverty line to median family income was 38%. Since then both ratios have fallen to the 30% level (Smeeding, 2005) while the ratio to median household income was 31%. Median household income ($38,855) is far below median family income ($47,469) because single persons living alone (or with others to whom they are not directly related) are both numerous and have lower incomes than do

families (US Census Bureau, 2003a, 2003b). Families include all units with two or more persons related by blood, marriage, or adoption; single persons (unrelated individuals) are excluded. In contrast, households include all persons sharing common living arrangements, whether related or not, including single persons living alone. Different adjustments for family or household size might also make a difference in making such comparisons.

4. One might even go so far as to compare immigrants in their destination vs. origin nations, though we do not do so in this chapter. In the US the incomes of migrants are mainly believed to be higher than in their source nation (Lerman, 2003; Haskins, 2008), but it is not clear how these incomes would compare to poverty rates of immigrants in their native nations using either appropriate relative or "absolute" lines in those source countries.
5. Market income includes earnings, income from investments, occupational (private and public-sector) pensions, child support, and other private transfers. For the calculation of poverty rates, MI refers to gross income in all countries but Austria, Belgium, Greece, Ireland, Italy, and Spain, where MI is net of taxes and social contributions.
6. Formally, adjusted disposable income (ADPI) is equal to unadjusted household income (DPI) divided by household size (S) raised to an exponential value (e), $ADPI = DPI/S^e$. We assume the value of e is 0.5. To determine whether a household is poor under the relative poverty measure, we compare its ADPI to 50% of the national median ADPI. National median ADPI is calculated by converting all incomes into ADPI and then taking the median of this "adjusted" income distribution. The equivalence scale which we employ is robust; especially when comparing families of different size and structure (e.g., elders and children). See Atkinson, Rainwater, and Smeeding (1995) for detailed and exhaustive documentation of these sensitivities.
7. Readers should also know that we do not separate native-born American Blacks from immigrants in this chapter; rather they are included in the majority definition. In later drafts, we plan to separately examine native and non-native Black minorities.
8. Austria and Belgium are already in LIS but the availability and counts of immigrant-minorities and fuller detail on their status for Austria are found in the homogenized public-use ECHP files. Portugal is not yet in LIS. These three datasets are noted by (e) in all analyses. The reader must take note that several ECHP files are used in both LIS and the three non-LIS countries. The problem with the ECHP is the same as with all "long" panels: the sample is drawn from a household roster in 1994, and thus no minorities who have emigrated since then were included unless they joined a sample household in the original panel. This reduces the number of households included and excludes most recent immigrants. Survey attrition and low immigrant-response rates have led us to exclude Spain, Ireland, and Greece as the samples are too small to report. As shown in Appendix Table WA2–1 (available online) the smallest samples we do include are for the three ECHP nations: Belgium in LIS (91 minority households); Portugal (100) and Austria (203).
9. Remember that these are "non-Australians" who include both non-naturalized and naturalized citizens.
10. Indeed, we worked with the Canadian survey takers to eliminate all incomplete records and those where the immigrant had so recently arrived as to have no Canadian income. Overall, 2.20% of the immigrant records and 2.15% of the immigrant population have been dropped due to this screen.
11. There is also a literature on how immigration affects US cities and how it affects incarceration (Butcher & Piehl, 2007). Also there is a wide literature on immigration patterns, political outcomes, public opinion and assimilation of non-natives into the cultural and political situation of nations (see chapters in Parsons & Smeeding, 2006).

References

Adsera, Alicia, & Chiswick, Barry. (2006). Divergent patterns in immigrant earnings across European destinations. In C. Parsons & T.M. Smeeding (Eds.), *Immigration and the transformation of Europe* (pp. 85–110). Cambridge: Cambridge University Press.

Amuedo-Dorantes, C., & Serrano-Padial, R. (2005). Fixed-term employment and its poverty implications: Evidence from Spain. *Focus, 23*(3), 42–45.

Atkinson, A. B., Cantillon, B., Marlier, E., & Nolan, B. (2002). *Social indicators: The EU and social inclusion.* Oxford: Oxford University Press.

Atkinson, Anthony B., Rainwater, Lee, & Smeeding, Timothy M. (1995). Income distribution in OECD countries: Evidence from the Luxembourg Income Study (LIS). *Social Policy Studies No. 18.* Paris: Organization for Economic Cooperation and Development.

Aydemir, A., & Sweetman, A. (2007). First and second generation immigrant educational attainment and labor market outcomes: A comparison of the United States and Canada. In B.R. Chiswick (Ed.), *Research in labor economics, volume 27: Immigration–Trends, consequences and prospects for the United States* (pp. 215–270). Amsterdam: Elsevier.

Banks, J., Disney, R.F., Duncan, A., & Van Reenen, J. (2005). The internationalization of public welfare. *The Economic Journal, 115*(502), 62–81.

Björklund, A., & Freeman, R. (1997). Generating equality and eliminating poverty—The Swedish way. In R.B. Freeman, R. Topel, & B. Swedenborg (Eds.), *The welfare state in transition: Reforming the Swedish model* (pp. 33–78). Chicago, IL: University of Chicago Press.

Borjas, George. (2006). Making it in America: Social mobility in the immigrant population. *The Future of Children, 16*(2), 55–71.

Borjas, George. (Ed.). (2007). *Mexican immigration to the United States.* Chicago, IL: University of Chicago Press.

Borjas, George, Grogger, Jeffrey, & Hanson, Gordon H. (2007). *Immigration and African-American employment opportunities: The response of wages, employment, and incarceration to labor supply shocks.* National Bureau of Economic Research Working Paper No. 12518.

Bradbury, B., & Jäntti, M. (1999). *Child poverty across industrialized nations.* Florence: UNICEF International Child Development Centre. Innocenti Occasional Papers, Economic Policy Series No. 71.

Bradbury, B., & Jäntti, M. (2005). *Child poverty, labor markets, and public policies across industrialized countries.* Sydney: University of New South Wales.

Bradbury, B., Jenkins, S.P., & Micklewright, J. (2001). *The dynamics of child poverty in industrialized countries.* Cambridge; New York: Cambridge University Press.

Bradshaw, J. (Ed.). (2002). *The well-being of children in the UK.* London: Save the Children.

Brucker, H., Frick, J.R., & Wagner, G.G. (2006). Economic consequences of immigration in Europe. In C. Parsons & T.M. Smeeding (Eds.), *Immigration and the transformation of Europe* (pp. 111–146). Cambridge: Cambridge University Press.

Butcher, K., & Piehl, A.M. (2007). Crime, corrections, and California: What does immigration have to do with it? *California counts.* Public Policy Institute of California, San Francisco, California, February 2008.

Capps, R., & Fortuny, K. (2006). *Immigration and child and family policy. The Urban Institute and Child Trends Roundtable on children in low-income families.* Retrieved April 5, 2009, from www.urban.org/url.cfm?ID=311362.

Chen, W.H., & Corak, M. (2005). *Child poverty and changes in child poverty in rich countries since 1990.* Syracuse, NY: Center for Policy Research, Syracuse University, Luxembourg Income Study Working Paper No. 405.

Clark-Kaufmann, E., Duncan, G.J., & Morris, P. (2003). How welfare policies affect child and adolescent achievement. *American Economic Review, 93*, 299–303.

Crul, M., & Vermeulen, H. (2006). Immigration, education and the Turkish second generation in five European nations: A comparative study. In C. Parsons & T.M. Smeeding (Eds.), *Immigration and the transformation of Europe* (pp. 235–250). Cambridge: Cambridge University Press.

Danziger, Sheldon, Heflin, Colleen M., Corcoran, Mary E., Oeltmans, Elizabeth, & Wang, Hui-Chen. (2002). Does it pay to move from welfare to work? *Journal of Policy Analysis and Management, 21*(4), 671–692.

Dennis, I., & Guio, A.-C. (2003). Poverty and social exclusion in the EU after Laeken Part 1. *Statistics in Focus*. Brussels: Eurostat.

Duncan, G.J., Gustafsson, B., Hauser, R., Schmauss, G., Messinger, H., Muffels, R., et al. (1993). Poverty dynamics in eight countries. *Journal of Population Economics, 6*, 215–234.

Esping-Andersen, Gøsta. (1990). *The three worlds of welfare capitalism*. Cambridge: Polity Press.

Esping-Andersen, Gøsta. (1999). *The social foundations of postindustrial economies*. Oxford: Oxford University Press.

Eurostat. (1998). Analysis of income distribution in 13 EU member states. *Statistics in focus, population and social conditions 1998–11*. Luxembourg: European Statistical Office.

Förster, M.F., & M. Pellizzari. (2005). *Trends and driving factors in income distribution and poverty in the OECD area*. Paris: Organization for Economic Cooperation and Development, Labour Market and Social Policy, Occasional Paper No. 42.

Garfinkel, I., Rainwater, L., & Smeeding, T.M. (2006). A reexamination of welfare state and inequality in rich nations: How in-kind transfers and indirect taxes change the story. *Journal of Policy Analysis and Management, 25*, 897–919.

Goodin, R.E., Headey, B., Muffels, R., & Dirven, H.-J. (1999). *The real worlds of welfare capitalism*. Cambridge: Cambridge University Press.

Haskins, Ron. (2008). Immigration, wages, education and mobility. In J.B. Isaacs, I. Sawhill, & R. Haskins (Eds.), *Economic mobility in America* (pp. 81–90). Washington, DC: Brookings Institution and Pew Foundation.

Hills, J. (2003). The Blair government and child poverty: An extra one percent for children in the United Kingdom. In I.V. Sawhill (Ed.), *One percent for the kids: New policies, brighter futures for America's children* (pp. 156–178). Washington, DC: Brookings Institution.

Hills, J., & Waldfogel, J. (2004). A "third way" in welfare reform: What are the lessons for the US? *Journal of Policy Analysis and Management, 23*, 765–788.

Islam, A. (2007). Immigration unemployment relationship: The evidence from Canada. *Australian Economic Papers, 46*(1), 52–66.

Jäntti, M., & Danziger, S. (2000). Income poverty in advanced countries. In A.B. Atkinson & F. Bourguignon (Eds.), *Handbook of income distribution* (pp. 309–378), Amsterdam: North-Holland.

Lerman, R. (2003). US income inequality trends and recent immigration. In John Bishop (Ed.), *Inequality, welfare and poverty: Theory and measurement* (pp. 289–307). Amsterdam: Elsevier.

Lindert, Peter H. (2004). *Growing public: Volume 1, The story: Social spending and economic growth since the eighteenth century*. New York: Cambridge University Press.

Marlier, Eric. (2008). *Child poverty and well-being in the EU: Current status and way forward*. Brussels: EU Social Protection Committee.

Menz, George. (2006). "Useful" *Gastarbeiter*, burdensome asylum seekers, and the second wave of welfare retrenchment: Exploring the nexus between globalization and the welfare state. In C. Parsons & T.M. Smeeding (Eds.), *Immigration and the transformation of Europe* (pp. 393–418). Cambridge: Cambridge University Press.

Micklewright, J., & Stewart, K. (2001). Child well-being in the EU—and enlargement to the east. In K. Vlaminck & T.M. Smeeding (Eds.), *Child well-being, child poverty and child poverty in modern nations: What do we know?* (pp. 99–127). Bristol: Policy Press.

Morrissens, Ann. (2006). Immigrants, unemployment and Europe's varying welfare regimes. In C. Parsons & T.M. Smeeding (Eds.), *Immigration and the transformation of Europe* (pp. 172–199). Cambridge: Cambridge University Press.

Munzi, T., & Smeeding, T.M. (2008). Conditions of social vulnerability, work and low income: Evidence for Spain in comparative perspective. In L. Costablile (Ed.), *Institutions for social well-being, alternatives for Europe* (pp. 33–69). New York: Palgrave-Macmillan Publishers.

Parsons, C., & Smeeding, T.M. (Eds.). (2006). *Immigration and the transformation of Europe*. Cambridge: Cambridge University Press.

Passel, J.S. (2005). *Estimates of the size and characteristics of the undocumented population.* Washington, DC: Pew Hispanic Center. Retrieved April 5, 2009, from http://pewhispanic.org/reports/report.php?ReportID=44.

Pear, R. (2003, October 13). Welfare spending shows huge shift from checks to service. *New York Times.*

Rainwater, L., & Smeeding, T.M. (2003). *Poor kids in a rich country: America's children in comparative perspective.* New York: Russell Sage Foundation.

Sapir, A. (2006). Globalisation and the reform of European social models. *Journal of Common Market Studies, 44,* 369–390.

Sassen, S. (2008). Fear and strange arithmetics: When powerful states confront powerless immigrants. *Open Democracy.* Retrieved April 5, 2009, from www.opendemocracy.net/article/fear-and-strange-arithmetics-when-powerful-states-confront-powerless-immigrants.

Sigle-Rushton, W., & McLanahan, S. (2004). Father absences and child well-being: A critical review. In D.P. Moynihan, L. Rainwater, & T.M. Smeeding (Eds.), *The future of the family* (pp. 116–158). New York: Russell Sage Foundation.

Smeeding, T.M. (2005). Public policy and economic inequality: The United States in comparative perspective. *Social Science Quarterly, 86*(5), 1–50.

Smeeding, T.M. (2006). Poor people in a rich nation: The United States in comparative perspective. *Journal of Economic Perspectives, 20,* 69–90.

Smeeding, T.M., O'Higgins, M., & Rainwater, L. (1990). *Poverty, inequality and the distribution of income in a comparative context: The Luxembourg Income Study (LIS).* London; Washington, DC: Harvester Wheatsheaf/Urban Institute Press.

Smeeding, T.M., Rainwater, L., & Burtless, G. (2001). United States poverty in a cross-national context. In S.H. Danziger & R.H. Haveman (Eds.), *Understanding poverty* (pp. 162–189). New York; Cambridge, MA: Russell Sage Foundation and Harvard University Press.

Statistics Canada. (2005). *LICOS—Low Income Cutoffs for 2003.* Ottawa: Statistics Canada.

UK Department for Work and Pensions. (2007). *Opportunity for all: Sixth annual report 2004.* London: Department for Work and Pensions.

UNICEF Innocenti Research Centre. (2000). *A league table of child poverty in rich nations.* Florence: UNICEF, Innocenti Report Card No. 1.

United Nations Development Programme. (1999). *Human development report 1999: Globalization with a human face.* New York: United Nations.

US Census Bureau. (2003a). Income in the United States: 2002. *Current Population Reports* P60–221. Washington, DC: Government Printing Office.

US Census Bureau. (2003b). Poverty in the United States: 2002. *Current population reports.* Washington, DC: US Department of Commerce, Economics and Statistics Administration.

Von Tubergen, F. (2006). Occupational status of immigrants in cross-national perspective: A multilevel analysis of seventeen Western societies. In C. Parsons & T.M. Smeeding (Eds.), *Immigration and the transformation of Europe.* Cambridge: Cambridge University Press.

Waldfogel, Jane. (2006). *What children need.* Cambridge, MA: Harvard University Press.

3 Disentangling Nativity Status, Race/ Ethnicity, and Country of Origin in Predicting the School Readiness of Young Immigrant Children

Jessica Johnson De Feyter and Adam Winsler

The extent to which children have a basic foundation of skills needed to begin and be successful in kindergarten has become a burgeoning topic in the fields of education, developmental psychology, and child policy. This is due in large part to a body of research showing that children who begin kindergarten already behind their peers in a range of developmental competencies have a hard time "catching up" later in schooling (NICHD Early Child Care Research Network, 2005) and are at risk for low academic achievement, grade retention, special education placement, and high school dropout (Ramey & Ramey, 1998). As has been discussed by Hernandez, Denton, and Macartney (this volume), immigrant children are quite diverse and although many live in optimal circumstances, many more live in poverty (Brandon, 2004) and face various social and institutional barriers that can present challenges to their long-term educational attainment, health, and psychological well-being (Fuligni, 1997; Leventhal, Xue, & Brooks-Gunn, 2006; Perreira, Chapman, & Stein, 2006). Fortunately, early education provides a promising solution; a quality preschool experience can help prepare children for kindergarten and have positive effects that last through adulthood (Campbell, Ramey, Pungello, Sparling, & Miller-Johnson, 2002; Schweinhart et al., 2004; Winsler et al., 2008). Early education can be a key factor in buffering immigrant children from adversities by affording them the opportunity to learn skills that can ease their transition to formal schooling.

Though growing attention to the educational attainment of immigrant youth has encouraged numerous studies on school-aged and adolescent populations, few studies exist to date on the state of immigrant children's development in early childhood, prior to entering formal schooling. The social sciences have only recently been able to access large early-childhood datasets with the necessary information about child and parent nativity and national origins to ask how well-prepared immigrant children are for kindergarten. Taking into account the "newness" of this area of study, the central goals of this chapter are two-fold and both relate to our own ongoing study on the school readiness of diverse, low-income, immigrant and non-immigrant children receiving subsidies to attend childcare in Miami, Florida (Winsler et al., 2008). The first goal of the chapter is to summarize the recently available literature on school readiness for immigrant children in the US, which finds that many immigrant children begin kindergarten somewhat behind their native-born peers, especially in areas like math (Crosnoe, 2007; Magnuson, Lahaie, & Waldfogel, 2006).

Second, we introduce the reader to some of the valuable research on older youth that highlights the sheer diversity of the immigrant child population (in terms of family background, generation, ethnicity, and national origins) and how this diversity is related to differences in educational outcomes. In our own study, discussed at the end of the chapter, we ask if this same heterogeneity of educational outcomes can be seen as early as the preschool age, and have found that indeed, children's backgrounds and nativity histories do matter for early developmental competencies and school readiness. There is really no single, one-dimensional story to tell about the state of immigrant children's educational progress, including their school readiness. Further, we find that even very young immigrant children bring with them important strengths, and our task as researchers, educators, and policy makers is to discern how best to leverage these strengths to promote their long-term academic success.

The School Readiness of Immigrant Children in the US

It is a little-known piece of history that kindergarten and preschool were originally implemented into US society in an attempt to minimize inequality in educational attainment based on factors like race and income (Meisels & Shonkoff, 2000). In fact, early education was seen as a means to integrate the multitudes of impoverished immigrant children into American society and provide supports for their long-term attainment (Braun & Edwards, 1972). Over 100 years later, as the US sociopolitical context and typical immigrant profile have changed dramatically, we are still invested in understanding the unique needs of children in immigrant families. This vision is not surprising, as it emerges from long-held American values of diversity and equality. Additionally, for hundreds of years, the success of the nation as a whole has been intricately tied to the contributions of immigrants and their children.

Studies that have investigated the early development and school readiness of children in immigrant families begin to shed light on their overall levels of preparedness for schooling, their progress in specific domains (e.g. cognitive and socioemotional development), and the effectiveness of the early-education programs they participate in. In one such study, using data from the nationally representative sample provided by the Early Childhood Longitudinal Study (ECLS-K), Magnuson et al. (2006) found that preschool had a larger positive effect (22% increase) on the English-language proficiency of children of immigrant mothers than it did for other children. Although there were no differences in the reading scores of English-proficient children in immigrant families and those in non-immigrant families, children in immigrant families did lag slightly behind children in non-immigrant families in math. Further, preschool attendance was associated with higher math and reading scores for both groups, even after controlling for family background. Therefore, the study found that preschool was just as beneficial for children in immigrant families as it was for children in native families, and it was most beneficial (in terms of English-language acquisition) for children whose mothers spoke a language other than English in the home.

When looking only at children in Mexican immigrant families, however, Crosnoe (2007) discovered that attending preschool did not seem to be as beneficial for these children as it was for children in native-born families. Like Magnuson and colleagues, and again using data from the ECLS-K, Crosnoe found that upon entering kindergarten, children in Mexican immigrant families lagged behind their native peers in mathematics. However, these differences were virtually eliminated when family socioeconomic (e.g., poverty status and presence of father) and family environmental factors (e.g., learning environment and parental involvement) were taken into account. On the other hand, children in Mexican immigrant families showed socioemotional strengths by exhibiting fewer externalizing behavior problems than children in native families, an effect that persisted even after family background factors were accounted for. They also showed more emotional maturity and competence in peer relations and in-class behavior (Crosnoe, 2006). That immigrant children demonstrate socioemotional and behavioral strengths is a finding that we substantiate in our own study of immigrant children's school readiness, and we elaborate on this point at the end of the chapter.

Crosnoe points out that without knowledge of childcare quality, family socioeconomic factors proved to be the most important factor for children's math achievement in kindergarten. Finally, he expresses concern that children in center-based care have been shown to exhibit slightly more behavior problems in later schooling than children who experience parental care (Belsky, 1999; NICHD, 2005) and feels increasing access to preschool for immigrant children is worth the investment as long as it does not jeopardize their socioemotional strengths. These studies highlight that many preschool immigrant children show both strengths and concerns in areas considered important for development, suggesting we should refrain from making global evaluations of their school readiness until we know more. It is notable, however, that immigrant children are often described as well-behaved with strong social skills (Suárez-Orozco, 2007) because kindergarten teachers often consider these areas to be more important for kindergarten readiness than academic knowledge and skills (Lin, Lawrence, & Gorrell, 2003; West, Hausken, & Collins, 1995). Future studies that address multiple developmental domains for young immigrant children will give us a more nuanced understanding of where their strengths and concerns lie, and how their strengths can be built upon to foster better long-term educational outcomes.

The Diversity of Immigrant Youth and their Educational Outcomes

Race, Ethnicity, and Country of Origin

There is great within-group variability in the academic success of immigrant children according to a variety of factors like race, ethnicity, and country of origin (Hao & Bonstead-Bruns, 1998). Though the extent of this variability is largely an open question with regard to school readiness for preschoolers (a key object of investigation in our own study), research on school-aged children and adolescents has demonstrated it unequivocally. For example, as part of the Project on Human Development in Chicago Neighborhoods, Leventhal et al. (2006) found distinct patterns of verbal development for each immigrant-race/ethnic group (Mexican-American, Black-American, White-American, Puerto Rican) reflecting the "unique socioeconomic, historical, and cultural circumstances of each sub-group" (p. 1372). Other factors, such as the amount immigrant parents pay for childcare and time spent in childcare, have similarly been found to vary by ethnicity and SES (Brandon, 2004).

One criticism that has come out of work with immigrant children is that ethnicity-based research on parenting and child development treats ethnicity as a static variable that defines a particular cultural group (Perreira et al., 2006). These researchers stress that educational practitioners need to move away from the conventional notion that equates each racial group with one culture and one ethnic identity and highlight the danger in assuming that, for instance, the racial identities of all Black youth are the same, regardless of community, country of origin, and social-cultural factors (Fuligni, 1997; Rong & Brown, 2001).

Some researchers have speculated that differences in outcomes for immigrant and native-born Black children and families may partly involve differences in their interpretations of how favorable conditions are for them in the host society (Portes, 1999). They highlight the importance of considering that involuntary minority groups like Native Americans, Mexican Americans, and African Americans have a history of oppression related to colonization and, in turn, have experienced widespread discrimination that has been institutionalized (Ogbu & Simmons, 1998). This outlook on their place within society can lead to feelings of marginalization that affect academic attitudes, motivation, and academic success. Conversely, the optimistic outlook and strong desire for upward mobility characteristic of many recent immigrants may contribute to higher self-regard, values, and motives when compared to same-race peers whose families have lived here for generations (Portes, 1999).

As with older immigrants, the few studies that exist on the competencies of very young immigrant children suggest segmented outcomes are evident even at a young age. Glick and Hohmann-Marriott (2007), for instance, found that after controlling for family structure and background, first-generation immigrant children who migrated in early childhood scored just as high as non-immigrant children on a math test in third grade. However, second-generation immigrant children scored significantly lower than both other groups. They also found interactions between generation and race/ethnicity for immigrant children, highlighting that both must be taken into consideration when predicting outcomes. The question is whether these racial, ethnic, and national boundaries, as well as their intersection with nativity history, matter for children's development prior to entering formal schooling in kindergarten. This question was an interest of ours and a major aim of our own study.

Generation and Its Implications for Child Outcomes

Though there would appear to be a clear distinction between immigrants (those who are foreign-born) and non-immigrants (those who are native-born), these broad conceptualizations are generally insufficient to answer questions relating to the achievement and success of immigrant children. Lost in these definitions are complexities and processes captured by details of children's migration histories. These include factors such as generation (whether it is the child (first-generation) or just the parent (second-generation) who was born in another country), children's ages at the time of migration, parents' ages at their time of migration, years spent in the US, and whether the child lives in a single status (both parents are immigrants) or mixed-status (only one parent is foreign-born) household (Oropesa & Landale, 1997; Rumbaut, 2004). Thus generational differences in children's early developmental competencies and school readiness were also a central question of our study.

Research has consistently shown that children's outcomes differ according to their age and level of schooling at the time of migration (Cortes, 2006; Kao & Tienda, 1995; Oropesa & Landale, 1997). In a comprehensive analysis of the unique characteristics of different generational groups, Rumbaut (2004) provides a typology that takes these nativity influences into account. He uses what he refers to as "decimal" generations to further divide the first- and second-generations into more meaningful groups. According to Rumbaut, research on immigrant children should take into account whether a child migrated during early childhood (ages 0–5), middle childhood (6–12), or adolescence (in their teens). Each of these age groups is faced with different developmental tasks and contexts of socialization, and therefore, the processes of migration and subsequent acculturative change will likely be experienced differentially by each age group. Children who arrive before the age of 5, for instance, (the 1.75 generation) will have almost no recollection of experiences in their home country and experience the bulk of their language development and socialization in the US. The first-generation immigrant children in our own sample are part of this 1.75 generation.

When the focus is on very young immigrant children, what may be more important for their outcomes is the nativity status and age at arrival of their parents rather than the timing of their own arrival (Glick & Hohmann-Marriott, 2007). This is because immigrant parents who themselves arrived at a young age may be more acculturated, speak more English, and use child-rearing practices that more closely resemble those of a native-born parent, while a more recent immigrant parent may be less acculturated, speak less English, and exhibit child-rearing and parenting that is more consistent with cultural norms in the home country. Often markers like ethnicity, country of origin, and generation are simply proxies for cultural, historical, or socioeconomic differences in the family that more directly influence children's outcomes. This next section will discuss the family background/home environment and child-rearing and how they can influence outcomes for young immigrant children.

Family Characteristics and Parenting

Though the particular influence of the home environment may differ with the age and developmental stage of the child, background characteristics of the family and strategies parents use are undoubtedly important for immigrant children during the time of transition. Indicators of human capital, such as family socioeconomic status and parental education, consistently predict outcomes for all children (Gershoff, Aber, & Raver, 2005; McLoyd, 1998), including those in immigrant families (Crosnoe, 2007; Magnuson et al., 2006), with higher income and parental education related to more favorable educational outcomes. As discussed by Hernandez et al. (this volume), there is more diversity in parental education among immigrant groups than any other demographic indicator, and similar diversity is found with regard to income. Other research has demonstrated the stifling influence that socioeconomic stratification and segregation based on race, ethnicity, or nativity can exert on children's success (García Coll et al., 1996), making the expansion of programs and policies that aim to reduce this disparity paramount to the discussion of the well-being of immigrant children.

Researchers have also gone beyond indicators of human capital and examined aspects of social capital to explain influential family processes in immigrant families. Social capital is generally defined as "a unique resource generated from social relationships" (p. 177), and within-family social capital is an important mechanism through which immigrant parents transmit and reinforce educational expectations, as well as strengthen the parent–child bond (Hao & Bonstead-Bruns, 1998). Perreira et al. (2006) call attention to the manner in which many immigrant parents actively seek to transform adversity and foster resilience in their children. The Latino parents in Perreira et al.'s study did this by respecting their children's capacity to adapt, expressing interest in learning about resources to foster support for their children, encouraging bicultural coping skills in their children, and maintaining high levels of communication with their children.

Because very young children are likely to spend more time at home in the care of parents than at any other age, home resources and parenting practices are important for children's outcomes in early childhood (Bornstein & Cote, 2004, 2007; Bradley, Corwyn, McAdoo, & García Coll, 2001). Glick and Bates (in press), using data from the Early Childhood Longitudinal Study—Birth Cohort (ECLS-B), found that for most immigrant mothers (except those of Chinese origin), migrating during their own middle childhood and/or adolescence was associated with fewer home resources and less-responsive parenting practices, which negatively impacted their children's cognitive development at 24 months.

General knowledge about how to care for a child, how children develop, and what parents can do to foster children's development all contribute to a parent's ability to provide a developmentally appropriate environment for their child's growth (Bornstein & Cote, 2007). Because beliefs about, and practices surrounding, child-rearing can be highly culture-specific (Bradley et al., 2001; Rogoff, 2003) it is possible that differences among immigrant groups in knowledge about child development can translate into real differences in child outcomes (Bornstein & Cote, 2004).

Bornstein and Cote (2004) investigated this relationship and found that although middle-class Japanese and South American immigrant mothers had strong knowledge about issues of health and safety, they made more errors than native-born mothers in areas concerned with universally normative aspects of children's development (Bornstein & Cote, 2004). The authors highlight that gaps in knowledge about normative child development can impact mothers' responsiveness to their children's needs, the mother–child relationship, and reporting of developmental progress to the child's pediatrician. They also note that in the home countries of many immigrant parents, the community takes a larger role in monitoring individual children's development than is commonly seen in the US. Therefore, immigrant mothers in the US often find themselves without the level of support they are accustomed to with regard to gaining access to knowledge of typical child development.

If continued research on the early developmental competencies and school readiness of diverse preschoolers does show variation according to nativity history, ethnicity, national origins, or generation (as described in our study), we can look to such aspects of the home environment and parenting to begin to contextualize and explain any persistent differences we find. We now turn to a discussion of our own study of the school readiness of ethnically diverse children in immigrant and non-immigrant families living in Miami.

School Readiness for Diverse Immigrant Children in Poverty in Miami

Study Description and Methods

The Miami School Readiness Project (Winsler et al., 2008), a large-scale, 5-year, university–community collaborative project that involved evaluation of a variety of different early-childhood programs and services, offers an excellent opportunity to examine multiple domains of school readiness for immigrant children. Essentially the entire (consenting) population of the county's ethnically and linguistically diverse preschool children receiving subsidies to attend a variety of (non-Head Start) early-childhood programs were assessed on a wide variety of school-readiness domains and are currently being followed as they progress through the early elementary school years. The location of the study was quite ideal because Miami has long been known as a "melting pot" with a large, diverse immigrant population. In fact, in 2004, the United Nations Development Program (UNDP) ranked Miami as the city with the highest foreign-born population in the world at 59% (UNDP Human Development Report, 2004). Consequently, the Miami preschool sample offers a unique opportunity to study and compare large samples of subgroups of young immigrant children.

Because the literature on adolescent immigrant children consistently finds that some groups of immigrant youth tend to thrive while others struggle, we found it important to examine whether these same patterns of disparity would be found in very young children, prior to starting formal schooling. If there prove to be substantial nativity group differences already in the skills considered important for kindergarten, the situation may call for early intervention and preschool curricula that are more targeted to unique issues faced by various groups of immigrant and non-immigrant preschoolers. If, however, these diverse groups are virtually indistinguishable at this young age in terms of pre-academic and socioemotional skills, and disparate patterns of achievement appear only later in development, there would be implications for focusing on the early grade school years for offsetting the sources of disparity among children with different nativity histories.

Child participants for the current study consisted of 2,194 4-year-old preschoolers attending some kind of childcare (center-based childcare, family daycare, or informal care) in the Miami community via childcare subsidies during the 2003–2004 academic year. The subsample discussed in this chapter consists only of those children who (a) had sufficient data on child country of origin and parent country of origin to determine generational status of the child, and (b) had at least some repeated measures (pre and post) child-assessment data during their 4-year-old preschool year.

Children were assessed for cognitive and language development with the Learning Accomplishment Profile-Diagnostic (LAP-D; Nehring, Nehring, Bruni, & Randolph, 1992) which was administered individually to children in a separate room of the child's school, both around the beginning and end of the academic year. The assessor chose the language to use for assessment (English or Spanish) after asking the teacher to report the child's strongest language and/or establishing which language was more comfortable for the child during brief initial interactions. For more methodological details about the instruments used and procedures, see Winsler et al. (2008).

Children's social-emotional strengths and behavior problems were measured with teacher-report using the Devereux Early Childhood Assessment (DECA; LeBuffe & Naglieri, 1999) at the beginning and end of the school year. The DECA was designed to create a profile of children's social-emotional strengths or "protective factors" within a resilience framework. Teachers reported on the frequency of children's behavior by rating them on items comprising four subscales: initiative, self-control, attachment/closeness with adults, and behavioral concerns. The first three subscales are combined to create an overall socioemotional total protective factors score (bigger numbers indicating greater strengths) and the behavior-concerns scale is scored such that larger numbers indicate greater concerns with behavior. Total protective factors and behavior concerns are the scales used here in the analyses in the form of standardized national percentiles. Teachers had the choice of completing the form in English or Spanish.

For the purposes of this study, and as is common in other research on immigrants, generational status of the child was determined by a combination of the country of origin of the child and the country of origin of the reporting parent. Three groups were created, namely, first-generation immigrant children, second-generation immigrant children, and third or later generation (hereafter referred to as non-immigrant) children. A first-generation immigrant child was defined as being born in a country other than the US. Using Rumbaut's (2004) delineation of the immigrant first generation, this group, given they are only 4 years old, would technically be considered a part of the 1.75 generation. A second-generation immigrant child was defined as having a US country of birth with the reporting parent having a country of birth other than the US. A non-immigrant child was defined as having a US country of origin with the reporting parent also having a US country of origin. While it is the case that we only received country-of-origin information for one (reporting) parent, a full 92% of children in this high-risk sample were living in single-parent households, and therefore we can be reasonably confident that the nativity status of the reporting parent is of greatest proximity and importance to the development of the child.

Regions were created geographically and were based on the most common geographical regions of immigrant parents in the sample, namely, South America, Central America, Cuba, and (non-Cuban) Caribbean islands. Because Cubans represent such a large and influential group in Miami, and are therefore strongly represented in the preschool population, we decided to analyze their data in two ways—as a separate "region" as well as include them when analyzing by country. Given the unique historical circumstances of the relationship between Cuba and the US, and the status of most Cubans as political refugees, it seemed appropriate to analyze outcomes for Cuban children separately.

The countries that constituted each region of origin are as follows, in descending order by largest number of families to smallest. Countries of origin in the South American region included Colombia, Venezuela, Peru, Chile, Brazil, Argentina, and Bolivia. Countries in the Central American region included Nicaragua, Honduras, Mexico, Panama, and Costa Rica. Countries in the non-Cuban Caribbean region included Haiti, Dominican Republic, Puerto Rico,[1] Jamaica, Bahamas, Virgin Islands, and Other West Indies. It should also be noted that because the sample is composed only of children receiving subsidies to attend childcare, these countries of origin are not likely representative of the entire population of Miami preschoolers nor Miami immigrants. The preschoolers in this sample are those whose families are in need of, and receive, financial assistance in order to provide their children with some type of childcare. There are surely countries not represented in our sample that are more represented in the higher-income demographic in Miami, and are therefore able to pay for childcare out of pocket. Also, there are likely other low-income immigrant families in the area with preschoolers who do not receive childcare subsidies who are systematically not in our sample.

Results[2]

Child and Family Background Characteristics

There were several differences across the nativity groups with regard to child and family characteristics. Though the entire sample was very low income and therefore at elevated risk for educational difficulties, it appeared first- and second-generation immigrant children had slight advantages in terms of family background and resources while non-immigrant children with native-born parents had slight disadvantages. On average, non-immigrant children were living in larger families and their parents were the youngest and least likely of the three groups to be married. The majority of non-immigrant children were Black/African American (57%), and although they were most likely to be English-proficient, almost 20% of non-immigrant children were still stronger in Spanish than English, and these children tended not to do so well in language skills overall, as will be discussed in more detail below.

First-generation immigrant children were highly likely to be Latino (89%) and highly unlikely to be English-proficient. Two distinct advantages first-generation immigrant children had over the other groups is that their parents were more likely to be married and hold a high school diploma or GED, which could translate into more social capital and resources available to their children. Second-generation immigrant children were also likely to be Latino (78%) and only 35% were English-proficient. Immigrant parents of second-generation immigrant children had slightly higher incomes (+$1,000) compared to the other groups but the lowest levels of education. Further, only 10% of these parents were married. This snapshot of the family lives, on average, of the different nativity groups helps to provide some context when interpreting their relative competencies in skills considered important for school readiness.

As is demonstrated by the above data on child and family background characteristics for the sample, it should be noted that the entire sample of children is low income and at higher than average risk for academic difficulties. As such, when we describe any one group's competence as "high" or "low," it is in relative terms within a sample of children who are all scoring generally low on these assessments. Results are reported here using national percentile scores where appropriate so the reader can more easily gauge the skill levels of the children relative to national norms. It should also be noted that controlling for the above demographic and family background factors did not change the outcomes of the analyses presented below, potentially because the sample is based on an already quite restricted range of family income.

During our study, we were interested in taking what we had learned from the literature on the diversity of educational outcomes for adolescent youth according to nativity, generation, ethnicity, and country of origin, and examining how it applies to preschool children, an understudied population in these areas. For each school-readiness domain (cognitive, language, socioemotional protective factors, and behavior concerns), we start with broad conceptualizations of the term "immigrant" and reach higher levels of specificity with each analysis. We first ask if children show similar levels of competence in these domains according to whether they are first-generation immigrants with foreign-born parents, second-generation immigrants with foreign-born parents, or non-immigrants with native-born parents. We then ask what importance race/ethnicity has for the school readiness of children with and without immigrant parents and examine whether the overall generational patterns persist within each race/ethnic group. Next we look deeper into the specific national origins of the first- and second-generation immigrant children, and ask whether diversity of school-readiness outcomes exists according to region or country of origin.

Cognitive Development

We first considered how each of the three nativity groups of first-generation immigrant, second-generation immigrant, and non-immigrant children performed in terms of cognitive skills. The first noteworthy pattern we observed was that all three nativity groups were making important and similar gains from the beginning to the end of the pre-kindergarten year in terms of cognitive skills. These gains are in terms of national percentiles, so it is not just maturation we are observing here. On average, children in the sample were improving their relative standing compared to national norms by about 5–6 percentile points across the year. Though the three groups were making similar gains, they differed in their overall level of cognitive competence at both time points. Specifically, non-immigrant children displayed stronger cognitive skills than both first- and second-generation immigrant children, who were not significantly different from each other. These differences were not accounted for by differences in parental income, education, family size, or marital status between the groups. Non-immigrant children reached the national average of the 50th percentile by the end of the year on average whereas the immigrant children started (39th–41st percentile) and ended the year (44th–45th percentile) at greater cognitive risk below national averages.

Because the ethnic composition of the nativity groups differed substantially, we investigated whether the nativity group differences discussed above held within each race/ethnic group.[3] Interestingly, while the same pattern showing non-immigrant advantage for cognitive skills was true for Black children, a different pattern emerged for Latino children. For Latino children, non-immigrant and first-generation immigrant children were indistinguishable in terms of cognitive skills, with only second-generation children lagging behind.

There were also geographic region and country-of-origin effects on immigrant children's cognitive functioning. Immigrant children from South America tended to demonstrate higher cognitive skills (48th percentile at post) than immigrants from other regions (40th–47th percentile at post), and Central American immigrant children appeared to be struggling the most (40th percentile at post). In terms of country of origin, there were both main effects for country but also significant country-by-time interactions. Children with family origins in Puerto Rico started the year showing the most cognitive competence (49th percentile), and thus did not show much improvement over the year. Comparatively, immigrant children from Honduras and the Dominican Republic appeared to be struggling the most with regard to cognitive skills at the beginning of the year (28th and 29th percentiles, respectively), but Dominican-origin children made excellent gains across the year, and by Spring, showed similar levels of cognitive skills as the other six groups. Children from Haiti began the year in the middle of the pack with regard to cognitive skills, but made great gains across the year and by Spring showed the highest levels of cognitive skills of any immigrant group (49th percentile). Though we predicted Cuban children may have an advantage in some domains due to their group's elevated social standing within the Miami community, we found they demonstrated average cognitive skills among this group of low-income, first- and second-generation immigrant children. Overall these results reveal that there is already substantial heterogeneity in cognitive outcomes and trajectories in preschool for immigrant children according to nativity status, ethnicity, region of origin, and country of origin.

Language Development

The LAPD language measure was administered in what appeared to be the child's strongest language, and thus was intended to measure general linguistic competence. As was seen earlier for cognitive skills, all three groups of children were at considerable risk but made excellent and similar gains (i.e., 10 national percentile points) in language skills across the preschool year. Again, however, they differed in overall competence at any time point. Non-immigrant children (about 82% of them assessed in English) demonstrated the strongest language skills (46th percentile at post). First-generation immigrant children (78% of them assessed in Spanish) showed intermediate levels of language facility (40th percentile at post), whereas second-generation immigrant children (65% of them assessed in Spanish) scored the lowest (35th percentile at post) in language skills. As was done with cognitive skills, we asked whether the overall nativity group differences held within each ethnic group (still overall, ignoring language of assessment). Within Latino children, it was second-generation immigrant children who lagged behind the other two groups in language and for Black children, non-immigrants scored significantly higher than the two immigrant groups.

A more interesting picture emerged when we analyzed just Latino children's language outcomes by nativity group separately for those assessed in English and Spanish. English-dominant/assessed Latino children followed the overall pattern that non-immigrant children were more linguistically advanced (in English) than first-generation immigrant children who, in turn, were more advanced than second-generation immigrant children. However, for Spanish-dominant/assessed Latino children, first-generation immigrant children were more linguistically advanced (in Spanish) than both second-generation and non-immigrant children.

So it appears first-generation children, if they are strong in their native language and are assessed in their native language, do quite well among the other groups in language skills considered important for kindergarten. On the other hand, second-generation and non-immigrant children tend to do better if they take their assessments in English. The finding that second-generation immigrant children tend to demonstrate the least competence of the three groups in language skills, regardless of whether they were assessed in English or Spanish, is quite important and suggests that the quality of language input in the home in both English and Spanish may be limited for second-generation immigrant children in poverty.

In terms of country and region of origin, the story is similar for language skills as it was for cognitive skills—immigrant children with origins in South America, Cuba, and the Caribbean islands all showed similar levels of language skills (36th–40th percentile at post), but children from Central America tended to be struggling by comparison (30th percentile at post). Puerto Rican and Cuban children started the year more advanced in language skills (31st and 29th percentiles, respectively) than children from other countries, and both groups made modest gains across the year. Children from Colombia and Haiti, on the other hand, began the year in the middle of the groups in terms of language competence, but made large gains across the year so that by Spring, they were scoring higher than all other groups (42nd and 39th percentiles, respectively). Immigrant children from Honduras (26th percentile at post) and the Dominican Republic (32nd percentile at post) appeared to be struggling the most with language, but Dominican-origin children made good gains and by the end of the year were more similar to other groups in language skills, while Honduran children still lagged behind. Again, we see that heterogeneity by country of origin, ethnicity, and language background is the key to understanding immigrant children's school readiness and that simple comparisons of nativity groups averaging across these factors are limited.

Socioemotional Development

In the area of socioemotional protective factors, which includes initiative, attachment/closeness with adults, and self-control, children in all groups started the year at less risk than they did in the cognitive/language area (around the national average for 4-year-olds) and made good and similar gains in social skills across the year. Most importantly, however, first-generation immigrant children showed considerable strengths in this area and were rated as higher on socioemotional protective factors by their preschool teachers (59th–66th percentile) than second-generation immigrants (52nd–58th percentile), who in turn were rated higher than non-immigrant children (50th–56th percentile) at both time points. When examined separately within each ethnic group, the same pattern of first-generation immigrant advantage in social skills was seen within each ethnic group at both time points.

Unlike what was seen in the cognitive and language domains, there were no differences in overall levels or gains in socioemotional protective factors among children with immigrant parents according to either region or country of origin. Rather, children with immigrant parents from all regions and countries showed similarly high socioemotional skills when compared to children with native-born parents.

Behavior Concerns

Overall, children in all groups either remained stable or improved their behavior slightly over the course of the school year according to teachers. However, as was seen with protective factors, the groups differed with respect to the mean levels of behavior problems displayed, with first-generation immigrant children displaying the fewest behavior concerns (46th percentile—just below national averages at post for problem behavior for 4-year-olds), followed by second-generation immigrant children (52nd percentile at post), and then non-immigrant children (57th percentile at post), who posed the greatest behavior problems for preschool teachers.

When immigrant groups were compared separately within Black and Latino children, we found that Black children followed the overall pattern, however, within just Latino children, non-immigrants were still the group with the most behavior concerns (57th percentile at post), but first- and second-generation immigrant children did not differ significantly from one another (47th and 52nd percentiles, respectively). There were few differences in children's behavior concerns according to region or country of origin. However, there was one exception worth pointing out—immigrant children with Haitian origins in Miami showed impressive reductions in behavior problems across the 4-year-old preschool year while the behavior concerns of children from all other countries remained relatively stable.

Conclusions

As is discussed throughout this book, immigrant children are extremely diverse in terms of language, skin color, religion, culture, and national origins, and this diversity has been shown to translate into disparities in educational outcomes for different groups (Crosnoe, 2007; García Coll et al., 1996; Magnuson et al., 2006). The first step in solving this puzzle, and closing the achievement gaps between children of varying national and ethnic backgrounds, is to start early and focus on how these children are doing before entering formal schooling. Once we have a good understanding of overall school-readiness patterns, we can begin to identify any familial, cultural, or sociohistorical processes involved in these educational disparities, and be more prepared to develop and implement relevant and informed educational policies and practices.

A major goal of our study was to investigate whether the same heterogeneity of educational outcomes found among older immigrant youth (according to factors like generation, ethnicity, and country of origin) would be found in the school-readiness outcomes of a sample of ethnically diverse, low-income preschool children. Our results revealed that even at the preschool age, children differed in a number of important ways according to family immigration history, generation, ethnicity, and national origins. Though the entire sample was low income and all the families likely faced a number of challenges, non-immigrant children tended to be slightly more disadvantaged in terms of family socioeconomic factors than either first- or second-generation immigrant children.

Overall, non-immigrant children showed stronger cognitive and language skills than first- or second-generation immigrant children. However, in the areas of socioemotional protective factors and behavior concerns, there was a clear immigrant advantage. First-generation immigrant children showed more socioemotional strengths than second-generation immigrant children, who in turn showed greater socioemotional strengths than non-immigrant children. Further, both first- and second-generation immigrant children displayed fewer behavior concerns than non-immigrant children. Unlike with cognitive and language skills, national origins did not seem to matter as much for socioemotional skills and behavior. First- and second-generation immigrant children displayed stronger socioemotional skills and fewer behavior concerns than non-immigrant children regardless of their family's national origins.

Perhaps there is something more universal about the immigration experience that helps young immigrant children attain stronger socioemotional skills in preschool. It could be the selection factor that parents who choose to migrate raise more socioemotionally competent children than parents who stay in the home country. Perhaps a more likely explanation is that parents from these non-US countries simply emphasize traits like initiative, self-control, and closeness with adults in children this age to a greater extent than do mainstream American parents, who often emphasize more academically focused socialization goals. Increased emphasis on social and behavioral competence by immigrant parents has been documented in other literature (Hao & Bonstead-Bruns, 1998; Okagaki & Sternberg, 1993; Perreira et al., 2006; Yearwood, 2001) and may be an area that educators can leverage in concert with immigrant parents to promote the academic achievement of immigrant children.

For most of the school-readiness domains, the effects of generational status depended somewhat on children's ethnicity. For Black children, non-immigrants demonstrated more language and cognitive competence than either of the immigrant groups. However, the pattern was different for Latino children, for whom first-generation immigrant children performed just as well as non-immigrant children. We also saw differences in cognitive and language skills according to national origins, whereby South American immigrant children showed the strongest skills and Central American immigrant children tended to be struggling, especially those from Honduras. We do know that many of the migrant farmworkers in South Florida originate from Central America, and that children in these families face additional risks such as increased mobility, crowded housing, and exposure to pesticides (Mehta et al., 2000). It is possible that these increased risks are being reflected in lower average cognitive and language skills for low-income Central American immigrant children as a whole.

Another interesting finding was that first-generation immigrant children, if they were strong in their native language and assessed in their native language, did quite well compared to the other groups in language skills considered important for kindergarten. On the other hand, second-generation and non-immigrant children tended to do better if they took their assessments in English. The low language performance in general (regardless of language of assessment) for second-generation immigrants is of some concern and suggests that interventions focusing on rich language input in home and in school for second-generation immigrant children may be needed. Clearly, further research on the how the home language and literacy environments differ between first- and second-generation immigrant children is needed and may shed more light on language patterns such as those found here.

In interpreting the overall results of our study, it is also important to consider the unique local context of Miami with regard to its history, demographics, and present policies toward immigration. First, Florida, and Miami-Dade County in particular, is unique with regard to the sheer number and concentration of recent immigrants. In the period between 2000 and 2005, the US-born population in Florida grew by 8.7%, while the state's immigrant population grew by 20.8% (totaling 3.2 million in 2005). Miami-Dade has the highest percentage of immigrants state-wide, with 51% of residents born in another country (Eisenhauer, Zhang, Hernandez, & Angee, 2007). This makes immigrants in Miami a majority, rather than a minority as in many other locales across the country. This concentration alone, and its implication for Miami as a receiving community with a first-hand understanding of the challenges of migration, could contribute to our finding that first-generation immigrant children have some developmental advantages. These advantages could act through better second-language accommodations in the community, enhanced resources available and accessible for recent immigrants, and/or increased social capital and support during the transition.

Further, we found that being a recent immigrant appeared to provide a larger advantage for Latino as compared to Black children. Here, it may be important to consider the local context and political climate in Miami. First, not only is the Latino population larger in number, but there exists a controversial US policy toward the differential treatment and repatriation of Cuban (the largest Latino immigrant group) versus Haitian immigrants (the largest Black immigrant group) seeking refuge on the Miami shores. Since the beginning of the Cold War, the US has taken in Cubans who make the 90-mile ocean voyage to US soil, defining them as political refugees seeking asylum from a Communist regime. Haitians, on the other hand, make a similar voyage to escape economic, and in some cases political, oppression, but have historically been sent back to Haiti (Dawkins, 2000). Further, in December 2001, there was a change in Immigration and Naturalization Service (INS; now US Citizenship and Immigration Services—USCIS) policy that resulted in the indefinite detention of Haitian refugees and asylum seekers in INS facilities and detention centers, rather than immediate release and repatriation. Because this policy applied specifically to Haitians, it attracted the attention of the American Civil Liberties Union (ACLU) and the Florida Immigrant Advocacy Center (FIAC) and was described by the organizations as "discriminatory" and "anti-Haitian" (US Commission on Civil Rights, 2002). It is quite possible that such policies could contribute to racial tensions in the community as well as feelings of marginalization for Black immigrant parents, somewhat neutralizing the immigrant optimism and advantage that has been described in other studies (Ogbu & Simmons, 1998; Portes, 1999).

It is further possible that US government support of Cuban refugees has "spillover effects" for Latino immigrants in general, at least in terms of language accommodations and resources. Research on older youth has found that retention of ethnic identity, values, and community ties can be beneficial for the educational attainment of some immigrant youth (Rong & Brown, 2001; Rumbaut, 1997) and while the Miami context likely facilitates this process for Latino immigrants, the same may not be the case, at least not to the same extent, for Black Caribbean immigrants, and we may be seeing this reflected in lower cognitive and language skills for their children. Though these are some of the unique immigration policy issues facing the Miami community, each community across the nation is experiencing increased recent immigration in its own way, and the local policies that are enacted directly affect the opportunities and resources available to immigrant children. A better understanding of how these local policies, in Miami and around the country, influence the lives of immigrant children is needed to evaluate their effects and drive policy toward more effective strategies for educating our diverse nation.

One "immigrant advantage" that persisted regardless of ethnicity or national origins was in socioemotional protective factors and behavior. Teachers consistently rated all groups of immigrant children as stronger than native-born children in these areas. These findings are similar to those by Crosnoe (2006, 2007) where Mexican immigrant children nationally showed fewer externalizing behavior problems and more emotional competence and maturity when compared to their non-immigrant peers. Considering that kindergarten teachers often place more importance on social skills and behavior for success in kindergarten than on academic skills (Lin et al., 2003; West et al., 1995), the strong initiative, self-control, attachment, and good behavior of immigrant children could be a valuable asset to build upon when they enter kindergarten. In fact, future longitudinal analyses with our sample will serve to answer the question of just how important immigrant children's socioemotional skills are to their later academic success.

If kindergarten teachers are aware of and can leverage these skills in immigrant children, then it is possible that socioemotional strengths could serve as a "bootstrapping" mechanism by which immigrant children can raise their level of skills in academic domains, perhaps through enhanced teacher–child and child–child interactions in the context of learning. Our preliminary follow-up research on this sample of children suggests that by second grade, first- and second-generation immigrant children no longer lag behind non-immigrant children in academic areas (grades and standardized test scores), and perform even better on behavioral measures like attendance and tardiness (De Feyter, Hutchison, & Winsler, 2008). Future analyses will determine whether the ability of children in immigrant families to "catch up" to non-immigrant children academically during the early years of school can be attributed, at least in part, to their socioemotional and behavioral strengths. Further, more detailed knowledge of the combinations of strengths and challenges held by many immigrant children in early childhood will help teachers and parents be more prepared to implement educational practices that can build on those strengths which, in turn, will serve to foster their later contributions as members of US society.

Finally, the provision of quality early-childhood education programs is seen by many as an important policy strategy for improving the school readiness and academic trajectories of children in poverty, immigrant or not, and for reducing the achievement gap (Entwisle & Alexander, 1993; Takanishi, 2004). Results from the Miami School Readiness Project so far (Winsler et al., 2008), and those presented here, suggest that immigrant and non-immigrant children who attend even garden-variety early childcare and pre-k programs make considerable progress in multiple domains of school readiness during their 4-year-old pre-k year. The fact that there were no nativity group-by-time interactions found here suggests that such early care and education experiences likely benefit both immigrant and non-immigrant children equally.

Immigrant children in the Miami community have benefited from the recent implementation of a voluntary universal pre-k program in the state of Florida (Florida House of Representatives, 2004), and as such, Miami can serve as a model for other communities wanting to increase access to early education and care for immigrant children. As pointed out by Crosnoe (2007) and discussed earlier, good-quality childcare and early-education programs for young immigrant children are a worthy investment, especially if they can build on and not jeopardize the existing socioemotional and behavioral strengths of young immigrant children. Evidence from our study in Miami suggests that immigrant children's social skills only increased over the course of the year in childcare and children's behavior problems as reported by teachers certainly did not increase over time. Thus, it would appear that early-childhood programs have much potential for improving the health and welfare of a diversity of immigrant families.

Acknowledgments

The Miami School Readiness Project was made possible and supported by the Early Learning Coalition of Miami-Dade/Monroe and other participating agencies including Miami-Dade County Child Development Services, and Miami-Dade County Public Schools.

Portions of this chapter were presented at the "On New Shores: Understanding Immigrant Children" conference in Guelph, Canada—October, 2007.

Work on this chapter was partially supported by The Children's Trust. The Trust is a dedicated source of revenue established by voter referendum to improve the lives of children and families in Miami-Dade County.

Notes

1. Though Puerto Rico is not a sovereign nation but a self-governing US territory, we found it appropriate to analyze their outcomes as a group distinct from mainland US children.
2. Throughout, we present only results that are statistically significant at least at the $p < 0.05$ level.
3. Unfortunately, because of the low numbers of White immigrants in Miami as compared to other groups, we were not able to investigate this point for children who were White.

References

Belsky, J. (1999). Quantity of nonmaternal care and boys' behavior/adjustment at ages 3 and 5: Exploring the mediating role of parenting. *Psychiatry: Interpersonal and Biological Processes, 62*(1), 1–20.

Bornstein, M.H., & Cote, L.R. (2004). "Who is sitting across from me?" Immigrant mothers' knowledge of parenting and children's development. *Pediatrics, 114*, 557–564.

Bornstein, M.H., & Cote, L.R. (2007). Knowledge of child development and family interactions among immigrants to America: Perspectives from developmental science. In J.E. Lansford, K. Deater-Deckard, & M.H. Bornstein (Eds.), *Immigrant families in contemporary society* (pp. 121–136). New York: Guilford Press.

Bradley, R.H., Corwyn, R.F., McAdoo, H.P., & García Coll, C. (2001). The home environments of children in the United States Part I: Variations by age, ethnicity, and poverty status. *Child Development, 72*(6), 1844–1867.

Brandon, P.D. (2004). The child care arrangements of preschool-age children in immigrant families in the United States. *International Migration, 42*(1), 65–87.

Braun, S.J., & Edwards, E.P. (1972). *History and theory of early childhood education.* Worthington, OH: C.A. Jones.

Campbell, F.A., Ramey, C.T., Pungello, E., Sparling, J., & Miller-Johnson, S. (2002). Early childhood education: Young adult outcomes from the Abecedarian Project. *Applied Developmental Science, 6*(1), 42–57.

Cortes, K. (2006). The effects of age at arrival and enclave schools on the academic performance of immigrant children. *Economics of Education Review, 25*(2), 121–132.

Crosnoe, R. (2006). *Mexican roots, American schools: Helping Mexican immigrant children succeed.* Stanford, CA: Stanford University Press.

Crosnoe, R. (2007). Early child care and the school readiness of children from Mexican immigrant families. *International Migration Review, 41*(1), 152–181.

Dawkins, M.P. (2000, April 27). Rethinking US immigration policy: Brief article. *Black Issues in Higher Education*. Retrieved April 5, 2009, from http://findarticles.com/p/articles/mi_m0DXK/is_5_17/ai_62297190.

De Feyter, J.J., Hutchison, L.A., & Winsler, A. (2008, November). After preschool: Follow-up on early schooling outcomes for diverse, low-income immigrant children. Poster presented at the conference: *On new shores: Understanding immigrant children*, Guelph, Ontario.

Eisenhauer, E., Zhang, Y., Hernandez, C.S., & Angee, A. (2007). *Immigrants in Florida: Characteristics and contributions*. Miami, FL: Florida International University, Research Institute for Social and Economic Policy. Retrieved April 5, 2009, from www.risep-fiu.org/reports/immigrants_spring_2007.pdf.

Entwisle, D.R., & Alexander, K.L. (1993). Entry into school: The beginning school transition and educational stratification in the United States. *Annual Review of Sociology, 19*, 401–423.

Florida House of Representatives. (2004). *Voluntary Prekindergarten Education Program* (1002.51 Florida Statute).

Fuligni, A. (1997). The academic achievement of adolescents from immigrant families: The roles of family background, attitudes, and behavior. *Child Development, 68*(2), 351–363.

García Coll, C., Lamberty, G., Jenkins, R., McAdoo, H.P., Crnic, K., Wasik, B.H., & Vázguez García, H. (1996). An integrative model for the study of developmental competencies in minority children. *Child Development, 67*, 1891–1914.

Gershoff, E.T., Aber, J.L., & Raver, C.C. (2005). Child poverty in the United States: An evidence-based conceptual framework for programs and policies. In R.M. Lerner, F. Jacobs, & D. Wertlieb (Eds.), *Applied developmental science* (pp. 269–324). Thousand Oaks, CA: Sage.

Glick, J.E., & Bates, L.A. (in press). The influence of mother's age at arrival in the United States on early cognitive development: Children of immigrants and natives in the ECLS-B. *Early Childhood Research Quarterly*.

Glick, J.E., & Hohmann-Marriott, B.E. (2007). Academic performance of young children in immigrant families: The significance of race, ethnicity, and national origins. *International Migration Review, 41*(2), 371–402.

Hao, L., & Bonstead-Bruns, M. (1998). Parent–child differences in educational expectations and the academic achievement of immigrant and native students. *Sociology of Education, 71*(3), 175–198.

Kao, G., & Tienda, M. (1995). Optimism and achievement: The educational performance of immigrant youth. *Social Science Quarterly, 76*(1), 1–19.

LeBuffe, P.A., & Naglieri, J.A. (1999). *The Devereux Early Child Assessment (DECA)*. Lewisville, NC: Kaplan, Early Learning Company.

Leventhal, T., Xue, Y., & Brooks-Gunn, J. (2006). Immigrant differences in school-age children's verbal trajectories: A look at four racial/ethnic groups. *Child Development, 77*(5), 1359–1374.

Lin, H.L., Lawrence, F.R., & Gorell, J. (2003). Kindergarten teacher views of children's readiness for school. *Early Childhood Research Quarterly, 18*, 225–237.

Magnuson, K.A., Lahaie, C., & Waldfogel, J. (2006). Preschool and school readiness of children of immigrants. *Social Science Quarterly, 87*(5), 1241–1262.

McLoyd, V. (1998). Socioeconomic disadvantage and child development. *American Psychologist, 53*, 185–204.

Mehta, K., Gabbard, S., Barrat, V., Lewis, M., Carroll, D., & Mines, R. (2000). *Findings from the National Agricultural Workers Survey (NAWS) 1997–1998: A demographic and employment profile of United States farmworkers* (Research Report No. 8). Washington, DC: US Department of Labor.

Meisels, S.J., & Shonkoff, P.J. (2000). Early childhood intervention: A continuing evolution. In P.J.

Shonkoff & S.J. Meisels (Eds.), *Handbook of early intervention* (2nd ed., pp. 3–31). New York: Cambridge University Press.

National Institute of Child Health and Human Development Early Child Care Research Network. (2005). *Child care and child development: Results from the NICHD study of early child care and youth development.* New York: Guilford Press.

Nehring, A.D., Nehring, E.F., Bruni, J.R., & Randolph, P.L. (1992). *Learning accomplishment profile: Diagnostic standardized assessment.* Lewisville, NC: Kaplan Press.

Ogbu, J., & Simmons, H.D. (1998). Voluntary and involuntary minorities: A cultural-ecological theory of school performance with some implications for education. *Anthropology & Education Quarterly, 29,* 155–188.

Okagaki, L., & Sternberg, R.J. (1993). Parental beliefs and children's school performance. *Child Development, 64,* 36–56.

Oropesa, R.S., & Landale, N.S. (1997). In search of the new second generation: Alternative strategies for identifying second generation children and understanding their acquisition of English. *Sociological Perspectives, 40*(3), 429–455.

Perreira, K.M., Chapman, M.V., & Stein, G.L. (2006). Becoming an American parent: Overcoming challenges and finding strength in a new immigrant Latino community. *Journal of Family Issues, 27*(10), 1383–1414.

Portes, P. (1999). Social and psychological factors in the academic achievement of children of immigrants: A cultural history puzzle. *American Educational Research Journal, 36*(3), 489–507.

Ramey, C.T., & Ramey, S.L. (1998). Early intervention and early experience. *American Psychologist, 53,* 109–120.

Rogoff, B. (2003). *The cultural nature of human development.* Oxford: Oxford University Press.

Rong, X.L., & Brown, F. (2001). The effects of immigrant generation and ethnicity on educational attainment among young African and Caribbean Blacks in the United States. *Harvard Educational Review, 71*(3), 536–565.

Rumbaut, R.G. (1997). Paradoxes (and orthodoxies) of assimilation. *Sociological Perspectives, 40*(3), 483–511.

Rumbaut, R.G. (2004). Ages, life stages, and generational cohorts: Decomposing the immigrant first and second generations in the United States. *International Migration Review, 38*(3), 1160–1205.

Schweinhart, L.J., Montie, J., Xiang, Z., Barnett, W.S., Belfield, C.R., & Nores, M. (2004). *Lifetime effects: The High/Scope Perry Preschool Study through age 40.* Ypsilanti, MI: High/Scope Press.

Suárez-Orozco, C. (2007, October). *Moving stories: Developmental and educational trajectories of newcomer immigrant children and youth.* Paper presented at the conference *On new shores: Understanding immigrant children,* Guelph, Ontario.

Takanishi, R. (2004). Leveling the playing field: Supporting immigrant children from birth to eight. *The Future of Children, 14*(2), 61–79.

United Nations Development Programme. (2004). *Human development report 2004.* http://hdr.undp.org/reports/global/2004/pdf/hdr04_frontmatter.pdf.

United States Commission on Civil Rights. (2002). *Briefing on Haitian asylum seekers and U.S. immigration policy: Executive summary.* www.law.umaryland.edu/marshall/usccr/documents/civilrightsbriefhaitianasylum.pdf.

West, J., Hausken, E.G., & Collins, M. (1995). *Readiness for kindergarten: Parent and teacher beliefs.* Washington, DC: Department of Education, National Center for Education Statistics.

Winsler, A., Tran, H., Hartman, S.C., Madigan, A.L., Manfra, L., & Bleiker, C. (2008). School readiness gains made by ethnically diverse children in poverty attending center-based childcare and public school pre-kindergarten programs. *Early Childhood Research Quarterly, 23,* 314–329.

Yearwood, E.L. (2001). "Growing up" children: Current child-rearing practices among immigrant Jamaican families. *Journal of Child and Adolescent Psychiatric Nursing, 14,* 7–17.

4 Preparing the Way

Early Head Start and the Socioemotional Health of Latino Infants and Toddlers

Krista M. Perreira, Linda Beeber, Todd Schwartz, Diane Holditch-Davis, India Ornelas, and Lauren Maxwell

Since 1995, Early Head Start (EHS) programs have been "preparing the way" for low-income infants and toddlers to enter school. They combine child-centered interventions with family support to help improve the socioemotional development of infants and toddlers and their readiness to engage in school. During the last decade, many EHS programs experienced a rapid increase in the number of enrolled infants and toddlers with Latina and immigrant mothers (Vogel et al., 2006). In 2006, 25% of children in EHS were Latino and many families served by EHS (16%) spoke primarily Spanish at home (Vogel et al., 2006).

Despite their increasing presence in EHS programs, we know substantially less about the early-childhood development of Latino children, especially the children of immigrants, than we do about the development of children with non-Hispanic White or African American parents. While some have studied the development of school-aged Latino children (Dennis, Parke, Coltrane, Blancher, & Borthwick-Duffy, 2003; Pachter, Auinger, Palmer, & Weitzman, 2006), few studies have examined the development of Latino infants and toddlers (Bradley, Corwyn, & McAdoo, 2001; Bradley, Corwyn, & Burchinal, 2001; Malik et al., 2007) and none that we know of have examined the development of Latino infants and toddlers with immigrant parents. The migration and acculturation experience of immigrant parents creates a unique ecological niche that shapes the development of their young children. Therefore, these families and the development of their children must be studied in context. Research conducted on the development of other population groups cannot be simply extrapolated to Latino children with immigrant parents.

This chapter examines how EHS programs can promote the well-being of young children of immigrants and ultimately their school readiness by treating the depressive symptoms of their mothers. Our research focuses on immigrant mothers from Latin America who participated in EHS programs in North Carolina, a state that saw a dramatic increase in the size of its Latino and immigrant communities between 1990 and 2000. In addition, our research integrates multiple methods of data collection (survey, observational, and unstructured personal interviews) to illustrate the interrelationships between depression, early-childhood development, and the context of migration and acculturation to life in the US.

Background

Latin American Migration and North Carolina

As shown by Hernandez (this volume), the Latino population is currently the fastest-growing population in the US. As these Latino populations in the US have grown, they have also dispersed geographically to new settlement communities throughout the US. Among these new settlement communities, the state of North Carolina ranked first in the percentage growth of the Latino population between 1990 and 2000.

At the time this study began in 2004, approximately 600,913 Latinos (7% of the state's population) lived in North Carolina and the Hispanic share of the population under age 5 had grown to 14% (Kasarda & Johnson, 2006; US Census Bureau, 2004). Despite perceptions to the contrary, the majority (56%) of Latinos living in North Carolina are legally present in the US. They were born in North Carolina (21%) or in another US jurisdiction (21%), or entered the US with a family or work visa (14%). Among foreign-born Latinos living in North Carolina in 2004, 76% had emigrated from Mexico.

The growth of the Latino population in North Carolina and other emerging Latino communities has substantial implications for early-childhood programs (e.g., Head Start and Early Head Start) that prepare young children for school. In 2000, Early Head Start (EHS) staff in North Carolina reported that many of their newest clients were Latina mothers who were struggling with depressive symptoms (Beeber, Canuso, & Emory, 2004). Since little was known about these mothers and their families, this study was undertaken to examine key factors associated with depression in immigrant Latina mothers enrolled in EHS and the effects of depression on parenting infants and toddlers in this unique community. Mothers with depression were subsequently enrolled in an intervention, called *ALAS* (i.e., "wings"), designed to help them nurture their children while reducing their depressive symptoms (Beeber et al., 2007).

Early Head Start Programs and Early Childhood Development

The EHS program grew out of the Head Start program launched by Lyndon Johnson in 1965 as part of the "War on Poverty" (National Head Start Association, 2005). As a comprehensive child-development program for low-income 4- and 5-year-olds, Head Start provided an enriched curriculum and family support services.[1] In 1994, Congress passed a sweeping reauthorization bill that authorized EHS. Currently, 750 EHS programs serve over 62,000 infants and toddlers across the US and Puerto Rico (Vogel et al., 2006).

Funded through the Department of Health and Human Services and administered by local grantees, EHS has established and upheld national standards for infant-toddler childcare while simultaneously permitting local communities to shape innovative early-enrichment programs to meet local needs (Chazan-Cohen, Stark, Mann, & Fitzgerald, 2007). One innovation has been a national performance standard requiring a focus on the promotion of infant-toddler mental health. Under this aegis, maternal depressive symptoms were addressed through EHS initiatives for the first time. Furthermore, EHS programs embraced a commitment to provide culturally and linguistically appropriate services and home-based services. As one of the few federally funded initiatives that serves the children of immigrant parents regardless of parents' immigration status, EHS has become an essential resource for children of immigrants in the post-welfare-reform era (National Head Start Association, 2005).

Since its inception, rigorous evaluations have shown that EHS improves the readiness of young children to engage in school (Love et al., 2005; Olsen & DeBoise, 2007). These evaluations suggest that it is possible to alter the development of cognitive, emotional, and social skills in young children through early-childhood intervention (Brooks-Gunn, 2004). Previous evaluations with very young children also support this claim (Cambell & Ramsey, 1994; Yoshikawa, 1995). Cognitive and language outcomes for at-risk children can improve when they are provided with stimulating, stable, and caring environments.

While studies have used treatment and control groups to evaluate the effectiveness of EHS and other early childhood interventions, few have evaluated the differential effects of EHS by three potentially critical moderators—race-ethnicity, primary language spoken at home, and maternal depression (Malik et al., 2007; Robinson & Emde, 2004). The current study contributes to the literature on EHS by focusing on a relatively understudied population—Spanish-speaking women who have recently immigrated from Latin America—and by evaluating the relationships between maternal depression, mother–child interactions, and child socioemotional development among these women.

Risk Factors for Maternal Depression Among Latinas

While few have studied maternal depression among Latinas (Dennis et al., 2003; Pachter et al., 2006), previous research has shown that the lifetime prevalence of depressive symptoms is higher among Latinos than either non-Hispanic Whites or African Americans (Vega & Rumbaut, 1991). Among Latinos there are significant differences in the lifetime prevalence of depression and other psychiatric disorders by country of origin (e.g., Mexico, Puerto Rico, or Cuba), immigrant status, and acculturation (Alderete, Vega, Kolody, & Aguilar-Gaxiola, 2000; Vega & Rumbaut, 1991).

Among mothers, economic hardship, social isolation, and family conflict can increase the risk for depression. Low-income mothers have up to four times the risk of developing severe depressive symptoms as middle-income mothers (Brown & Moran, 1997; Lanzi et al., 1999; Pascoe, Stolfi, & Ormond, 2006). Unmarried women and women who report low levels of social support are more at risk of depression (Dawson et al., 2003; DeKlyen, Brooks-Gunn, & McLanahan, 2006; Pascoe et al., 2006). Finally, women who experience family conflict including marital discord and domestic violence are more likely to experience depression (Coker et al., 2003; Malik et al., 2007; Martin et al., 2006).

Each of these risk factors is prevalent among Latina immigrant women. New immigrants from Mexico and other Latin American countries move to the US to find work and to build a better future for their children (Portes & Rumbaut, 1996). Despite their aspirations, Latina immigrant mothers often encounter challenges that prevent them from creating the strong, intact families and better lives that they have idealized (Portes & Rumbaut, 1996). Moving to the US exposes them and their children to acculturative stress, the weakening of protective cultural social supports, social marginality, and identity disintegration (Acevedo, 1999; Alderete et al., 2000). These experiences place them at risk for depressive symptoms.

A mother's sense of self-efficacy can help to counter the migration and acculturation experiences that place her at risk for depressive symptoms. Moreover, a strong sense of self-efficacy can mediate the relationship between depression and its potential consequences for parenting and child well-being. Considered a trait-like attribute (Mallinckrodt, 1992), self-efficacy refers to a person's beliefs in his or her ability to achieve goals and influence the events that affect his or her life. "Perceptions of self-efficacy determine the amount of effort an individual expends and how long they will persist in the face of adversity, which in turn shapes affective responses to stressful situations" (Haslam, Pakenham, & Smith, 2006, p. 279). For Latina mothers, the act of migration from Latin America to the US demonstrates some degree of self-efficacy (Hondagneu-Sotelo, 1994). Those with higher self-efficacy may be more resilient to the stresses of acculturation, less likely to develop depressive symptoms, and more able to cope with the demands of parenting.

At the same time that immigrant Latina mothers are at high risk for depression, they are also unlikely to receive mental health treatment (Vega & Alegria, 2001). Most do not have public or private health insurance (Fremstad & Cox, 2004). Furthermore, most mothers are able to work best with mental health providers who speak Spanish and who are familiar with Latino culture (Perreira & Smith, 2007). However, low-cost, bilingual, culturally sensitive mental health providers are scarce or nonexistent in many areas of the US. Finally, Latina mothers may fear that acknowledging a mental health problem and seeking assistance will lead to trouble with authorities (Pincay & Guarnaccia, 2007). As a result, many Latina mothers struggle with depressive symptoms in isolation, placing their children at even more risk for difficulties that will eventually require costly interventions (Heckman & Masterov, 2004).

Maternal Depression and Early-Childhood Development

The mental health of EHS Latino infants and toddlers is influenced directly by maternal mental health and indirectly by income, cultural norms of child-rearing, and sociopolitical forces (Pachter & Harwood, 1996; Phillips & Cabrera, 1996). Altered maternal behaviors associated with depressive symptoms can compromise an infant's socioemotional health and the attainment of developmental milestones (NICHD Early Child Care Research Network, 1999; Petterson & Albers, 2001). For example, infants and toddlers of mothers with depressive symptoms have demonstrated less vocalization, greater negative affect, poor socialization skills, negative self-concept, and intractable tantrums (Cicchetti, Rogosch, Toth, & Spagnola, 1997; Hart, Jones, Field, & Lundy, 1999; Murray, Fiori-Crowley, Hooper, & Cooper, 1996). By targeting depressive symptoms, mental health interventions can help at-risk Latina mothers regain the energy to talk and play with their children and to provide the affection and security their young children need to achieve optimal socioemotional health (Jones, Lamb-Parker, Schweder, & Ripple, 2001).

Although the ways in which depressive symptoms limit maternal support for optimal infant-toddler development have been well-documented in non-Latina mothers, limited data exists on Latina mothers and their infants/toddlers. The study of

Latina mothers is complicated by their diversity and a tendency in early studies to combine Spanish-speaking mothers into a homogeneous group. Latinas differ by country of origin, length of time since immigration, acculturation to the US, and other socioeconomic factors. In addition, they differ in terms of their migration experiences, events surrounding their entry to the US, and the degree of governmental and non-governmental support they receive following immigration and settlement in the US (Perreira & Smith, 2007). These individual and contextual factors can influence both mother's risk for depression and the effects of maternal depressive symptoms on their young children (García Coll, 1990). As a result, it is increasingly important that studies on maternal depression and child development fully explore the unique experiences of Latina immigrant women and the contexts in which their children develop.

Methods

Setting

This project took place in three Early Head Start programs in North Carolina. Although the three participating programs were in different geographical regions of the state, they served similar populations of Latinos. They were located in areas where young Latinos, mostly Mexicans, had immigrated to find work in poultry-processing plants, construction, landscaping, farming, and service industries. In addition, each program served between 75 and 100 families (both Latino and non-Latino) and offered both center- and home-based services, a mixed-method approach to service delivery. The percentage of EHS enrolled children that were Latino in each site ranged from 30% to 60% during the data-collection period (August 2003–August 2006).

Procedures

Beginning in June 2003, all Spanish-speaking women enrolling in these three EHS program sites were asked if they would consent to completing the Center for Epidemiologic Studies Depression (CES-D) questionnaire. After completing the initial screening, women were asked to participate in baseline data collection and, if symptomatic for depression, an intervention study called ALAS or "wings."[2] Some 169 women were screened for depression between June 2003 and July 2006. Of those screened, 95 (56%) were found to have significant symptoms of depression (i.e., a score of 16 or higher on the CES-D) and 74 were asymptomatic (i.e., score below 16 on the CES-D). Those who were symptomatic were directed to the intervention study and completed baseline data collection. The first 25 of those who were asymptomatic were also asked to complete baseline data collection. Due to the limited reading abilities of some mothers, all consent forms and questionnaires were read aloud in Spanish.

The baseline data collection for both symptomatic and asymptomatic mothers consisted of a 1-hour questionnaire, a HOME observation, and a 45-minute videotaped observation. Additionally, nine of the asymptomatic and seven of the symptomatic mothers who participated in the baseline data collection also agreed to complete a 1–2 hour, in-depth personal interview on a second visit. Symptomatic mothers were interviewed only after completing the intervention.

Data and Measures

ALAS Baseline Survey

In the baseline survey, ALAS researchers collected information about maternal depressive symptoms, family conflict, general self-efficacy, maternal stress, and the socioemotional development of their children. Additionally, descriptive data on the acculturation and sociodemographic characteristics of mothers and their children were collected.

Maternal depressive symptom severity was evaluated using the 20-item Center for Epidemiological Studies Depression Scale—Spanish version (CES-D) (Radloff, 1977). Respondents completed the CES-D on two occasions, once during their initial screening and again during the baseline data collection. For the CES-D, respondents rate symptom frequency in the previous week. Each item is scored 0 to 3, with total scores ranging from 0 to 60. A score of 16 or above indicates clinically significant symptoms with a linear relationship between increasing scores and the likelihood of a diagnosis of major depressive disorder (Radloff, 1977). Approximately 85% of Latino respondents who score over 16 are presumed to have clinically significant depressive symptom severity (Vega, Kolody, Valle, & Hough, 1986). In our sample of Latina mothers, the Cronbach's alpha (α) was 0.84.

Family conflict was measured by five items from the Family Environment Scale (Moos & Moos, 1984). Respondents rate statements about family interactions (i.e., people in their family fight a lot, lose their tempers, throw things, criticize each other, and hit each other) on a four-point ordinal scale. These statements are summed to yield a score ranging from 5 to 20. In our sample, the α was 0.81 for this scale.

Maternal self-efficacy was measured by the General Self-Efficacy Scale (GES—Spanish version). This 20-item instrument measures perceived self-efficacy in coping with minor and major stressful life events and contains 10 general items and 10 items added specifically for this study (Bäßler & Schwarzer, 1996). The 10 specific self-efficacy items measure daily functioning with symptoms, management of life issues, use of social support, and parenting. Respondents rate the statements on a four-point ordinal scale. They are summed to yield a score ranging from 20 to 80 ($\alpha = 0.90$ for this study).

Parenting stress was measured using the short form (17-item) version of the Parental Stress Index (Loyd & Abidin, 1985; Reitman, Currier, & Stickle, 2002). In addition to obtaining a total parenting stress score, the short form includes two subscales—modified parental distress ($\alpha = 0.83$ for this study) and parent–child dysfunctional interaction ($\alpha = 0.88$ for this study). The Total Parenting Stress score ranges from 17 to 75; the modified parental distress score ranges from 5 to 25; and the parent–child dysfunctional interaction score ranges from 5 to 60.

The Child Behavior Checklist (CBCL), aggression subscale was used to measure irritability and social-emotional competence of infants and toddlers. The CBCL is designed for optimal use with children above 18 months of age. Therefore, it is scored in this study on only the subsample of children aged 18 to 60 months. The CBCL aggression subscale has 19 items and parents rate their child's behavior using a three-point Likert scale. Thus, raw scores range from 0 to 38. In our sample, the α for this scale was 0.91 at baseline.

Mother's acculturation to the US was measured using three sets of variables: (1) months lived in the US; (2) age at migration to the US; and (3) four language items from the Short Acculturation Scale for Hispanics (SASH) by Marin and colleagues (1987). The four-item SASH had an excellent internal reliability in our sample, with $\alpha = 0.87$, and possible scores ranging from 4 (limited English skills) to 20 (limited Spanish skills). However, because our sample consisted primarily of recent immigrants, there was little variability in the measure and the scale was dichotomized to identify participants with limited English skills (i.e., Spanish monolinguals). Limited English skills were associated with having spent less time in the US ($r = -0.25$) and having moved to the US at an older age ($r = 0.16$).

Other sociodemographic data included information on mother, child, and household characteristics. For mothers, we measured the mother's age, mother's Latino heritage (coded as Mexican = 1), mother's marital status (married = 1), and mother's employment status (employed = 1). We also collected data on self-reported health using the standard question, "How would you describe your health in the last 3 months?" (1 = poor ... 5 = excellent). This single-item question has been used in many large national surveys and has been found to be the single best measure of general health status across a wide variety of population groups (Finch, Hummer, Reindl, & Vega, 2002; McGee, Liao, Cao, & Cooper, 1999). For children, we collected data on their father's age, their Latino heritage (coded as Mexican = 1; 0 otherwise), their gender (female = 1; 0 otherwise), their age, whether they had a medical visit in the last month (= 1; 0 otherwise), and whether they had any health problems (= 1; 0 otherwise). Data on household characteristics included whether the mother was currently living with a spouse or partner (= 1; 0 otherwise), whether the spouse or partner was employed (= 1; 0 otherwise), the number and age of household members, total monthly income and the number of people living off that income, whether the family needed transportation assistance in the past month (= 1; 0 otherwise), and financial strain (i.e., whether the mother worried about debts sometimes or often = 1; 0 otherwise).

HOME Observation

Administered using both a maternal interview and observation, the HOME inventory (0–3 version) was designed to identify children under 3 years who are at risk for developmental delay due to a home environment lacking appropriate stimulation (Caldwell & Bradley, 1980). The HOME consists of 45 items arranged in 6 subscales: (1) verbal and emotional stimulation; (2) avoidance of restrictions and punishment; (3) organization of the environment; (4) provision of appropriate play materials; (5) maternal involvement; and (6) variety in daily stimulation. Each item is scored as present or absent, and the total score equals the number of present items with a range of 0 to 45. Higher scores indicate a more stimulating, affirming home environment. The current study found an $\alpha = 0.78$ at baseline.

Videotaped Observations

Videotapes of mother–infant interactions in the home were made for 45 minutes at baseline. Videotapes were scheduled at a time when the child was awake and not eating a meal. The mother was told that the purpose was to record the child's and mother's behaviors when they were home together. The mother was asked to carry out her usual activities in their home, and the child was free to do whatever he or she wanted and the mother would allow.

Using a mother–child coding system for mothers interacting with infants to 3-year-old children (Table 4.1), the occurrence of child and mother behaviors were scored in 10-second intervals with each behavior counted only once in each interval (Holditch-Davis, Bartlett, & Belyea, 2000). To adjust for variation in the lengths of videotapes, most variables were measured as a percentage of the scoreable videotape. Play with objects was measured as a percentage of the time that the child was *not playing* with the mother so that it measured the child's ability to play independently. Coders were blinded to maternal depressive symptom status and achieved interrater reliability ratings (kappas) of at least 0.65 on each behavioral code (mean = 0.82). A bilingual research assistant reviewed and corrected the coding of all verbal behaviors.

Spiker-Crawley Sensitivity Rating Scale. The videotaped observation was also rated using the Maternal Sensitivity Sub-Scale from the Mother–Child Rating Scales developed by Crawley and Spiker (1983) and revised by Goldman and Martin (1986). A composite variable reflecting the mother's contingent responses to child cues was created from the mean scores of five highly correlated behaviors (i.e., elaborateness, sensitivity, stimulation value, mood, and mutuality) each rated on five-point scales (Table 4.1). Two coders, trained to 85% agreement, rated each videotape and a consensus score was used. The Cronbach's alpha for this score was 0.95 in this study.

Qualitative Interviews

On a second visit, 16 mothers participated in 1.5- to 2-hour personal interviews in their primary language, Spanish. Following an interview guide that contained questions on migration and parenting experiences, the interviewer engaged in a flexible, semi-structured interview process. All interviews were audiotaped, transcribed verbatim by the interviewer, and translated into English prior to content analysis. Following Miles and Huberman (1994), all interviews were initially read and coded by a bilingual, bicultural team member of Mexican background who used ATLAS.ti to assist with analysis. Reviews and additional coding were conducted by the interviewer and the two Principal Investigators—a psychiatric nurse and a bilingual, bicultural immigration scholar with substantial experience working with Latina immigrants. To enhance reliability, each interview was coded by at least two members of the research team. The team compared codes and concepts from different interviews, examined their universality, identified aberrant cases, and developed matrices to identify linkages among concepts (Miles & Huberman, 1994). Similar codes were grouped together into broader themes that included Parenting, Mother's Emotional Health, Migration, Family Stressors and Family Supports, and Early Head Start Experience. Quotes reported in this chapter reflect this analysis and represent the full body of coded interviews.

Statistical Analysis

A total of 105 Spanish-speaking mothers with children enrolled in EHS participated in this study. Our analysis proceeded in two stages. First, using CES-D scores at screening and baseline, we defined a subsample of N = 83 mothers that were consistent in terms

Table 4.1 Interactive Behaviors Scored During the Videotapes

Mother behaviors	*Child behaviors*	*Definitions*
Body Contact	–	Mother and child trunks are in contact
Eye-to-eye	–	Mother and child make eye-to-eye contact
Gesture	Gesture	Gestures or directs facial expression at mother or child
Hold	–	Holds or carries the child
Interact	–	Talks to, touches, gestures toward, or plays with child
Look	Look	Looks at mother or child
Near	–	Close enough to achieve eye contact but not holding or having body contact with the child
Negative	Negative	Directs negative affect towards mother or child (e.g., frown or scold)
No adult	–	No adult is in the room with the child
Other care	–	Someone other than mother is caring for or interacting with the child
Play with child	–	Initiates or takes part in child's play activity or games
Positive	Positive	Directs positive affect to mother or child (e.g., smile or kiss)
Talk	Talk	Speaks words to mother or child
Teach	–	Instructs child (e.g., names an object, demonstrates an activity)
Touch	Touch	Touches mother or child (e.g., pat or caress)
Uninvolved	–	Not interacting with, playing with, or looking at the child.
–	Competing Activities	Activities that compete with play (eating, toileting, working)
–	Inactive	Child is still or moves less than two steps in 10 seconds
–	Locomotion	Moves body but without walking (e.g., belly creep or scoot)
–	Object Play	Plays with an object but not with a person
–	Play	Plays with a person, object, or self
–	Uninvolved with Play	Not playing and not engaged in activities that compete with play
–	Vocalize	Makes a non-fussy sound but does not say words
–	Walk	Walks independently or by supporting self on objects or people
Elaborativeness	–	The extent to which the mother follows the child's lead and builds on the child's initiative
Mood	–	Expressed warmth and positive affect of mother
Mutuality	–	The degree to which mother and child are in harmony or synchrony with each other
Sensitivity	–	Reflects the mother's awareness of the child's cues or signals
Stimulation value	–	Encompasses optimal cognitive development

of being classified as having depressive symptoms (CES-D total score of at least 16) or not across the two time periods (i.e., screening and baseline). We excluded N = 22 mothers from this subsample who had discordant classifications across these two time periods. This allowed for sharper contrasts between groups and the relationship between depressive symptoms, maternal behaviors, and child behaviors. With this sample, we then used two-sample (independent group) t-tests to evaluate mean differences on several maternal, child, and family characteristics across mothers who were above the threshold for substantial symptoms of depression (i.e., symptomatic mothers, CES-D $\geqslant$ 16) and those below the threshold (i.e., asymptomatic mothers, CES-D < 16). We also tested for mean differences in maternal behaviors and child behaviors between mothers with and without substantial symptoms of depression. Due to small cell sizes, we used Fisher exact tests to evaluate differences in proportions for categorical and dichotomous variables.

Next, we returned to our full sample (N = 105) and used ordinary least squares regression analysis to examine maternal depressive symptoms and their relationship to maternal and child behaviors.[3] To allow for greater stability in the measurement of depressive symptoms, we averaged CES-D scores from each participant's initial screening and the baseline data collection that occurred approximately 2 weeks later.

In our regression analyses, we focused on two maternal behavior variables—total parenting stress and total HOME score—and two child behaviors—aggressive behaviors (CBCL subscale) and negative child behavior from our videotape observation data. In conducting these analyses, we first evaluated risk and protective factors for depressive symptoms. Then, we explored the extent to which: (1) self-efficacy mediated the relationship between depressive symptoms and the HOME environment; (2) self-efficacy mediated the relationship between depressive symptoms and parenting stress; and (3) self-efficacy mediated the relationship between depressive symptoms and child behaviors (i.e., aggression and/or negative behavior). Following Baron and Kenny (1986), we estimate a series of three regressions to test for mediation and calculate Sobel's test for the approximate significance of each mediation pathway. Covariates used in all regressions included mother's age, whether the mother was currently living with a spouse or partner, and whether the mother had limited English skills. Correlations and means for all variables used in regression analyses are reported in Tables 4.2 and 4.3. To allow for easier comparisons of their relative effects, the variables used in the regression analyses are standardized and standardized coefficients are presented. These standardized coefficients reflect the change in the dependent variable that results from a change of one standard deviation in an independent variable.

Our understanding of the results and interpretation of the data are interwoven with findings from the qualitative interviews. Because the data are cross-sectional, the associations found in our regressions should not be interpreted as causal. Future analyses with longitudinal data will be needed to further evaluate any causality suggested by our models.

Table 4.2 Correlation Matrix of Variables in Full Sample (N = 105)

		(1)	*(2)*	*(3)*	*(4)*	*(5)*	*(6)*	*(7)*	*(8)*	*(9)*	*(10)*	*(11)*	*(12)*	*(13)*	*(14)*	*(15)*	*(16)*	*(17)*
(1)	mother's age	1.00																
(2)	father's age[a]	**0.71**	1.00															
(3)	Mexican mother	0.05	0.03	1.00														
(4)	living with spouse or partner	0.01	–0.03	0.10	1.00													
(5)	limited English language skills[b]	0.00	–0.01	–0.15	0.04	1.00												
(6)	number of children aged 6–18	0.06	–0.10	**0.19**	**–0.12**	–0.12	1.00											
(7)	mother's education	0.10	–0.09	0.05	–0.05	–0.33	–0.11	1.00										
(8)	mother's employment	–0.01	0.02	**–0.18**	**–0.29**	0.06	–0.10	0.01	1.00									
(9)	female child	–0.08	–0.12	0.03	–0.06	0.11	0.09	0.03	–0.03	1.00								
(10)	child's age	0.10	0.11	–0.07	0.02	0.03	–0.14	**0.16**	**0.26**	0.15	1.00							
(11)	family conflict	–0.08	–0.06	**–0.28**	0.13	0.11	–0.14	–0.07	0.11	0.03	**0.22**	1.00						
(12)	general self-efficacy score	**0.18**	**0.21**	0.13	0.03	–0.11	0.05	–0.07	**0.26**	0.00	**0.22**	**–0.27**	1.00					
(13)	total home	**0.16**	**0.22**	0.13	0.11	–0.15	–0.08	0.13	0.03	–0.07	0.12	**–0.23**	**0.21**	1.00				
(14)	total parenting stress score	–0.08	**–0.19**	**–0.17**	**–0.01**	0.13	–0.13	–0.13	–0.16	0.02	0.02	**0.23**	**–0.44**	**–0.41**	1.00			
(15)	CES-D score	**–0.20**	–0.14	–0.20	–0.10	**0.23**	**–0.12**	–0.02	–0.07	0.01	0.01	**0.47**	**–0.54**	**–0.42**	**0.42**	1.00		
(16)	CBCL t-score[c]	0.09	0.02	0.02	0.08	0.22	–0.07	0.15	–0.09	0.03	**0.25**	**0.41**	**–0.49**	**–0.40**	**0.35**	**0.42**	1.00	
(17)	Child negative behavior[b]	0.08	0.00	–0.11	–0.04	**0.27**	0.00	0.00	–0.03	–0.01	**–0.26**	0.09	**–0.36**	**–0.11**	0.14	**0.28**	**0.27**	1.00

Note

Bold and shading indicates $p < .1$. N varies for a few correlations due to missing data.

a N = 81.

b N = 104.

c N = 50.

Table 4.3 Means of Variables for Full Sample

Variable	*N*	*Means*	*Std. Dev.*
Mother's age	105	26.90	5.72
Father's age	81	29.16	5.04
Mexican Mother	105	0.64	0.48
Living with spouse or partner	105	0.89	0.32
No English-language skills	104	0.72	0.45
Number of children aged 6–18	105	0.78	0.91
Mother's education	105	8.68	2.82
Mother's employment	105	0.36	0.48
Female child	105	0.50	0.50
Child's age	105	15.85	11.05
Family conflict	105	8.12	3.07
General self-efficacy score	105	56.28	12.39
Total home	105	34.40	6.66
Total parenting stress score	105	36.61	9.92
CES-D score	105	21.47	13.12
CBCL: Aggression T-score	50	58.60	10.74
Negative child behavior	104	7.22	6.91

Note
Ns vary due to missing data.

Results

Maternal Depression and General Self-Efficacy

Women with depressive symptoms (N = 58) and those without depressive symptoms (N = 25) were similar in several respects (Table 4.4). The vast majority had migrated to the US from Mexico when they were in their early 20s, had lived in the US for approximately 5 years, and were poorly educated with between 8 and 9 years of schooling. Their youngest child (i.e., child enrolled in EHS) was slightly under 1.5 years old. While over 60% of the women were not employed full- or part-time, nearly all the women had a spouse or partner who was employed and contributed to the household's income. On average household income for our participants was approximately $1,200 per month and this income supported 4–5 individuals living in the household. Given their limited incomes and laws in North Carolina that restrict access to driver's licenses for persons without a Social Security number, many (30%–32%) women experienced economic hardship and strained to pay their monthly debts. Most (60%–62%) needed transportation assistance at least once per month.

In reflecting on the hardships of their lives in the US, the following two quotes capture the frustrations of many:

1 You leave many people behind in Mexico and the bills keep on adding up. So, we have to find work quickly to be able to pay the [coyotes] who brought us here and to provide for the families we left in Mexico.

Table 4.4 Means/Percentages of Selected Characterists for Mothers With and Without Depressive Symptoms (Std. Dev)[a]

Variable	*Symptomatic (N = 58)*		*Asymptomatic (N = 25)*		*Effect Size*[d]
Mother's characteristics					
T1: Mother's age	25.3	(5.3)	28.7	(4.7)	–0.66***
T1: Mother Mexican (%)	58.6	–	72.0	–	0.13
T1: Mother currently married (%)	46.6	–	64.0	–	0.16
T1: Mother's years of school completed	8.8	(2.9)	8.5	(2.6)	0.11
T1: Mother employed (%)	36.2	–	32.0	–	0.04
T1: Mother's months lived in the US[c]	59.0	(44.6)	66.1	(27.7)	–0.18
T1: Mother's age when came to US[c]	20.5	(5.4)	22.1	(4.9)	–0.32
T1: No English-language skills (%)[c]	73.7	–	52.0	–	–0.21*
T1: General self-efficacy score	51.0	(11.8)	64.5	(7.8)	–1.25***
T1: Number of mother's medical visits last month	0.3	(0.6)	0.2	(0.4)	0.23
T1: Self-reported health very good to excellent (%)	63.8	–	16.0	–	0.24***
T1: CES-D score	30.2	(10.4)	4.4	(3.5)	2.90***
Child's characteristics					
T1: Child's father's age[b,c]	28.1	(4.8)	30.8	(4.9)	–0.56*
T1: Child Mexican (%)	37.9	–	40.0	–	0.02
T1: Female child (%)	51.7	–	44.0	–	0.07
T1: Child's age in months	16.3	(11.7)	15.6	(9.6)	0.06
T1: Children had any medical visits last month (%)	55.2	–	40.0	–	–0.14
T1: Child has health problems (%)	20.7	–	12.0	–	0.10
Household characteristics					
T1: Living with spouse or partner (%)	81.0	–	96.0	–	0.20*
T1: Spouse or partner employed (%)	94.1	–	100.0	–	0.24
T1: Number of people in the home	5.1	(1.5)	5.4	(1.9)	–0.21
T1: Number of children 0–5	1.8	(0.8)	1.8	(1.0)	–0.03
T1: Number of children 6–12	0.4	(0.6)	1.1	(0.9)	–1.08***
T1: Number of children 13–18	0.2	(0.5)	0.0	(0.2)	0.43**
T1: Number of adults	2.7	(1.0)	2.6	(0.9)	0.13
T1: Number of moves in past year[c]	0.5	(0.8)	0.5	(0.8)	–0.01
T1: Total monthly income (c)	1141.6	(405.1)	1170.2	(279.4)	–0.08
T1: Number people living off income[c]	4.3	(1.1)	4.9	(1.6)	–0.52
T1: Monthly income per capita[c]	275.6	(101.7)	257.9	(87.5)	0.18
T1: Needed transportation assistance last month (%)	62.1	–	60.0	–	0.02
T1: Financial strain experienced (%)	29.3	–	32.0	–	0.03
T1: Family conflict score	9.2	(3.5)	6.6	(1.5)	0.87***

Notes

a Sattertwaite adjustment for unequal variances used to calculate differences in means. Fisher's Exact tests were used to calculate differences for categorical variables.

b Ten missing values for asymptomatic cases, N < 25

c A small number (1–5) of missing values for symptomatic cases, N < 58

d Effect sizes are based on Cramer's φ for categorical variables and Cohen's d for interval variables.

* $p < 0.1$, **$p < 0.05$, ***$p < 0.01$.

> 2 The problem of life here is that really there is not a lot of public transportation. There are buses and everything but they don't come very frequently. And I want to learn how to drive. It's just that, you know, I'm afraid of the police. They tell me that you have to get your license to be able to drive but they don't give out licenses any more [to persons without social security numbers].

While these frustrations and economic hardships were shared by all women in our study, participants with depressive symptoms experienced additional hardships that women with fewer symptoms of depression had not experienced (Table 4.4). Symptomatic women were less likely to live with a spouse or partner; they had fewer children aged 13–18 available to help them around the home; they had more negative family interactions (i.e., family conflict); and they were less likely to have English-language skills. In addition, women with symptoms of depression tended to be younger and had a lower sense of self-efficacy, when compared to asymptomatic women.

Our regression analyses demonstrated that family conflict,[4] limited English-language skills, and the absence of a spouse or partner were strongly associated with both more depressive symptoms and a lower sense of self-efficacy (Table 4.7, Part A). Moreover, depressive symptoms were negatively associated with general self-efficacy. In other words, women who reported feeling sad, alone, and sleepless also reported difficulties in figuring out how to resolve problems, get help when they needed it, best to help their children, and overcome challenging situations.

The importance of a partner's support in raising and nurturing children was a common theme in our interviews. As one woman said,

> What makes it easier for me [is] having my husband's help because, when he is not here and I am alone with my children, it is really difficult for me. The support of having him there, to say, "I am here" is [what makes my life as a mother] easier.

Another commented, "I have support from my husband because we have to share. Since we work, we have to share the childcare."

For many women, the support for child-rearing from their male partners was novel and reflected a substantial change in gender roles that occurred in the US. As one women explained,

> Over there in Mexico, it is like, well, your husband works, you have your children, you educate them, you [the mother] know what to do with them. The husband is just working. Here [in the US], I tell my husband that he has to help me because they [the children] are also yours.

Not only were women able to share child-rearing responsibilities with their male partners but they were also able to share other homemaking responsibilities. Another women commented,

> [In Mexico,] even though he had a jar of water here [*she motions to her side*] and a glass, he didn't serve himself. I had to serve him because he was a man.... He has changed a lot and he is really different now.

Finally, women living in the US had more freedom to work outside the home than they had had in Mexico. As a third women explained,

> In Mexico, machismo is that the woman is at home even though the man only earns enough to eat, or whatever. But the culture is really different [here]. Here, if you want to go to out to work, to have also a little more money and not to only be stuck at home, [you can].

While potentially a source of family conflict, these changes in gender relations within the family were most often accompanied by reductions in domestic violence, as women learned that they could seek support from authorities in the US. Echoing the words of many, one mother remarked,

> Over there [in Mexico], even though the woman decides to accuse the man because he beats her, he mistreats her, the only thing that she receives is, well, negative. Because they say, "Well, he is your husband." In other words, he has the right. But I think that no one has the right to beat or to mistreat his woman even though he is her husband. And here it is different because here if the man mistreats [his wife], she can accuse him and then the authorities come.

The relationship between maternal depression and self-efficacy was also reflected in our interviews. Telling a story about a challenging time for her, one woman said,

> For me, [the most difficult challenge] has been the language. I let him [her 3-year-old son] get books at the library and he gets them in English. And he tells me, "Read them to me Mama!" And I only see the pictures.... If I knew English, I could ... [she interrupts herself] ... Also something happened to us, well it happened to me. I went to the park ... And there were a lot of parents, but Americans. There were kids, a ton of kids, that were going up like a little mountain [a rock-climbing wall]. And, well, I couldn't ask what [children] needed to go up. Because I didn't know their language and they were only Americans. Then, what we did was leave. Because I was ashamed ... And Claudia [her daughter] wanted to climb. And I couldn't communicate with them to ask what we would need so that Claudia could climb.

Maternal Behaviors

At the same time that maternal depressive symptoms were associated with low self-efficacy, they were also associated with more difficulty in parenting along several dimensions of maternal behavior (Table 4.2). Women with depressive symptoms (CES-D ≥ 16) had significantly higher total parenting stress levels than women with fewer depressive symptoms. Moreover, these differences were significant along the two subscales of parenting stress—parenting distress and parent–child dysfunction. In other words, women with depressive symptoms felt trapped in their parenting role, had

Table 4.5 Means/Percentages of Maternal Behaviors and Home Environment for Mothers With and Without Depressive Symptoms (Std. Dev)[a]

Variable	*Symptomatic (N = 58)*		*Asymptomatic (N = 25)*		*Effect Size*[d]
Survey data					
Mother spanks child (%)	24.1	–	12.0	–	0.01
PSI: Modified parental distress	16.9	(4.2)	11.8	(3.8)	1.23***
PSI: Parent–child dysfunctional interaction	23.6	(7.6)	18.9	(4.6)	0.68***
PSI: Modified total stress	40.4	(10.2)	30.8	(5.7)	1.06***
Home observation data					
HOME: Reads to child at least 3 times/week (%)	67.2	–	76.0	–	0.09
HOME: Emotional and verbal	9.0	(2.2)	10.5	(0.7)	–0.93***
HOME: Avoidance of restriction and punishment	5.9	(1.2)	6.4	(1.2)	–0.80*
HOME: Organization of environment	4.8	(1.1)	5.2	(0.6)	–0.43**
HOME: Play materials	6.1	(2.4)	7.3	(1.8)	–0.39**
HOME: Maternal involvement with child	4.0	(2.1)	5.5	(0.9)	–0.53***
HOME: Variety in daily stimulation	3.1	(1.2)	3.8	(1.3)	–0.81**
HOME: Total score	32.9	(6.9)	38.7	(4.1)	–0.59***
Videeotaped observation data[b]					
Body contact	17.7	(21.4)	13.1	(13.9)	0.24
Eye-to-eye	14.8	(15.5)	19.9	(11.2)	–0.36*
Gesture	18.2	(15.0)	23.3	(12.5)	–0.36
Hold	20.8	(25.9)	14.2	(16.6)	0.28
Interact	59.0	(27.0)	62.9	(19.7)	–0.16
Look	45.4	(23.5)	56.1	(16.2)	–0.49**
Near	63.6	(26.5)	71.2	(20.7)	–0.30
Negative affect	0.3	(0.7)	0.3	(0.6)	0.01
No adult	13.4	(17.4)	12.3	(14.1)	0.06
Other care	2.2	(5.4)	2.4	(7.6)	–0.03
Play with child	13.6	(18.2)	12.8	(10.6)	0.05
Positive affect	8.4	(10.0)	9.8	(6.5)	–0.15
Talk	36.0	(25.3)	46.3	(20.0)	–0.43*
Teach	1.3	(2.4)	2.5	(3.3)	–0.43
Touch	17.0	(15.4)	15.7	(14.1)	0.09
Uninvolved	34.1	(25.4)	28.8	(17.1)	0.23
SC: Elaborateness[c]	3.3	(1.1)	3.7	(0.9)	–0.45*
SC: Mood[c]	1.7	(0.9)	1.5	(0.7)	0.27
SC: Mutuality[c]	3.9	(0.9)	4.1	(0.5)	–0.23
SC: Sensitivity[c]	3.8	(0.9)	4.0	(0.8)	–0.17
SC: Stimulation value[c]	3.1	(1.2)	3.6	(0.9)	–0.47*
Spiker-Crawley (SC) Composite[c]	3.7	(0.9)	3.9	(0.7)	–0.29

Notes

a T-tests using the Sattertwaite adjustment for unequal variances were used to compare differences in means. Fisher's Exact tests were used to compare differences in proportions.

b N = 24 for videotaped observation data among asymptomatic mothers.

c Spiker-Crawely (SC) data were available for only 48 of the symptomatic cases and 14 of the asymptomatic cases. Possible scores range from 1 to 5 for all items except Mood. Scores on mood range from –3 to 3.

d Effect sizes are based on Cramer's φ for categorical variables and Cohen's d for interval variables.

* $p < 0.1$, **$p < 0.05$, ***$p < 0.01$.

a low sense of their child-rearing competence, and felt little of the reciprocity in love and affection from their infants and toddlers that makes parenting rewarding.

In addition to reporting higher levels of parenting stress, women with depressive symptoms engaged in fewer of the HOME activities known to stimulate children and promote their cognitive development (Bradley et al., 1994). In contrast to mothers with minimal depressive symptoms, they provided significantly less emotional and verbal stimulation for their infants and toddlers, fewer materials for and involvement with their child's play activities, and less variety in the types of activities used to stimulate their child's development.

These survey and HOME observation-based results were also reflected in our videotaped observations. A mother's eye-to-eye contact with her infant or toddler, looks toward her child, and talking to her child are known to be essential for the child's healthy socioemotional development. However, these types of interactions occurred less frequently among mothers with versus those without substantial depressive symptoms. Consistent with data from the HOME, we also identified less elaborateness in play among women with symptoms of depression and found that maternal child behaviors among these women were not promoting optimal stimulation for cognitive development. Thus, children of mothers with depressive symptoms were at high risk of developmental delays.

Controlling for potential confounders (e.g., mother's age, limited English skills, and child's age), our regression analyses further demonstrated the significance of interrelationships between depressive symptoms, parenting stress, and maternal behaviors in the HOME environment (Table 4.7, Part B). In addition, our results suggested that depressive symptoms and parenting stress are separately, and nearly equally, related to maternal behaviors in the HOME environment (Table 4.7, Model B3). Finally, our regression results supported our hypothesis that general self-efficacy partially mediates the relationship between maternal depression and parenting stress ($t_{sobel}=2.32$, $p=0.02$). However, there was no direct nor mediation effect of self-efficacy on maternal behaviors in the HOME environment. Thus, women with a stronger sense of self-efficacy may be better able to cope with depressive symptoms, and depressive symptoms then interfere less with their parenting behaviors.

Several of the mothers we interviewed recognized the link between maternal depression and their parenting. As one women with depression lamented,

> I believe that the depression is my biggest defect. My son is growing and as he grows he is more rebellious. So, sometimes I say, "Ay! How difficult!" ... I get angry and, "Ay, no please!" and I also get in a bad mood.... I tell you, sometimes I don't know how to treat him; I don't know what to say to him.

In discussing the challenge of parenting through depression, another stated,

> I didn't know how to express to my children the tenderness or the caring that I felt. Because I felt it here [*points to her heart*], but I didn't know how to express it. So, it was, [*she falters*] it was very difficult to express [*she falters again*] to express my caring to my children.

Child Behaviors

Though the infants and toddlers in our study were just beginning their developmental journeys, the effects of their mothers' depressive symptoms on their own behaviors were already beginning to show (Table 4.6). Though it did not approach significance, mothers with depressive symptoms reported that their child had more learning difficulties than mothers without depressive symptoms. In addition, they reported significantly more aggressive behaviors in their children than mothers without depressive symptoms reported. Some 20% of children with symptomatic mothers had clinically significant scores on the aggression subscale of the CBCL; whereas none of the children of asymptomatic mothers had clinically significant scores. Our videotape observational data confirmed the higher prevalence of negative affect among children with symptomatic vs. asymptomatic mothers. In fact, the rate of negative behavior in children with symptomatic mothers was nearly double the rate in children with asymptomatic mothers. In addition, children with depressed mothers engaged in significantly more activities (e.g., vocalization and gesturing) designed to get their mothers' attention.

Table 4.6 Means/Percentages of Child Behaviors for Mothers With and Without Depressive Symptoms (Std. Dev)[a]

Variable	*Symptomatic (N = 58)*		*Asymptomatic (N = 25)*		*Effect Size*[d]
Survey data					
T1: Child has learning difficulties (%)	17.2	–	16.0	–	–0.02
CBCL: Aggression raw score at T1b	17.0	9.0	8.1	5.2	1.16***
CBCL: Aggressive behavior t-score at T1b	62.2	10.8	52.2	4.4	1.14***
CBCL: Clinically significant score (%)b	24.0	–	0.0	–	–*
Videotaped observation data[c]					
Competing activities	16.8	(11.2)	22.7	(14.4)	–0.48*
Gesture	18.0	(11.5)	12.5	(7.2)	0.53**
Inactive	73.1	(20.9)	73.2	(22.9)	–0.01
Locomotion	4.7	(6.9)	5.1	(9.0)	–0.06
Look	27.4	(16.9)	31.4	(13.6)	–0.25
Negative behavior	8.1	(7.5)	4.5	(4.0)	0.54***
Object play	37.1	(23.9)	35.3	(16.9)	0.08
Play	51.3	(25.1)	50.4	(17.0)	0.04
Positive behavior	6.0	(6.9)	4.6	(4.3)	0.22
Talk	11.4	(19.4)	12.3	(17.7)	–0.05
Touch	12.4	(9.9)	11.3	(12.2)	0.11
Uninvolved with play	31.9	(20.2)	27.0	(16.2)	0.26
Vocalize	29.4	(15.4)	23.8	(11.0)	0.40*
Walk	16.8	(17.9)	19.2	(20.7)	–0.13

Notes:

a T-tests using the Sattertwaite adjustment for unequal variances were used to compare differences in means. Fisher's Exact tests were used to compare differences in proportions.

b Data collected only for children ages 18 to 60 months. Therefore, N = 25 for symptomatic cases and N = 17 for asymptomatic cases.

c N = 24 for videotaped observation data among asymptomatic mothers.

d Effect sizes are based on Cramer's φ for categorical variables and Cohen's d for interval variables.

* $p < 0.1$, ** $p < 0.05$, *** $p < 0.01$.

In our regression results (Table 4.7, Part C), we found that depressive symptoms were significantly associated with both children's aggression and children's negative behavior. In addition, maternal self-efficacy fully mediated these relationships (respectively, $t_{sobel}=2.11$, $p=0.03$; $t_{sobel}=1.96$, $p=0.05$). Once maternal self-efficacy was added to models of aggression and negative behavior, the coefficient on depressive symptoms became nonsignificant. At the same time, parenting stress and maternal HOME behaviors were not directly associated with child behavior. Although there were significant bivariate relationships and correlations between parenting stress, the HOME, and child behaviors, parenting stress was not significantly related to negative child behavior after controlling for the child's age and the mother's English-language skills. In models (not shown) of child aggressive behavior, there were direct effects between parenting stress and maternal HOME behaviors. However, these effects disappeared after entering CES-D scores or general self-efficacy scores into the regression equations. When taken together with earlier results, this suggests a story of common causality (i.e., common cause acting on both the independent and the dependent variable) rather than mediation. High levels of depressive symptoms and low levels of maternal self-efficacy promote both difficulties in parenting and negative or aggressive child behaviors. But difficulties in parenting have no direct relationship with negative or aggressive child behaviors in our sample.

Although many of the immigrant Latina women we spoke with were struggling with depression and their symptoms compromised the socioemotional well-being of their children, mothers were also able to find moments of happiness and delight in their children's behaviors. As one women with depression remembered,

> There are a lot of times when I feel proud. For example, when Pedro comes to me and he hugs me and he gives me a kiss and he tells me, "I love you." Or [I feel proud] when the two children hug each other, because at times they do that. They are playing or something and they hug each other. [At those times,] I feel like maybe I am not doing so badly in my role [as a mother].

Another commented,

> It makes me happy to see my children playing [and] to see them amusing themselves.... [It makes] me proud that my son has become accustomed to asking for something. [He says] "Please" and you give him something and [he says] "Thank you." So, I like it because at times people say to me, "Ay, what a well behaved boy you have."

Moreover, mothers very much appreciated the services of Early Head Start and felt, whether they were experiencing depressive symptoms or not, that EHS helped them to learn more about being a good parent and provided them with resources that partially alleviated the stress they experienced as new parents. One woman stated simply,

> Here [at Early Head Start], if you feel sad, you get depressed; there are people that help you. If you need someone to take care of a baby, they take care of it for you. If you are alone with your baby, there is someone to help you.

Table 4.7 Regression Analyses with Full Dataset (N = 104)

A. Maternal Depressive Symptom (CES-D) and General Self-Efficacy

	Avg. CES-D Score *(1)*	*General Self-Efficacy* *(2)*
Avg. CES-D score	–0.44***	
Mother works	–	0.20**
Family conflict	0.49***	–0.16*
Mother's age	–0.15*	0.07
Living with spouse or partner	–0.17**	0.06
Limited English-language skills	0.19**	–0.01
Child's age	–0.08	0.18**
Intercept	0.00	–0.02
Model statistics		
R-squared	0.32	0.41
F Value	9.08***	9.26***

B. Parenting Stress and the Home Environment

	Parenting Stress		*HOME Score*		
	(1)	*(2)*	*(1)*	*(2)*	*(3)*
Total parenting stress (PSI)	–		–		–0.33***
General self efficacy	–	–0.34***	–	–0.04	–0.15
Avg. CES-D score	0.41***	0.23**	–0.37***	–0.40***	–0.32**
Mother's age	–0.01	0.01	0.07	0.07	0.08
Living with spouse or partner	0.04	0.02	0.08	0.08	0.09
Limited English-language skills	0.03	0.04	–0.08	–0.07	–0.06
Child's age	0.02	0.09	0.13	0.14	0.17*
Intercept	0.00	0.00	0.01	0.01	0.01
Model statistics					
R-squared	0.18	0.25	0.21	0.21	0.29
F Value	4.18***	5.32***	5.11***	4.25***	5.70***

C. Child Behavior

	CBCL: Aggression T-Score[a]				*Negative Child Behaviors*			
	(1)	*(2)*	*(3)*	*(4)*	*(1)*	*(2)*	*(3)*	*(4)*
Total HOME score	–	–	–0.21	–0.17	–	–	0.04	0.03
Total parenting stress (PSI)	0.04	0.01	–	–	0.02	–0.04	–	–
General self efficacy	–	–0.42**	–	–0.41**	–	–0.25**	–	–0.24**
Avg. CES-D score	0.33**	0.13	0.26*	0.07	0.25**	0.14	0.28***	0.14
Mother's age	0.19	0.09	0.18	0.08	0.15*	0.17*	0.15	0.16*
Living with spouse or partner	0.23	0.12	0.28*	0.15	–0.02	–0.02	–0.02	–0.03
Limited English-language skills	0.21	0.21	0.17	0.18	0.21**	0.22**	0.22**	0.22**
Child's age	0.18	0.22	0.16	0.20	–0.27**	–0.22**	–0.27**	–0.22**
Intercept	–0.14	–0.08	–0.10	–0.05	0.00	0.00	0.00	0.00
Model Statistics								
R-squared	0.28	0.36	0.30	0.38	0.21	0.25	0.21	0.25
F Value	2.67**	3.35***	2.98**	3.57***	4.27***	4.47***	4.29***	4.45***

Notes

Standardized beta coefficients shown. Standard errors, t values and p values not shown due to space limitations.

a Sample size reduced to N = 49 for regressions on CBCL.

* $p < 0.1$, ** $p < 0.05$, *** $p < 0.01$.

Another explained in detail,

> [Early Head Start] helps you in many ways. Even though you want to change, you come from Mexico with a certain mind set. So, for example, I use to say to my children, "Why should I buy you different toys every month? If I am buying toys and they are very expensive, one that I buy you should last a while. This is what I thought.
>
> But, [my EHS home visitor] brought different toys and I saw that my son entertained himself with them and they interested him. What I learned a little with her is that for example, I brought them, how do you call them, puzzles. I had never bought one for my son. And he liked it.
>
> It was strange to me because I wanted to help him to put it together and he told me, no, that he wanted to do it by himself. I wouldn't say that he was able to put it all together. But, for one or two, he was able to put them in their places, because, for example, we [the home visitor and I] filled it in, and then he wanted to do it alone. And like, yes. I think that this is what Early Head Start helped me with. They helped me to know a little about toys and how to know what he wanted.

Discussion

Early Head Start programs were designed with the understanding that the social, emotional, and behavioral development of infants and toddlers is critical to their school readiness and intervention at these young ages can change later developmental outcomes. In the decade following the programs' inception, research showing a strong link between maternal depression and early-childhood development has accumulated (Cicchetti et al., 1997; Hart et al., 1999; Murray et al., 1996). However, most studies of this relationship have focused on non-Hispanic White and middle-class families. As a result, we know little about how culture, ethnicity, and the context of poverty shape the relationship between maternal depression and the behavior of infants and toddlers among low-income, immigrant families from Latin America (Harwood, Leyendecker, Carlson, Asencio, & Miller, 2002). Though small (N = 105), our sample is, as far as we know, the largest study of maternal depression and infant-toddler behavior among Latina immigrant mothers living in the US.

Our research with Latina mothers in EHS yielded four critical findings. First, focusing on women (mostly Mexican) who had immigrated to North Carolina from Latin America, this study confirmed that depressive symptoms are common among this population and that maternal depression is strongly associated with both aggressive and negative behaviors in young children with Latino immigrant mothers. In addition, depressive symptoms were associated with parenting stress and maternal behaviors that can impede the socioemotional and cognitive development of infants and toddlers.

In studies of primarily non-Hispanic, White, middle-class women, maternal psychosocial well-being has been found to be essential to early child development. As found in this study, infants and toddlers with depressed mothers from White, middle-class backgrounds also exhibit more negative emotions, more aggressive externalizing behaviors, vocalize less, and have lower activity levels (Abrams, Field, Scafidi, & Prodromidis,

1995; Field, 1995). In addition, other studies have found infants and toddlers with depressed mothers display fewer positive emotions, have higher levels of withdrawal and irritability, have lower levels of attachment security, engage in less play and exploratory behavior, exhibit poorer mental and motor development, and show signs of atypical brain activity (Atkinson et al., 2000; Dawson et al., 2003; Grace, Evindar, & Steward 2003). These developmental delays during infancy increase children's risks for a range of socioemotional and behavioral problems in preschool, elementary school, and early adulthood (Downey & Coyne, 1990; Pachter et al., 2006). Though we only measure a small subset of these developmental milestones, our research strongly suggests that these same patterns can be expected among lower-income, Spanish-speaking Latinas.

Second, we found that the relationship between depression, parenting stress, and maternal behaviors in the HOME environment was partially mediated by a mother's sense of self-efficacy. Moreover, maternal self-efficacy fully mediated the relationship between maternal depression and child behavior problems. Although few have studied these relationships in the past, research on maternal self-efficacy and maternal coping skills supports our findings (Coleman & Karraker, 2003; Lee, 2003). High maternal self-efficacy and adaptive coping skills have been associated with fewer maternal-perceived child problem behaviors and positive parenting practices (Coleman & Karraker, 2003; Lee 2003). In addition, previous observational studies have found strong relationships between maternal depression and parenting behavior, especially among disadvantaged women and mothers of infants. Women with depressive symptoms tend to display increased hostility, higher rates of negative interactions with their children, and impatient use of directives in guiding child behavior (Lovejoy, Graczyk, O'Hare, & Neuman, 2000). Thus, our results are consistent with those of earlier studies and add to the literature by focusing on Latinas and exploring the interrelationships between depression, self-efficacy, parenting stress, and maternal behaviors.

In contrast to previous research with primarily non-Hispanic White and non-Hispanic African American mothers (Cummings, Keller, & Davies, 2005; Malik et al., 2007), we did not find a direct relationship between family conflict and child behavior after accounting for maternal depressive symptoms. In our sample of Latinas, family conflict influenced only the presence of depressive symptoms in women and their sense of self-efficacy. Thus, this research supports the need to study children's behaviors within an ecological framework (García Coll, 1990). Moreover, as has been found in studies of older children (Pachter et al., 2006), it suggests that the pathways from maternal depression to early child development differ across ethnic and socioeconomic groups.

Third, we found that limited English skills among Latina women were associated with both the prevalence of depressive symptoms and negative child behaviors. This finding suggests that acculturative stress may play a direct role in the development of depression among Latina mothers and in the development of their infants and toddlers. Defined as the stress associated with interactions between two distinct cultures and their adjustment to one another, acculturative-stress measures commonly include items on discrimination, legal status, and language conflict (Finch, Frank, & Vega, 2004). Research with more detailed measures of acculturative stress may yield even stronger results.

Future research on acculturation and parenting may also benefit from further attention to changing gender roles in families with immigrant parents. Hondagneu-Sotelo

(1994) and others (Donato, Gabaccia, Holdaway, Manalansan, & Pessar, 2006) have demonstrated how migration can be understood as a gendered system. Gender relations in families and social networks shape migration patterns and acculturation experiences in the US. Moreover, immigration can lead to the reconstruction of gender relations in families who have immigrated to the US. Our qualitative data suggested that Latina women gain freedom to work outside the home after migrating to the US while their male partners share more responsibility for childcare and homemaking. Thus, migration would appear to facilitate gender equality. However, others have shown that migration also disrupts the social bonds and supports of women and promotes husband–wife dependency (Parrado & Flippen, 2005). Finally, many Latino fathers also suffer from depression but the interaction between maternal and paternal depression has yet to be evaluated in Latino populations (Vega & Rumbaut, 1991; Mezulis, Hyde, & Clark, 2004). Consequently, research on parenting and child development in immigrant families needs to pay more attention to the roles of fathers in early childhood and how changes on social networks, husband–wife dependency, and both paternal and maternal depression affect families' abilities to nurture their children.

Fourth, our study suggests that interventions with Latina women that focus on reducing symptoms of depression and/or improving their sense of self-efficacy can enhance their capacity to create the nurturing and stimulating home environments their children need for optimal development. The ALAS "wings" project is currently being implemented to test this approach (Beeber et al., 2007). The intervention uses Interpersonal Psychotherapy (IPT) and is designed to help women develop new skills and strategies to manage stressful interpersonal issues. In collaboration with an intervention nurse and their EHS home visitor, women in the intervention work through several visually enhanced, modular skill sheets written for low-literacy readers. These skill sheets are designed to promote self-efficacy and to develop a mother's competence in four interpersonal problem areas—daily functioning in the presence of depressive symptoms, effective use of social support, management of stressful life issues, and effective parenting. We hope that this and other interventions being tested as part of the Early Head Start Infant Mental Health Initiative are successful.

Given the cross-sectional design of our study and relatively small sample size, our results are suggestive but not conclusive. The relationships evaluated in this study will need to be reassessed using a larger longitudinal sample where causality can be more fully explored. In particular, evidence suggests that not only can maternal depression lead to child problem behaviors, but child problem behaviors can lead to family conflict, parenting stress, and maternal depression (Elgar, Curtis, McGrath, Waschbusch, & Stewart, 2003; Garstein & Sheeber, 2004). In addition, poorer child outcomes can ultimately validate a mother's sense of lowered self-efficacy (Harnish, Dodge, & Valente, 1995). Thus, a vicious cycle between lower maternal self-efficacy, depression, and poorer child outcomes can be established. Studies capable of teasing out the bidirectional relationship between maternal depression and child problem behaviors are needed. With a better understanding of these relationships, research can design effective interventions capable of disrupting this negative cycle.

While Latina immigrant mothers at risk for depression can be hard to identify and engage in the community, Early Head Start programs provide a safe and structured environment through which to connect with them. Consequently, Early Head Start programs can reach out to Spanish-speaking immigrant women and become a critical bridge between their cultures of origin and American mainstream culture. Efforts to build this bridge early in children's lives can promote school readiness and allow the children of immigrants to reach their full educational potential.

Acknowledgment

This project was supported by funding to the first author from the Foundation for Child Development, young scholars program and funding to the second author from the Department of Health and Human Services, ACYF Early Head Start–University Partnership Grant 90YF0042/01. We would like to thank Ginny Lewis and Hjordis Blanchard for their excellent management of this project and Amy Moose, Maria Garuti, Louise Noble, and Natalia Garcia for assistance with data collection.

Notes

1. To qualify as low-income, families must have income at or below 100% of the federal poverty level (Administration for Children and Families [ACF], 2008).
2. Mothers participating in the intervention study were required to be at least 15 years of age, not in psychotherapy or addiction therapy, and not on psychotropic medication. They were also required to have an EHS-enrolled child between 6 weeks and 30 months old. Of the women screened for depressive symptoms, only 14 refused to participate and six were ineligible for participation.
3. The regressions used in this analysis reflect a fully recursive model. To further evaluate our system of regressions, we conducted path analysis using MPLUS computer software (Muthén and Muthén, 2004). Path analysis using SEM techniques allows researchers to account for correlation between residuals, measurement error, and latent constructs measured by sets of variables. However, for our analysis, the SEM results differed little from the OLS results. Therefore, we present only the OLS results. SEM results are available upon request.
4. In regression analyses, family conflict was never directly associated with any other outcomes including parenting stress, HOME scored, child aggression, or child negative behavior. Therefore, it was not included in the final estimations of these models.

References

Abrams, S.M., Field, T., Scafidi, F., & Prodromidis, M. (1995). Newborns of depressed mothers. *Infant Mental Health Journal, 16*, 233–239.

Acevedo, M.C. (2000). The role of acculturation in explaining ethnic differences in the prenatal health-risk behaviors, mental health, and parenting beliefs of Mexican American and European American at-risk women. *Child Abuse Neglect, 24*(1), 111–127.

Administration for Children and Families. (2008). *Program design and management, eligibility and enrollment.* Retrieved February 15, 2008, from www.ehsnrc.org/InformationResources/Index.htm.

Alderete, E., Vega, W.A., Kolody, B., & Aguilar-Gaxiola, S. (2000). Effects of time in the U.S. and Indian ethnicity on DSM-III-R psychiatric disorders among Mexican origin adults. *Journal of Nervous and Mental Disease, 188*, 90–100.

Atkinson, L., Paglia, A., Coolbear, J., Niccols, A., Parker, K.C.H., & Guger, S. (2000). Attachment security: A meta-analysis of maternal mental health correlates. *Clinical Psychology Review, 20*, 1019–1040.

Baron, R.M., & Kenny, D.A. (1986). The moderator-mediator variable distinction in social psychological research: Conceptual, strategic, and statistical considerations. *Journal of Personality and Social Psychology, 51*(6), 1173–1182.

Bäßler, J., & Schwarzer, R. (1996). Evaluación de la autoeficacia: Adaptación española de la escala de autoeficacia general [Measuring generalized self-beliefs: A Spanish adaptation of the General Self-Efficacy scale]. *Ansiedad y Estrés, 2*(1), 1–8.

Beeber, L.S., Chazan-Cohen, R., Squires, J., Jones Harden, B., Boris, N.W., Heller, S. S., et al. (2007). Five approaches to improving infant/toddler mental health in Early Head start from the Early Promotion and Intervention Research Consortium (E-PIRC). *Infant Mental Health Journal, 28*, 130–150.

Bradley, R.H., Caldwell, B.M., Rock, S.L., Casey, P.M., & Nelson, J. (1987). The early development of low-birthweight infants: Relationship to health, family status, family context, family processes, and parenting. *International Journal of Behavioral Development, 10*, 301–318.

Bradley, R.H., Corwyn, R.F., & Burchinal, M. (2001). The home environments of children in the United States. Part II: Relations with behavioral development through age thirteen. *Child Development, 72*(6), 1868–1886.

Bradley, R.H., Corwyn, R.F., & McAdoo, H.P. (2001). The home environments of children in the United States. Part I: Variations by age, ethnicity, and poverty status. *Child Development, 72*(6), 1844–1867.

Bradley, R.H., Mundfrom, D.J., Whiteside, L., Caldwell, B.M., Casey, P.H., Kirby, R.S., & Hansen, S. (1994). A reexamination of the association between HOME scores and income. *Nursing Research, 43*, 260–266.

Brooks-Gunn, J. (2004). Intervention and policy as change agents for young children. In P.L. Chase-Lansdale, K. Kieman, & R.J. Friedman (Eds.), *Human development across lives and generations: The potential for change* (pp. 293–340). New York: Cambridge University Press.

Brown, G.W., & Moran, P.M. (1997). Single mothers, poverty and depression. *Psychological Medicine, 27*(1), 21–33.

Caldwell, B., & Bradley, R. (1980). *Home observation for measurement of the environment.* Little Rock, AR: University of Arkansas at Little Rock.

Chazan-Cohen, R., Stark, D.R., Mann, T.L., & Fitzgerald, H.E. (2007). Early Head Start and infant mental health. *Infant Mental Health Journal, 28*, 99–105.

Cicchetti, D., Rogosch, F., Toth, S., & Spagnola, M. (1997). Affect, cognition, and the emergence of self-knowledge in the toddler offspring of depressed mothers. *Journal of Experimental Child Psychology, 67*, 338–62.

Coker, A.L., Davis, K.E., Arias, I., Desai, S., Sanderson, M., Brandt, H.M., et al. (2002). Physical and mental health effects of intimate partner violence for men and women. *American Journal of Preventive Medicine, 23*(4), 260–268.

Coleman, P.K., & Karraker, K.H. (2003). Maternal self-efficacy beliefs, competence in parenting, and toddlers' behavior and developmental status. *Infant Mental Health Journal, 24*, 126–148.

Crawley, S.B., & Spiker, D. (1983). Mother-child interactions involving two-year-olds with Down syndrome: A look at individual differences. *Child Development, 54*, 1312–1323.

Cummings, E.M., Keller, P.S., & Davies, P.T. (2005). Towards a family process model of maternal and paternal depressive symptoms: Exploring multiple relations with child and family functioning. *Journal of Child Psychology and Psychiatry, 46*, 479–489.

Dawson, G., Ashman, S.B., Panagiotides, H., Hessl, D., Self, J., Yamada, E., et al. (2003). Preschool outcomes of children of depressed mothers: Role of maternal behavior, contextual risk, and children's brain activity. *Child Development, 74*, 1158–1175.

DeKlyen, M., Brooks-Gunn, J., & McLanahan, S. (2006). The mental health of married, cohabiting, and non-coresident parents with infants. *American Journal of Public Health, 96*(10), 1836–1841.

Dennis, J.M., Parke, R.D., Coltrane, S., Blancher, J., & Borthwick-Duffy, S.A. (2003). Economic pressure, maternal depression, and child adjustment in Latino families: An exploratory study. *Journal of Family and Economic Issues, 24*(2), 183–202.

Donato, K.M., Gabaccia, D., Holdaway, J., Manalansan, M., & Pessar, J.R. (2006). A glass half full? Gender in migration studies. *International Migration Review, 40*(1), 3–26.

Downey, G., & Coyne, J. (1990). Children of depressed parents: An integrative review. *Psychological Bulletin, 108*, 50–76.

Elgar, F.J., Curtis, L.J., McGrath, P.J., Waschbusch, D.A., & Stewart, S.H. (2003). Antecedent–consequence conditions in maternal mood and child adjustment: A four-year cross-lagged study. *Journal of Clinical Child and Adolescent Psychology, 32*, 362–374.

Field, T. (1995). Infants of depressed mothers. *Infant Behavioral Development, 18*, 1–13.

Finch, B.K., Frank, R., & Vega, W.A. (2004). Acculturation and acculturation stress: A social-epidemiological approach to Mexican migrant farmworkers' health. *International Migration Review, 38*(1), 236–262.

Finch, B., Hummer, R.A., Reindl, M., & Vega, W.A. (2002). Validity of self-rated health among Latino(a)s. *American Journal of Epidemiology, 155*, 755–759.

Fremstad, S., & Cox, L. (2004). *Covering new Americans: A review of federal and state policies related to immigrants' eligibility and access to publicly funded health insurance.* San Francisco, CA: Kaiser Family Foundation.

García Coll, C. (1990). Developmental outcome of minority infants: A process-oriented look into our beginnings. *Child Development, 61*, 270–289.

Gartstein, M.A., & Sheeber, L. (2004). Child behavior problems and maternal symptoms of depression: A mediational model. *Journal of Child and Adolescent Psychiatric Nursing, 17*, 141–150.

Goldman, B.D., & Martin, N. J. (1986). *Revision of Crawley and Spiker's 1983 Mother-Child scale.* Chapel Hill, NC: University of North Carolina at Chapel Hill.

Grace, S.L., Evindar, A., & Steward, D.E. (2003). The effect of postpartum depression on child cognitive development and behavior: A review and critical analysis of the literature. *Archive of Women's Mental Health, 6*, 263–274.

Harnish, J., Dodge K., & Valente, E. (1995). Mother-child interaction quality as a partial mediator of the roles of maternal depressive symptomatology and socioeconomic status in the development of child behavior problems. *Child Development, 66*, 739–53.

Hart, S., Jones, N., Field, T., & Lundy, B. (1999). One-year-old infants of intrusive and withdrawn depressed mothers. *Child Psychiatry and Human Development, 30*(2), 111–120.

Harwood, R., Leyendecker, B., Carlson, V., Asencio, M., & Miller, A. (2002). Parenting among Latino families in the U.S. In M.H. Bornstein (Ed.), *Handbook of parenting: Social conditions and applied parenting* (2nd ed., pp. 21–46). Mahwah, NJ: Lawrence Erlbaum Associates.

Haslam, D.M., Pakenham, K.I. & Smith, A. (2006). Social support and postpartum depressive symptomatology: The mediating role of maternal self-efficacy. *Infant Mental Health Journal, 27*(3), 276–291.

Heckman J., & Masterov, D. (2004). *The productivity argument for investing in young children.* Committee for Economic Development. Retrieved February 15, 2008, from http://jenni.uchicago.edu/Invest.

Holditch-Davis, D., Bartlett, T.R., & Belyea, M. (2000). Developmental problems and the interactions between mothers and their three-year-old prematurely born children. *Journal of Pediatric Nursing, 15*(3), 157–167.

Hondagneu-Sotelo, P. (1994). *Gendered transitions: Mexican experiences of immigration.* Berkeley, CA: University of California Press.

Jones, S.M., Lamb-Parker, F., Schweder, A., & Ripple, C. (2001). *Parent involvement in Head Start: Context and consequences.* New York: Columbia University.

Kasarda, J., & Johnson, J.H. (2006). *The economic impact of the Hispanic population on the State of North Carolina*. Chapel Hill, NC: Frank Hawkins Institute of Private Enterprise.

Lee, K. (2003). Maternal coping skills as a moderator between depression and stressful life events: Effects on children's behavioral problem in an intervention program. *Journal of Child Family Studies, 12*, 425–437.

Love, J.M., Kisker, E.E., Ross, C., Constantine, J., Boller, K., Chazan-Cohen, R., et al. (2005). The effectiveness of Early Head Start for 3-year-old children and their parents: Lessons for policy and programs. *Developmental Psychology, 41*, 885–901.

Lovejoy, C.M., Graczyk, P.A., O'Hare, E., & Neuman, G. (2000). Maternal depression and parenting behavior: A meta-analytic review. *Clinical Psychology Review, 20*, 561–592.

Loyd, B., & Abidin, R. (1985). Revision of the parenting stress index. *Journal of Pediatric Psychology, 10*(2), 169–177.

Malik, N.M., Boris, N.W., Heller, S.S., Jones Harden, B., Squires, J., Chazan-Cohen, R., et al. (2007). Risk for maternal depression and child aggression in Early Head Start families: A test of ecological models. *Infant Mental Health Journal, 28*, 171–191.

Mallinckrodt, B. (1992). Childhood emotional bonds with parents, development of adult social competencies and availability of social support. *Journal of Counseling Psychology, 39*, 453–461.

Marin, G., Sabogal, F., Marin, B., Otero-Sabogal, R., & Perez-Stable, E. (1987). Development of a short acculturation scale for Hispanics. *Hispanic Journal of Behavioral Sciences, 9*, 183–205.

Martin, S.L., Li, Y., Casanueva, C., Harris-Britt, A., Kupper, L.L., & Cloutier, S. (2006). Intimate partner violence and women's depression before and during pregnancy. *Violence Against Women, 12*(3), 221–239.

McGee, D.L., Liao, Y. Cao, G., & Cooper, R.S. (1999). Self-reported health status and mortality in a multiethnic US cohort. *American Journal of Epidemiology, 149*, 41–46.

Mezulis, A.H., Hyde, J.S., & Clark, R. (2004). Father involvement moderates the effect of maternal depression during a child's infancy on child behavior problems in Kindergarten. *Journal of Family Psychology, 18*(4), 575–588.

Miles, M., & Huberman, M. (1994). *Qualitative data analysis: An expanded sourcebook* (2nd ed.). London: Sage.

Moos, R.H., & Moos, B.S. (1984). *Family Environment Scale test and manual.* Palo Alto, CA: Consulting Psychologists Press.

Murray, L., Fiori-Crowley, A., Hooper, R., & Cooper, P. (1996). The impact of postnatal depression and associated adversity on early mother-infant interactions and later infant outcome. *Child Development, 67*, 2512–2526.

National Head Start Association. (2005). *Head Start: The nation's pride ... celebrating 40 years of success.* Alexandria, VA: Author. Retrieved February 15, 2008, from www.paheadstart.org/UserFiles/File/Legislative_History.pdf.

NICHD Early Child Care Research Network. (1999). Chronicity of maternal depressive symptoms, maternal sensitivity, and child functioning at 36 months. *Developmental Psychology, 35*(5), 1297–310.

Olsen, L., & DeBoise, T. (2007). Enhancing school readiness: The Early Head Start model. *Children & Schools, 29*(1), 47–50.

Pachter, L.M., Auinger, P., Palmer, R., & Weitzman, M. (2006). Do parenting and the home environment, maternal depression, neighborhood, and chronic poverty affect child behavioral problems differently in different racial-ethnic groups? *Pediatrics, 117*(4), 1329–1338.

Pachter, L., & Harwood, R. (1996). Culture and child behavior and psychological development. *Journal of Developmental and Behavioral Pediatrics, 17*(3), 191–198.

Pascoe, J.M., Stolfi, A., & Ormond, M.B. (2006). Correlates of mothers' persistent depressive symptoms: A national study. *Journal of Pediatric Health Care, 20*(4), 261–269.

Perreira, K., & Smith, L. (2007). A cultural-ecological model of migration and development: Focusing on Latino immigrant youth. *The Prevention Researcher, 14*(4), 6–8.

Petterson, S.M., & Albers, A.B. (2001). Effects of poverty and maternal depression on early child development. *Child Development, 72*(6), 1794–1813.

Phillips, D., & Cabrera, N. (1996). *Beyond the blueprint: Directions for research on Head Start's families.* Washington, DC: Microfiche National Academy Press.

Pincay, I.E., & Guarnaccia, P.J. (2007). "It's like going through an earthquake": Anthropological perspectives on depression among Latino immigrants. *Journal of Immigrant and Minority Health, 9*(1), 17–28.

Portes, A., & Rumbaut, R.G. (1996). *Immigrant America: A portrait.* Berkeley and Los Angeles, CA: University of California Press.

Radloff, L. (1977). The CES-D scale: A self-report depression scale for research in the general population. *Applied Psychological Measurement, 1*, 385–401.

Robinson, J., & Emde, R.N. (2004). Mental health moderators of Early Head Start on parenting and child development: Maternal depression and relationship attitudes. *Parenting: Science and Practice, 4*(1), 73–97.

US Census Bureau. (2004). *2004 American community survey*, S0201 Selected Population Profile. Washington, DC: US Census Bureau. Retrieved February 15, 2008, from http://factfinder.census.gov/servlet/DatasetMainPageServlet?_program=ACS&_submenuld=&_lang=en&_ts=.

Vega, W., & Rumbaut, R. (1991). Ethnic minorities and mental health. *Annual Review of Sociology, 17*, 351–383.

Vega, W.A., & Alegria, M. (2001). Latino mental health and treatment in the United States. In M. Aguirre Molina, C. Molina, & R. Zambrana (Eds.), *Health issues in the Latino community* (pp. 179–208). San Francisco, CA: Jossey-Bass.

Vega, W., Kolody, B., Valle, R., & Hough, R. (1986). Depressive symptoms and their correlates among immigrant Mexican women in the United States. *Social Science and Medicine, 22*, 645–652.

Vogel, C., Aikens, N., Burwick, A., Hawkinson, L., Richardson, A., Medenko, L., et al. (2006). *Findings from the survey of Early Head Start programs: Communities, programs, and families.* Washington, DC: US Department of Health and Human Services, Administration for Children and Families. Retrieved February 15, 2008, from www.acf.hhs.gov/programs/opre/ehs/survey_ehs/reports/findings_ehs/findings_ehs_survey.pdf.

Yoshikawa, H. (1995). Long-term effects of early childhood programs on social out comes and delinquency. *The Future of Children, 5*(3), 51–75.

5 Latinos and Early Education

Immigrant Generational Differences and Family Involvement[1]

Eugene E. García, Kent Scribner, and Delis Cuéllar

Introduction

The generational status of Latino families is an important variable to explore when interpreting why Latinos experience the educational system in vastly different ways (Hernandez, 2006; Galindo & Reardon, 2006; Reardon & Galindo, 2006). Furthermore, parental educational participation in children's education has been documented as critical to understanding differences in how children experience education (Lee & Bowman, 2006; Raikes et al., 2006; Brooks-Gunn & Markman, 2005). For these reasons, this chapter examines young Latino children's demographics, educational circumstances, and family characteristics by generational status. Additionally, promising early childhood and education programs and a promising school district in Phoenix, Arizona, all of which serve mainly Latino immigrant families, are presented.

Demographics of Young Hispanic Children

Recently there has been much national attention given to the burgeoning Hispanic population in the US. The rapid growth is due both to an expanding wave of immigration from Latin American countries and to the relatively high birth rate among Hispanic families living here. As shown in Table 5.1, young Hispanic children are projected to have a higher percentage growth for several decades than Black and White non-Hispanic children.

Table 5.1 Actual and Projected Population Percentage Growth of Children under the Age of Five for Hispanic, Black and White Non-Hispanic Children

Children under age 5	*Year 2000 actual no.*	*Year 2025 Projected no. and percentage growth*	*Year 2050 Projected no. and percentage growth*
Hispanic	3,668,905	5,862,000 (+59.8%)	8,551,000 (+45.9%)
Non-Hispanic White	2,744,783	3,345,000 (+21.87%)	3,982,000 (+19%)
Blacks	11,171,157	12,024,000 (+7.3%)	12,287,000 (+2.2%)
Total (All children under age 5)	19,175,798	22,551,000 (+17.6%)	26,914,000 (+19.3%)

Note
Table adapted from Collins and Ribeiro, 2004.

Meanwhile, the high proportion of Hispanic children from often-underprivileged immigrant families redoubles the fact that too many face circumstances related to low levels of school readiness and achievement. In combination, these facts make clear the urgent imperative for the nation's school system to adapt and find ways to better serve the largest and fastest-growing group of children (Ramirez & de la Cruz, 2003; Hernandez, 2006).

Based on national demographic data (and considering each statistic separately), a Hispanic child is most likely American-born (88%), of Mexican descent (65%), living in California (31%) with both parents (77%)—at least one of whom is an immigrant (64%)—and is likely at least somewhat proficient in English (70%). Her/his family is probably low-income (58%) and the mother probably did graduate high school, but has no college degree (47%). However, our hypothetical child, despite having been categorized as Hispanic, belongs to a very diverse group of individuals with widely varying nationalities, generational statuses, and socioeconomic status (SES) levels. In fact, less than 1% of all Hispanic children fit the profile outlined above.

Most young children of Hispanic descent come from immigrant families. In the year 2000, 64% of these children were either immigrants themselves (first-generation American) or were US-born children of immigrants (second-generation American). Of these 64%, most (88%) fit the latter category (Hernandez, 2006). The remaining 36% were third-generation Americans and beyond. As expected, immigration status is a category where much variability is found. The likelihood that a given child will be from an immigrant family depends heavily on the family's national heritage. Roughly 90% of Dominican, Central American, and South American families are immigrant families. By comparison, about two-thirds of Mexican and Cuban youngsters belong to immigrant families. Puerto Rican children are the least likely to belong to immigrant families, with nearly half having two native-born parents.

Hispanic families have and continue to arrive from various countries and represent many different cultures. Figure 5.1 represents this diversity by displaying the percentage of young Hispanic children in each major national Latino heritage group (Hernandez, 2006).

Other demographic studies suggest that these percentages have remained steady through the recent past (Martin et al., 2005).

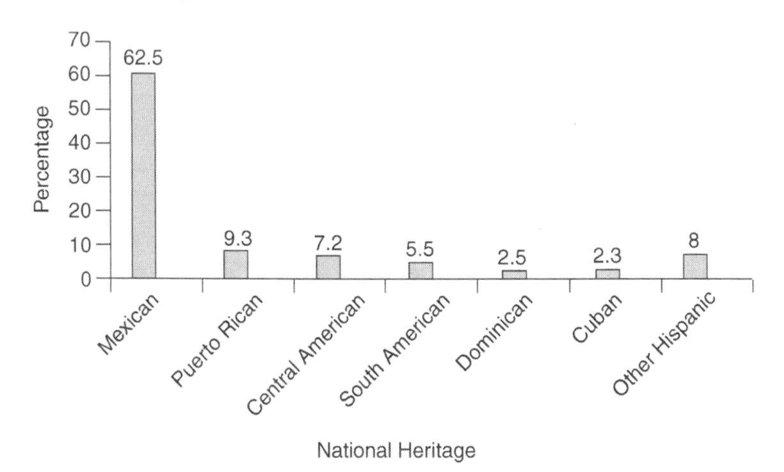

Figure 5.1 Percentage of young Hispanic Children by National Origin, 2000.

The educational-attainment patterns of the parents of young Hispanics vary substantially based on immigration status. The variability in terms of the mothers' educational attainment is indicated in Figure 5.2.

At the national level, in 2000, native-born mothers of young Hispanic children were more than 50% more likely to hold a college degree than immigrant mothers, were almost twice as likely to have finished high school and were more than eight times as likely to have progressed beyond the eighth grade (Hernandez, 2006). The educational attainment of Hispanic fathers varies with their immigration generational status too. As shown in Figure 5.3, all Hispanic immigrant fathers are less likely to have attained a high school diploma than native-born Hispanic fathers.

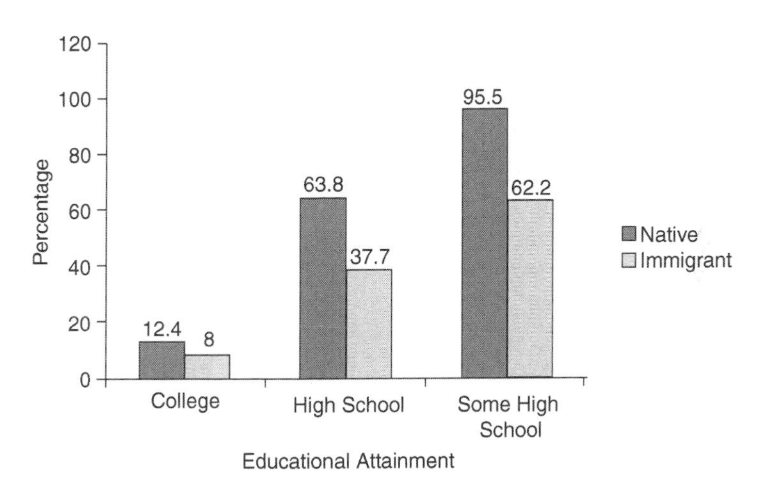

Figure 5.2 Percentage of Mothers of Young Hispanic Children with Various Educational Attainment by Immigration Status.

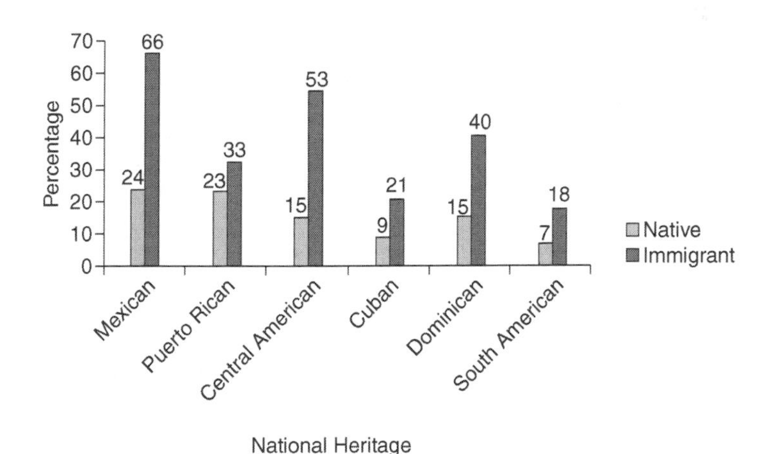

Figure 5.3 Percentage of Fathers of Young Hispanic Children Who Did Not Graduate High School by Immigrant Group and National Origin.

Galindo and Reardon (2006) point out that the parental educational circumstances are most disadvantaged for first- and second-generation Mexican-origin students and students from Central America. First- and second-generation Mexican students are three times as likely to have parents with less than a high school education than are third-generation and beyond Mexican students. Furthermore, Mexican-American mothers are the least likely to hold a college degree, with only 6.2% having a college degree in 2000. In that year, young children of Mexican descent had a 51.4% probability of having a mother without a high school diploma. This is the case for 49.9% of Central American children, 35.5% of Dominican children, 29.5% of Puerto Rican children, and 17.1% of South American children. Cubans, who make up the smallest percentage of Hispanics in the country, had the highest level of education. More than a quarter (29.2%) of young Cuban children have mothers who have attained a college degree and 84.6% had mothers that graduated high school, figures that are very similar to those for White mothers (30.2% and 91.1%, respectively) and well above the national averages (23.8% and 81.8%, respectively) (Hernandez, 2006).

Given the lower average level of education for the parents of young Hispanic children, it is perhaps unsurprising that Hispanic youths experience very high levels of poverty in the US. More than one-quarter (26%) of Hispanic children aged 8 or younger live below the poverty line and more than half (58%) come from low-income families (those with incomes less than twice the national poverty line). This compares to only 9% of White children living below the poverty line and 27% of White children belonging to low-income families.

Notably, the pattern of economic success mirrors that of educational attainment with respect to immigration status and national heritage. Young Hispanic children are 31% more likely to live in poverty or under low-income conditions when they come from an immigrant family (63%) as compared to those with native-born parents (48%). Mothers of young Mexican-American children, who have the lowest average educational attainment among Hispanic national heritage groups, also showed the lowest rates of economic success, with 68% of their children living in low-income families (Hernandez, 2006).

The population of Hispanic children is indeed diverse in terms of generational status, national heritage, economic success of their families, and the ultimate education attained by their parents. These facts, combined with the overall unequal numbers and growth rates of Hispanics in different regions, means that policy makers, administrators, and teachers will all face their own unique set of challenges as they prepare to serve this large and rapidly growing population.

Young Hispanic Children's Educational Circumstances

On average the early academic standing of Hispanic children lags behind that of children from other ethnic groups in the country (Reardon & Galindo, 2006). To better understand this gap and the educational circumstances of young Latinos, their academic standing in the early years, the types of schools they attend, their early education participation and effects of this participation are presented by generational status.

Latino Children's Academic Standing

The early academic standing of Hispanic children lags behind that of children from other ethnic groups in the country. Although this gap is not found in children at 9 months old (Lopez, Barrueco, & Miles, 2006), academic differences are found at the start of preschool, in kindergarten, and throughout the elementary years and beyond (Galindo & Reardon, 2006). In a report using ECLS-K—the Early Childhood Longitudinal Study-Kindergarten Class of 1998–1999, a nationally representative database that includes standardized test scores for children starting in kindergarten through the fifth grade, Galindo and Reardon (2006) report on important educational experiences of Hispanics by Hispanic subgroups and for Mexican Americans by generational status. They found that half of Hispanic kindergarteners are classified as language-minority students and that 30% at the beginning of kindergarten are not considered English-proficient. This is an important fact, because English-language proficiency has been documented to be an important determinant of educational success (Gandara, Rumberger, Maxwell-Jolly, & Callahan, 2003). However, the percentage of language-minority students varies by generational status. For instance, among Mexican students, more than 90% of first-generation children are language-minority students compared to only 14% of third-generation and beyond. Additionally, first-generation Mexican-American students are much more likely to live in a household where only Spanish is spoken (75.2%), in comparison to second-generation Mexican-American students (53.1%) or third-generation and above (4.9%). This generational difference in English proficiency is found among all Hispanic subgroups. Hernandez (2006) shows that a higher percentage of children in immigrant families than in native families are considered limited-English-proficient (LEP). For example, for native-born Puerto Rican families the percentage of children who were considered LEP in 2000 was only 12% compared to 30% of children from island-origin families. For children in native-born families with Central American heritage, the percentage of young children who were considered LEP was 11% and 38% for children in immigrant families. For Cubans, Dominicans, and South Americans the percentages of children who were considered LEP were as follows (the first percentage is for native-born families and the second for immigrant families): 9% and 24%; 18% and 39%; and 9% and 23% respectively.

Hispanic children also start kindergarten behind in mathematics in comparison to their White non-Hispanic, Asian American and African American counterparts (Reardon & Galindo, 2006). Generational status again is an important variable in explaining the gap in mathematics knowledge. For example, first- and second-generation Mexican-origin students and Central American students start kindergarten with math scores more than one standard deviation below those of White students. However, third-generation Mexican-American children start kindergarten with math scores less than one-half a standard deviation below White students. Interestingly, the Hispanic–White test scores gap narrows substantially in the first two years of schooling, especially for Latino subgroups with lower English-proficiency levels, recent immigrants, and those from non-English-speaking homes. This narrowing, Reardon and Galindo (2006) suggest, is due to the process of increased oral and written English-language acquisition. Despite the Hispanic–White gap narrowing in math and reading, by the end of the fifth grade, the gap in math is one-half a standard deviation and three-eighths of a standard deviation in reading (Reardon & Galindo, 2006). By the end of fifth grade, Hispanic children who come from low socioeconomic circumstances have similar proficiency levels in reading as White fifth-grade children from low socioeconomic circumstances (Reardon & Galindo, 2006).

Even though there is rapid progress for children from Spanish-speaking homes (who are in the main first- and second-generation Hispanic children) in math and reading in the first two years of schooling, these children do not score as well as children from English-speaking homes. It is important to note, however, that the non-English-proficient students make more progress in math skills in relation to White students from kindergarten to fifth grade. But this progress does not suffice to eliminate the considerable initial gaps. In fact, in reading, by fifth grade, Hispanic children with low English proficiency still remain over a standard deviation behind Hispanic students who were proficient in English in kindergarten and behind non-Hispanic White students (Reardon & Galindo, 2006).

Types of Schools Young Latino Students Attend

In a study conducted by the Civil Rights Project housed at Harvard University using data from 2000, it was found that Latino students experience more educational segregation in the public school system than any other ethnic group in the country (Frankenber, Lee, & Orefield, 2003). Researchers have shown that Hispanic students are likely to attend schools with a high concentration of non-English-proficient and poor students (Crawford, 1997; Schmid, 2001; Van Hook & Stamper Balistreri, 2002). In California, students of color and first- and second-generation immigrant students who are English learners (the majority of these English learners are of Mexican origin) are often housed in overcrowded and deteriorating facilities. These students are almost exclusively the only ones who appear on the state's "critically overcrowded" list (Oakes, 2004).

The types of schools that Mexican-American students attend are highly correlated to the generational status of their families. A larger percentage of first-generation Mexican-American students (97%) and second-generation (96%) attend public kindergarten than third-generation and beyond Mexican-American children (90%) (Galindo & Reardon, 2006). Overall, throughout the K–fifth-grade period, first- and second-generation Mexican-American students attend schools that are larger in size, located in communities with higher levels of disorganization and have more safety problems when compared to the schools that third-generation and beyond Mexican-American students and Hispanics in general attend (Galindo & Reardon, 2006). Moreover, these schools also have less-experienced teachers, and are more likely to have a high proportion of minority and poor students than the elementary schools attended by children from other racial/ethnic communities. What is critical is that these problems seem to have a bearing on children's development and academic performance (Crosnoe, 2005). Weak educational foundations and problematic early-childhood education settings are likely to lead to pessimistic prospects.

Latino Education Participation and Outcomes in the Early Years

According to the Pat Brown Institute for Public Affairs (2006), national trends on preschool participation (as the primary care arrangement) by ethnicity show that Latino families have the least percentage of their children attending a preschool in comparison to families from all other major ethnic groups. Only 43% of Latino 3- to 5-year-olds attends center-based preschool programs vs. 59% of Whites and 66% of Blacks (National Center for Education Statistics, 2006). This is a perplexing finding when one considers that in a recent survey almost all Latino families (97%) mentioned that if high-quality preschools were available in their community they would enroll their preschool children in center-based preschool programs (Zarate & Perez, 2006; Garcia & Gonzalez, 2006). Research shows it is not a lack of Latino interest in preschools that is to blame for Latino children attending preschool in such low numbers, but rather the fact that in heavily Latino communities the availability of high-quality, publicly funded programs is very limited (Bridges & Fuller, 2006).

The preschool participation of Hispanic children varies with the generational status of their families. Hernandez (2006) demonstrates that all native-born Hispanic families are more likely to enroll their children in preschool/nursery school than their immigrant counterparts. For first- and second-generation Mexican-American families, the percentage of their children who were enrolled in preschool/nursery school in 2000 was 36% and for their native-born counterparts this percentage rose to almost half (48%). For Puerto Ricans, Central Americans, Cubans, Dominicans, and South Americans the percentages rose from 49% to 57%, 43% to 61%, 61% to 66%, 52% to 55%, and 57% to 67% respectively.

Nonetheless, young Latino children achieve significant cognitive development when enrolled in high-quality state-funded preschool programs. In an assessment of Tulsa, Oklahoma's preschool program it was discovered that Hispanic and Black children, but not White children, gained considerably in cognitive and language development (Gormley & Gayer, 2005; Gormley & Phillips, 2005). In a different study of Oklahoma's universal pre-K program, Gormley, Gayer, Phillips, and Dawson (2005) found that children from all ethnic groups fared well in the letter–word identification, spelling, and applied-problem tests. The classrooms in these schools accommodate a substantial proportion of Hispanic children from Spanish-speaking families. Gormley et al. (2005) found that Hispanic children improved their letter–word identification scores by 4.15 points (1.50 above the standard deviation for the control group), spelling scores by 2.66 points (0.98 above the standard deviation for the control group), and their applied-problems scores by 4.97 points (0.99 above the standard deviation for the control group). Given conditions like those in the Oklahoma universal pre-K program study, it becomes apparent that Hispanic children are capable of developing and improving their language, cognitive, and problem-solving skills in high-quality settings.

Hispanic Family Characteristics

Although Hispanic children often start school under disadvantaged academic circumstances, the literature has shown that Hispanic families possess positive attributes that are likely to work as a safeguard against these risk factors. For example, a foundational attribute in Hispanic families is familism. Familism expresses important values such as family identification, obligation, and support (Velez-Ibanez & Greenberg, 1992). Familism has been found to positively affect Latino students' academic performance (Valenzuela & Dornbusch, 1994). Valenzuela and Dornbusch used survey data from

3,158 (2,666 Anglo and 492 Mexican-origin) high school students to investigate the impact of familism on students' academic performance. Behavioral, attitudinal, and structural dimensions of familism were related to students' self-reported grades. The authors found that for both the White and Mexican-American groups, familism was important but the Mexican group was able to achieve academic gains because of it. It is important to note that this was the case for the Mexican-descent students whose parents had at least 12 years of education. For the Mexican-descent group, neither familism nor parental education on their own related to higher educational outcomes. However, it was the interaction of the two variables that accrued the gains.

Another important attribute is the high percentage of intact families within the Hispanic community. Mexican immigrant families have the highest percentage of intact families when compared to all immigrant families and all US native families, including White families (Hernandez, 2006). The generational status of Latino families is an important variable to understand the variability in intact families within the Hispanic community. For instance, for Mexican-American children from immigrant families this percentage in 2000 was 86%, and 65% for Mexican-American children in native-born families. The following percentage pairs represent the percentages in each (immigrant and native) group for Puerto Ricans, Central Americans, Cubans, Dominicans, and South Americans respectively: 64% and 52%; 81% and 52%; 85% and 71%; 66% and 33%; and 85% and 67%. Importantly, research shows that children who grow up in stable, two-parent households when compared to children who lack these attributes, achieve higher levels of education, earn higher incomes, enjoy higher occupational status, and report fewer symptoms of depression, even after controlling for parental income and education (Amato, 2005). Specifically, for Mexican-American families, it has been suggested that the high rate of intact marriages helps contribute to Mexican-American children's high levels of psychological well-being (Crosnoe, 2006). Moreover, Latino children often live in households that include nuclear and extended family. This affects Hispanic children positively. Latino households that include grandparents and other extended-family members are conducive to communal caregiving and family-wide participation in children's early learning experiences (Buriel & Hurtado-Ortiz, 2000).

Parent Involvement in Education

Parent involvement in children's education has been documented as important in the academic well-being of children in the academic literature (Barrera & Warner, 2006; Lee & Bowman, 2006; Raikes et al., 2006). Using ECLS-K data, Qiuyun (2006) studied the effects of parent involvement of language-minority parents in their children's academic outcomes (reading, math, and science) and social-emotional outcomes in the years of kindergarten through third grade, in a four-year longitudinal study. The findings suggest that English-language learners (ELL) count with less parent involvement through the early academic years and that they lagged behind their non-ELL peers at the beginning of kindergarten through the end of third grade.

Promising Educational Practices for Districts or Programs Working with Latino Families

AVANCE, Project FLAME (Family Literacy: Aprendiendo, Mejorando, Educando), PIQE, HIPPY, and the Isaac School District have been found to have a positive effect on Latino educational parental involvement and Latino children's early academic performance. These educational entities ameliorate several key issues that in the past have proved to be barriers for successful parent involvement for Latino immigrant parents. For instance, research has shown that in order for parent-involvement programs to succeed, they need to include Latino parents as legitimate collaborators in the development of the programs (Delgado-Gaitan, 1992), should use the language that the parents speak best (Rodriguez-Brown, 2009), explicitly teach new immigrants about the expectations of and how to navigate the American school system (Delgado-Gaitan, 1992), and incorporate the family's funds of knowledge (Moll, Amanti, Neff, & Gonzalez, 1992). The programs above have successfully addressed these important issues and thus are highlighted in this document.

AVANCE: A Parent–child Education Program

AVANCE, a non-profit organization established in 1973 with the mission of "Unlocking America's potential by strengthening families within at-risk communities through effective parent education and support programs," is a parent–child education program that focuses on parent education, early childhood development, brain development, literacy, and school readiness. The program largely supports Latino immigrant families under conditions of economic stress in underserved communities and aims to prepare parents to be supporters and role models for their children to succeed in school.

The AVANCE program (AVANCE, 2007), with chapters throughout Texas and in Los Angeles, California, is a 9-month course built on the assumption that parents can improve their parenting skills, that they are the most influential teachers and role models for their children, and that the years between childbirth and age 3 are critical to influencing a child's educational success.

The program serves parents with children from 0–3 years of age and operates in housing projects, schools, and community centers. AVANCE instructors make parents aware of the learning and development their children undergo, including the emotional, physical, social, and cognitive processes. This awareness-raising practice is based on the discussion of topics that range from the importance of effective discipline and nutrition to reading and math. Parents are also encouraged to attend classes in literacy, learning English, and preparing for the GED.

Project FLAME

A program that came about with the purpose of improving the parent involvement and academic achievement of children of limited-English-proficient parents is Project FLAME (Family Literacy: Aprendiendo, Mejorando, Educando) (Rodriguez-Brown & Shanahan, 1989). FLAME is housed at the University of Illinois, Chicago and is carried out in public schools. Presently, the program model has been nationally circulated to over 50 sites to train family-literacy professionals. FLAME offers wide-ranging services to Latino families with children between the ages of 3 and 9 with the purpose of increasing parents' ability to provide literacy opportunities for their children, increasing parents' ability to act as positive literacy models for their children, improving parents' literacy skills so that they may efficiently initiate, encourage, support, and extend their children's learning, and improving the relationship between parents and school officials. An important aspect of Project FLAME is the emphasis on using the language in which the parents feel most comfortable.

Following are some of the skills that are imparted by the program to Hispanic parents and the ways in which the program has improved Hispanic children's early education. For example, parents learn what types of books are appropriate for the age of their children, and are encouraged to reach out in the community to access literacy materials and create at-home literacy centers. Parents are also provided with English-as-a-second-language courses and encouraged to engage in reading and writing activities with their children. Through workshops in the program parents learn the value of interacting with their children in activities such as talking, singing, and playing. The program emphasizes talking with children about books. In order to improve parent–school communication, parents learn about what schools expect from their children academically and are encouraged to volunteer in their children's classrooms. Through the participation with the program, children's knowledge of basic concepts, letter knowledge, and print awareness increase. Furthermore, parent-involvement activities such as volunteering and implementing teacher suggestions also increased within the Latino parents (Rodriguez-Brown, 2009).

In a quasi-experimental study, children of parents who attended FLAME and who did not attend preschool were compared to children who attended a state-funded preschool program and whose parents did not take part in FLAME. The children were compared in terms of their print awareness, recognition of lower and uppercase letters, and knowledge of basic concepts via the Boehm test. All children came from similar socioeconomic backgrounds, and most of these families asserted that Spanish was their dominant language. On the pretest, the children who attended the state-sponsored preschool outperformed the FLAME children, but on the posttest there were no differences detected. This was after adjusting for the pre-existing differences between the FLAME and the comparison group. The fact that this study included a comparison group was important in learning that the improvements among the FLAME children were due to their parents' participation in the FLAME project (Rodriguez-Brown & Mulhern, 1993).

Parent Institute for Quality Education

Parent Institute for Quality Education (PIQE)—a program whose underlying assumption is that the most promising way to enhance their children's education is by transforming the working partnership between parents, school, and community—aims to teach parents how to become important supporters of their children's educational performance and development (Vidano & Sahafi, 2004; Zellman, Stecher, Klein, & McCaffrey, n.d.). Since its inception in 1987, PIQE has graduated over 154,000 parents from schools all over California and has begun to expand outside California, opening new offices in Dallas and Phoenix.

The fundamental premise of PIQE is that low-income, recently immigrated parents need information about the dynamics of the US educational system, about how to collaborate with the school and teachers, and about how to assist their children at home (PIQE, 2007). PIQE offers this information through a program that consists of eight 90-minute sessions in which a range of topics are discussed, including home–school collaboration, the home, motivation, and self-esteem, communication and discipline, academic standards, how the school functions, and the road to university (Chrispeels & Rivero, 2001; Chrispeels, Gonzales, & Arellano, 2004; Golan & Peterson, 2002). Each PIQE session emphasizes the centrality of parents to their children's future and encourages parents to interact with each other and with the instructor to talk about the topic at hand. Multiple classes are scheduled to accommodate the family's needs (e.g., morning or evening classes). Instructors who share the ethnic backgrounds and similar life experiences to those of the parents conduct the classes.

Evaluations of PIQE have suggested that as a result of parents' participation in the program, these parents have become more engaged with their children, the school, and especially their children's teachers (Chrispeels & Rivero, 2001; Chrispeels et al., 2004). Likewise, data from a performance evaluation that focused on the children of parents that graduated from the PIQE suggest that the program has had a bearing on school persistence, reduced the dropout rate, and increased college enrollment (Chrispeels & González, 2004; Chrispeels et al., 2004; Vidano & Sahafi, 2004). PIQE instructors have played a key role in achieving these goals by utilizing specific collaborative and supportive practices that effectively retain parents and remove barriers to their participation, as well as using parent- and community-centered activities that encourage parents to complete the 8-week sessions of the program (Golan & Peterson, 2000).

Home Instruction for Parents of Preschool Youngsters

The Home Instruction for Parents of Preschool Youngsters (HIPPY) program is a free, 2-year, home-based early-intervention program for 4- and 5-year-old children. HIPPY is an internationally acclaimed early-childhood education program presently used in 157 sites, 26 states, and 7 countries. In the US, it is intended to provide educational enrichment to at-risk children from poor and immigrant families, increase school readiness, and foster parent involvement in their children's education (HIPPY USA, 2007a). The main purpose of the program is to increase school readiness and to foster parent involvement in their children's education and in community life. The 30-week HIPPY curriculum is made up of lessons that are designed to develop a child's skills in three major areas: language development, problem solving, and sensory and perceptual discrimination (HIPPY USA, 2007b).

A study conducted by Garcia (2006) investigated the academic effects of HIPPY on Hispanic English-language learners in Texas. Using standardized measures in reading, mathematics, and language arts, the author compared Hispanic youngsters who were part of HIPPY starting at age 4 (HIPPY 4-Preschool) and age 5 (HIPPY 5-Kindergarten) to Hispanic students who attended an early-childhood school and did not participate in HIPPY. The curriculum used was in Spanish. The treatment group statistically outperformed the control group in the reading, language, and mathematics long after they experienced the intervention. These statistically significant results were still found at the end of third grade.

The Isaac School District Embraces the Isaac Initiatives for Latino Families

The Isaac School District is located in central Phoenix and serves a student population that is almost exclusively (94%) Hispanic, where 80% of students come from homes where English is not the primary language; 46% are English-language learners and low-income; and 93% of students in the district live at or below the federal poverty line. Here, we document some important initiatives that were adopted within the district that have improved the education that Hispanic children receive.

In 2002, the Arizona Department of Education (ADE) identified only two Isaac schools as "Academically Performing." Through a much-improved participatory and democratic decision-making process, the district's ADE 2007 results showed eight schools designated by the ADE as "Performing" or better, including the district's first "Highly Performing" school. These positive changes came about because district- and site-level leaders have worked collaboratively with teachers, parents, and support staff to establish an organizational culture that persistently attempts to discover the community assets and funds of knowledge (Moll et al., 1992; Reyes, Scribner, & Paredes Scribner, 1999; Scheurich & Skrla, 2003) that exist within the school community and capitalize on them. Action-oriented initiatives along with a sustained vision for improvement in academic achievement were established cooperatively.

These initiatives were established through participatory democratic decision making among all stakeholders, including parents, teachers, students, principals, and school staff, and central and classified staff (Beck & Murphy, 1996; Blasé & Blasé, 1997; Bredeson, 1994). Understanding that leadership is a shared responsibility, one premise that has framed a great deal of our leadership style is the understanding that "those closest to the problem often have the best solution" (Heckman & Peterman, 1996). Each member of the learning community has the potential to provide insight, offer feedback or ask questions that could add value to considerations of the larger school community (Reyes et al., 1999). Effective leadership, as defined in the Isaac School District, empowers all stakeholders with the responsibility to create conditions and establish a culture in which these ideas are able to emerge for consideration. Leaders are responsible for building communication systems and a culture of continuous improvement where problem solving and participation take place in an orderly, systematic manner, grounded always in the best interests of student learning and student well-being (Senge, 1990; Beck & Murphy, 1996).

Five years ago the Isaac District was characterized as a community of talented, well-intentioned people with a great "care-ethic" (Noddings, 1999, 2003). The school community, however, lacked effective communication with internal and external stakeholder groups, including a significant disconnect between school leaders and parents. In July 2003, a functional leadership cabinet was nonexistent. Department heads never met regularly to discuss operational short-term issues, nor to engage in any longer-term strategic planning. Parental involvement was characterized by a "one-way" flow of information where school officials offered anecdotal data and superficial diagnosis of "what these parents need to do" or through the identification of a litany of community ills which were preventing the schools from experiencing success. It was clear that weak communication and loose accountability systems allowed individuals and specific departments to create subcultures and norms that perhaps served specific individual's or group's interests, rather than the larger organization and its community in a productive way.

Immediately, three Superintendent's Advisory Councils were established. Each addressed "organizational priorities" of the respective stakeholder group. The "Superintendent's Certified Advisory Council," made up of teachers and certified employee leaders, addressed issues and established priorities from the classroom teacher's perspective. Support-staff leaders collaborated with the superintendent simultaneously using an identical model for information gathering, meeting facilitation and decision making on the "Superintendent's Classified Advisory Council." Among these three groups, the largest membership was, and continues to be, those participating on the "Superintendent's Parent Advisory Council." This group, which averages over 100 participants, addresses issues relevant to parents' lives, parent-involvement activities, and building and strengthening relationships with their school and the school district. Agendas of this group are set in conjunction with our school-site parent coordinators. Discussion topics include issues such as the following: parents as instructional support at home; implications of child safety and security at school in the context of Arizona's new immigration laws; the importance of having parents in parent-education programs; networking with other parents; and creating good questions for upcoming parent–teacher conferences.

These advisory groups have been an integral part of creating the Isaac District's new instructional paradigm and an inclusive organizational culture. Representative leaders from certified, classified, and administrative groups have worked together to successfully implement the "interest-based negotiations process" for the first time in the district among the employee bargaining units. Certified employees, classified staff, and parent groups have all played important roles in establishing the district's mission, vision, values, and goals.

The district's mission has been distilled into three easy-to-remember concepts that guide all of the work at the district. These are *The Isaac Initiatives* that are embraced by Isaac School District stakeholders. The three "I's" for Isaac commit all those involved with the students to (1) increase student achievement for every student throughout the district, (2) improve customer service to both the internal and external customers and (3) integrate parents and community into each decision made. The Isaac Initiatives replaced the paragraph-long, run-on sentence which previously served as the rarely cited district mission statement. District staff members were enthusiastically encouraged to follow the three "I's" by the often-cited phrase: "Keep an Eye on Isaac."

These initiatives framed the district's mission and vision. They have concentrated on a three-legs-of-the-stool approach. Given the low educational level of the Latino parents (Hernandez, 2006), it may seem more effective to concentrate on the opportunity to raise schooling success by focusing on the child with strong educational interventions with little focus on the parents. The approach at Isaac is an example of an attempt to address both—it cannot be one or the other. Therefore, in conjunction with a governing board, a participatory and democratic decision-making process was created, resulting in improvements in student achievement and success in community engagement over the past 5 years. By embracing these initiatives, a conscious effort was made to create a school district with high-impact schools, serving high-performing Latino students.

Conclusion

Several conclusions arise from this review. Latino children are the fastest growing segment of the US population; their families vary greatly, they often attend poor-quality schools, and educationally lag behind children from other ethnic groups. However, Latino families possess many attributes that positively affect their children's educational well-being. Furthermore, although Latino children are the least likely group of children to attend preschool programs, Latino parents have displayed a great deal of interest in enrolling their children in high-quality preschools if the schools became available in their community. Additionally Latino families are benefiting greatly from the early-childhood and education programs created to manage their specific needs. Moreover, school districts that establish collaborative governance and leadership and build collaborative relationships with Latino parents can have an impact on student achievement and success. Given such great diversity it is pivotal that practitioners working with the Latino community are cognizant that every family depending on a variety of variables will face very different challenges. Finally, researchers need to continue to explore specific ways in which educational problems can be ameliorated for specific segments of the Latino population.

Note

1. Latino and Hispanic are both used interchangeably to identify persons of Mexican, Puerto Rican, Cuban, and Central and South American backgrounds.

References

Amato, P. (2005). The impact of family formation change on the cognitive, social and emotional well-being of the next generation. *The Future of Children, 15*, 76–96.

AVANCE (2007). *About AVANCE.* Retrieved October 4, 2007, from www.avance.org.

Barrera, J.M., & Warner, L. (2006). Involving families in school events. *Kappa Delta Pi Records, 42*(2), 72–75.

Beck, L.G., & Murphy, J. (1996). *The four imperatives of a successful school.* Thousand Oaks, CA: Corwin Press.

Blasé, J., & Blasé, J.R. (1997). *The fire is back!* Thousand Oaks, CA: Corwin Press.

Bredeson, P.V. (1994). Empowered teachers—empowered principals: Principals' perceptions of leadership in schools. In N.A. Prestine & P.W. Thurston (Eds.), *Advances in educational administration* (vol. 3, pp. 195–220). Greenwich, CT: JAI Press.

Bridges, M., & Fuller, B. (2006). *Access of Hispanics to center-based programs for 3- to 4-year olds and infants and toddlers.* Unpublished analysis for the National Task Force on Early Childhood Education for Hispanics.

Brooks-Gunn, J., & Markman, L.B. (2005). The contribution of parenting to ethnic and racial gaps in school readiness. *Future Child, 15*(1), 139–168.

Buriel, R., & Hurtado-Ortiz, M.T. (2000). Child care practices and preferences of native- and foreign-born Latina mothers and Euro-American mothers. *Hispanic Journal of Behavioral Sciences, 22*(3), 314–331.

Chrispeels, J., & González, M. (2004). *Do educational programs increase parents' practices at home?: Factors influencing Latino parent involvement.* Cambridge, MA: Harvard Family Research Project.

Chrispeels, J., González, M., & Arellano, B. (2004). *Evaluation of the effectiveness of the Parent Institute for Quality Education in Los Angeles Unified School District September 2003 to May 2004.* Santa Barbara, CA: University of California.

Chrispeels, J.H., & Rivero, E (2001). Engaging Latino families for student success: How parent education can reshape parents' sense of place in the education of their children. *Peabody Journal of Education, 76*(2), 119–169.

Collins, R., & Ribeiro, R. (2004) Toward an early care and education agenda for Hispanic children. *Early Childhood Research and Practice, 6*(2), 1–10.

Crawford, J. (1997). *Best evidence: Research foundations of the Bilingual Education Act.* Washington, DC: National Clearing House for Bilingual Education.

Crosnoe, R. (2005). Double disadvantage or signs of resilience? The elementary school contexts of children. *American Education Research Journal, 42*(2), 269–314.

Crosnoe, R. (2006). *Mexican roots, American schools: Helping Mexican immigrant children succeed.* Palo Alto, CA: Stanford University Press.

Delgado-Gaitán, C. (1992). School matters in the Mexican-American home: Socializing children to education. *American Educational Research Journal, 29,* 495–513.

Frankenber, E., Lee, C., & Orfield, G. (2003). *A multiracial society with segregated schools: Are we losing the dream?* Cambridge, MA: The Civil Rights Project, Harvard University.

Galindo, C., & Reardon, S.F. (2006). *Hispanic students' educational experiences and opportunities during kindergarten.* Tempe, AZ: National Task Force on Early Childhood Education for Hispanics.

Gandara, P., Rumberger, R., Maxwell-Jolly, J., & Callahan, R. (2003). English learners in California schools: Unequal resources, unequal outcomes. *Educational Policy Analysis Archives, 11*(36). Retrieved April 5, 2009, from http://epaa.asu.edu/epaa/v11n36.

García, E., & Gonzales, D.M. (2006). *Pre-K and Latinos: The foundation for America's future.* Washington, DC: Pre-K Now.

García, E., Jensen, B., & Cuellar, D. (2006). Early academic achievement of Hispanics in the United States: Implications for teacher preparation. *The New Educator, 2,* 123–147.

Garcia, M. (2006). *The impact of the home instruction for parents of preschool youngsters on reading, mathematics and language achievement of Hispanic English language learners.* Unpublished Dissertation, University of North Texas.

Golan, S., & Petersen, D. (2000). *Promoting involvement of recent immigrant families in their children's education.* Menlo Park, CA: SRI International.

Gormley, W., & Gayer, T. (2005). Promoting school readiness in Oklahoma: An evaluation of Tulsa's pre-K program. *Journal of Human Resources, 40,* 533–558.

Gormley, W.T., Gayer, T., Phillips, D., & Dawson, B. (2005). The effects of universal Pre-K on cognitive development. *Developmental Psychology, 41*(6), 872–884.

Gormley, W., & Phillips, D. (2005). The effects of universal pre-K in Oklahoma: Research highlights and policy implications. *Policy Studies Journal, 33,* 65–82.

Heckman, P.E., & Peterman, F. (1996). Indigenous invention: New Promise for school reform. *Teachers College Journal, 98*(2), 307–327.

Hernandez, D. (2006). *Young Hispanic children in the U.S.: A demographic portrait based on Census 2000.* Tempe, AZ: National Task Force on Early Childhood Education for Hispanics.

HIPPY USA. (2007a). *About HIPPY.* Retrieved October 1, 2007, from www.hippyusa.org/About_HIPPY/about_HIPPY.html.

HIPPY USA. (2007b). *The HIPPY curriculum.* Retrieved October 1, 2007, from www.hippyusa.org/Model/curriculum.html.

Lee, J., & Bowman, N. (2006). Parent involvement, cultural capital, and the achievement gap among elementary school children. *American Educational Research Journal, 43*(2), 193–218.

Lopez, M.L., Barrueco, S., & Miles, J. (2006). *Latino infants and their families: A national perspective of protective and risk factors for development.* Tempe, AZ.: National Task Force on Early Childhood Education for Hispanics.

Martin, J.A., Hamilton, B.E., Sutton, P.E., Ventura, S.J., Menacker, F., & Munson, M.S. (2005). Births: Final data for 2003. *National Vital Statistics Report, 52*(2), 1–114. US Department of Health and Human Services, Center for Disease Control and Prevention.

Moll, L.C., Amanti, C., Neff, D., & Gonzalez, N. (1992). Funds of knowledge for teaching: Using a qualitative approach to connect homes and classrooms. *Theory Into Practice, 31*(2), 132–141.

National Center for Education Statistics. (2006). *Conditions of education 2006.* Washington, DC: US Department of Education.

Noddings, N. (1999). Caring and competence. In G. Griffen (Ed.), *The education of teachers* (pp. 205–220). Chicago, IL: National Society of Education.

Noddings, N. (2003). *Caring: A feminine approach to ethics and moral education* (2nd ed.). Berkeley, CA: University of California Press.

Oakes, J. (2004). Investigating the claims in Williams v. State of California: An unconstitutional denial of education's basic tools? *Teachers College Record, 106*(10), 1889–1906.

Orfield, G., & Yun, J. (1999). *Resegregation in American schools.* Boston, MA: The Civil Rights Project, Harvard University.

Pat Brown Institute for Public Affairs. (2006). *Preschool after proposition 82: Should spatial targeting be the natural next step?* Brief No. 4. California State University, Los Angeles, CA. Retrieved November 25, 2007, from www.patbrowninstitute.org/publications/documents/PolicyBrief-4.pdf.

PIQE. (2007). *PIQUE Home.* Retrieved October 6, 2007, from www.piqe.org.

Qiuyun, L. (2003). *Parent involvement and early literacy.* Retrieved September 28, 2007, from www.gse.harvard.edu/hfrp/projects/fine/resources/digest/literacy.html.

Qiuyun, L. (2006). *Beyond cultural deficit approach: Disentangling language minority parents' involvement in the early grades.* Paper presented at the American Educational Research Association, San Francisco, CA.

Raikes, H., Alexander Pan, B., Luze, G., Tamis-LeMonda, C.S., Brooks-Gunn, J., & Constantine, J. (2006). Mother-child bookreading in low-income families: correlates and outcomes during the first three years of life. *Child Development, 77*(4), 924–953.

Ramirez, R., & de la Cruz, P. (2003). *The Hispanic population in the United States: March, 2002.* Washington, DC: US Census Bureau.

Reardon, S.F., & Galindo, C. (2006). *Patterns of Hispanic students' math and English literacy test scores in the early elementary grades.* Tempe, AZ.: National Task Force on Early Childhood Education for Hispanics.

Reyes, P., Scribner, J.D., & Paredes Scribner, A. (1999). *Lessons from high-performing Hispanic schools: Creating learning communities.* New York: Teachers College Press.

Rodríguez-Brown, F.V. (2009). *Home-school connection: Lessons learned in a culturally and linguistically diverse community.* New York: Taylor & Francis.

Rodríguez-Brown, F.V., & Mulhern, M.M. (1993). Fostering critical literacy through family literacy: A study of families in a Mexican-immigrant community. *Bilingual Research Journal, 17*(3/4), 1–16.

Rodríguez-Brown, F.V., & Shanahan, T. (1989). *Literacy for the limited English proficient child: A family approach.* Chicago, IL: University of Illinois.

Scheurich, J., & Skrla, L. (2003). *Leadership for equity and excellence: Creating high achievement classes, schools, and districts.* Thousand Oaks, CA: Corwin Press.

Schmid, C. (2001). Educational achievement, language minority and the new second generation. *Sociology of Education, 73,* 71–87.
Senge, P. (1990). *The fifth discipline: The art and practice of the learning organization.* New York: Currency Doubleday.
Valenzuela, A., & Dornbusch, S.M. (1994). Familism and social capital in the academic achievement of Mexican origin and Anglo adolescents. *Social Science Quarterly, 75,* 18–36.

6 Diversity in Academic Achievement

Children of Immigrants in US Schools

Jennifer E. Glick and Littisha Bates

Introduction

Perhaps one of the easiest conclusions to draw about children of immigrants in the US today is that they are a diverse group with considerable variation in academic performance and subsequent educational attainment. Perhaps one of the most difficult tasks, therefore, is to draw substantive conclusions about the determinants of immigrant children's paths through school. Scholarship on the academic performance of immigrants often compares those who arrived in childhood to their higher-generation counterparts. These studies find somewhat mixed support for a classic assimilation model of improved performance over generations (i.e., from immigrants themselves to the second-generation children of immigrants then compared to those in the third or subsequent generations). On the one hand, some studies point to lower test scores and school completion rates for immigrant adolescents than their higher-generation peers (Portes & Rumbaut, 2001). These differences may attenuate as adolescents move through school (Glick & White, 2003). Yet, increasing achievement over time or across generations is not as assured for all groups. Thus, the segmented assimilation perspective clearly calls for consideration not only of the considerable diversity of immigrant origins but the diversity of the context encountered in the US as well (Portes & Rumbaut, 2001; Suárez-Orozco & Suárez-Orozco, 2001).

For schools, educating children from diverse national-origin and linguistic backgrounds presents challenges in several areas. Many children of immigrants come from low-income backgrounds, live in households where no one speaks English well, and may be isolated in ethnically or racially segregated neighborhoods (Garcia, 2002; Hernandez, Denton, & Macartney, 2008). Further, accessing social services and resources can be difficult even for those families with documented status and US-citizen children (Capps, Fix, & Reardon-Anderson, 2003). This rather bleak picture is also accompanied by strengths from close immigrant communities or families with great interest in helping their children succeed in their new country (Crosnoe, 2006; Suárez-Orozco & Suárez-Orozco, 2001). The best policy approach for enhancing the educational success of children of immigrants must consider these strengths and challenges. But first, we must understand just which characteristics of families and their communities create barriers to educational success for children of immigrants.

In this chapter, we focus on academic achievement of a large sample of children in kindergarten and follow their achievement over time. Our first goal is to illustrate the considerable diversity evidenced among children in immigrant families. We note the variety of family backgrounds and school characteristics experienced by children from across these groups. We then follow earlier studies to compare the mathematics achievement of children of immigrants to their peers in native families in order to determine whether the differences observed in kindergarten are attenuated or expanded over time. Although there is little agreement on the correct temporal scale, all studies of assimilation or segmented assimilation posit some form of change, whether that change occurs across generations or for individuals and families over time.

We focus on several characteristics of immigrant families and schools that may be associated with children's academic outcomes. Research on school readiness, early school performance and academic achievement all point to the importance of family characteristics and socioeconomic status (Entwisle & Alexander, 1993). Thus, the diverse family backgrounds of children of immigrants likely contribute to the large variations in academic achievement. In addition, parental involvement is an important aspect of children's academic success yet here too there is great diversity as some immigrant parents participate more than others (García Coll et al., 2002; Kao, 2004). Finally, schools are the key setting for academic instruction, yet children of immigrants do not all experience the same academic settings (Portes & Rumbaut, 2001). This chapter examines the relative impact of these characteristics on initial math-test scores of children from diverse origins in their kindergarten year. The analyses then focus on growth in math-test scores through fifth grade. The goal is not only to demonstrate how much of the variation in initial performance can be explained by the variations in backgrounds among children in immigrant families and their peers in native families but to demonstrate which characteristics lead to greater divergence over time.

Diversity of Immigrant Origins

Immigrants in the US today come from many different origins. This diversity is reflected in the top countries of birth for foreign-born residents counted in the last census: Mexico, China, Philippines, India, Vietnam, Cuba, Korea, Canada, El Salvador, and Germany (US Bureau of the Census, 2003). While some countries, such as Mexico, have very long histories of migration to the US, much of the current migration from Latin America and Asia represent newer sources of migrants when compared to decades past. This diversity of national origins also represents very different selection processes for international migration that may have implications for children. For example, selection of adult immigrants with high status relative to those in the sending country may explain high expectations and positive outcomes for children born in the US (Feliciano, 2006). Besides their very different family cultural backgrounds, children of immigrants from historically disadvantaged minority groups in the US face barriers that children from other immigrant groups do not (Zhou, 1997). The resulting cultural and racial diversity that has emerged from recent immigration leads to questions about the relative academic achievement of children who are affected by the experiences of their immigrant parents (Fernandez-Kelly & Schauffler, 1994; Portes & Zhou, 1993).

The diversity of immigrant origins is also reflected in the underlying differences across groups. Asian-origin immigrants in particular vary widely by linguistic background, motivations and selectivity of migrants, as well as cultural practices (Zhou &

Xiong, 2005). So, while some studies point to superior academic performance of children of Asian immigrants (Kao & Tienda, 1995), others caution that the Asian panethnic group is far too diverse to characterize as a monolithic high-performing group (Kim, 2002; Zhou & Xiong, 2005). And, while many Hispanic immigrants are united by linguistic background, their patterns of migration and socioeconomic characteristics also differ. Thus, it is very difficult to simply paint immigrant family patterns or children's outcomes with one brush or even several panethnic brushes (see Bankston, Caldas, & Zhou, 1997; Kim, 2002; Portes & Rumbaut, 2001; Suárez-Orzoco & Suárez-Orzoco, 2001; Zhou & Xiong, 2005).

This chapter examines children from diverse immigrant and non-immigrant origins and pays particular attention to the race and ethnic origins of children in combination with their parents' (primarily mothers') immigrant origins. The term "first generation" is broadly applied to all born outside of the US. However, some researchers have noted that those who arrive as very young children face different adaptation processes from those who arrive as adolescents or young adults (Oropesa & Landale, 1997). So, we compare children with at least one immigrant parent (regardless of the child's birthplace) to children with no immigrant parents in the same racial and ethnic groups where data are sufficient. Guided by the sometimes conflicting perspectives on immigrant adaptation, including a segmented assimilation perspective, our analyses attend to variations in family background, parental school involvement and school characteristics across groups. We briefly review the literature on each of these domains here.

Family Background, Parental Involvement, and School Characteristics

Family Background

Models of academic achievement and status attainment both emphasize the importance of family and parental characteristics for positive achievement outcomes. Family socioeconomic status and parental education, for example, are often cited as key determinants of children's own orientation toward schooling and resources available for assistance in learning. So, variations in family structure, parental education and income may all play a role in differential achievement for children from diverse immigrant and ethnic origins (Battle, 2002; Feliciano, 2006; Teachman, 2008). For some groups, disadvantages in the form of low parental education or income may be offset by advantages such as having two parents present and strong support for academic achievement (Hagen, MacMillan, & Wheaton, 1996; Sanders & Nee, 1996; Valenzuela & Dornbusch, 1994).

Another factor associated with immigrant families that may serve as a disadvantage for children is the lack of familiarity with English. But, not all children in immigrant families have limited English ability or come from non-English backgrounds, while not all children with parents born in the US are fluent English speakers (Van Hook & Fix, 2000). Thus, it is important to distinguish language background from nativity status itself; language skills are so critical to academic success in the US that children may be more differentiated by their English ability than by their nativity. A study of first-through sixth-graders finds Spanish home-language background has a significant effect on children's academic performance net of their socioeconomic status or race/ethnicity

(Rosenthal, Baker, & Ginsburg, 1983). The home language environment is also an important factor in determining maintenance of immigrant parents' mother tongue (Alba, Logan, Lutz, & Stults, 2002). In this case, linguistic background or children's own language status may be more meaningful predictors of school readiness and academic trajectories regardless of parental nativity.

Schools too are perhaps more impacted by the challenges posed by English learners than by the immigrant status of their students (Gershberg, Dannenberg, & Sanchez, 2004). Although there is considerable concern about the burden placed on schools faced with the challenge of teaching children with limited English proficiency, it is not clear if language background per se has a cumulative impact on children's academic achievement over time. If children from non-English backgrounds face initial difficulties in school they may fall further behind over time. Alternatively, non-English background could be associated with initial divergence in academic performance but play a smaller role by the time children have been in school for several years.

Parental Involvement

In addition to family structure and economic status, it may be useful to consider parental resources or investments in children's education that are not necessarily dependent on family income (Hao & Bonstead-Bruns, 1998; Fuligni, 1997). The degree to which immigrant families are able to provide broad support and invest in their children's schooling despite low economic status or limited familiarity with schooling in the US has been viewed as a potential explanation for higher school performance among children from some groups. Many immigrant parents are optimistic about their children's opportunities for education in the US and the chance for academic success (Kao & Tienda, 1995, 1998).

Social relations among parents, teachers, and other key members of a child's social group are fundamental to increasing human capital in the form of skills and achievement (Coleman, 1990). Positive parent interactions with teachers or other school personnel provide support for the student that may encourage school achievement (Lareau, 1989). For example, parental involvement in children's schooling enhances academic achievement and provides some explanation for group disparities in educational outcomes (Lee & Bowen, 2006; Hao & Bonstead-Bruns, 1998). Interactions of family and school may serve as a key resource for young children in schools (Lareau & Horvat, 1999; Parcel & Dufur, 2001; Zellman & Waterman, 1998). Despite their high level of interest in involvement in their children's schooling, language barriers and unfamiliarity with US schools may also limit parental involvement in children's schooling (García Coll et al., 2002; Crosnoe, 2006; Wong & Hughes, 2006).

Of course parental involvement in children's schooling may change over time. Overall, parental involvement in children's schooling tends to decrease from the entrance to school through later grades (Eccles & Harold, 1996). Perhaps immigrant parents will become more involved, relative to their involvement in the beginning, as their comfort with US schools increases and their children move through school. Alternatively, parents may perceive their involvement as not being effective or welcomed and may decrease over time at a sharper rate than their US-born counterparts. Thus, while parental involvement in schooling declines over time in general, it is not clear if this will be the case to the same degree for parents from diverse origins.

School Context

Finally, studies of early education point to the importance of stratification for shaping even the very initial academic trajectories of children in the US (Entwisle & Alexander, 1993; Lee & Burkam, 2002). Children of immigrants are also likely to face very different school characteristics that shape their outcomes over time as well (Portes & MacLeod, 1996). School context could help explain some of the racial/ethnic differences in academic progress if children from some minority groups are more likely to encounter contexts that are less supportive of their academic achievement (Roscigno, 1998; Zhou, 2003). Children in immigrant families are not evenly distributed in schools throughout the US (regional concentration of immigrants is also large), so these measures could help explain differential outcomes by national origin as well (Hernandez et al., 2007). There is, of course, some selectivity into schools as families choose which schools their children attend. We can control for family socioeconomic status (i.e., family income and parents' education) as a way to somewhat reduce the effect of this selectivity.

We have less of an understanding of when in the schooling process the children of immigrants are most likely to be impacted by this disparity in the US educational system. Children of immigrants may face an advantage by being in a school with children from similar linguistic backgrounds and in a school that may be better able to serve students of limited English proficiency. Conversely, the children of immigrants may face a disadvantage if they become segregated in poorer schools with fewer resources over time (Contrearas & Stephens, 1997). Overall, school context seems likely to provide some of the explanation for highly variable trajectories among children of immigrants from different origins.

Data and Methods

Data for the study come from the Early Childhood Longitudinal Study-Kindergarten (ECLS-K) Cohort. The sample here consists of nearly 10,000 children entering kindergarten in the US and follows these same children through fifth grade (US Department of Education, 2002). Children of foreign-born mothers, including children entering the US before age 5 and children born in the US, are compared to children of US-born mothers. We compare children with at least one immigrant parent to their native peers. Our "immigrant children," therefore, include children who are immigrants themselves (i.e. entered the US before kindergarten) as well as those born in the US to immigrant parents.

Children are also identified based on the race/ethnic (or where data are limited, panethnic) background. In this way, we can observe the initial performance of children from diverse origins as they enter kindergarten and trace these same children's growth in achievement over time. We arrived at 12 groups with sufficient data to compare. First, non-Hispanic White children of US-born mothers are the reference group for all analyses. Then, we identify non-Hispanic White children of foreign-born mothers. This combines mothers from diverse origins but primarily combines those from European countries. The third group includes non-Hispanic Black children of US-born mothers. We then identify non-Hispanic Black children of foreign-born mothers (primarily of Afro-Caribbean origins). The next groups include Mexican-origin children with US-born mothers, Mexican-origin children of Mexican-born mothers, other Hispanic-origin children of US-born mothers and other Hispanic children of foreign-born mothers (primarily Central and South American). There are not enough cases of children from Hispanic origins to separately identify their ethnicity so we are confined to this panethnic grouping. Similarly, Asian-origin children of US-born mothers are combined. However, we are able to separately identify Chinese-origin children of foreign-born mothers and Filipino-origin children of foreign-born mothers. This leaves one additional category for "other" Asian-origin children of foreign-born mothers. Our interpretations of the results will be primarily focused on those groups we can identify by specific ethnic or racial origins.

There are many ways to measure academic achievement. The analyses here require a measure that will be consistent across school settings and is measured repeatedly over time to assess growth. Thus, the dependent variable for these models reflects children's scores on standardized test scores in math. These scores are based on Item Response Theory (IRT) which relies on patterns of correct answers to obtain final scores (Tourangeau, Nord, Le, Pollack, & Atkins-Burnett, 2006). The kindergarten math IRT scores form the baseline through the final wave of the data when children are in fifth grade. These scores have been employed in similar investigations of the children of immigrants in the first few waves of the ECLS-K data (Glick & Hohmann-Marriott, 2007; Magnuson, Lahaie, & Waldfogel, 2006). Here, growth-curve models predicting changes in math scores from the spring of kindergarten through the fifth grade round of the data are presented.[1]

Multilevel growth-curve regression models are estimated using SAS 9.1 Proc Mixed in conjunction with Proc MIANALYZE. The growth-curve modeling is advantageous for several reasons. In particular it allows us to model children's growth in math scores as a function of time up to fifth grade (Raudenbush & Bryk, 2002; Raudenbush, 2001). This method also allows us to account for time varying and fixed characteristic of children and the schools they attend (Raudenbush & Bryk, 2002; Raudenbush, 2001). The models here are constrained to one slope for growth which smoothes over the variations that are occurring in the rates of growth throughout the period (see McCoach, O'Connel, Reis, & Levitt, 2006, for example of differential growth in reading scores in ECLS-K). The Proc MIANALYZE procedure accounts for missing data via multiple imputation. All models include measures for child gender and time as well as appropriate weights. Time is centered on the mean age of children in spring of kindergarten. The centering of time is important because it dictates how the intercept and coefficients are interpreted. In this case, since time is centered on age in spring of kindergarten the intercept represents children's math scores at baseline.

Models examine the mediating role of family background, parent–school involvement, and school characteristics on racial/ethnic/nativity differences in test-score growth. Several measures of the family structure and socioeconomic status of children come from the kindergarten wave. One of the most important measures of family background is language-use in the home. According to prior research, children from homes in which a non-English language predominates will have lower initial academic performance. This will likely explain some of the variation across children of immigrants and their peers from non-immigrant families. However, because our sample is based on children who all enter school in the US, it seems likely that non-English home backgrounds will play a minimal role in explaining divergence in scores over time as all children will be exposed to approximately the same duration of schooling in the US.

Other measures of family background may be important at least when explaining initial academic performance. Two-parent families are contrasted to step-parent families and single-parent families. In addition, we control for the mother's education. This is likely to be very important for explaining ethnic and nativity differences because the educational selectivity of immigrants will vary across groups (Feliciano, 2005). Likewise, groups vary according to economic status as well so the models include a continuous measure for household income in kindergarten.

Although not the focus of the current analyses, childcare arrangements in the year prior to kindergarten are included as a measure of prior exposure to educational or formal care settings. Immigrants, particularly Hispanic immigrants, are less likely to rely on formal care arrangements in the years prior to formal schooling (Brandon, 2004). Differential exposure to these environments does appear to be associated with the initial performance in kindergarten (Magnuson et al., 2006).

Involved parents may be able to translate their socioeconomic status and social capital into children's academic success. There are, of course, many ways for parents to be involved in their children's education. Here we select those measures that are available across waves in the ECLS-K and reflect parental contact with the schools themselves. The measures include parent attendance at parent–teacher conferences, school open-houses or Parent–Teacher Association (PTA) meetings at each wave of the data. Thus, we will be able to show the extent to which this involvement increases or decreases over time and whether these changes alter the test-score trajectories of different groups.

Finally, scholarship concerned with the possibility of downward trajectories among some groups suggests that school context may be an important predictor of changes in student achievement once schooling is well under way. Here measures are included to reflect school type (private, non-religious; private, religious; and public) and school composition. To capture the extent to which the school serves low-income or other high-risk populations, we include a measure of whether the school receives Title 1 funding. Title 1 funding is federal funding provided to districts and schools based on a formula that takes into account the concentration of low-income students served. Finally, we include a variable that identifies the proportion of the student body in the school designated as having limited English proficiency (LEP). We adjust for changes in school characteristics that may occur as students change schools across waves. There is some racial/ethnic variation in the likelihood of changing schools throughout the observation period.

Results

There is considerable diversity in the family backgrounds, parental school involvement and school context of children from the racial/ethnic groups included in the analyses. Table 6.1 presents some of the descriptive characteristics of the sample and demonstrates clearly that some children of immigrants are more advantaged than others. Mexican-origin children of immigrants, for example, are more likely to have mothers with very low levels of education, to come from a home in which a non-English language is dominant, and to attend schools with very high proportions of children designated as having limited English proficiency than most other groups of children. Chinese-origin children of immigrants, on the other hand, appear particularly

Table 6.1 Children's Backgrounds by Ethnic and Immigrant Origins, Kindergarten Year

	Child of immigrants							*Child of US born parents*				
	Chinese origin	*Filipino origin*	*Other Asian origin*	*Mexican origin*	*Other Hispanic*	*Non-Hisp. Black*	*Non-Hisp. White*	*Asian origin*	*Mexican origin*	*Other Hispanic*	*Non-Hisp. Black*	*Non-Hisp. White*
Mother's education												
Less than high school	7.6%	8.4%	22.4%	56.8%	34.3%	9.6%	6.5%	6.5%	16.4%	14.0%	15.6%	7.4%
High school grad.	27.4%	18.7%	29.4%	34.3%	31.0%	35.4%	19.7%	37.4%	36.5%	41.2%	43.4%	33.7%
Some college	9.3%	16.8%	15.6%	6.0%	24.1%	26.9%	36.3%	29.4%	33.7%	28.3%	33.2%	27.9%
4 year degree	27.0%	46.0%	18.7%	1.9%	8.3%	16.6%	22.3%	17.8%	6.3%	11.6%	4.9%	19.2%
More than 4 years	28.0%	8.1%	12.8%	0.6%	2.1%	3.7%	14.0%	7.5%	4.7%	3.7%	1.4%	9.7%
Non-English home	90.8%	43.6%	55.6%	87.9%	73.7%	11.2%	22.7%	10.0%	16.7%	12.4%	0.1%	0.5%
Parent–school involvement												
Attends PTA	28.1%	34.7%	36.7%	37.0%	35.0%	38.3%	34.2%	35.9%	28.4%	28.4%	32.8%	34.3%
Attend Open House	59.8%	62.6%	57.7%	55.9%	56.8%	71.4%	69.9%	76.6%	71.4%	74.1%	68.2%	80.3%
Parent/teacher conf.	89.4%	75.5%	83.8%	79.1%	80.7%	75.7%	79.4%	89.5%	86.7%	86.7%	71.0%	88.3%
School context												
Private religious school	4.1%	14.8%	8.2%	2.3%	6.5%	6.6%	13.6%	10.0%	8.3%	10.5%	7.4%	13.4%
Other private school	10.8%	17.5%	7.4%	0.1%	3.5%	3.9%	7.2%	8.4%	1.9%	3.9%	2.5%	4.5%
Public school	85.1%	67.7%	84.3%	97.5%	90.0%	89.5%	79.2%	81.7%	89.8%	85.6%	90.0%	82.1%
Title 1 school	29.7%	41.4%	50.0%	83.7%	67.8%	63.5%	48.9%	44.6%	65.8%	60.0%	76.5%	0.57%
Percent LEP	8.2	15.0	11.9	38.4	22.1	8.2	6.0	6.5	17.6	9.0	2.0	2.23

Source: Early Childhood Longitudinal Study – Kindergarten Cohort (n = 8,895).

advantaged by mother's education. Yet, many of these children also come from non-English-language homes. Ethnic group differences are also evident among children of US-born parents. Black, Mexican, and Hispanic-origin children have mothers with comparatively low levels of education. We also note that Asian-origin, Mexican and other Hispanic children of US-born parents are more likely to come from a non-English-speaking home than their non-Hispanic White or Black counterparts. This likely reflects that some of these children come from homes in which the grandparent generation is the immigrant generation while among White and Black children, the first-generation is further removed.

Overall, parental involvement in schooling is similar across many of the groups we compare here but there does appear to be some difference by parental nativity in the likelihood of participating in their child's schooling. This is depicted even more clearly in the first panel of Figure 6.1 which separates children according to parental nativity alone and demonstrates how parental involvement changes over time. Parental involvement tends to increase in the first few years of children's schooling among immigrant and US-born parents with considerable leveling off by fifth grade. What is more, immigrant parent involvement increases more steeply from the time children are in kindergarten to third grade when compared to children with US-born parents.

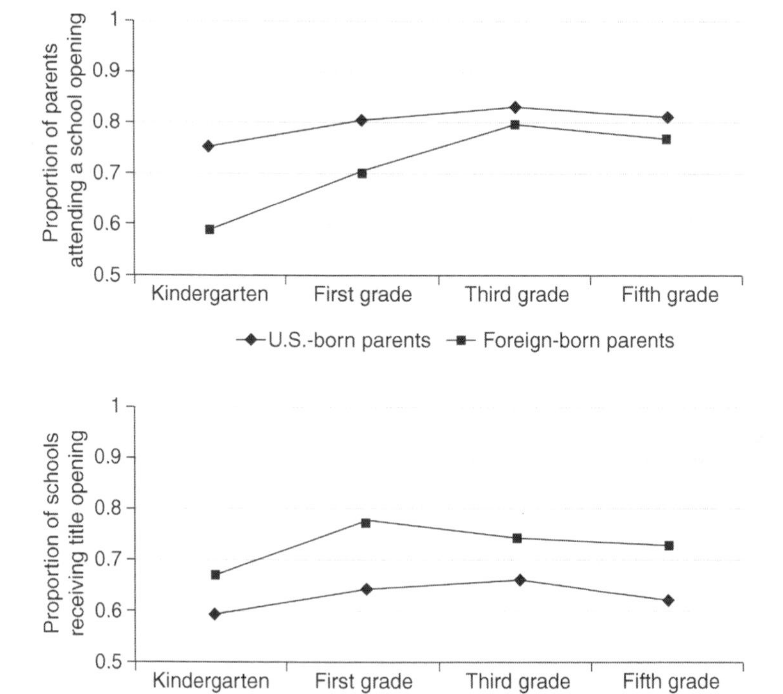

Figure 6.1 Changes in Parental Involvement and School Type Over Time by Parent's Nativity (source: ECLS-K (n = 8,895)).

Table 6.1 also demonstrates the considerable diversity in children's school environments in kindergarten. Clearly non-Hispanic White children are the least likely to attend Title 1 schools and attend schools with a comparatively low percentage of children designated as Limited English Proficient (LEP). And, these patterns of school characteristics by race/ethnicity and nativity are maintained throughout fifth grade. Children who attend disadvantaged schools in kindergarten are also likely to be attending similarly disadvantaged schools by fifth grade even if they change schools during this period of observation. An examination of children's school environments over time reveals that children of immigrant parents are still more likely to be in disadvantaged schools by fifth grade. The second panel of Figure 6.1 demonstrates this gap for attendance at schools receiving Title 1 funds from kindergarten through fifth grade.

Children of immigrants also display diversity in initial academic performance. Figure 6.2 shows the test scores among all children in the kindergarten year. Math scores are already highly divergent across race/ethnic groups at the outset. The scores also diverge according to mother's place of birth. Thus, we find non-Hispanic White children of US-born parents score above many of their peers with the exception of Chinese-origin children of immigrants. Children of Mexican and other foreign-born Hispanic parents do not score as favorably at the outset. There are also interesting contrasts within racial groups by parental nativity. Non-Hispanic Black children of immigrant parents score approximately 3 points higher on the math test than non-Hispanic Black children of US-born parents. But the opposite is the case among Mexican-origin children where those with US-born parents outscore their peers with immigrant parents. This suggests there is not one simple conclusion about the performance of children of immigrants and their peers overall. However, these scores presented in Figure 6.2 do not adjust for the wide variation in family background, home language, parental involvement, or school characteristics.

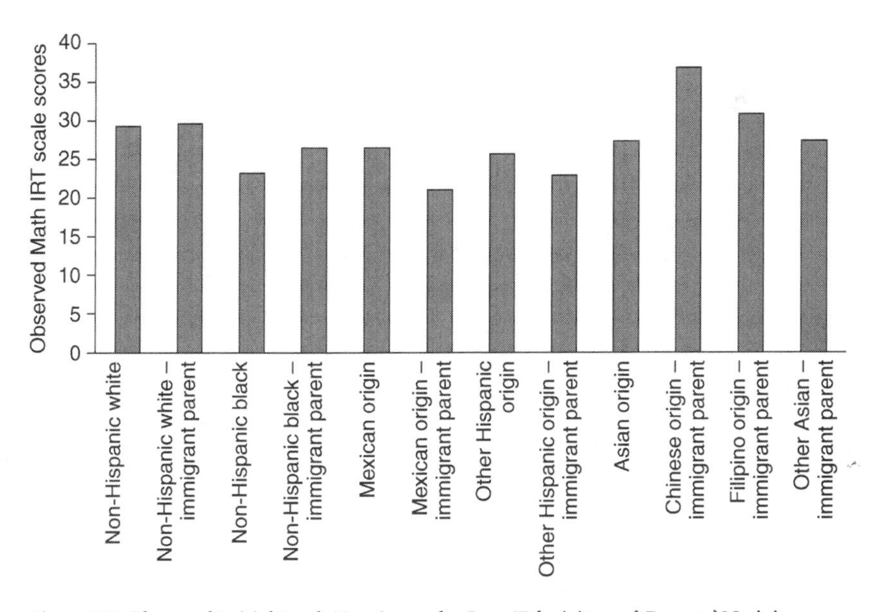

Figure 6.2 Observed Initial Math Test Scores by Race/Ethnicity and Parents' Nativity.

The multilevel growth-curve models predict the changes in math scores from the initial kindergarten scores described above through the final wave of data when children are in fifth grade. These models are presented in Table 6.2. The first model simply depicts the relative growth in scores by the child's race/ethnicity and parental nativity. It is clear from this model that the observed differences in scores found in the kindergarten year (and shown in Figure 6.2) are carried forward through fifth grade. The interactions with time demonstrate significant differences in "slopes" in addition to the main terms that depict significant differences in the "intercept." Thus, it appears that those children scoring below non-Hispanic White children of US-born parents in the first year also fall further behind over time; non-Hispanic Black, Mexican and other Hispanic children lag even further behind. Conversely, the scores of Chinese children of immigrant parents increase even more over time. In other words, over time scores grow even more disparate among children differentiated by race/ethnicity and parental nativity. The question to be answered is whether family background, parental involvement, school context, or a combination of factors can provide further explanation for this growing divergence in scores.

Model 2 adds the family background measures to the models. Family structure, mother's education, and family income all play a role in explaining differences in children's scores at the outset (main effects) and over time (interaction terms predicting slopes). Note that half of the deficit in initial scores for Black children of US-born parents relative to non-Hispanic White children of US-born parents is accounted for by the inclusion of these measures. Similar reductions are observed among other groups including Mexican and other Hispanic-origin children, Asian-origin children of US-born parents, and Filipino-origin children of immigrants. The model also demonstrates the long-term impact of low family socioeconomic status on children's trajectories. Mother's education and family income, for example, continue to have an impact on children's scores over time.

Model 2 also adds the measure for non-English home backgrounds to the models. The main effect and interaction terms have opposite signs indicating that, while children from non-English-speaking homes have lower initial scores, these children begin to catch up from their starting point. This is an important finding as states grapple with providing sufficient resources for children with limited English proficiency. These results suggest that children from non-English-speaking homes are able to acquire appropriate skills and move toward their peers from English-only backgrounds as they move through school. It is also important to note that the differences between non-Hispanic White children of US-born parents and Mexican-origin children of immigrant parents are greatly attenuated by the inclusion of the home language and parental education variables (separate models with only these variables are not presented here). Although Mexican-origin children of immigrant parents still have slightly negative trajectories, family background including home-language background appears to be a particularly important mediator here.

The next model (Model 3) addresses the importance of parental involvement on children's math-score growth. Children whose parents attend events at their schools have higher scores at the outset as well as positive growth in scores over time. However, very little of the racial/ethnic or nativity variation in scores is altered by the inclusion of these measures in the model. Model 4 then adds the school variables to the models.

Children in schools receiving Title 1 funds, schools with larger proportions of students receiving free lunch, and schools with a greater proportion of the student body with limited English proficiency all show less growth in scores than their peers. School context is an important determinant of differential academic outcomes in the long run and children of immigrants are impacted not only by their own home-language background but by the schools they attend in the US.

It is clear that achievement trajectories over time are more divergent as children move through their elementary school years. Figure 6.3 depicts the predicted growth in math scores across the groups for whom significant differences remain after Model 4 in Table 6.2. By fifth grade, the growth in math test scores has been lower for Black children of US-born parents, Mexican and Hispanic children of immigrants relative to the large non-Hispanic White native reference group. What is more, Chinese-origin children of immigrant parents see greater growth in their scores over time. These distinctive trajectories exist despite our extensive set of controls for family background, parental school involvement, and school context. In fact, very little change in coefficients for the Chinese-origin group is observed across our models. Although considerable variation has been explained by family background, parental involvement, and school context, it is clear that additional work is needed to elucidate the remaining divergence in academic achievement across these groups.

Conclusions

Children of immigrants in the US are a diverse group with considerable variation in academic performance and subsequent educational attainment. Academic achievement, here measured with growth in math test scores over time, is strongly predicted by a combination of family background characteristics, variation in parental school involvement, and the diverse school contexts children encounter. The results also indicate that substantial variation remains even net of these characteristics. But, the analyses show that immigrant status alone does not predict a single trajectory for children's achievement. There is great diversity within the population of children of immigrants in the US today and they trace different achievement patterns over time.

Some characteristics are associated with negative academic trajectories but other traits are not as predictive of academic progress over time. For example, children from families with lower socioeconomic status, and non-English backgrounds have lower initial school performance than their peers from English-only homes or higher socioeconomic status. Thus, a focus on improving school readiness among socioeconomically disadvantaged and non-English-speaking populations may be effective in reducing initial performance gaps (Garcia, Jensen, & Cuellar, 2006; Gershberg et al., 2004). But, these characteristics do not forecast the same growth in academic performance over time. While low socioeconomic status is predictive of lower gains in math scores, for example, coming from a non-English-speaking home has a diminished impact on growth in scores over time. In other words, children from non-English-speaking homes do not fall further behind their peers but low economic status seems to have a cumulative effect for children's progress through school. Policy directed at children from non-English-speaking backgrounds may be best targeted to initial school experiences but more long-term programs may be needed to reduce the socioeconomic gaps in achievement.

Table 6.2 Growth Models Predicting Math Test Scores, Kindergarten through Fifth Grade

	Model 1	*Model 2*	*Model 3*	*Model 4*
Race and nativity (vs. Non-Hispanic White-US parents)				
Non-Hispanic White-Immigrant parent	–0.56***	–1.02+	–0.95+	–1.03+
× Time	0.97***	0.62***	0.59**	0.65**
Non-Hispanic Black	–4.90***	–2.12***	–2.07***	–2.05***
× Time	–3.04***	–2.03***	–2.03***	–2.06***
Non-Hispanic Black-Immigrant parent	–3.14***	–1.50+	–1.43	–1.34
× Time	–0.42***	0.07	0.04	0.02
Mexican origin	–2.08***	–0.11	–0.10	–0.08
× Time	–0.62***	–0.04	–0.07	–0.03
Mexican origin-immigrant parent	–5.79***	–0.32	–0.38	–0.34
× Time	–1.65***	–0.34+	–0.37+	–0.32+
Other Hispanic origin	–3.13***	–1.67***	–1.66***	1.68***
× Time	–0.91***	–0.52***	–0.53**	–0.49**
Other Hispanic origin-immigrant parent	–4.71***	–1.15*	–1.18*	–1.19*
× Time	–0.48***	0.19	0.20	0.26
Asian origin	–0.49***	0.06	0.06	–0.01
× Time	–0.41***	–0.34	–0.36	–0.32
Chinese origin-immigrant parent	5.04***	5.65***	5.74***	5.81***
× Time	1.82***	1.39***	1.38***	1.38***
Filipino origin-immigrant parent	0.09***	0.55	0.67	0.54
× Time	0.37***	0.01	0.02	0.15
Other Asian-immigrant parent	–0.05***	1.51**	1.62**	1.58**
× Time	0.66***	0.77***	0.76***	0.80***
Male	–0.87***	–0.83***	–0.84***	–0.83***
× Time	0.76***	0.77***	0.78***	0.78***
Family structure (vs. two married parents)				
Step-parent family		–0.62***	–0.55	–0.51
× Time		–0.33*	–0.32*	–0.35*
Single-parent family		–1.04+	–0.88***	–0.96***
× Time		–0.21+	–0.18+	–0.19+
Non-parental family		–2.23***	–2.18**	–2.11***
× Time		–0.71**	–0.67**	–0.69**
Mother's education (vs. less than high school)				
High School grad.		1.83***	1.81***	1.81***
× Time		0.49***	0.45**	0.45**
Some college		2.11***	2.10***	2.09***
× Time		0.80***	0.76***	0.76***
4-year degree	2.74***	2.72***	2.70***	
× Time		1.26***	1.21***	1.23***
More than 4 year		3.39***	3.37***	3.29***
× Time		1.35***	1.32***	1.35***
Family income quintiles (vs. the 5th quintile)				
1st quintile		–5.30***	–5.11***	–4.81***
× Time		–1.93***	–1.86***	–2.03***
2nd quintile		–3.67***	–3.59***	–3.34***
× Time		–1.30***	–1.25***	–1.39***
3rd quintile		–3.03***	–2.98***	–2.77***
× Time		–0.76***	–0.72***	–0.83***
4th quintile		–1.70***	–1.68***	–1.54***
× Time		–0.67***	–0.65***	–0.72***

Table 6.2 continued

	Model 1	*Model 2*	*Model 3*	*Model 4*
Non-English Home		−1.27**	−1.23**	−1.18**
× Time		0.32*	0.32*	0.32*
Child care arrangements Pre-K (vs. parent only care)				
Multiple Care Arrangements		0.64*	0.61*	0.58*
× Time		−0.18+	−0.20+	−0.17+
Head Start only		−0.99*	−1.05*	−100*
× Time		−0.47***	−0.44**	−0.48**
Centre Based Care only		1.16***	1.13***	1.07***
× Time		0.13	0.11	0.14
Relative Care only		0.05	0.06	0.08
× Time		−0.07	−0.08	−0.10
Parent-School Involvement				
Attends PTA			0.21+	0.21+
× Time			0.04	0.05
Attends Open House			0.49**	0.52***
× Time			0.35***	0.34***
Parent/teacher conf.			0.13	0.19
× Time			0.22**	0.20**
School Context (vs. Public School)				
Private Religious school				0.75***
× Time				−0.65***
Other private school				2,11***
× Time				−1.21***
Title 1 school				−0.19
× Time				0.05
Percent LEP				−0.04
× Time				−0.22**
Time	17.86***	17.72***	17.22***	17.51***
Intercept	30.53***	29.84***	29.20***	28.96***

Source: Early Childhood Longitudinal Study – Kindergarten Cohort (n = 8,895).

Notes
***$p < 0.001$, **$p < 0.01$, *$p < 0.05$, and +$p < 0.10$.

There is also evidence that immigrant families take advantage of opportunities to participate in their children's schooling rather than becoming discouraged over time. It is instructive that immigrant parents increase their involvement in children's schooling more steeply from kindergarten through the first few years of children's schooling when compared to their US-born counterparts. The data employed here do not elucidate the possible reasons for this increase in involvement; perhaps immigrant parents are increasingly aware of the opportunities to participate or gain sufficient comfort communicating with school personnel. Regardless of the reasons, it seems children of immigrant parents are benefiting from their parents' involvement. Parental attendance at open-house events is associated with initial math scores. Attendance at school open-house events and parent–teacher conferences is also associated with positive growth in math scores. This suggests that those programs encouraging parental participation,

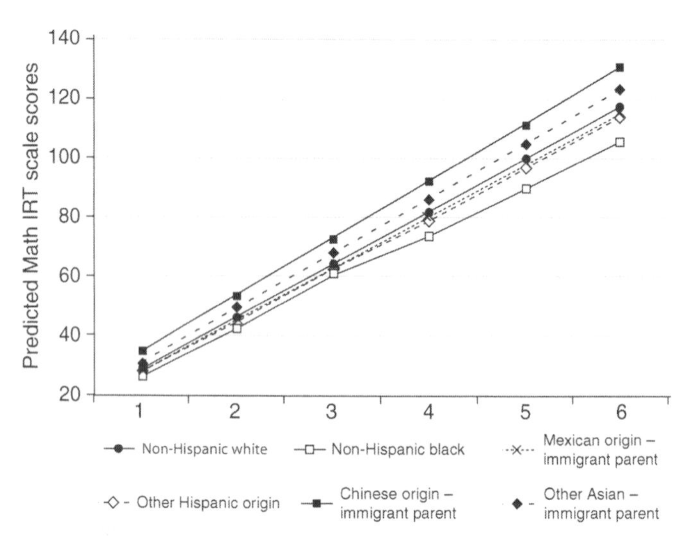

Figure 6.3 Predicted Math Achievement Trajectories by Race/Ethnicity and Parents' Nativity (source: ECLS-K (n = 8,895)).

Note
Predicted Scores based on full model. Groups with growth significantly different from non-Hispanic Whites are presented.

particularly those available in the home language of immigrant children, may also help reduce gaps in achievement (García Coll et al., 2002).

The analyses presented here suggest that school characteristics are associated with differential growth in scores over time. Some characteristics are associated with differential scores at the outset, perhaps reflecting differential selection of students into some environments. For example, children in private schools outperform their peers in public school initially but the interactions suggest this advantage is not carried forward to differential growth over time. Other characteristics are associated with outcomes over time. In particular, children in schools with a greater proportion of students designated as LEP have less growth in math scores over time than children in schools with fewer students so designated. Further, concentration in schools with higher proportion of LEP students appears to explain some of the remaining divergence in scores for Mexican-origin children of immigrant parents from their non-Hispanic White peers of US-born parents. Differences in school context also explain some of the divergence in trajectories across groups of children. Children of Mexican immigrants and Black children appear to be particularly disadvantaged in this respect.

The results here suggest that reducing educational disparities among children of immigrants could be enhanced by a focus on their initial school readiness and ability to participate in English instruction. Coming from a home in which a non-English language predominates is associated with lower initial academic performance in kindergarten. But by fifth grade, there is relatively little long-term effect and, if anything, these children show a positive trajectory. In other words, the long-term achievement trajectories of these children are determined less by their immigrant status than by other characteristics. Although some of the racial/ethnic and nativity differences in initial math scores and growth in scores over time are explained by differences in family background, parental involvement, and school characteristics, the results presented here point to persistent racial gaps. Even when adjusting for family and school characteristics, non-Hispanic Black children of US-born parents continue to fall behind their peers by fifth grade. If anything, the results reaffirm concerns about the racial gaps in education while ameliorating some concern about children of immigrants overall.

Acknowledgment

This research is supported by a grant from the National Institute of Child Health and Human Development, number RO3 HD044006.

Note

1. We rely on the mathematics standardized test scores because this assessment was given to the majority of students in the ECLS-K. Spanish speaking children who were not deemed to be English proficient were given a Spanish version of the math test. Children from other language backgrounds who failed the English-language screener (OLDS) were not given the math test. The majority of children are assessed in math by first grade (US Department of Education, 2002).

References

Alba, R., Logan, R., Lutz, A., & Stults, B. (2002). Only English by the third generation? Loss and preservation of the mother tongue among the grandchildren of contemporary immigrants. *Demography, 39*(3), 467–484.

Bankston, C.L., III, Caldas, S.J., & Zhou, M. (1997). The academic achievement of Vietnamese American students: Ethnicity as social capital. *Sociological Focus, 30,* 1–16.

Battle, J. (2002). Longitudinal analysis of academic achievement among a nationwide sample of Hispanic students in one-versus dual-parent households. *Hispanic Journal of Behavioral Science, 24*(4), 430–447.

Brandon, P.D. (2004). The childcare arrangements of preschool age children in immigrant families. *International Migration, 42*(1), 65–87.

Capps, R., Fix, M.E., & Reardon-Anderson, J. (2003). Children of immigrants show slight reductions in poverty, hardship. *Snapshots, 13.* Washington, DC: Urban Institute.

Coleman, J. (1990). *Foundations of social theory.* Cambridge, MA: The Belknap Harvard University Press.

Contrearas, R., & Stephens, J. (1997). Forty years after Brown: The impact of immigration policy on desegregation. *Education and Urban Society, 29*(2), 182–191.

Crosnoe, R. (2006). *Mexican roots, American schools: Helping Mexican immigrant children succeed.* Stanford, CA: Stanford University Press.

Eccles, J.S., & Harold, R. (1996). Family involvement in children's and adolescents' schooling. In A. Booth & J. Dunn (Eds.), *Family–school links: How do they affect educational outcomes?* (pp. 3–34). Mahwah, NJ: Lawrence Erlbaum Associates.

Entwisle, D.R., & Alexander, K.L. (1993). Entry into school: The beginning school transition and educational stratification in the United States. *Annual Review of Sociology, 19,* 401–423.

Feliciano, C. (2005). Does selective migration matter? Explaining ethnic disparities in educational attainment among immigrants' children. *International Migration Review, 39,* 841–871.

Feliciano, C. (2006). Beyond the family: The influence of premigration group status on the educational expectations of immigrants' children. *Sociology of Education, 79*(4), 281–303.

Fernandez-Kelly, M.P., & Schauffler, R. (1994). Divided fates: Immigrant children in a restructured U.S. economy. *International Migration Review, 28*, 662–689.

Fuligni, A. (1997). The academic achievement of adolescents from immigrant families: The roles of family background, attitudes and behavior. *Child Development, 68*, 351–363.

García Coll, C., Akila, D., Palacios, N., Bailey, B., Silver, R., DiMartino, L., & Chin, C. (2002). Parental involvement in children's education: Lessons from three immigrant groups. *Parenting, 2*(3), 303–324.

García, E.E. (2002). Bilingualism and schooling in the United States. *International Journal of the Sociology of Language, 2002*(155–156), 1–92.

García, E.E., Jensen, B., & Cuellar, D. (2006). Early academic achievement of Hispanics in the United States: Implications for teacher preparation. *The New Educator, 2*, 123–147.

Gershberg, A.I., Dannenberg, A., & Sanchez, P. (2004). *Beyond "bilingual" education: New immigrants and public school policies in California.* Washington, DC: The Urban Institute.

Glick, J., & Hohmann-Marriott, B. (2007). Academic performance of young children in immigrant families: The significance of race, ethnicity and national origins. *International Migration Review, 41*, 371–402.

Glick, J., & White, M. (2003). The academic trajectories of immigrant youth: Analysis within and across cohorts. *Demography, 40*, 759–784.

Hagen, J., MacMillan, R., & Wheaton, B. (1996). New kid in town: Social capital and the life course effects of family migration on children. *American Sociological Review, 61*, 368–385.

Hao, L., & Bonstead-Bruns, M. (1998). Parent–child differences in educational expectations and the academic achievement of immigrant and native students. *Sociology of Education, 71*, 175–198.

Hernandez, D.J., Denton, N.A., & Macartney, S. (2007). Children in immigrant families: The U.S. and 50 states: national origins, language, and early education. *Child Trends & the Center for Social and Demographic Analysis.* Albany, NY: State University of New York, 2007 Research Brief Series. Publication #2007-11.

Kao, G. (2004). Social capital and its relevance to minority and immigrant populations. *Sociology of Education, 77*, 172–175.

Kao, G., & Tienda, M. (1995). Optimism and achievement: The educational performance of immigrant youth. *Social Science Quarterly, 76*(1), 1–19.

Kao, G., & Tienda, M. (1998). Educational aspirations of minority youth. *American Journal of Education, 106*, 349–384.

Kim, R.Y. (2002). Ethnic differences in academic achievement between Vietnamese and Cambodian children: Cultural and structural explanations. *The Sociological Quarterly, 43*(2), 213–235.

Lareau, A. (1989). *Home advantage: Social class and parental intervention in elementary education.* New York: Falmer Press.

Lareau, A., & Horvat, E.M. (1999). Moments of social inclusion and exclusion: Race, class and cultural capital in family–school relationships. *Sociology of Education, 72*, 37–53.

Lee, J., & Bowen, N.K. (2006). Parent involvement, cultural capital and the achievement gap among elementary school children. *American Educational Research Journal, 43*, 193–218.

Lee, V.E., & Burkam, D.T. (2002). *Inequality at the starting gate: Social background differences in achievement as children begin school.* Washington, DC: Economic Policy Institute.

Magnuson, K., Lahaie, C., & Waldfogel, J. (2006). Preschool and school readiness of children of immigrants. *Social Science Quarterly, 87*(5), 1241–1262.

McCoach, D.B., O'Connel, A.A., Reis, S.M., & Levitt, H.A. (2006). Growing readers: A hierarchical linear model of children's reading growth during the first 2 years of school. *Journal of Educational Psychology, 98*(1), 14–28.

Oropesa, R.S., & Landale, N.S. (1997). In search of the new second generation: Alternative strate-

gies for identifying second generation children and understanding their acquisition of English. *Sociological Perspectives, 40*(3), 429–455.
Parcel, Toby L., & Dufur, Mikaela J. (2001). Capital at home and at school: Effects on student achievement. *Social Forces, 79*(3), 881–912.
Portes, A., & MacLeod, D. (1996). Educational progress of children of immigrants: The roles of class, ethnicity and school context. *Sociology of Education, 69*, 255–275.
Portes, A., & Rumbaut, R. (2001). *Legacies. The story of the immigrant second generation.* Berkeley, CA: University of California Press.
Portes, A., & Zhou, M. (1993). The new second generation: Segmented assimilation and its variants. *The Annals of the American Academy of Political and Social Science, 530*, 74–96.
Raudenbush, S.W. (2001). Comparing personal trajectories and drawing causal inferences from longitudinal data. *Annual Review of Psychology, 52*, 501–525.
Raudenbush, S.W., & Bryk, A.S. (2002). *Hierarchical linear models* (2nd ed.). Thousand Oaks, CA: Sage.
Rosenthal, A.S., Baker, K., & Ginsburg, A. (1983). The effect of language background on achievement level and learning among elementary school students. *Sociology of Education, 56*, 157–169.
Roscigno, V.J. (1998). The reproduction of educational disadvantage. *Social Forces, 76*, 1033–1060.
Sanders, J.M., & Nee, V. (1996). Immigrant self-employment: The family as social capital and the value of human capital. *American Sociological Review, 61*(23), 1–49.
Suárez-Orozco, C., & Suárez-Orozco, M.M. (2001). *Children of immigration.* Cambridge, MA: Harvard University Press.
Teachman, J.D. (2008). The living arrangements of children and their educational well-being. *Journal of Family Issues, 29*, 734–761.
Tourangeau, K., Nord, C., Le, T., Pollack, J.M., & Atkins-Burnett, S. (2006). *Early childhood longitudinal study, kindergarten class of 1998–99 (ECLS-K), combined user's manual for the ECLS-K fifth-grade data files and electronic codebooks* (NCES 2006-032). US Department of Education, Washington, DC: National Center for Education Statistics.
US Bureau of the Census. (2003). *The foreign-born population: 2000.* Census 2000 Brief, C2KBR-34.
US Department of Education, National Center for Education Statistics. (2002). *Early childhood longitudinal study-kindergarten class of 1998–99 (ECLS-K), psychometric report for kindergarten through first grade,* NCES 2002-05. Donald A. Rock and Judith M. Pollack, Educational Testing Service, Elvira Germino Hausken, project officer. Washington, DC.
Valenzuela, A., & Dornbusch, S.M. (1994). Familism and social capital in the academic achievement of Mexican origin and Anglo adolescents. *Social Science Quarterly, 75*, 18–36.
Van Hook, J., & Fix, M. (2000). A profile of the immigrant student population. In J. Ruiz de Velasco, M. Fix, & B. Chu Clewell (Eds.), *Overlooked and underserved: Immigrant students in U.S. secondary schools* (pp. 9–33). Washington, DC: Urban Institute.
Wong, S., & Hughes, J.N. (2006). Ethnicity and language contributions to dimensions of parental involvement. *School Psychology Review, 35*(4), 645–662.
Zellman, G.L., & Waterman, J.M. (1998). Understanding the impact of parent school involvement on children's educational outcomes. *Journal of Educational Research, 91*, 370–380.
Zhou, M. (1997). Segmented assimilation: Issues, controversies and recent research on the new second generation. *International Migration Review, 31*(4), 975–1008.
Zhou, M. (2003). Urban education: Challenges in educating culturally diverse children. *Teachers College Record, 105*, 208–225.
Zhou, M., & Xiong, Y.S. (2005). The multifaceted American experiences of the children of Asian immigrants: Lessons for segmented assimilation. *Ethnic and Racial Studies, 28*(6), 1119–1152.

7 Latino/a Immigrant Parents' Voices in Mathematics Education

Marta Civil and Núria Planas

In this chapter we draw on a decade of research with working-class, Latino/a families and their engagement in their children's mathematics education. Most of the families in our work are of Mexican origin; some are recent immigrants, while others have been in this part of the country for generations since this area was at one time part of Mexico. Throughout our years of working in these communities, we have noticed that, often, immigrant students who were recent arrivals and had been schooled in Mexico came in with a strong command of mathematics, particularly in terms of arithmetic procedures and knowledge of formulas (e.g., knowing the formula for finding the area of a triangle) and tended to outperform (at least in the more skill-type activities) their classmates who had been mostly (if not completely) schooled in the US. Valenzuela (1999) also documents this difference in performance in more general terms, not specific to mathematics.

As a group, Latinos (Hispanic is the term used in the reports) continue to underperform in mathematics compared to White students on the National Assessment of Educational Progress (NAEP). In the 2007 NAEP the mathematics average scores for fourth graders were 248 for White students and 227 for Hispanic students; the mathematics average score for ELL (English Language Learner) fourth graders was 217 and the average score for non-ELL fourth graders was 242. (The scale is from 0 to 500.) Although the performance has shown improvement for all groups in the recent years, the gaps between groups persist. Our work takes place in schools that overall do not perform well in state assessments. These schools are in low-income communities, with a majority of Latino students, some of whom are ELLs.

Immigration is often strongly related to both economic and social disadvantage. Rainwater and Smeeding (2003) show that poverty rates for Latinos/as are about three times that for the so-called group of Anglo-Americans. They point to the necessity of new pedagogies and relationships so that such social differences do not persist over the next decades. In their portrayal of the circumstances surrounding different groups of immigrants, Hernandez, Denton, and Macartney (this volume) provide ample evidence for the rather challenging conditions that affect Mexican immigrant families (in particular in terms of educational background and economic situation). These authors state that children of Mexican origin are among the most likely (from several groups of different origins) to have a parent who is limited-English-proficient. They are also most likely to have parents with low levels of formal education (67% of the Mexican-origin children in their data had a father who had not completed high school).

The parents in our work cover the whole spectrum of educational attainment but overall the median is a sixth-grade level of schooling. Our findings confirm what Hernandez et al. (this volume) write in terms of immigrant parents having high hopes for the education of their children yet often are not familiar with the school system in the US. These authors point out the importance "for educators to focus attention on the needs of children in immigrant and native-born families who are most likely to have parents who have completed no more than elementary school or who have not graduated from high school" (p. 13). This chapter presents an effort in this direction.

Building on our prior work and in particular the involvement of the first author in projects grounded on the Funds of Knowledge concept (González, Moll, & Amanti, 2005), we have developed an approach to working with immigrant and minoritized students that relies on understanding and involving these students' community (i.e., primarily their family members) in the in-school learning. We assume that a community approach (Civil, 2007) can help overcome the social use of school mathematics as a gatekeeper. We have documented students' engagement in the learning of mathematics when this learning is grounded on their experiences (Civil, 2002a, 2002b, 2007; Kahn & Civil, 2001). Throughout some of this work it became evident to us that parents, and in particular immigrant parents, needed to be brought to the foreground of our efforts to improve the teaching and learning of mathematics for the students with whom we work. In Civil and Andrade (2003), we highlight the concept of parents as intellectual resources. We argue that by establishing relationships of trust and a two-way dialogue between home and school, we may be able to address issues of social valorization of knowledge (Abreu & Cline, 2005) that could lead to conflict between parents and school personnel with children being caught in the middle (Suárez-Orozco & Suárez-Orozco, 2001). In this chapter we focus on the voices of immigrant parents because they are an important (yet often invisible) part of the school community and a significant influence on their children's learning. Latino/a parents and their children can inform us about their norms of schooling, which may differ from those found in other cultures (Okagaki & Frensch, 1998; Okagaki & Sternberg, 1993), in particular the local school culture. We begin with a brief overview of why a focus on mathematics education is important when talking about immigration, diversity, and education.

Immigration, Diversity, and Mathematics Education

At the end of the 1980s, Bishop (1988) argued that different cultures have in common the same mathematical patterns: counting, measuring, locating, designing, playing, and explaining. He based his ideas on results from cross-cultural studies developed by anthropologists. One of the most relevant findings was that different groups develop universal mathematical patterns through situated mathematical practices. A distinction between *universal* patterns and *situated* practices was stated and the extended idea of mathematics as being culturally neutral was strongly contested. Researchers have carried out studies centered on the idea that mathematical practices are socially mediated by the contexts where they are developed (Chronaki, 2005; H.P. Ginsburg, 1999). Different studies document how people tend to perform virtually error-free mathematics in contexts that relate to their everyday activities (Lave, 1988; Nunes, Schliemann, &

Carraher, 1993), while they may be unsuccessful in the "traditional" pencil-and-paper school mathematics.

D'Ambrosio (1985) used the term "ethnomathematics" to refer to the mathematics which is practiced among identifiable cultural groups, such as national-tribal societies, labor groups, children of a certain age bracket, professional classes, and so on. In our work, we have used principles of ethnomathematics to develop mathematical teaching innovations that build on the backgrounds and experiences of the culturally diverse students with whom we work (Civil, 2002a, 2007; Civil & Kahn, 2001). In Civil (2002b, 2007) we discuss dilemmas related to the connection between in-school and out-of-school mathematics. Some of these dilemmas, we argue, are related to our beliefs as to what we are willing to count as being mathematics. We are aware of issues of transfer across contexts (Lave, 1988) and of the fact that there are many differences between in-school and out-of-school mathematics. Civil (2002a, 2002b, 2007) has written on these differences and on how one of the premises behind this community approach to the teaching and learning of mathematics is not to attempt to reproduce the everyday contexts in the classroom but to use those as contexts from which to develop the mathematics that children are expected to learn in school. The everyday contexts provide us with a way to connect with the families' (and children's) knowledge, experiences, and ways of learning (e.g., by apprenticeship) but our responsibility is to ensure that these children advance in their mathematical learning in school.

Some researchers have looked into the issue of contextualization and its interaction with social class in an attempt to explain differences in approaches to doing mathematics. Cooper and Dunne (2000) present data from two children (a middle-class girl and a working-class boy) that illustrate differences as to how these two children approached "real-context" type problems, with the working-class child taking the contexts more seriously in a way that it sometimes interfered with his being able to successfully solve the task. Lubienski (2004) argues that working-class students tend to become immersed in real-world constraints of problems, and are also more deferential to the authority of the teacher. Planas (2007) examines the diversity of norms in the mathematics classroom and how different participants had difficulties when expected to show the knowledge associated to the representations for a "good student." It is assumed that an understanding of immigrant students' interpretations of classroom norms was not possible without considering their out-of-school contexts of experience, and primarily their home contexts. We argue that in the case of immigrant students, the access to their home contexts, by means of the access to their parents' voices, may be an effective way of gaining knowledge about their mathematical daily practices, beyond stereotypes and misconceptions reinforced by dominant negative social representations on them.

Our position when addressing challenges and difficulties that Latino/a students may experience when learning mathematics is a rejection of a deficit model that tends to blame the students and their environment (i.e., family and community) for these problems (see Valencia & Black, 2002, for a discussion regarding the myth that Mexican Americans do not care about education). Instead, we argue that the issue is systemic and that is related to schools not considering these students' expectations and experiences. The context of immigration, the role of language, and the general living conditions of a minoritized group are realities that need to be taken into account when assessing these students' mathematics learning experiences. This information is also needed when interpreting Latino/a students' behaviors as learners. Although many Latino/a students are not immigrants themselves, their parents' experiences of immigration have an influence on them. If parents experience contradictions between mathematics instruction in the US and preserving certain school values and approaches to doing mathematics learned in Mexico, they may communicate these contradictions to their children (Civil, Planas, & Quintos, 2005). Children may not experience the contradictions themselves but they still will have to cope with transition processes between the school culture and certain home values (Civil & Andrade, 2002).

Research Method

Our approach to research with parents is grounded on a phenomenological perspective (Van Manen, 1990). Thus, the lived experiences of the parents as they participate in the mathematics workshops are at the center of our attention. We try to understand the nature of these lived experiences through dialogue with the parents. In this chapter we draw on work that spans over a decade and that includes three projects[1] (Civil & Andrade, 2003; Civil & Bernier, 2006; Civil, Bratton, & Quintos, 2005; Civil & Quintos, 2006). Although there were some differences among the projects, our approach to working with parents retained some common characteristics. Engaging in conversations about mathematics teaching and learning is key to our research. Parents participate in a series of workshops (sometimes called Math For Parents courses, or "tertulias matemáticas" (mathematical get-togethers)). These sustained experiences allow us to promote a two-way dialogue in a safe and supportive environment in which the parents (most of whom are mothers) bring in their questions not only about mathematics but also about their children's schooling.

We rely on multiple sources of data, including observations and field notes, focus groups, individual interviews, and classroom visits and debriefings. To analyze our data we use Glaser and Strauss (1967) constant comparative method. This process leads to the development of themes that tend to be highly interrelated. In this chapter, we consider three such themes from a community approach perspective. The first can be seen as a general theme that includes the other two themes: (1) Latino parents' perceptions of their children's mathematics education; (2) Latino parents' valorizations of school mathematical practices; and (3) Latino parents' views of language in their children's mathematics education. For this third theme, we focus on issues related to language and mathematics as they occur in parents' interactions with their children around homework.

To us, mathematics education is a process of *enculturation* (Bishop, 1988) through the reconstruction of practices that are highly conditioned by the contexts where they are developed. In the case of home contexts, the parents' perceptions of their children conducting certain practices at school, their valorization of these practices, and their forms of communicating perceptions and valorizations to their children may be seen as significant social issues of influence.

Latino Parents' Perceptions of Their Children's Mathematics Education

In this section we present some of our findings on parents' perceived differences between mathematics education in schools in the US and schools in Mexico. This has been a constant theme in our research into parents' perceptions about the teaching and learning of mathematics (Civil, Planas, & Quintos, 2005; Civil & Quintos, 2006). Many of the families have frequent contact with relatives across the border in Mexico. Most parents (and children too) comment that they find that mathematics instruction is more advanced in Mexico:

ERNESTO[2]: The level in Mexico is much higher. I have nieces and nephews there and here and there, I see that they have learned more things at school. [Referring to a nephew in Mexico] He's in fourth grade and my son is in fourth grade too. What they're giving my son now, he [the nephew] learned in second grade. So, the educational level is lower and they learn more slowly than they learn in Mexico.

BERTHA: No, I'm not happy. I feel that there is repetition of a lot of things; I don't understand why the teaching is so slow, I don't like it, I don't like the system, I don't like it at all. When we go to Mexico ... my nieces and nephews or my husband's nieces and nephews, they are children that are more or less the same age as Jaime [their son] and I see that Jaime is behind. Here they tell me that Jaime [is] really excellent.

It is not our goal to engage in a discussion of whether mathematics instruction is more advanced in Mexico or in the US. This is a complex issue that we are trying to understand better in our current research. We do have some evidence that students who have been schooled in Mexico and have recently arrived in the US tend to have a better command of arithmetic skills and formulas. But there is much more to knowing mathematics than skills and facts. Our goal in this chapter is to highlight immigrant parents' perceptions, not to determine whether these perceptions are "accurate" or not. These perceptions affect the interactions between children and parents and between parents and the schools their children attend. Furthermore, these perceptions go beyond opinions in that the parents provide evidence for their assertions. Whether they refer to what their relatives in Mexico are doing (as the quotations above illustrate) or, as we will show later, what their children tell them or what they see themselves happening in the US classrooms, these parents based their perceptions on data. Granted, their perceptions are influenced by their views of what counts as mathematics, which in most cases consists of arithmetic and procedures and do not usually encompass other topics or approaches such as problem solving.

One of our goals in the mathematics workshops is to widen parents' views of what counts as mathematics by engaging the parents in problem-solving tasks and in exploring topics such as geometry, measurement, and data analysis. Although we encourage discussions in which parents bring up these perceived differences between Mexico and the US, we tend to be very cautious about our own participation in these conversations since not only do we believe that this is a very complex comparison, but also it is an emotionally charged subject that often brings up memories of these parents' own experiences as learners of mathematics as well as a realization that they are not "there" anymore, where "there" is both a time—their school years—and a place—Mexico. As one mother, Gabriela, told another mother in a discussion on the differences between Mexico and the US,

GABRIELA: But for one thing, here we are in the US and here is where they are going to grow up, they are going to study here.

Even more poignant was a focus group at the house of one of the parents. Several of the parents (in particular two fathers, Francisco and Rogelio) had been quite persistent throughout the conversation in their comments about the teaching of mathematics in Mexico as being at a higher level than what their children were currently experiencing. After a while of this persistence, one of the mothers, Irene, said in a rather upset tone:

IRENE: But, let's leave Mexico, OK? We are not in Mexico anymore.
FRANCISCO: Yes, we are not…
IRENE: Let's focus on what we are living here.

Most of the parents' comments express a concern for the fact that their children do not know arithmetic well enough (e.g., the multiplication facts) or that they seem to be going at slower pace than at schools in Mexico:

VICTORIA: And you know, with the children, in fourth grade, it's hard for them because here they don't ask them to memorize the tables and in Mexico yes, when I went to school, I had to memorize the multiplication tables, 1 through 10, and they quizzed on them; and here no, children struggle a lot; just to do a computation they take out the notebook that has all the tables in the back, and I say, "no, you have to learn them."

Victoria goes on to describe how she tries to get her children to learn the multiplication tables, and how they do that for a while but it is a struggle. Victoria is one of many parents concerned about what they perceive as problematic with the teaching of mathematics at their children's school; the fact that they are not expected to memorize the multiplication tables is a common topic of discussion in our conversations with parents (for similar results with Pakistani parents in the U.K., see Abreu & Cline, 2005). Another point of concern is the repetition, going over material that they had already seen in Mexico. In the quotation below, a mother is talking about her child, a fourth grader, who was getting upset in class and not paying attention because he had already seen the content before:

LUCRECIA: More advanced [in Mexico]; because my son here is doing division by one digit and over there, they are already dividing by three digits, so it's lower. It's lower, yes, because here they are going over the multiplication tables and over there, by second grade, the tables … for that reason, I find it a lower level here, and my son finds it easier here, because since he comes more advanced from there, maybe that's why he finds it easier. And the teacher said that he wasn't paying attention but if he had already seen this [the material], then he already knew it and he didn't pay much attention, yes, he was getting a bit upset.

The case of this child is not unique; we have similar evidence from other parents and from the children themselves, who comment on how they are studying things in mathematics that they had already seen in Mexico. Below is an excerpt from an interview with a sixth grader who had recently arrived from Mexico:

RESEARCHER: Describe yourself as a math student.
STUDENT: I am advanced because in Mexico the schools are a year ahead. I am very fast at doing things. The teacher gives me harder work....
RESEARCHER: What is your best subject in math?
STUDENT: Algebra.
RESEARCHER: You already know algebra?
STUDENT: Yes
RESEARCHER: Where did you learn algebra?
STUDENT: In Mexico, they had already taught me algebra. And the teacher here is barely starting to teach some algebra.

We do not want to imply that these students are necessarily successful in the US mathematics classrooms. Although some of them may indeed arrive with a better command of certain aspects of mathematics, the transition to schooling in the US may be less than smooth. Language plays a key role, as we will see later. Mathematics instruction is very language dependent, probably even more so in reform-oriented mathematics classrooms, with their emphasis on communication. But, as Valdés (2001) points out, "students should not be allowed to fall behind in subject-matter areas (e.g., mathematics, science) while they are learning English" (p. 153). Her account of immigrant middle-school students shows, like our data, how some of them who had a strong mathematics background when they arrived were not placed in classes that challenged them (mathematically), hence getting bored and missing out on opportunities to advance in their learning of this subject.

Latino Parents' Valorizations of School Mathematical Practices

Closely related to this topic of difference in instruction between the two countries is the notion of valorization of knowledge (Abreu, 1995). We will focus on aspects of elementary mathematics, that is, algorithms for arithmetic operations. Arithmetic takes up most of the teaching time in elementary mathematics. Our work with teachers and preservice teachers shows unawareness on their part for the idea that different parts of the world have different ways to do the four basic operations. When presented with these different ways, their reactions often show a preference toward "their own" ways:

A PRESERVICE TEACHER: This is nice but they need to learn to do things the US way.
A FIFTH-GRADE TEACHER: And now every Wednesday we are teaching division and multiplication, and the children are doing it the way we ask. This Wednesday when

> we did it, Eliseo said, "Oh no, my mama did it different." And he went to the board and did it that way, and I say "Yes, but that's in mama's home. Let's do it the way that we do it in the school." And it was again very close, but it was an approximation. It was an approximation.

We do not know what the teacher meant by "it was an approximation." Exploring these different algorithms is not easy, as our work with teachers and preservice teachers shows. Thus, their reactions to these different ways may be a combination of valorization of knowledge and lack of understanding of these approaches to do arithmetic.

To further illustrate this point, we focus on division algorithms since this topic arises in every discussion with parents schooled in Mexico. Figure 7.1 illustrates the standard approach to division in Mexico and in the US. The difference is that in Mexico the subtractions are done in your head; you do not write them down. It may seem like a simple difference because it has to do with the representation of the algorithm and not with the algorithm itself. Yet, it is a subject of controversy. The Mexican parents with whom we work have a clear preference for their method, which they consider more efficient and cleaner.

This is what Marisol and Verónica said about the division algorithms:

MARISOL: When I looked at how he [her son] was dividing, he subtracted and subtracted and that he wrote all the equation complete I said, I even said, "this teacher wants to make things complicated. No, son, not that way! This way!" And he learned faster with this [Marisol's] procedure.

VERÓNICA: I tried to do the same with my child with divisions, that he didn't write everything, but he says, "no, no, mom, the teacher is going to think that I did it on the computer." "You don't need to write the subtraction son," I say, "you only put what is left." "No, no, my teacher is going to think that I did it on the computer, I have to do it like that." "Ok, you think that…, but I want to teach you how we learned." And I did teach him, but he still uses his method, and that way he feels safe that he is doing his homework as they told him to. The same thing with writing above what they borrow and crossing it out, I tell him, "I remember our homework did not have to have any cross-outs," whereas his does.

Verónica and Marisol both said that they showed their children their method to divide. Verónica, however, points out that her son would rather use his teacher's method to be on the safe side. We do not know whether his teacher would have accepted this other method ("his mom's method"), but we suspect that this method

Mexico	U.S.
29	29r6
42 ⟌1224	42 ⟌1224
384	−84
6	384
	−378
	06

Figure 7.1 Division in Mexico; Division in the US (field notes).

may have been rejected given the evidence we have collected from teachers. Many of them were unaware of this representation of the algorithm of division and were surprised when they saw it and said that they did not understand it. This lack of knowledge for what is a common representation for division in Mexico happened at a school where 90% of the students are Latino and many of them have at least one parent who was schooled in Mexico. At a parent workshop, all the parents divided using this representation of the algorithm, while none of the teachers had ever seen it. One of these teachers who has been at that school for over 10 years and who lives in the community said, "no, that's not our old way [in response to a question as to whether this was an old way to divide]; that's the Mexican way because I don't understand that."

In Civil and Andrade (2003) we argue for the concept of parents as intellectual resources, which would bring knowledge such as this approach to division to the forefront in the schools, thus valuing immigrant parents' knowledge. Although all families have cultural and social capital, working-class and immigrant families often do not possess the kind of capital that schools recognize as valid (Lareau & Horvat, 1999). In our work with parents we address this inequity in how the forms of capital among low-income, ethnic/language "minority" families are perceived by schools. As Bourdieu (1986) points out, the difference in distribution of cultural capital among different groups (and, we add, on how each group's capital is valued) may explain some of the differences in children's school achievement. What our work has revealed is a richness of mathematical knowledge among these parents, many of whom were educated in Mexico. Their approaches are different, yet no less valid. Schools, however, do not often recognize these differences.

Some of the parents we work with are caught in a dilemma. On one hand they perceive the education in Mexico to be more advanced, yet on the other hand, some of them know that their children will be educated and most likely stay in the US, and they do not want to create a conflict between "their ways" and what their children are learning in school. We illustrate this point with an interaction between two immigrant mothers:

LUCINDA: Well, what I say is, for example my daughter tells me "come to learn how they teach here, come see that I am right," when we are upset at each other here around the table, and sometimes she is the one who makes me upset, because I want to explain things to her as I know them, and I tell her, "m'hija, the way I explain it to you, I know it's much better for you," but she sticks to her [way].

GABRIELA: But for one thing, here we are in the US and here is where they are going to grow up, they are going to study here, and I wanted to do the same thing as you, but then I say, but why, if they are teaching him things from here, and he is going to stay here, and so, one wants to teach them more so that they know more, but what they are teaching them is because they are going to stay here, and they are going to follow what they teach them here.

One could say that this is typical generational discourse—parents trying to show their children how they were taught because they feel that it was a "better" way. But there is more to this when one looks at it in the context of immigration and trying to navigate two cultures (at least) (and in our case, two languages). Conversations such as that between Lucinda and Gabriela bring up the issue of conforming or not to the new system. Okagaki and Sternberg (1993) point out that the immigrant parents in their study (from Cambodia, Mexico, the Philippines, and Vietnam) seemed to value conformity over autonomy. They provide a possible explanation for this, "if one goal of immigrant parents is to help their children adapt to the American school environment, an emphasis on conformity may be viewed as an appropriate vehicle for accomplishing this goal" (p. 52). This explanation seems to agree with what some of the parents in our study (e.g., Gabriela) have shared with us.

We argue that these differences in approach take on a different light when those affected are low-income, immigrant families, whose knowledge has historically not been recognized by institutions such as schools (Abreu, Cline, & Shamsi, 2002). As Takanishi (this volume) writes, "global migration can lead to diversity, innovation, and renewal in the receiving country, but it is often accompanied by social conflict" (p. 1). We claim that indeed immigration could become an opportunity for diversity, innovation, and renewal to be brought into the mathematics teaching and learning in classrooms with immigrant students, but that, in our experience, this does not seem to be the case and in fact these different ways of doing things can lead to conflict. What we witness are situations of potential conflict between children and parents as they try to adjust to the new setting while trying to keep connected to the former. As Suárez-Orozco and Suárez-Orozco (2001) write, "(I)mmigrants are by definition in the margins of two cultures. Paradoxically, they can never truly belong either 'here' nor 'there'" (p. 92). These authors write about the identity issues that immigrant children face when caught between their parents' culture and the culture in their new country.

Immigrant children seem to be caught in the middle, in the boundaries of at least two cultures. They are not fully a member of the home culture when adjusting to the teachers' demands, neither are they fully a member of the local school culture when adjusting to their parents' demands. Some children may seek to become "bicultural" but even this option may create tensions. This feeling of "caught between two cultures" impacts parent–child interactions around mathematics, as the case of Lucinda shows. When we interviewed Lucinda, her daughter was in fifth grade; they had been in the US for 2 years. In the quote given earlier, we see Lucinda struggling with her daughter over what it means to know. She talks about how she and her daughter were having differences of opinion when it came to ways to do mathematics. Lucinda wanted to show her the way she had learned in Mexico and her daughter wanted to "stick" to the way they do things here. The daughter seemed to have adapted to her new school system, while the mother was less willing to let go. Yet, in the quote below, Lucinda reflects on how when they first arrived, the daughter was the one being unhappy with the mathematics class in the US because she found it too easy, and the mother was telling her how she was going to learn "the way from here" (the US)

LUCINDA: When I came from there [Mexico], [my daughter] was in third grade; when we came here, she said that the school looked like play, "why, m'hijita?"; "Because they are making me do 4 + 3, mom, I don't want to go to this school. It's weird." And I would tell her, "but you are going to learn the way from here," well, at that time, that's what I thought, but then I visited my relatives [in Mexico] [and then she goes on to talk about the difference in levels Mexico vs. US and her concern at the difference in levels].

The case of Lucinda points to the complexity of people trying to adapt to and make sense of situations that are different from what they have previously experienced. In our local context of immigration, we wonder about the effect that this adaptation to the new context has on the family dynamics. As the quote below shows, it may not be an easy road:

MÓNICA: Last night my son said to me that school from Mexico was not valued the same as school here, that is, it doesn't count. What I studied there doesn't count here, and he said, "Mom, do you know this problem?" "No, to tell you the truth, I don't," I said to him. "See," he says, "see, that's why I said that they didn't teach you [there] what they teach me here." ... He knows that what is taught here is different from what is taught there and so he says, "why would I ask my mom for help if she's not going to know?" So, there is a barrier.

There is another dimension to this valorization of knowledge that although it is not exclusive to immigrant parents, it is important to point out in our field of mathematics education. Since the 1990s some new curricula grounded on constructivist principles of teaching and learning have been developed in mathematics education in the US. Our work is primarily located in schools that are using reform-based curricula. In some of these curricula the approaches to computation move away from procedures and emphasize invented strategies that build on children's concept of number and their number sense. Thus, one of our goals in the parents' workshops is for parents to learn about these different approaches to doing arithmetic. This brings up again the valorization of knowledge as parents judge these approaches within the framework of what they would expect for their children's education.

At a parents' workshop on addition and subtraction, the first author was asked to explain to one of the mothers an approach to subtraction from a handout from the reform-based curriculum the second/third-grade teacher was using. The example showed that to find 51−22, one could do 30−22, which gives 8; then one needs to add 21 (what is missing from 30 to 51) to 8, thus the answer is 29 (in the handout, the adding of 21 is done in steps, by adding 10 to 30, so 10 to 8; then 10 more, so 50 and 28, and then 1 more, 51 and 29). When the mother was invited to try this strategy on 42−13, instead she said, "to me, this is much easier" and went back to 51−22, set it up vertically and started explaining to her son (a second grader) the "standard" subtraction procedure, "when the number on top is smaller, you ask for 1 from the one next to it,...". The mother walked him through 51−22 and then encouraged him to try 42−13. The mother helped him make the "2" into "12" and then the child asked, "do I put a 5?" pointing to the 4 in 42. The mother said, "no, no 3." The child did not understand the regrouping strategy. We are not claiming that he would have understood the alternative strategy any more easily, since these strategies are often based on a flexible understanding of numbers (e.g., being able to break numbers apart and regroup in different ways), which this child did not have at that point. He was having difficulties with mathematics, which is why his mother wanted to come to the workshops. The "standard" algorithm for subtraction (regrouping) seems straightforward compared to many of these alternative methods, but it is not conceptually obvious, as we saw the child stumbling over how to regroup and whether to decrease or increase the number that he was using to regroup. What seemed clear to us is that the mother valued the "standard" algorithm and appeared to be skeptical about the alternative approaches. We can see how different views about teaching and learning mathematics are in play and can potentially come into conflict, even with the parents who are coming to the workshops and therefore being exposed to how and why their children are being taught this "different" way.

Latino Parents' Views of Language in Their Children's Mathematics Education

In the previous section we brought up the potential conflict between children and parents when their ways of doing mathematics do not match. We argue that these differences in approaches may be particularly sensitive in an immigration context. In fact, this potential conflict between parents and children and between parents and schools is exacerbated when we add the language factor. In this section we focus on the interactions between parents and children around homework, particularly in our context where the children's instruction is in English but the language in the home (at least with the parents) is Spanish.[3] Some of the parents do not seem to think that language plays much of a role in mathematics:

RESEARCHER: Do you think that the language affects your son's learning of mathematics?
DOROTEA: No, because numbers are the same in English than in Spanish; it's the same thing, that is, if you add in Spanish or in English, it's the same thing.
LUCRECIA: Mathematics is a language that doesn't need translation.

Language, however, plays a key role in the teaching and learning of mathematics, particularly in those classrooms using reform-based curricula. Although many of these textbooks do include computation exercises, they also have activities that are quite language rich, and by this we mean language in the sense of the English language, but also the mathematical language. We are not referring just to typical word problems, but to tasks that use rather complex sentences in the instructions or the context and that may ask students to provide written explanations. There are resources in Spanish for many of these curricula; however, due to the non-bilingual emphasis in our local context, some schools do not seem to have these materials to send home in Spanish. Parents comment on the difference between being in a bilingual program and not:

CÁNDIDA: Well, I remember that they would give her homework in English and in Spanish, and so I could help her a little more.... But when it was all in English, no. Then I couldn't. I felt bad. I would be very frustrated because I couldn't explain it to them, I would have liked to explain it to them and I couldn't. I was frustrated.
VERÓNICA: I liked it while they were in a bilingual program, I could be involved ... When he was in kindergarten it was easy to cut out things, pass out the projects to the kids, gather them up, I even brought work home to take for the teacher the next

day. In first grade it was the same thing, I went with him and because the teacher spoke Spanish, she gave me things to grade and other jobs like that. My son saw me there, I could listen to him, I watched him. By being there watching, I realize many things. And then when David went to second grade into English-only and with a teacher that only spoke English, then I didn't go, I didn't go.

Teachers have also shared their concern with homework. In some cases teachers assign the more standard type of worksheet in part because it is less language demanding but also it gives something that parents recognize and want—practice of basic skills. It is hard to separate what is due to a reform-based curriculum (i.e., topics that may be unfamiliar to the parents) and what is due to the language, but parents often said that their reason for coming to the parents' workshops was to be able to help their children with homework (see L. Ginsburg, 2006, for her work with African American parents and reform-based mathematics homework; see also Jackson & Remillard, 2005; Remillard & Jackson, 2006). One obvious way in which the language plays a role is that parents feel they cannot help their children with homework, even though in many cases they say that they know the mathematics. One mother, Selena said that as a student she had no problems with mathematics in Mexico, but that now, here in the US she is having a hard time helping her son because:

SELENA: Sometimes I cannot explain it to him because I hardly know English. There are things that he reads them to me and he translates them into Spanish; sometimes I understand what he's telling me in English, but others, definitely I don't understand anything ... And so, I put a circle around the parts I did not understand.

Verónica, a mother who had attended college in Mexico and had some teaching experience there, told us that she was confident she had enough mathematics background to help her son who was in middle school at the time, but:

VERÓNICA: It takes a lot of work when it is difficult to translate something for me, so he prefers to go early to school or ask someone else and that is something I don't like. He doesn't feel very sure that I understand him because the problem is written in English. I don't know how to read it and he doesn't know how to translate it well for me because he speaks Spanish and reads Spanish ... but when kids learn Spanish here, their vocabulary is not as developed and he doesn't translate like he should so that I'm able to help him.... I think he thinks I studied differently.

Verónica was concerned because she knew the mathematics, yet she felt that her son did not value her knowledge. Her comment also points out to the issue of academic language (for more on language and mathematics with Latino students, particularly in the context of reform-based instruction, see Khisty, 2006; Moschkovich, 2002). Because Verónica's child had been schooled in English since second grade (he had been in a bilingual class prior to that), he did not have a command of academic Spanish. He knew how to speak Spanish, as this was the home language, but could not talk about mathematics in Spanish. This is a common situation in our context now that access to bilingual education has been restricted. In a series of focus-group interviews with fourth through sixth graders, we asked them, "whom do you go to when you need help with your homework?" Although many of them said that they asked their parents, they also brought up that language was an issue:

DANIELA (fifth grade): Well, since I have two brothers that are already working and my mother does not understand everything in English, I need to ask one of my brothers or a cousin who is in high school.

RESEARCHER (asking a group of fifth graders): And you have never tried to ask your questions to your parents in Spanish?

[The children in the group all laughed and shook their heads (indicating no).]

RESEARCHER (to a group of sixth graders): So, what you know how to say about mathematics in English, you cannot say it in Spanish?

IGNACIO: Practically not.

JULIÁN: Practically not.

These excerpts point to another issue that, although we do not directly address it in this chapter, is quite present in our everyday work with immigrant families: the waste of a resource. We agree with Hernandez et al. (this volume) when they write about the importance of bilingualism in global economy. The children in our work could be fully bilingual both at the social and academic levels yet due to the current language policies in place in our context, they are not.

In terms of parent–children interactions around homework, there are several factors at play. Although some of the issues are language-based (i.e., parents use Spanish while children are not strong enough with academic Spanish), some of them are once again related to different approaches to doing mathematics. Next we present excerpts from an exchange during a home interview in which the mother (Margarita) and the father (Sergio) are trying to help their daughter (Berta, in third grade) with a homework subtraction problem. The mathematics task is very relevant for everybody in the room, including the interviewer Beatriz, because it builds on an activity they had just seen six days earlier at the parent workshop. The whole interaction was in Spanish. To give the flavor of the conversation and to highlight the issues around language and mathematics, we have left the first few lines in Spanish (with the translation into English next to it).

MARGARITA: ¿Qué dice? Dímelo en español. [*What does it say? Tell me in Spanish.*]

BERTA: Jack tiene 73 pennies, cuando él agarró ... [*Jack has 73 pennies, when he got...*]

[...]

BERTA: 100 pennies, él ... [*100 pennies, he...*] [long pause]

MARGARITA: Él puede ... [*he can*]

BERTA: Él puede ... puede ... cambiarlo por un dólar! [*he can... can ... change it for one dollar*]

MARGARITA: Aha.

BERTA: How many more pennies Jack need? Cuántos más pennies el Jack necesita?

MARGARITA: Primero, primero lo vamos a hacer con 100 pennies, a cien pennies la ... [*First, first we'll do it with 100 pennies, to 100 pennies...*]

BERTA: Pero, pero, pero, pero no me digas! [*But, but, but, but don't tell me*]

[A few minutes later] [Translated into English from here on]

MARGARITA: Seventy-three; seventy-three; it's what we did with the clips. But these are pennies, right, "mi'hijita"? And we found how many pennies were left?

Here the mother relates the situation to an activity that she and her daughter had worked on at the parents' workshop in which they took out a handful of paper clips from a box of 100, they counted how many they took out and then they had to find how many were left in the box; the given problem (Jack has 73 pennies; how many more does he need to be able to exchange them for $1?) that Berta is solving is similar to the paper clip one, as Margarita notices. But Berta does not seem to see (or hear) the connection to that activity. After a few seconds she turns to her father for help.

BERTA: Dad! I need help.
SERGIO: Look m'hija. It's very easy; look, just pay attention. You put...
BERTA: I have to do it! [raising her voice]
SERGIO: I know, I know; look; I'm not going to do it for you; if you have seventy, eighty, ninety, one hundred, how much; how much is it? Ten, twenty, thirty. But since you already have three, it wouldn't be thirty. It would be, how much? If you have thirty...
BERTA: One, one ... one thousand!
SERGIO: No. You have three here...
BERTA: Ninety!
SERGIO: No, just a moment...
BERTA: Eighty! Seventy!
SERGIO: Wait, wait. If you have seventy-three here, seventy-three to eighty, it's seven. From eighty to ninety, it's ten. From here to there, another then. How much would it be? Seven, ten, and ten, how much?
BERTA: Twenty-seven!!! [yelling]
SERGIO: That's it; so, erase, erase; do it well!
BERTA: [at the same time and screaming] Dad, dad but I have to do it this way.
SERGIO: And how did they teach you?
BERTA: Like this, I have to do it like this; like one, one, and how much, and then plus zero, plus six zeros...

In this exchange the father is looking at the subtraction 100–73, as first from 70 to 100, which gives him 30, and then, since it was 73 and not 70, he is asking her to account for that difference of 3, which would give 27. This strategy of adding up from the number you are subtracting is similar to one of the strategies the teacher is using in the classroom. It is one of these "reform" approaches, as opposed to the traditional subtraction algorithm (regrouping and so on). At the workshop a few days earlier, Sergio did not seem to show much interest in this alternative approach and in fact in videotaped interactions between him and his daughter, we see Sergio trying to teach the traditional algorithm to Berta. Yet in this interaction in the home, he is using one of the approaches discussed in the workshops and hence, used in the classroom too. But Berta does not think that this is the way she has to do it. We cannot tell from her explanation what that other way is. Several minutes later, Berta is still concerned that her father's method is not going to be accepted, in part because she is worried that she is not going to know how to explain it, which is an expectation of many reform-based classrooms:

BERTA: But if you did it for me, and then they tell me, what was it? Because the teacher is going to say, "how did you do it?" And I'm not going to know, and then she's going to say, "who did it for you?" So ... I'm not going to know how these things work in the head.

Her father explains it to her again and then:

BERTA: Ah, look, you are doing it wrong.
SERGIO: Ten; ten and ten and seven, right? How much is that? Count. It's easier this way, but I don't know how your teacher tells you, how she wants us to do it.
BERTA: Well, she wants us to do it well, and that we do it like this...
SERGIO: Well, I don't know how they want me to do it.

This excerpt illustrates again the concept of valorization of knowledge. Berta thinks her father is doing it the wrong way and that the teacher "wants us to do it well." It also illustrates the conflict between the father and daughter, and Sergio ends up giving up "well, I don't know how they want me to do it." The interviewer, Beatriz, then intervenes because she notices that Sergio's way is very similar to one of the approaches in the classroom.

BEATRIZ: How he did it, how he did it for you, how he explained it to you, it's similar to what they explain to you, right Berta?
SERGIO: It's very hard to explain to Berta.... And for more than I want to explain it to her...

Between Margarita and Beatriz they bring up another tool that they have been using in the classroom—the 100 chart. It seems that Berta was under the impression that to solve this problem she needed to use this chart to count from 73 to 83, then to 93, and then to 100. This interaction highlights several issues. One, that is hard to capture in the transcription, is related to the difficulty for a child like Berta who has been schooled in English to talk about mathematics in Spanish. A second issue is related to the reform approaches; not only are the strategies different but also there is an expectation that the child will be able to explain her thinking, which requires communication in English (yet, it is in Spanish in the home). It is no longer "just" about filling out worksheets with subtraction exercises. A third issue is more typical of interactions between parents and children (unrelated to whether they are immigrant or not); it has to do with the parents' way versus the teacher's (or the school's) way. In this case, the father used a strategy that we know would have been fine in the classroom but the daughter did not seem to recognize it as one of the approaches they had been discussing and was convinced that she needed to use the 100 chart. A fourth issue, that encompasses the previous ones, is about the potential effect that these issues may have on parental engagement and on the relations between parents and children on academic subjects. Both the father and the child were getting frustrated with each other in the previous exchange.

In the workshops we address several of the issues highlighted in this section by (a) engaging parents in activities that reflect what their children are learning; this allows us to discuss the different methods and introduce English terms that the children are likely to bring home (some workshops are bilingual but others are mostly in Spanish), and (b) (in some workshops) parents and children work together on tasks that are based on what the children are studying; this allows us to address issues of language and content that may come up.

Conclusion

In this chapter we have focused on the importance of establishing a dialogue with Latino/a immigrant parents about mathematics education. Although our emphasis has been on the parents, there are clear implications from this work for mathematics instruction in general and for possible roles for teachers and schools. The workshops we have described are a powerful arena for dialogue between parents and teachers. Teachers become aware not only about parents' perceptions about their children's education but also about other approaches to doing mathematics (as is the case with the division algorithm). Teachers can then bring these different approaches into their class, thus valuing these forms of knowledge. In one of our projects, we had teams of parents and teachers (and school administrators) facilitating workshops for parents in the community. This approach pushed parents and teachers to reconsider their roles, as they were sharing similar responsibilities as workshop facilitators. In Civil and Bernier (2006) we discuss some of the challenges and possibilities associated with this approach. Some of the challenges were associated with issues of power, as teachers saw themselves as experts while parents did not want "to be relegated to handing out papers or greeting the people coming to the workshop" (p. 327). Some of the possibilities showed teachers embracing their new relationship with the parents and an appreciation for their contributions to the mathematical learning of their children.

In terms of implications for mathematics instruction, immigrant parents have expressed their concern that maybe their children are not learning the kinds of mathematics and approaches to doing mathematics that they were expecting. This concern needs to be addressed. One approach is what we have suggested, through both dialogues and workshops in which parents not only learn about the approaches to mathematics instruction in their children's schools but also share their approaches to doing mathematics. On one hand, by engaging parents with the mathematics that their children are learning, we seek to address an issue brought up by earlier research that suggests that Latino parents (particularly Mexican/Mexican-American) want to help their children with homework but may not know how to do that (Delgado-Gaitan, 1992; Okagaki & Frensch, 1998; Okagaki, Frensch, & Gordon, 1995). As Okagaki et al. (1995) write, "some Mexican American parents may not have the practical knowledge to help their children on schools tasks and … children's school performance will improve as parents become better educated and more able to provide effective instrumental support" (p. 175). Our research thus fits within the primary cultural discontinuities theory by which "parents may have less practical knowledge about how to do school tasks and about the school system itself. This lack of knowledge—not a low valuation of education—is what affects parental support for school" (Okagaki et al., 1995).

On the other hand, however, our approach moves beyond "teaching" parents about the mathematics their children are learning and emphasizes listening to parents. This idea of listening to parents and engaging with them in a mutual exchange of information is at the basis of our concept of parents as intellectual resources (Civil & Andrade, 2003). The quotation below captures this approach, as Ana reflects on the impact of the workshops on herself as a learner and shows a sense of ownership of her learning:

ANA: I am so happy with all these mathematics workshops because I realize how to help my children understand mathematics in a different way, from a fun approach, all together as a family.... And also for us, because one never knows when we may need it, and this way we move forward, and no one is going to mandate that is has to be the way they say, because we also think and solve problems.

Our findings point to the need for respect and positive valorizations of different groups' knowledge. This has implications for schools. Immigrant children interpret their values and meanings according to the mediation of their families' values and meanings. In this process of mediation, both parents and children interact with positive and negative valorizations, suggested by themselves and by other members of the educational context—teachers, non-immigrant students, school administrators, other immigrant students, etc. The contents of these valorizations have an influence on the children's positioning when learning mathematics. Children who experience respect for their home culture at school, and for their school culture at home, may see their learning as a smooth transition process among cultures instead of a place for conflict. Negative valorizations limit the learner's possibilities for their learning and they also limit the learner's possibilities to understand what other learners know.

The construction of a more equitable society is not the only reason why we should be concerned with promoting positive valorizations among different cultural groups. There are also reasons related to mathematics education. Mathematical patterns are universal, but mathematical practices are necessarily situated. Lack of respect for others' knowledge makes it difficult to develop a positive disposition toward learning different mathematical practices. Prior to the learning of different representations and algorithms we need a positive attitude toward the cultures where these are used. But in addition to gaining knowledge about other groups' ways of doing mathematics, learning about different types of representations and algorithms for subtraction or division is a way of better understanding the concepts behind these operations. Interaction between children and parents concerning each other's mathematical knowledge is a means of gaining knowledge. However, it is not an easy interaction. When immigrant parents talk with their children they are interacting with members of another culture—or should we say, "other cultures"—not only due to generational differences. Children are at some point of the distance between their home cultures and their school and classroom cultures. The dialogue between children and parents is to be seen as a form of multicultural dialogue that needs to overcome negative valorizations. In order to seek similarities between different mathematical practices concerning the same notion, children and parents need to interpret each other's knowledge as complementary, and accept the possibility of working together on a common school task, as a way of getting to know each other better and understanding mathematics better as well. We close with the words of a 15-year-old, which capture this idea of working together and exchanging information:

> Now that she [his mother] is attending the mathematical workshops, she can teach me other ways of learning mathematics ... She shares it with the entire family and we all get involved in a mathematical gathering that is fun. We are all teachers and students at the same time, there is no difference and that there be much respect and "confianza" [trust] is most important.

Notes

1. Project Bridge (Linking home and school: A bridge to the many faces of mathematics) was supported under the Educational Research and Development Centers Program, PR/Award Number R306A60001, as administered by the OERI (US Department of Education). Project MAPPS (Math and Parent Partnerships in the Southwest) and CEMELA (Center for the Mathematics Education of Latinos/as) are funded by the National Science Foundation (NSF) under grants ESI-9901275 and ESI-0424983. The views expressed here are those of the authors and do not necessarily reflect the views of the funding agencies.
2. All names are pseudonyms. All the quotations from parents have been translated from Spanish.
3. Proposition 203 was a ballot initiative approved by Arizona voters in 2000, now codified as part of the Arizona Education Statutes. This law severely restricts bilingual education programs, replacing them with "Structured English Immersion" classes for a period "not normally intended to exceed one year" (ARS, 15–752). The law allows teachers to use a minimal amount of the child's native language for clarification, but "all children in Arizona public schools shall be taught English by being taught in English and all children shall be placed in English language classrooms" (ARS, 15–752).

References

Abreu, G. de (1995). Understanding how children experience the relationship between home and school mathematics. *Mind, Culture, and Activity: An International Journal, 2*, 119–142.

Abreu, G. de, & Cline, T. (2005). Parents' representations of their children's mathematics learning in multiethnic primary schools. *British Educational Research Journal, 31*, 697–722.

Abreu, G. de, Cline, T., & Shamsi, T. (2002). Exploring ways parents participated in their children's school mathematical learning: Case studies in multi-ethnic primary school. In G. de Abreu, A.J. Bishop, & N.C. Presmeg (Eds.), *Transitions between contexts of mathematical practices* (pp. 123–147). Boston, MA: Kluwer.

Bishop, A.J. (1988). *Mathematical enculturation*. Dordrecht: Kluwer.

Bourdieu, P. (1986). The forms of capital. In J.G. Richardson (Ed.), *Handbook of theory and research for the sociology of education* (pp. 241–258). New York: Greenwood Press.

Chronaki, A. (2005). Learning about "learning identities" in the school arithmetic practice: The experience of two young minority Gipsy girls in the Greek context of education. *European Journal of Psychology of Education, 20*(1), 61–74.

Civil, M. (2002a). Culture and mathematics: A community approach. *Journal of Intercultural Studies, 23*(2), 133–148.

Civil, M. (2002b). Everyday mathematics, mathematicians' mathematics, and school mathematics: Can we bring them together? In M. Brenner & J. Moschkovich (Eds.), *Everyday and academic mathematics in the classroom. Journal of Research in Mathematics Education Monograph #11* (pp. 40–62). Reston, VA: NCTM.

Civil, M. (2007). Building on community knowledge: An avenue to equity in mathematics education. In N. Nasir & P. Cobb (Eds.), *Improving access to mathematics: Diversity and equity in the classroom* (pp. 105–117). New York: Teachers College Press.

Civil, M., & Andrade, R. (2002). Transitions between home and school mathematics: rays of hope amidst the passing clouds. In G. de Abreu, A.J. Bishop, & N.C. Presmeg (Eds.), *Transitions between contexts of mathematical practices* (pp. 149–169). Boston, MA: Kluwer.

Civil, M., & Andrade, R. (2003). Collaborative practice with parents. The role of researcher as mediator. In A. Peter-Koop, V. Santos-Wagner, C. Breen, & A. Begg (Eds.), *Collaboration in teacher education: Examples from the context of mathematics education* (pp. 153–168). Boston, MA: Kluwer.

Civil, M., & Bernier, E. (2006). Exploring images of parental participation in mathematics education: Challenges and possibilities. *Mathematical Thinking and Learning, 8*(3), 309–330.

Civil, M., Bratton, J., & Quintos, B. (2005). Parents and mathematics education in a Latino community: Redefining parental participation. *Multicultural Education, 13*(2), 60–64.

Civil, M., & Kahn, L. (2001). Mathematics instruction developed from a garden theme. *Teaching Children Mathematics, 7*, 400–405.

Civil, M., Planas, N., & Quintos, B. (2005). Immigrant parents' perspectives on their children's mathematics. *Zentralblatt für Didaktik der Mathematik, 37*(2), 81–89.

Civil, M., & Quintos, B. (2006). Engaging families in children's mathematical learning: Classroom visits with Latina mothers. *New Horizons for Learning Online Journal, XII*(1). Retrieved April 5, 2009, from www.newhorizons.org/spneeds/ell/civil%20quintos.htm.

Cooper, B., & Dunne, M. (2000). *Assessing children's mathematical knowledge: Social class, sex and problem solving.* London: Open University Press.

D'Ambrosio, U. (1985). Ethnomathematics and its place in the history and pedagogy of mathematics. *For the Learning of Mathematics, 5*, 44–48.

Delgado-Gaitan, C. (1992). School matters in the Mexican-American home: Socializing children to education. *American Educational Research Journal, 29*, 495–513.

Ginsburg, H.P. (1999). The myth of the deprived child: New thoughts on poor children. In A.B. Powell & M. Frankenstein (Eds.), *Ethnomathematics: Challenging eurocentrism in mathematics education* (pp. 129–154). New York: State University of New York Press.

Ginsburg, L. (2006, July). *Adult learners go home to their children's math homework: What happens when the parent is unsure of the content?* Paper presented at the 13th Annual Conference of Adults Learning Mathematics, Belfast, U.K.

Glaser, B., & Strauss, A. (1967). *The discovery of grounded theory: Strategies for qualitative research.* Chicago, IL: Aldine.

González, N., Moll, L., & Amanti, C. (Eds.). (2005). *Funds of knowledge: Theorizing practice in households, communities, and classrooms.* Mahwah, NJ: Lawrence Erlbaum.

Jackson, K., & Remillard, J.T. (2005). Rethinking parent involvement: African American mothers construct their roles in the mathematics education of their children. *The School Community Journal, 15*(1), 51–73.

Kahn, L., & Civil, M. (2001). Unearthing the mathematics of a classroom garden. In E. McIntyre, A. Rosebery, & N. Gonzalez (Eds.), *Classroom diversity: Connecting school to students' lives* (pp. 37–50). Portsmouth, NH: Heinemann.

Khisty, L.L. (2006). Language and mathematics: Toward social justice for linguistically diverse students. In J. Novotná, H. Moraová, M. Krátká, & N. Stehlíková (Eds.), *Proceedings of the 30th Conference of the International PME Group* (vol. 3, pp. 433–440). Prague: Charles University.

Lareau, A., & Horvat, E. (1999). Moments of social inclusion and exclusion race, class, and cultural capital in family–school relationships. *Sociology of Education, 72*(1), 37–53.

Lave, J. (1988). *Cognition in practice: Mind, mathematics and culture in everyday life.* Cambridge: Cambridge University Press.

Lubienski, S.T. (2004). Decoding mathematics instruction: A critical examination of an invisible pedagogy. In J. Muller, A. Morais, & B. Davies (Eds.), *Reading Bernstein, researching Bernstein* (pp. 150–175). London: Routledge Falmer.

Moschkovich, J.N. (2002). A situated and sociocultural perspective on bilingual mathematics learners. *Mathematical Thinking and Learning, 4*(2/3), 189–212.

Nunes, T., Schliemann, A.D., & Carraher, D.W. (1993). *Street mathematics and school mathematics.* Cambridge: Cambridge University Press.

Okagaki, L., & Frensch, P.A. (1998). Parenting and children's school achievement: A multiethnic perspective. *American Educational Research Journal, 35*, 123–144.

Okagaki, L., Frensch, P.A., & Gordon, E.W. (1995). Encouraging school achievement in Mexican American children. *Hispanic Journal of Behavioral Sciences, 17*, 160–179.

Okagaki, L., & Sternberg, R.J. (1993). Parental beliefs and children's school performance. *Child Development, 64*, 36–56.

Planas, N. (2007). The discursive construction of learning in a multiethnic school: perspectives from non-immigrant students. *Intercultural Education, 18*(1), 1–14.

Rainwater, L., & Smeeding, T.M. (2003). *Poor kids in a rich country.* New York: Russell Sage Foundation.

Remillard, J.T., & Jackson, K. (2006). Old math, new math: Parents' experiences with *Standards*-based reform. *Mathematical Thinking and Learning, 8*, 231–259.

Suárez-Orozco, C., & Suárez-Orozco, M. (2001). *Children of immigration.* Cambridge, MA: Harvard University Press.

Valdés, G. (2001). *Learning and not learning English: Latino students in American schools.* New York: Teachers College Press.

Valencia, R., & Black, M. (2002). "Mexican Americans don't value education!"—On the basis of the myth, mythmaking, and debunking. *Journal of Latinos and Education, 1*(2), 81–103.

Valenzuela, A. (1999). *Subtractive schooling: U.S.-Mexican youth and the politics of caring.* Albany, NY: State University of New York Press.

Van Manen, M. (1990). *Researching lived experience: Human science for an action sensitive pedagogy.* London, Ontario: The University of Western Ontario.

8 Cultural Incongruence Between Teachers and Families

Implications for Immigrant Students

Selcuk R. Sirin and Patrice Ryce

Schools are often the first places where many immigrant families began to negotiate their cultural differences with the mainstream society. Upon entering the US school system, the cultural background of most immigrants is often mismatched with the cultural background of their teachers. In addition to the more typical language and cultural barriers, certain immigrant groups, such as Muslim immigrants and undocumented immigrants, have to overcome increasingly negative perceptions of their group to effectively advocate for their children's educational success. Learning to navigate through these cultural barriers holds difficulties for all immigrant families with school-age children, but undocumented immigrants as well as Muslim immigrants face particular challenges as they are increasingly perceived as the ultimate "other" in the popular discourse.

Prior research on marginalized groups show that teachers' lack of experience or understanding of their students' cultures can lead to negative educational and psychological outcomes due to diminished expectations of academic achievement, biased decisions on teacher grading and tracking decisions, and increased referrals for learning disability and psychological evaluations (Delpit, 1995; Hauser-Cram, Sirin, & Stipek, 2003; Ladson-Billings, 1995). In this chapter we will examine how the increasingly negative perceptions of certain immigrant groups may put their children at risk in schools. Specifically we will attempt to uncover the potential implications of the cultural incongruence between teachers who are members of mainstream society and students who come from immigrant families. In the first half of the chapter, we will provide a conceptual framework and a general understanding of cultural incongruence for immigrant families and schools. In the second half of the chapter we will focus primarily on Muslim immigrants to illustrate the implications of such incongruence for this specific population in the post-9/11 US context. Whenever possible we will provide empirical evidence from research conducted with specific populations of interest (i.e., undocumented and/or Muslim immigrants). In the absence of such work, we will rely on other marginalized groups to draw some parallels with the hope of inspiring others to tackle the implications of cultural incongruence for children of increasingly marginalized immigrant groups.

I Background

More than half of the foreign-born population live in California, New York, and Texas (Hernandez et al., this volume), where school systems are presumably accustomed to serving immigrant students. However, what is unique about the most recent wave of immigration that started in 1990s is that cities and states that have not traditionally experienced large immigrant populations have recently encountered large influxes of new immigrants. For example, between 1990 and 2000, the number of foreign-born residents increased by 88% in the south and 65% in the Midwest (Malone, Baluja, Costanzo, & Davis, 2003). The entrance of large numbers of children of immigrants into the nation's schools has created an immediate need for schools to address the educational, social, and psychological needs of these children and their families.

While some of the historical immigrant destination cities may have school systems that are familiar with the specific issues that stem from serving immigrant students, the newly settled communities may not yet have systems in place to accommodate the special needs of children of immigrants and their parents. As the number of children of immigrants is expected to grow even higher in the next several decades, school districts across the country face the double challenge of finding teachers who are trained to successfully teach an increasingly diverse student population and an anticipated shortage of teachers in the next decade.

As the numbers of immigrants and the places where they settle diversify, the topic of immigration and its implications for schooling has also become an important aspect of the American public discourse. While the US is the quintessential immigrant nation where an overwhelming proportion of the population can trace back their ancestry to somewhere outside North America, new waves of immigration almost invariably provoke anti-immigrant feelings. Some worry that immigrants will "take over" and threaten the American way of life (Suárez-Orozco & Suárez-Orozco, 2001). For others, immigrants' desire to hold on to their culture and language is perceived as a threat to the union (Huntington, 2004). As a result, American history is full of periods when the mainstream public threatened the health and well-being of immigrants, either due to the zeitgeist of the historical period or based on the public's negative perceptions of certain immigrant groups.

Currently, we are in yet another cycle of growing anti-immigrant sentiments. According to a June 2007 national poll, 45% of respondents believed that the amount of immigration into the US should be decreased from its current level and 35% stated that immigration was a "bad thing" for the US today. In the same poll, 58% thought that immigration was making the crime situation in the US worse, 34% thought that immigration was making the job situation worse for themselves and their family, 46% thought that immigration was making the economy in general worse, and 55% thought that immigration was making taxes worse (Gallup, 2007). These negative perceptions are not likely to go away as several political figures and public intellectuals seem to exploit economic and cultural anxieties of the American public. This creates increasingly negative perceptions of immigration and immigrants, which are likely to have long-term consequences for the children of immigrants who start schools in the US.

A specific group of immigrants who currently go through public scrutiny is the immigrants who come from Muslim countries. Relatively comfortable in the middle- and upper-middle-class fraction of urban and suburban life, Muslims prior to the 9/11 attacks had the social capital to belong to the mainstream US culture (Deaux, 2006). Citizenship rates, educational degree, and income brackets indicate that Muslim immigrants were, if provisionally, part of the upwardly mobile middle-class American society. However, after the terrorist attacks of 9/11, mainstream US society took notice of this particular group of immigrants and pronounced anti-Muslim sentiment became commonplace. Before 9/11, 80% of Americans agreed that racial profiling was wrong. However, after 9/11, 60% favored racial profiling "at least as long as it was directed at Arabs and Muslims" (Maira, 2004, p. 3). Over 30% of Americans thought we should intern Arab Americans after 9/11 (see Swiney, 2006, for a general review). Another national opinion poll indicated that 46% of adults in the US agreed that "it is OK to detain Muslims indefinitely to protect 'us'" (Deane & Fears, 2006).

These pronounced anti-Muslim sentiments in the American public raises the issue of how children of these immigrant groups fare in schools surrounded by teachers, administrators, and families who may echo some of these very opinions. In the next section, we will discuss how cultural differences between immigrant families and their schools, and between teachers and parents, can affect the academic and psychological well-being of immigrant students. This issue is of particular concern for those who come from stigmatized groups, such as Muslims in post-9/11 US.

II Cultural Congruence: A Conceptual Framework

Today, more than 20% of school-aged children come from immigrant families and 80% of them are of color, coming from Latin America, Asia, and the Caribbean. In comparison, according to the US Department of Education (2007), in the 2003–2004 school year, 83.3% of full-time teachers in public and private schools were White, with only 7.8%, 6.2%, and 1.4% self-identifying as Black, Hispanic, and Asian, respectively. What are the implications of this racial/ethnic difference between teachers and students? Are students who come from different social and ethnic backgrounds at risk whenever there is a mismatch between teachers and parents in terms of racial or ethnic backgrounds?

According to Bronfenbrenner (1979), one of the mesosystems that shapes individual development in school years is the links between home and school. The quality and frequency of home and school interactions have important implications for students, particularly in the early school years. Students suffer academically in an impoverished mesosystem where there is very little interaction between home and school or when different microsystems (i.e., home and school) endorse different value systems. As the seminal work of Epstein (1983) showed, effective two-way interactions between parents and teachers positively affect students' academic progress.

The degree to which schools' and families' systems can cooperate, especially in early school years, largely shapes how the child adjusts to school. Conversely, the lack of understanding of home contexts of students by teachers and the lack of understanding of the schooling system by parents may put the child at risk for academic failure. There have been several conceptual approaches to address this phenomena of home and school disconnect using terms like "cultural discontinuity" (Delpit, 1995; Ogbu, 1993), "cultural incongruence" (Au & Kawakami, 1994), or "cultural mismatch" (Ladson-Billings, 1995; Villegas, 1988). Although all three of these terms are typically used interchangeably in the literature, we will use cultural incongruence as it reflects a continuum more than the other two alternatives. While the source of incongruence is the cultural mismatch between teachers and parents, this may not always lead to cultural incongruence as many schools make an attempt to bring the culture of the students into the classroom (Au & Kawakami, 1994).

Many strongly argue that the US public school system is oriented around European-American cultural values (Slater, 2008), which can cause children from other cultural backgrounds to suffer academically. Ogbu (1982) offered "cultural discontinuity" as an anthropological model for why certain racial and ethnic groups fail in the US education system. According to Ogbu, children from certain minority, immigrant, and lower socioeconomic status groups failed because their cultures are not congruent with the culture of their schools. In his widely cited article, Ogbu also wrote that the use of the cultural-discontinuity hypothesis dates back to 1905 when Edgar Hewitt criticized "American public school system for failing to understand the cultural backgrounds of children of immigrants" (p. 291). Delpit (1995) asserts that when significant differences exist between a student's home culture and his/her school culture, teachers can "easily misread students' aptitudes, intents, or abilities as a result of the difference in styles of language use and interactional patterns" (p. 167). In addition, the presence of these differences may also result in teachers using styles of instruction and/or discipline that conflict with the norms of the child's home.

Addressing the same phenomena, Phelan, Davidson, and Yu (1991) proposed a more general model to explain how the differences across family, school, and peer cultures play out in the lives of children. Specifically, according to their "multiple worlds" model, students can either live in: (a) congruent worlds that support smooth transitions; (b) different worlds that require transitions to be negotiated; (c) diverse worlds that lead to difficult transitions; or (d) highly discordant worlds that create resistance. For immigrant students who come from cultures that are not similar to the schools they attend, the first path is typically not available. This leaves them with having to negotiate the differences, which can make the transitions between these seemingly different worlds quite difficult and at times impossible. Students who live in different "worlds" at home, in schools, or even with their peers, suffer the most when the differences are vast and unmanageable.

Due to the increasing numbers of immigrants in our nation's schools coupled with a comparatively less-diverse teaching staff, it is important to examine the potential implications of cultural incongruence on the educational experiences of immigrant groups. In the following section, we will discuss these implications, utilizing findings from past empirical work.

III Implications of Cultural Incongruence for Immigrant Students

Children of immigrants enter the schools in the US with a variety of linguistic, religious, and cultural traditions, many of which our nation's teachers may have little to no knowledge about. Parents who are not fully aware of their children's rights may be reluctant to demand high-quality education. The consequences of teacher misunderstanding and potentially negative attitudes resulting from this misunderstanding may have a profoundly negative effect on the academic achievement of their students. Lasky (2000), for example, found that teachers were more comfortable with parents who shared a similar value system to their own and often became demoralized, angry, and discouraged with parents who did not share the same values. Consequently, the cultural discontinuity between children of immigrants and their teachers is likely to play a much larger role in the lives of immigrant students who come from cultures often markedly different from that of mainstream US. In this section we will briefly review the literature on cultural incongruence to identify the areas within which the effect of cultural incongruence is most pronounced.

Before we further this discussion, however, it is important to note that "matching" individual families and teachers by certain fixed categories can only be helpful as long as we remind ourselves that cultures are fluid and they vary greatly within. Furthermore, as Sen (2004) argues "culture *absolutely* does not sit still" (p. 43) and it is perhaps more the case for immigrants and immigrant-receiving cultures (Suárez-Orozco & Suárez-Orozco, 2001). For this reason *family and school cultures* should also be understood as fluid and not fixed—particularly when embodied in children who travel between the two worlds. As such the following sections where we go into specific domains wherein cultural incongruence may play a role for immigrant students should be read with caution. There are always variations within each group; school cultures are also varied and may also change over time in their responses to the new realities of their student population.

One domain in which cultural discontinuity could have a profound effect on the educational experience of immigrant children is in teacher expectations. According to Jussim, Eccles, and Madon (1996) teacher-expectancy effects are much stronger among stigmatized social groups, such as African Americans, children from families with low SES, and, to a lesser extent, girls. Furthermore, teachers' expectations can have a profound influence on students' actual achievement. In a study of 712 low-income African American sixth graders, Gill and Reynolds (2000) found that teacher expectations had a powerful direct impact above and beyond several other critical factors on academic achievement. Thus, children in certain marginalized groups are prone to lowered academic expectations by teachers, which have sustaining effects on school performance over time.

Teachers may also lower their expectations when they encounter families who do not share their educational values or views about discipline and child-rearing practices. In previous work, we tested this very hypothesis through our examination of the relationship between teacher–parent value differences and teacher ratings of literacy and math skills of 105 kindergarten children from low-income families (Hauser-Cram et al., 2003). We found that teachers held significantly lower academic expectations when they perceived value differences with parents, and this was true even after we controlled for students' actual skills and parental education.

Another negative outcome of the cultural discontinuity in our nation's classroom for the educational experiences of children of immigrants is special education referrals. When teachers do not understand or have limited exposure to the cultural norms of their students, they may misinterpret these students' behavior (Osher et al., 2004). Utilizing data from 11 large urban school districts in Southern California, Rueda, Artiles, Salazar, and Higareda (2002) found that the number of Latino English-Language Learners placed in special education tripled between the years of 1993 and 1999. De Valenzuela, Copeland, Qi, & Park (2006) examined the composition of 17,824 special education students from preschool through 12th grade and also found a disproportionate amount of English-Language Learners in special education. These findings are of particular relevance for children of immigrants who may not speak English in the home. Inappropriate placement in special education can have detrimental effects on the academic success of young students due to the attachment of stigmatizing labels and restricted access to general education settings (Hosp & Reschly, 2004).

A third potential fallout from cultural congruence for immigrant students is in the area of tracking. If teacher expectations are greatly influenced by their perception of cultural differences between themselves and their minority students' families, their lowered expectations may have a profound effect on their direct assessment of these children. Tracking (often called ability grouping) is the separation of children by ability and curriculum and is a pervasive practice in the US educational system. Utilizing data from a nationally representative sample of 17,212 first graders, Condron (2007) found that Black and Hispanic students were significantly more likely to be placed in lower reading groups than White students. In addition, children of immigrants are disproportionately represented in non-college tracks (Oakes, 1985; Olsen, 1997). The academic success of students in lower tracks often suffers as a result of their placement. In addition, the work is often less challenging and imaginative than that of higher tracks (Pallas, Entwisle, Alexander, & Stluka, 1994). Often, teachers hold lower expectations for students in lower tracks (Wheelock, 1992) and these students experience less teaching time and attention from their teachers.

Teachers and immigrant parents may also view certain child-rearing practices quite differently. Child-rearing practices in the US are largely dominated by the work of Baumrind (1966) who argued that authoritative parenting yields the most optimal developmental outcomes for children. Although many research findings have confirmed her approach, some argued that her theoretical model is limited because it is largely based on middle-class European-American parents. In a study of 324 first- and second-generation Chinese American adolescents and 248 adolescents of European descent from greater Los Angeles, Chao (2001) demonstrated that a number of Baumrind's (1966) characteristics failed to describe optimal child-rearing practices for Chinese American families. Thus, expecting immigrant groups to raise their children according to standards that they are not accustomed to may create potential for misunderstanding between teachers and certain immigrant parents.

The previous discussion on the nature and potential implications of cultural incongruence demonstrates the influence such incongruence can have on the academic experiences of immigrant-origin students, particularly those stigmatized and misunderstood by mainstream society. In the remaining sections, we will focus on Muslim immigrants as a group particularly relevant to the current discourse on immigration in the US and for which cultural incongruence may be particularly salient in the contemporary US educational system.

IV Immigrant Muslim Students in US Public Schools: A Potential for Cultural Incongruence?

The terrorist attacks of 9/11 created a double bind for many Muslim immigrants.[1] As residents of the US, they felt vulnerable to terrorism as did all Americans, but as Muslims, they also found that they were perceived as a potential threats by the larger society, including certain government agencies and the media. Since the attacks,

Congress passed the Patriot Act, which increased the government's powers for surveillance, search warrants, and detention, and is impacting primarily Muslim immigrant communities. As part of the new measures, Muslim immigrant adult men with legal documents from 16 predominantly Muslim countries were required to register with Immigration and Naturalization Services. In addition to detentions, deportations, and surveillance, there has also been a significant increase in hate crimes against Muslims. In the year following the attacks, the Federal Bureau of Investigation reported a 17-fold increase in hate crimes against Muslims and the rate has remained at this level since that time.

Muslim American Immigrants

It is estimated that there are 2–6 million Muslims in the US and they come from more than 100 different countries (Capps, Fix, Ost, Reardon-Anderson, & Passel, 2005). As in other immigrant groups (Grewal, 2003), young children represent a much larger portion of this population. About two-thirds of Muslims are immigrants to the US while the remaining third are mostly African American converts to the religion.

The first major wave of Muslim immigration to the US began late in the 19th century. The majority of Muslim immigrants during this first wave came from the Middle East, Albania, and South Asia. They were mostly illiterate peasants and, as a result, had more difficulties in adapting to life in the US in comparison with the Christian Arabs from the Middle East who migrated in large numbers around the same time. Muslims of this era moved to places like North Dakota, Indiana, and Iowa. Muslim Arabs also joined Christian Arabs in large numbers in search of work at the Ford Company around Detroit and in Dearborn, Michigan, which became the home of a large Muslim and Arab community in the US. Around 1915, the first mosques in the US began to appear in places like Cedar Rapids, Iowa, and Biddeford, Maine. This first wave of Muslim immigration ended with the 1925 Johnson–Reed Immigration Act, which restricted all Asians from coming to the US, including those from most of the Muslim and Arab countries which were also classified as Asian.

The second wave of Muslim immigration to the US began with the immigration reforms of 1965, which, among other things, made it possible for Muslims from the Middle East and South Asia to immigrate to the US. The Muslim immigrants of this era arrived with much stronger religious and national identities than previous generations of Muslim immigrants, due to popular movements that had shifted the Muslim and Arab world onto a more Islamic and nationalistic path. As in the previous era, these immigrants also came from Palestine, Egypt, Syria, and Iraq, but unlike the previous wave, they also came from the South Asian countries of India, Pakistan, and Bangladesh in much larger numbers. Another shift was the composition of Arab immigrants; unlike the first wave of immigrants when an overwhelming majority of Arabs were Christians, the second wave was composed of mostly Muslim Arabs. Perhaps the most striking difference between the two waves of immigrants was that, compared to the earlier immigrants, most of the migrants of this era either had a college degree or came to the US to pursue one. This change likely reflects shifts in US immigration policy. Given these differences, both immigration status and generations spent in the US are two critical factors to consider when it comes to understanding Muslim American identity formation.

In addition to immigrant Muslims, there is also a growing "indigenous" Muslim population in the US composed of converts from other religions. The majority of this group is African American. Although there always have been Muslims among African Americans since the arrival of slaves, the followers of the Nation of Islam, once led by Elijah Muhammad and popularized by the charismatic leadership of Malcolm X, became a major force within the African American community. Thus, within both immigrant and indigenous groups, Muslim Americans are diverse in terms of race, ethnicity, religious practice, immigration status, and historical roots in the US. Given this diversity, it is reasonable to question the very category "Muslim American" that emerged during the past decade. The popular media, government agencies, and, more importantly, Muslims themselves increasingly adopted the label "Muslim American" to refer to immigrants of specific religious or Middle Eastern geographical origins (Zine, 2001). Particularly since the 9/11 attacks, a growing number of immigrants have formed organizations under the label of "Muslim" both at the national and local levels.

Muslim Immigrants in the United States

Muslim Americans as a group are one of the fastest-growing segments of the US population. According to the American Religious Identification Survey (ARIS) the number of Muslims in the US grew over 108% in a single decade during the 1990s (Kosmin, Mayer, & Keysar, 2001). A public survey by the Pew Research Center (2007) indicated that Muslim Americans are also a much younger group compared to the general US population. Some 56% are between the ages of 18 and 39, compared to 40% in the general public. These numbers parallel other immigrant populations like Latinos and some Asian groups, reflecting the nature of recent immigration.

The Muslim immigrant population in the US is also unique from other immigrant groups in that it is a very highly educated and wealthy group. According to the Zogby International (2004) survey of Muslims immigrants in the country, close to two-thirds of Muslim Americans have at least a college degree, compared to the US average of 28%. Additionally, one-third of respondents reported incomes of $75,000 or more and an additional 20% reported incomes of $50,000–75,000. The Pew Research Center survey (2007) found that foreign-born Muslims reported much higher income levels compared to their US-born Muslim counterparts. The occupational statuses of Muslim Americans also reflect the middle-class status of the majority of Muslims. About 23% of adults work in professional/technical jobs, with an additional 10% working in managerial positions and 9% in medical fields.

Despite these statistics, it is important to note that not all Muslim groups fare as well. Despite the high numbers of professional degrees and the low numbers of college dropouts among Muslims, they are on par with the national average when it comes to having no high school degree, both around 5%, indicating the possibility of a segment of immigrants who came here with no formal education (Zogby International, 2004). According to an analysis of the 2000 Census data by Hernandez, Denton, and Macartney (2008), compared to 8% of White children, 29% of Afghani American children, 26% of Iraqi American children, and 22% of Pakistani/Bangladeshi American children of immigrant families were living in official poverty in 2000.

Finally, unlike other immigrant groups, an overwhelming number of Muslims in the

US have legal status. According to the American Muslim survey conducted by Zogby International, close to 90% of adults are US citizens. This is surprisingly high considering the finding from the same survey that two-thirds of Muslim adults in the US were not born in the US. The higher percentage of citizenship may also be a result from the 1965 Immigration Act which encouraged highly educated professionals to enter the US from mostly Muslim countries. Given the large numbers of deportations after the 9/11 attacks, suspicious attitudes toward Muslims in general and international Muslim students in particular, and stricter visa screenings adopted by consulates in Muslim and Middle Eastern countries, it is likely that undocumented immigration among Muslims will continue to be much lower than among other groups in the near future.

Muslim immigrants are also quite well-integrated into the fabric of the mainstream US society as illustrated by the use of English at home and intermarrying across religious lines. According to US Census data (2000), around 80% of families from Pakistan, Bangladesh, Iraq, and Afghanistan were bilingual, exceeded only by African immigrants (88%), and much higher than all the other groups, including 61% of Vietnamese Americans, and 63% of Mexican Americans. Additionally, the rate of intermarrying with other religions is more common among Muslim Americans than many other immigrant groups in the US. According to one survey, about one in five Muslim Americans intermarry (Kosmin et al., 2001). It is quite likely that the rate of intermarriage will go up dramatically with each successive generation in the US, as is commonly observed in other immigrant groups.

The status of Muslims in the US is quite different than those in Europe. On average, Muslim immigrants to the US are more likely to be professionals or students at higher education than their counterparts who migrate to Europe (Rath & Buijs, 2002). While Muslim immigrants enjoy high citizenship rates in the US, most Muslims in Europe still struggle with gaining access to civic life in their newly adopted countries. For example, after more than 40 years of legal employment in Germany, the majority of Muslim immigrants (mostly of Turkish origin) have still not been granted full citizenship. A similar comparison could also be made between American Muslims and French Muslims, the latter of whom struggle with a national discourse that denies them any right to "Frenchness." These differences between the US and other nations may be due to selective migration, different policies of integration, and less societal discrimination in the US.

Muslim Students in Public Schools

The American public school system poses many challenges for Muslim students. Many Muslim students report feelings of alienation and marginality at school because of their religion (Zine, 2001). Female Muslim students feel they are stereotyped as not valuing education, and feel their success is limited by discouragement from teachers (Mastrilli & Sardo-Brown, 2002). The teaching of Islam in American public schools often includes stereotypical portrayals of Muslims, distortions, omissions, and textbook inaccuracies (Hermansen, 2003; Kassam, 2003), further exacerbating negative perceptions of Muslims already prevalent in the US.

Furthermore, Muslim students often face difficulty adhering to religious requirements due to conflicting school policies. Muslim girls have experienced harassment for wearing their headscarves in school or refusing to wear t-shirts and shorts during physical education classes. In 2003, the Muskogee Public School District in Alabama suspended an 11-year-old Muslim girl twice for refusing to remove her headscarf, claiming that other students were "frightened" by her scarf. The issue could only be resolved after the family went to the courts system and when the US Justice Department intervened on behalf of the family. The school system now has a new dress code that allows for the wearing of headscarves for religious reasons (Associated Press, 2004).

In addition to issues surrounding manner of dress, Muslim students often have difficulty adhering to other religious requirements. For example, mandatory mixed-gender physical education classes commonly found in US public schools directly conflict with Islamic cultural values (Zine, 2001). Muslims are also required to pray five times per day, two of which would fall during the school day (Hoot, Szecsi, & Moosa, 2003). In addition, the special Jum'ah prayer requires group prayer at a certain time on Friday. Securing accommodations for prayer within a busy public school schedule can prove challenging. Adhering to dietary requirements in school cafeterias may also pose a challenge for Muslim students as most devout Muslims follow strict dietary rules based on religiously sanctioned halal and pork-free food products not commonly found in public school cafeterias (Hoot et al., 2003). Although adhering to many traditions such as these is not required before puberty, some Muslim parents encourage their children to follow religious practices at a younger age. Such institutionalized imposition of American cultural values which directly contradict Islamic religious tenets sets an environment of failure and alienation, which, when internalized by these adolescents, can lower self-esteem.

Some school districts across the country have made accommodations for Muslim students. For example, at Carver Elementary School in San Diego, students in the Arabic language program are given the option of praying at the specific times needed during the day. In Dearborn, Michigan, where at least one in three students is of Middle Eastern descent, two vacation days are scheduled during Ramadan (Dotinga, 2007). On October 11, 2007, the Cliffside Park school district in New Jersey closed for the first time in observance of Eid al-Fitr, the last day of Ramadan (Fagan, 2007). Schools have also recently made changes in their lunch offerings to accommodate Muslims students' dietary requirements. Schools in Dearborn, Michigan also give students the option of eating hot dogs and chicken nuggets slaughtered in accordance with Muslim law (Dotinga, 2007). However, although required by law, accommodations may not be easily acquired and may stigmatize Muslim students. Many Muslim families are met with resistance when requesting accommodations. Critics claim that Muslim students are being given accommodations not available to other religious groups (Dorell, 2007; Fagan, 2007)

Partly because of these challenges, some parents choose to send their children to private Islamic schools. In 2001, there were 170 private Islamic schools in the US, with each school serving an average of 150 students (Nimer, 2002). Muslim parents choose Islamic schools for a variety of reasons. For example, many view sending their child to an Islamic school as an important way to ensure their child feels a sense of Muslim identity and belonging (McCreery, Jones, & Holmes, 2007). These schools follow Muslim beliefs and practices, familiarizing their students with Islamic sources of knowledge and ethical values. Furthermore, in contrast to public schools, Islamic schools conform to halal dietary standards, and schedule classes and activities around daily prayers, Ramadan, and other significant Islamic holidays. Thus, students are able to easily adhere to their religious requirements while in attendance. In addition, Islamic schools place significant emphasis on reading, math, and science and adhere to high academic standards. Parents send their children to Islamic schools not only to teach them Muslim values and practices, but also to ensure that their child is competitive for jobs and college (Nimer, 2002).

Teacher Perspectives of Muslim Students

Although Muslim students are entering the nation's public school classrooms in large numbers, teachers often have a limited knowledge of Islam (Hoot et al., 2003). In their survey of 218 preservice teachers, Mastrilli and Sardo-Brown (2002) found that an alarming number indicated an extremely limited knowledge of the Islamic faith or the extensive global influence of Islam. For example, one in seven respondents indicated that there were less than 20,000 Muslims in the US. In reality, it is estimated that the figure is close to six million. In addition, an alarming one-third of the participants did not know how to answer the question about the commonalities they shared with Muslims. What was even more surprising was the finding that one in seven preservice teachers indicated that they had nothing in common at all with Muslims. One-fourth of responses did not respond when asked how they would facilitate the learning of an Islamic student in their classroom. Finally, about one-third of the participants reported a negative reaction upon hearing the word Islam. Thus, not only are teachers extremely limited in their understanding and knowledge about the cultural background of their Islamic students, but they may also be influenced by the anti-Muslim sentiments common in post-9/11 US.

Findings from a Study of Muslim Parent and Teacher Perspectives

Learning to navigate through this historical period holds difficulties for everyone, but Muslim immigrants who send their children to schools in the US face particular challenges (Leonard, 2003). To date, very little research has been conducted with young Muslim children or their immigrant families. In our own research study, we extended our previous work examining the influence of teacher perceptions of value differences between themselves and parents on their math and literacy expectations for their students. In a three-wave longitudinal study of 191 immigrant children of Muslim and non-Muslim backgrounds, we have drawn a sample from both Islamic and public schools. Mean age of the children was 6.35 years ($SD = 0.72$). There were 101 Islamic school students and 90 public school students (54% girls and 46% boys). All students had at least one parent who was not born in the US and at least one parent who is fluent in English.

In our preliminary analyses from the first wave of data, we asked teachers from Muslim and public school settings to rate their students' academic competence in a number of ways. We measured teacher expectations with a scale originally used in our previous work (see Hauser-Cram et al., 2003) which asked the teachers to rate the child's current reading and math skills in comparison to their same-age peers. Teachers were also asked to rate how well they expected the child to perform in reading and math the following year and then at the end of fifth grade. The results showed that there is evidence for potential cultural incongruence when it comes to teachers in Islamic and public schools. Islamic school teachers, who are all Muslim and who presumably have much deeper understanding of the culture of the child, held higher academic expectations than their public school teachers when it comes to immigrant students' literacy ($M=2.52$, $SD=0.81$ vs. $M=2.07$, $SD=0.94$), $t\ (189)=3.50$, $p < 0.01$, and math ($M=2.44$, $SD=0.74$ vs. $M=2.09$, $SD=0.85$), $t\ (187)=3.05$, $p < 0.01$. Because the students were not randomly assigned to Islamic vs. public schools, it is possible that these differences in teacher perception may be due to certain parent characteristics that we are not controlling for in our design. However, given the findings from our previous study about the implications of value differences that shapes teachers' perspectives even after controlling for student cognitive functioning at school entry, it is plausible to argue that teachers' views of immigrant students shape their ratings of their students who come from cultural backgrounds that are different from teachers.

In order to further understand how teachers view immigrant Muslim families, we also asked them to rate each parent in terms of a number of domains that are highly relevant to education. Specifically, we asked teachers to rate how involved each child's parents were on the following four areas: "making sure that s/he can take advantage of schooling (e.g. getting to school on time, dressed properly, with materials)," "communicating with the teacher or school," "working at school," and "advocating for the child." Teachers were provided with the response choices of "don't know," "not very much," "somewhat," and "quite a lot." The results show that Islamic school teachers ($M=3.16$, $SD=0.71$) rated their parents as significantly more involved than public school teachers ($M=2.95$, $SD=0.63$), $t\ (188)=2.12$, $p < 0.05$. Again, it is difficult to make any causal assumption about the implications of school type beyond highlighting the notion that when parents and teachers share similar cultural background, parents are more likely to be involved in schools.

We also wanted to know more about the degree to which teachers are aware of potential barriers to academic success for their students across two school types. We asked teachers to rate potential barriers to each of their students' academic success. The academic scale comprised the following factors: "English proficiency," "tardiness/absenteeism," "special learning problems," "poor academic skills," "lack of motivation/interest," and "attentional problems." Psychological barriers were assessed with the items "child health," "emotional upset/family crises," "difficulty with peer relationships," and "psychological problems." Teachers responded using the items "not a problem," "minor problem," "moderate problem," and "serious problem." Public school teachers rated their students as having significantly more academic barriers than Islamic school teachers did ($M=7.43$, $SD=2.34$ vs. $M=9.21$, $SD=4.39$, respectively), $t\ (187)=-3.52$, $p < 0.01$ and psychological barriers ($M=4.51$, $SD=1.19$ vs. $M=4.99$, $SD=1.93$, respectively), $t\ (186)=-2.06$, $p < 0.05$. It is plausible, then, to argue that somehow when teachers are not quite in congruence with parents in terms of cultural background, teachers are more likely to report barriers for parents.

These findings, albeit preliminary and only descriptive at this point, show significant variation across school contexts in terms of how teachers view their immigrant students and parents. Islamic school teachers held significantly higher academic expectations for their students than public school teachers held for their students, rated their parents as more involved, and rated their students as having fewer academic and psychological barriers. Thus, these findings provide evidence for the potential negative consequences of cultural congruence for the academic and psychological well-being of immigrant students in public schools. As we move forward with this longitudinal study, it is our goal to gain a more nuanced understanding of parent–teacher interactions across these school contexts.

Our research also included qualitative data to examine the experiences of Muslim parents in the US. Parents were asked to describe instances where they have experienced discrimination in their daily lives. Responses revealed themes discussed previously in the chapter, including experiencing negative attitudes toward Muslims. One parent wrote, "because I cover my hair anybody knows that I'm Muslim. So when I drive or when I walk anybody [sic] look at me or at the children like we are different ... did not feel that before 2001." Another parent also disclosed experiencing negative reactions to her Islamic heritage, writing "The people stare at you. They give us passing remarks; especially when shopping." A third parent wrote, "they do treat us different than American people. They look at your name (Example Mohammed or Ahmad)" and stated she experienced "some un-welcomed comments about being Muslim or Arab." Yet another parent wrote, "People judge that since my husband has a Muslim name that we are Arabic/Muslim and are terrorist [*sic*]." Parents also wrote about discrimination experienced by their children. One parent wrote, "My kids were playing with neighbors' kids. My kids fought with them because of that neighbors' kids told to my kids 'we don't like Muslims.' My kids feel bad." Parents also disclosed their difficulties assimilating into the American culture. For example, one parent wrote that her family experienced "Problem [sic] to keep up between our traditions, culture and the life style here in the US." Another parent wrote that she experienced difficulty "Teaching our son our cultural values while enabling him to assimilate."

Our qualitative data reveals the discrimination and difficulties with assimilation that Muslim families in both Islamic and public schools experience in contemporary America. However, public school and Islamic school parents did contrast in their description of their children's school experiences. One public school parent expressed frustration about the scarcity of Muslims in their neighborhood, stating, "There is no[t] enough Muslim children around us." Another parent wrote, "I cannot talk with teachers because I don't understand them." In contrast, an Islamic school parent wrote, "Thanks God, in the Islamic school [*sic*] there is rarely stress due to being immigrant, just small school issues." In conjunction with our descriptive quantitative data, these results demonstrate that the cultural congruous context in Islamic schools may alleviate some of the stresses experienced by immigrant Muslim parents. In contrast, in the potentially culturally incongruous public school context, the difficulties experienced by immigrant Muslims in the outside world may also be experienced in their child's school.

V Addressing Adverse Affects of Cultural Congruence in Teacher Training

There have been several approaches to address the negative implications of growing cultural incongruence between home and school cultures for certain student populations. These efforts can be grouped under two categories: school-based organizational interventions and teacher-based interventions. The school-level approaches focus on involving parents in the educational process, making sure that the school curriculum reflects the lives of diverse students in a given school system, and providing additional services for certain groups of parents. The teacher-level approaches focus on professional development to ensure that teachers are culturally competent, sensitive, and professionally prepared to address the needs of a diverse student population.

In her review of the literature on education needs of young children of immigrants, birth to age 8, Takanishi (2004) noted that "the most serious current challenge is the preparation of teachers ... to educate newcomer children more effectively" (p. 72). The fields of education and psychology have embraced the idea that training school professionals should involve multicultural training to work with diverse students (Villegas & Lucas, 2002). Although there have been many attempts to educate school-based professionals in order to increase tolerance, embrace diversity, and overcome stereotypes (e.g. Marshall, 1999), there is little empirical research regarding the effectiveness of these programs and when evidence is provided, it is often conflicting (Rogers-Sirin, 2008). Despite these efforts, research consistently shows that teachers feel insufficiently prepared to address the needs of their diverse learners who come from an increasingly large number of countries and languages. So what is the best way to make sure that teachers in today's schools are ready to serve the students in our public schools?

A quick review of teacher-based intervention efforts show that there have been three general trends in preparing teachers for a diverse school population. The first approach is the focus on learning the backgrounds of different cultures. Typically focused on the most common racial and ethnic groups, this approach provides basic information about specific cultures, providing historical, anthropological, and at times, psychological profiles of different racial or ethnic groups. Though this approach may work with school systems where there are only a few groups represented, in most cases, a large number of countries, languages, and cultures are represented in the same school, or classroom, which makes it almost impractical to follow this model. Furthermore, as noted elsewhere in this chapter and book, several districts in the US are experiencing large influxes of immigrants in a short period of time, making it almost impossible to track and prepare teachers by focusing singularly on teaching them about certain groups. Furthermore, even when a stable group is represented in a certain school system, in many cases families within a certain group differ greatly from one another. As such, without falling into certain stereotypes, it is hard to make any use of the general knowledge about a certain group.

The second approach, self-awareness, was originally developed within the field of psychology and has found its way into several teacher-education programs. Workshops and professional educational sessions have been devoted to raising teachers' understanding of their own cultural backgrounds in order to appreciate the role of culture in the lives of humans in general. The rationale behind this approach is that if the teachers were in touch with their own background and their stereotypes and misconceptions about different cultures along the way, they would be more likely to relate to the experiences of other people who come from different ethnic backgrounds (Phinney, 1990). In most cases, those who are open to self-awareness would welcome such efforts to educate themselves about their biases, but there will always be those who simply do not take part in such platforms and when they are required to conform, they will leave the training more biased than before.

The third approach, professional standards, is rooted in the larger movement toward professionalization of the field of teaching overall (Brabeck et al., 2000; Sirin, Brabeck, Satiani, & Rogers-Sirin, 2003). According to this approach, serving the needs of each student is an ethical requirement demanded by professional standards outlined by school-related professions. An ethical teacher, or school professional, must do whatever is needed to make sure that each child is served regardless of their background. Unlike the prior two models, this approach is a specified job requirement. Serving the needs of each student, no matter who they are, is not a personal choice, but an ethical requirement to be sensitive to the needs of each child.

Special Recommendations for Teachers Serving Muslim Students

Hoot et al. (2003) compiled a list of information teachers should have in order to better support the rights and needs of Muslim children. Among their suggestions includes providing a safe place for Muslim students to pray. Teachers should also have knowledge of Islamic dietary needs. The Qur'an distinguishes between *haram* (forbidden) and *halal* (permissible) food, and pork products are forbidden. Furthermore, attention to the preparation and serving of food must also be attended to. For example, simply removing pepperoni from pizza may not make the pizza acceptable because of the possibility of remaining pork grease.

Hoot and colleagues (2003) also emphasize the importance of teachers understanding Muslim students' fasting practices. During Ramadan, the ninth month in the Islamic lunar calendar, Muslims abstain from all food and drink between sunrise and sunset. At these times, teachers can provide a separate area during snack and lunch for students who choose to fast. In addition, teachers should ensure that children do not undertake too much strenuous physical activity while they are fasting.

The authors also stress the importance of understanding the Muslim belief in modesty, particularly its relevance to clothing choices for Muslim children. Muslims are expected to wear clothes that are modest and cover most of their body. Clothing requirements may have implications for gym time, for example, where children may be given shorts to wear. Hoot and colleagues (2003) encourage teachers to provide sweatpants as an alternative for Muslim children.

Gender and privacy issues are also an important consideration for teachers of Muslim students. In mixed-gender situations such as physical education classes and co-ed bathrooms, teachers should be conscious of Muslim restrictions regarding mixing of the sexes. Furthermore, Muslim children may feel uncomfortable changing and showering in public or common areas such as gym locker rooms. In addition, teachers should provide a method for Muslim children to fulfill their religious obligation to wash their private areas after using the bathroom (Hoot et al., 2003).

Hoot and colleagues (2003) also state that teachers should be aware of Muslim beliefs and practices that may be relevant when developing music and art projects. Islamic law prohibits loud, violent, or depressing music. In addition, when engaging in holiday celebrations, teachers should be cognizant of the fact that Muslim parents may be concerned about the pagan origins of holidays such as Halloween and Valentine's day.

Finally, Hoot and colleagues (2003) state that teachers must intervene when Muslim students are being teased. When teachers observe Muslim students being teased for their clothing or dietary regulations, for example, the authors encourage teachers to share the reasons for these traditions with other children in a respectful, open environment.

VI Conclusions

In this chapter we highlighted current demographic trends that show an increasingly diverse student body and continuingly stable teaching profession that is overwhelmingly White and middle-class. The cultural-congruence model that we presented suggests that when there is a greater divide between how teachers and parents view certain cultural and educational values, students are the ones who pay the price with lowered teacher expectations, disproportionate special education referrals, and placement in lower educational tracks. At times the general mood of the nation turns negative toward certain communities, as it has been recently against Muslims or undocumented immigrants, and the potential implications of incongruence becomes even more problematic for children and families who come from these communities. In our own study, we found that Islamic school teachers held significantly higher academic expectations, viewed their parents as more involved, and perceived their students as having fewer academic and psychological barriers to their academic success compared to public school teachers. Given the difficulty in diversifying the teaching profession, it is important to turn the focus to teacher training and more productive teacher–parent collaboration. In the light of current demographic trends and the increasingly hostile anti-immigrant environment that seems to have emerged in the public discourse, we will need to pay even more attention to how school professionals perceive their students' culture. With our specific focus on Muslim immigrants in this chapter we hope to introduce Muslim families and special needs of Muslim students in particular with the hope that with more understanding we can begin to build effective bridges between teachers and families regardless of their background.

Note

1. Although the labels "Muslim" and "Arab" are often used interchangeably to refer to the same group of people in the public discourse, they signify two distinct characteristics of a person; the former referring to one's religion and the latter referring to one's ethnicity. Not all Arabs are Muslims and not all Muslims are Arabs. Indeed, one out of four Arab Americans are Muslims and the remainder are Christians.

References

Associated Press. (2004). *Muslim student, Oklahoma district settle hijab lawsuit.* Retrieved January 5, 2008, from www.firstamendmentcenter.org/news.aspx?id=13379.

Au, K., & Kawakami, A. (1994). Cultural congruence in instruction. In E. Hollins, J. King, & W. Hayman (Eds.), *Teaching diverse populations* (pp. 5–23). New York: State University of New York Press.

Baumrind, D. (1966). Effects of authoritative parental control on child behavior. *Child Development, 37*(4), 887–907.

Brabeck, M.M., Rogers, L.A., Sirin, S., Henderson, J., Benvenuto, M., Weaver, M., et al. (2000). Increasing ethical sensitivity to racial and gender intolerance in schools: Development of the racial ethical sensitivity test. *Ethics and Behavior, 10*(2), 119–137.

Bronfenbrenner, U. (1979). *The ecology of human development.* Cambridge, MA: Harvard University Press.

Capps, R., Fix, M.E., Ost, J., Reardon-Anderson, J., & Passel, J.S. (2005). *Health and well-being of young children of immigrants.* Washington, DC: Urban Institute.

Chao, R.K. (2001). Extending research on the consequences of parenting style for Chinese Americans and European Americans. *Child Development, 72*(6), 1832–1843.

Condron, D.J. (2007). Stratification and educational sorting: Explaining ascriptive inequalities in early childhood reading group placement. *Social Problems, 54*(1), 139–160.

Deane, C., & Fears, D. (2006, March 9). Negative perception of Islam increasing. *Washington Post.* Retrieved April 23, 2007, from www.washingtonpost.com/wp-dyn/content/article/2006/03/08/AR2006030802221.html.

Deaux, K. (2006). A nation of immigrants: Living our legacy. *Journal of Social Issues, 62*(3), 633–651.

Delpit, L. (1995). *Other people's children: cultural conflict in the classroom.* New York: The New Press.

De Valenzuela, J.S., Copeland, S.R., Qi, C.H., & Park, M. (2006). Examining educational equity: revisiting the disproportionate representation in special education. *Exceptional Children, 72*(4), 425–441.

Dorell, O. (2007, July 26). Some say schools giving Muslims special treatment. *USA Today.* Retrieved 5 January, 2008, from www.usatoday.com/news/nation/2007-07-25-muslim-special-treatment-from-schools_N.htm.

Dotinga, R. (2007, July 12). Public schools grapple with Muslim prayer. *The Christian Science Monitor.* Retrieved 5 January, 2008, from www.csmonitor.com/2007/0712/p01s03-ussc.html.

Epstein, J.L. (1983). *Effects on parents of teacher practices in parent involvement.* Baltimore, MD: Johns Hopkins University, Center for Social Organization of Schools.

Fagan, A. (2007, October 2). Muslims' needs roiling schools: Fast-growing religion forces making of accommodations. *The Washington Times.* Retrieved January 5, 2008, from www.washingtontimes.com/news/2007/oct/02/muslims-needs32roiling-schools/.

Federal Bureau of Investigation. (2002). *2001 Hate crime report.* Retrieved January 5, 2008, from www.fbi.gov/filelink.html?file=/ucr/01hate.pdf.

Gallup. (2007). *Gallup's pulse of democracy: Immigration.* Retrieved January 5, 2008, from www.gallup.com/poll/1660/Immigration.aspx.

Gill, S., & Reynolds, A.J. (2000). Educational expectations and school achievement of urban African American children. *Journal of School Psychology, 37*, 403–424.

Grewal, I. (2003). Transnational America: Race, gender and citizenship after 9/11. *Social Identities: Journal for the Study of Race, Nation & Culture, 9*(4), 535–561.

Hauser-Cram, P., Sirin, S.R., & Stipek, D. (2003). When teachers' and parents' values differ: Teachers' ratings of academic competence in children from low-income families. *Journal of Educational Psychology, 95*(4), 813–820.

Hermansen, M. (2003). How to put the genie back in the bottle: "Identity Islam" and Muslim youth cultures in America. In O. Safi (Ed.), *Progressive Muslims: On justice, gender and pluralism* (pp. 306–319). Oxford: Oneworld Publications.

Hernandez, D.J., Denton, N.A., & Macartney, S.E. (2008). *U.S. Nationwide data, Circumstances of U.S. Children by Race-Ethnicity or Country of Origin.* Albany, NY: University at Albany, Center for Social and Demographic Analysis (CSDA), Retrieved February 24, 2008, from http://mumford.albany.edu/children/data_list_national.htm.

Holbrook, T. (2005, February 7). Muslim garb spurs dress-code protest. *The Courier Journal,* Retrieved April 23, 2007, from www.courier-journal.com.

Hoot, J.L., Szecsi, T., & Moosa, S. (2003). What teachers of young children should know about Islam. *Early Childhood Education Journal, 31*(2), 85–90.

Hosp, J.L., & Reschly, D.J. (2004). Disproportionate representation of minority students in special education: Academic, demographic, and economic predictors. *Exceptional Children, 70*(12), 185–200.

Huntington, S.P. (2004). *Who are we? The challenges to America's national identity.* New York: Simon and Schuster.

Jussim, L., Eccles, J., & Madon, S. (1996). Social perceptions, social stereotypes, and teacher expectations. In M.P. Zanna (Ed.), *Advances in experimental social psychology* (vol. 28, pp. 281–388). San Diego, CA: Academic Press.

Kassam, T. (2003). On being a scholar of Islam. In O. Safi (Ed.), *Progressive Muslims: On justice, gender and pluralism* (pp. 128–145). Oxford: Oneworld Publications.

Kosmin, B.A., Mayer, E., & Keysar, A. (2001). *American religious identification survey.* New York: City University of New York.

Ladson-Billings, G. (1995). Toward a theory of culturally relevant pedagogy. *American Educational Research Journal, 32*(3), 465–491.

Lasky, S. (2000). The cultural and emotional politics of teacher–parent interactions. *Teaching and Teacher Education, 16,* 843–860.

Leonard, K.I. (2003). *Muslims in the United States: The state of research.* New York: Russell Sage Foundation.

Maira, S. (2004). Youth culture, citizenship and globalization: South Asian Muslim youth in the United States after September 11th. *Comparative Studies of South Asia, Africa, and the Middle East, 24,* 221–235.

Malone, N., Baluja, K.F., Costanzo, J.M., & Davis, C.J. (2003). *The foreign-born population: 2000,* US Census Bureau. Retrieved January 5, 2008, from www.census.gov/prod/2003pubs/c2kbr-34.pdf.

Marshall, P.L. (1999). Teachers' racial identity and the single course in multicultural education. *Action in Teacher Education, 20,* 50–69.

Mastrilli, R., & Sardo-Brown, D. (2002). Novice teachers' cases: A vehicle for reflective practice. *Education, 123*(1), 56–62.

McCreery, E., Jones, L., & Holmes, R. (2007). Why do Muslim parents want Muslim schools? *Early Years: An International Journal of Research and Development, 27*(3), 203–219.

Nimer, M. (2002). *The North American Muslim resource guide: Muslim community life in the United States and Canada.* New York: Routledge, Taylor & Francis.

Oakes, J. (1985). *Keeping track: How schools restructure inequality.* New Haven, CT: Yale University Press.

Ogbu, J. (1982). Cultural discontinuities and schooling. *Anthropology and Education Quarterly, 13*(4), 290–307.

Ogbu, J.U. (1993). Variability in minority school performance: A problem in search of an explanation. In E. Jacob & C. Jordan (Eds.), *Minority education: Anthropological perspectives* (pp. 83–111). Norwood, NJ: Ablex Publishing Corporation.

Olsen, L. (1997). *Made in America: Immigrant students in our public schools.* New York: New Press.

Osher, D., Cartledge, G., Oswald, D., Sutherland, K.S., Artiles, A.J., & Coutinho, M. (2004). Cultural and linguistic competency and disproportionate representation. In R.B. Rutherford, M.M. Quinn, & S.R. Mathur (Eds.), *Handbook of research in emotional and behavioral disorders* (pp. 54–77). New York: Guilford Press.

Pallas, A.M., Entwisle, D.R., Alexander, K.L., & Stluka, M.F. (1994). Ability-group effects: Instructional, social, or institutional? *Sociology of Education, 67,* 27–46.

Pew Research Center. (2007). *Muslim Americans: Middle class and mostly mainstream.* Retrieved May 30, 2007, from http://pewresearch.org/pubs/483/muslim-americans.

Phelan, P., Davidson, A.L., & Yu, H.C. (1991). Students' multiple worlds: Navigating the borders of family, peer, and school cultures. In P. Phelan & A.L. Davidson (Eds.), *Cultural diversity: Implications for education* (pp. 52–88). New York: Teachers College Press.

Phinney, J.S. (1990). Ethnic identity in adolescents and adults: Review of the research. *Psychological Bulletin, 108*, 499–514.

Rogers-Sirin, L. (2008) Approaches to multicultural training for professionals: A guide for choosing an appropriate program. *Professional Psychology: Research and Practice, 39*(3), 313–319.

Rueda, R., Artiles, A.J., Salazar, J., & Higareda, I. (2002). An analysis of special education as a response to the diminished academic achievement of Chicano/Latino students: an update. In R.R. Valencia (Ed.), *Chicano school failure and success: Past, present, and future* (2nd ed., pp. 310–332). London: Routledge/Falmer.

Sen, A. (2004). How does culture matter? In V. Rao & M. Walton (Eds.), *Culture and public action* (pp. 37–58). Stanford, CA: Stanford University Press.

Sirin, S.R., Brabeck, M.M., Satiani, A., & Rogers-Sirin, L. (2003). Validation of a measure of ethical sensitivity and examination of the effects of previous multicultural and ethics courses on ethical sensitivity. *Ethics and Behavior, 13*(3), 221–235.

Slater, R. (2008). American teachers: What do they believe? *Education Next, 8*(1), 46–52.

Suárez-Orozco, C., & Suárez-Orozco, M.M. (2001). *Children of immigration.* Cambridge, MA: Harvard University Press.

Swiney, C.F. (2006) Racial profiling of Arabs and Muslims in the US: Historical, empirical, and legal analysis applied to the war on terrorism. *Muslim World Journal of Human Rights, 3*(1). Retrieved January 5, 2008, from www.bepress.com/mwjhr/vol. 3/iss1/art3.

Takanishi, R. (2004). Leveling the playing field: Supporting immigrant children from birth to eight. *Future of children, 14*(2), 61–80.

US Census Bureau. (2000). *United States Census 2000.* Retrieved January 5, 2008, from www.census.gov/main/www/cen2000.html.

US Department of Education. (2007). *The condition of education 2007.* Retrieved January 5, 2008, from http://nces.ed.gov/pubs2007/2007064.pdf.

Villegas, A.J. (1988). School failure and cultural mismatch: Another view. *The Urban Review, 20*, 253–265.

Villegas, A.J., & Lucas, T. (2002). Preparing culturally responsive teachers: Rethinking the curriculum. *Journal of Teacher Education, 53*(1), 20–32.

Wheelock, A. (1992). *Crossing the tracks.* New York: Norton Press.

Zine, J. (2001). Muslim youth in Canadian schools: Education and the politics of religious identity. *Anthropology and Education Quarterly, 32*(4), 399–423.

Zogby International. (2004). *Muslims in the American public square: Shifting political winds and fallout from 9/11, Afghanistan, and Iraq.* Retrieved January 5, 2008, from www.zogby.com/AmericanMuslims2004.pdf.

9 Special Educational Needs of Children in Immigrant Families

Dylan Conger and Elena L. Grigorenko

As demonstrated in chapters throughout this volume, the research community has accumulated a substantial amount of knowledge on the academic achievement and English-language needs of young newcomers to the US. There is also a growing body of research on the physical and mental health prospects of immigrant youth. In stark contrast, and in spite of an abundance of anecdotal evidence, very little empirical work has examined immigrant youth's rates of disabilities and participation in special education programs. This chapter provides an overview of what we do know so far about immigrant children and special education. We first provide empirical evidence from three data sources on the rates of disability and special education among immigrant youth compared to native-born children. We find that immigrant youth are less likely to participate in special education programs and offer some explanations for their underrepresentation. We conclude with implications for policy and practice.

Immigrants and Disability Rates: Selective Migration?

The various theories regarding the health and education outcomes of immigrant children in the US have been well described in earlier chapters. To summarize, though immigrants tend to be poorer and less proficient in English than native-born individuals, most immigration scholars agree that immigrants are a positively selected group who possess a strong work ethic, cultural cohesion, and an optimistic outlook that benefits their children (e.g., Feliciano, 2005; Kao & Tienda, 1995). At the same time, they encounter substantial barriers that may prevent them from receiving the services they require in times of need, such as proper medical care and educational services. Many of these barriers will be described more fully below.

To begin our inquiry into the special education rates of immigrant children, we first compare their rates of disability to those of native-born children. Selective migration could render the immigrant population quite different from the native-born population on underlying disabilities. Parents with disabled children may be more or less likely to emigrate depending upon their resources and the quality of the education and care provided to special needs children in their home countries relative to the services provided in the US. For instance, if parents with disabled children tend to be less resourced or less able to migrate than other potential migrants, then foreign-born children in the US can be expected to have a lower rate of disability than native-born children.

Related work on the health of immigrant children and youth suggest mixed findings. On some surveys, immigrant parents are more likely to report that their children are in fair or poor health than native-born parents (Capps, Fix, Ost, Reardon-Anderson, & Passel, 2004; Capps, Ku, & Fix, 2004; Hernandez, 2004; Hernandez & Charney, 1998). Yet they are also less likely to report that their children have chronic conditions or neurological impairments (Hernandez & Charney, 1998) and immigrant adolescents are less likely to report physical or psychological problems than native-born adolescents (Harker, 2001; Harris, 1999). And despite the lower rates of prenatal care among immigrant mothers, their children have lower prevalence of both low birth weight and infant mortality than the children of native-born mothers of the same ethnicity (Hernandez & Charney, 1998).

This chapter reports on immigrant children's reported disabilities as compared to native-born using data from two sources. The first is the Early Childhood Longitudinal Study-Kindergarten Cohort (ECLS-K), a national probability sample of kindergarteners established in the US in 2000.[1] The second is the National Survey of America's Families (NSAF), a national sample of adults established in 2002. Both data sources report on the disability and special education rates of children and permit distinctions to be made between children of immigrants and children of native-born individuals. Following methods from earlier chapters that use the ECLS-K (see Van Hook & Baker, this volume), we identify children of immigrants as such if at least one of the parents reported being foreign-born during any of the interviews. Using the NSAF, we focus on the difference between foreign-born and native-born children.[2] Nativity groups can also be examined separately by race/ethnicity and gender in both data sources. The two data sources rely on parental reports, thus the reliability may be compromised if immigrant parents are more or less likely than native-born parents to report disability or participation in special education.

Using both data sources, we find some difference in disability rates between native-born and children of immigrants (see Table 9.1 for ECLS-K and Table 9.2 for NSAF). Using the ECLS-K, a random sample of US kindergarteners, we find that the parents of immigrant children are less likely to report that their children have a learning disability (5.7% vs. 12.4%). Though parental reports of other disabilities are lower among the children of immigrants than among natives (8.2% vs. 8.6%), the difference is not statistically significant at conventional levels. There is also substantial variation in the magnitude of the difference across racial/ethnic groups. Immigrant children are reported by their parents to have far lower rates of learning disabilities among Black, Mexican, and other Hispanic children, but not among White children (insufficient numbers of Asian children of natives prevented comparisons among Asians). The gap in learning disabilities between Mexican-origin children and Hispanic children of native-born is roughly 11 percentage points. Only the Hispanic (non-Mexican) immigrant children have lower rates of other disabilities than their co-ethnic native-born peers, however. To summarize, though some of the differences are statistically insignificant, immigrants of Black and Hispanic origin are either less or equally likely to be disabled than co-ethnic native-born children. The differences among Whites are insignificant and the differences among Asians cannot be determined.

Table 9.2 provides results from the NSAF in which the operationalization of being immigrant is slightly different (foreign-born vs. all native-born), disability is reported

Table 9.1 Disability Rates by Immigrant Status and Race/Ethnicity, ECLS-K

	Learning disability		*Other disability*	
	Children of immigrants	*Children of natives*	*Children of immigrants*	*Children of natives*
All children	5.7	12.4	8.2	8.6
Asian	3.0	NA	6.3	NA
Black	1.3	9.2	3.0	6.1
Mexican	3.5	14.5	9.6	11.8
Other Hispanic (excluding Mexican-origin immigrants)	7.0	14.5	5.6	11.8
White	11.6	13.0	10.4	8.8

Data source: ECLS-K.

Notes

i All differences between children of immigrants and children of natives are statistically significant at $p < 0.05$ except for the following: learning disabilities – white; other disability – all children, white, black, Mexican.

ii The sample size for Asian children of natives was too small to reliably calculate the average.

iii Percentages are weighted to reflect national population.

Table 9.2 Disability Rates by Nativity Status and Race/Ethnicity, NSAF

	Foreign-born	*Native-born*
All children	6.9	10.2
Asian/Pacific Islander	8.1	5.4
Black	4.6	11.5
White	6.5	10.1
Hispanic	6.4	10.2
Non-Hispanic	7.4	10.2

Data source: Urban Institute's National Survey of America's Families Focal Child File, 2002. Disability question: "Does (CHILD) have a physical, learning, or mental health condition that [limits (his/her) participation in the usual kinds of activities done by most children (his/her) age/limits (his/her) ability to do regular school work]?"

Notes

i All differences between native-born and foreign-born are statistically significant at $p < 0.05$. except for the difference within Asian/Pacific Islanders.

ii Percentages are weighted to reflect national population.

in one category, and ethnic groups are defined slightly differently. Despite these differences, the general findings are similar to those using the ECLS-K with parents of foreign-born children reporting lower or equivalent rates of disability to parents of native-born children. Using the NSAF, we are also able to compare Asian native-born to Asian foreign-born and we find that the rates are slightly higher for immigrant children but not statistically different from zero.

The results from both of these datasets suggest that the children of immigrants are either less likely to be disabled or that immigrant parents are less likely to report a disability than native-born parents. If the former explanation is what drives these findings, then there may be some credence to the theory that parents with disabled children from other nations may be less likely to emigrate to the US than parents with non-disabled children. The fact that we observe lower rates of disability among children born abroad (not just those whose parents are immigrants) supports this selective migration story. Correspondingly, immigrant children may be less (or, at most, equally) likely to require special education services. In the next section, we explore whether higher or lower rates of special education participation are observed for immigrants relative to native-born children.

Immigrant Receipt of Special Education: Disproportionate Under- or Overrepresentation?

Despite the absence of much empirical work, there is a great deal of anecdotal and small-sample evidence that immigrant children receive special education services at a rate that is not consistent with their need. Interestingly, the concerns originate from two rather different points of view. On the one hand, given the extensive documentation that minorities are over represented in special education, many assume that foreign-born students, because they tend to be racial and linguistic minorities, are over-referred to special education (Schemo, 1992). Some have also examined special education diagnostics, which sometimes associate limited proficiency in English with cognitive limitations (Guillory, 2000).

Others have complained that immigrant students are less likely to be enrolled in special education programs due to communication barriers and the limited availability of bilingual paraprofessionals or combined bilingual/special education classes (Advocates for Children (AFC), 2000). In one qualitative study of immigrants in New York City, for instance, immigrant students were reported by educators to be "over-referred" to special education programs, perhaps reflecting their parents' reluctance to challenge special education diagnoses (Gershberg, 2002).

As mentioned above, however, it appears that immigrants may be slightly less likely to have a disability than native-born children (though caution should be taken since these are reported results). Absent a centralized data source that documents special education use among US students when stratified by place of birth, we have somewhat limited empirical evidence to refute or provide support for these claims. In this section, we use data from three sources to examine the special education rates of the two groups. The first are data from the New York City Department of Education; these data have been reprinted by permission from Conger, Schwartz, and Stiefel (2003). The second two are the same sources described above: the ECLS-K and the NSAF.

Despite reports among some advocates and educators that immigrants are overrepresented in special education programs, the available evidence from all three sources suggests that immigrants are less likely to participate in special education programs than native-born children (see Tables 9.3, 9.4, and 9.5). We begin with data from the New York City Department of Education, which distinguishes between children who are receiving full- vs. part-time special education, the former of which is for students with somewhat more severe disabilities. Unlike the survey data, these data rely on educator diagnoses and, in that respect, may overcome some reporting biases. In addition, in these data, foreign-born children are all those born abroad (the birthplace of parents is not collected). For both types of special education, foreign-born children are substantially less likely to participate, a gap of approximately four points in part-time and three points in full-time. Again, the gaps vary by racial group with the largest gaps found among Hispanics and the smallest among Asian students (Conger et al., 2003). In a companion paper (Conger, Schwartz, & Stiefel, 2007), it was also found that nativity differences in special education rates tend to be larger among children in the higher elementary and middle school grades than among children in the early elementary school grades.

The survey data provide somewhat smaller differences, but again, the rates of participation are generally lower for immigrant than for native-born children. Table 9.4

Table 9.3 Special Education Rates by Nativity Status, New York City Public Schools

	Part-time special education		*Full-time special education*	
	Foreign-born	*Native-born*	*Foreign-born*	*Native-born*
All children	3.1	7.2	2.5	5.9
Asian	2.3	3.4	1.2	1.3
Black	3.7	6.6	3.5	7.1
Hispanic	3.4	7.9	3.6	6.8
White	3.2	8.6	1.4	3.1

Data source: New York City Department of Education. Sample includes 658,951 students who were enrolled in an elementary or middle public school in academic year 1999–2000. Table reprinted from Conger, Schwartz, and Stiefel (2003).

Notes
i All differences between native-born and foreign-born are statistically significant at $p < 0.05$.
ii Part-time special education refers to students who receive services for mild to moderate disabilities, such as speech impediments. Full-time special education refers to students who receive services for more severe disabilities, such as blindness.

Table 9.4 Special Education Rates by Immigrant Status, Disability, and Race/Ethnicity, ECLS-K

	Children of immigrant	*Children of natives*
All children		
Has disability	32.9	34.8
Does not have disability	5.1	4.4
Asian	3.5	NA
Black	2.8	9.4
Mexican	10.7	11.0
Other Hispanic (excluding Mexican-origin immigrants)	8.7	11.0
White	10.6	11.1

Data source: ECLS-K.

Notes
i All differences between children of immigrants and children of natives are statistically significant at $p < 0.05$ except for the following: all children, Mexican, Other Hispanic, and white.
ii The sample size for Asian children of natives was too small to reliably calculate the average.
iii Percentages are weighted to reflect national population.

Table 9.5 Special Education Rates by Nativity Status, Disability, and Race/Ethnicity, NSAF

	Foreign-born	*Native-born*
All children	9.9	11.8
Has disability	57.5	59.4
Does not have disability	6.5	5.6
White	11.0	11.7
Black	5.1	12.1
Asian/Pacific Islander	8.7	6.7
Hispanic	8.0	13.3
Non-Hispanic	11.9	11.5

Data source: Urban Institute's National Survey of America's Families Focal Child File, 2002. Special education question: "Does (CHILD) now receive special education services?" Disability question: "Does (CHILD) have a physical, learning, or mental health condition that [limits (his/her) participation in the usual kinds of activities done by most children (his/her) age/limits (his/her) ability to do regular school work]?"

Notes
i All differences between native-born and foreign-born are statistically significant at $p < 0.05$ except for the differences among whites, Asian Pacific Islanders, and non-Hispanics.
ii Percentages are weighted to reflect national population.

provides the ECLS-K data with the first two rows showing the special education rates for children of immigrants vs. children of natives among those who reported a disability and those who did not. There is no difference in the special education rates between children of immigrants and children of native-born in both categories, suggesting that needs are being met at the same rate for the two groups. A different pattern emerges within racial/ethnic groups, however. Black immigrant children are much less likely to receive special education than Black native-born, 2.8% and 9.4% respectively. The differences among White, Mexican, and other Hispanic children are statistically insignificant, and the difference among Asian children cannot be determined.

The NSAF survey results tell a similar story. First, there is no difference between the average foreign-born and native-born child in special education participation, among both those who report a disability and those who do not report a disability. Second, Black foreign-born children are far less likely to participate than Black immigrant children, 5.1% and 12.1% respectively.

The balance of the evidence presented here suggests three important findings. First, immigrant parents are less likely to report that their children have a disability than native-born parents. Second, most immigrant parents are equally (or slightly less) likely to report that their children receive special education services with one exception: the parents of Black immigrant children are much less likely to report that their child participates in a special education program than the parents of Black native-born children. Third, using school system data, where students are professionally evaluated, immigrant children of all racial/ethnic groups are much less likely to be participating in special education programs, particularly older immigrant children. At the very least, we can confirm that immigrant children are probably not more disabled than their native-born peers. It is also quite possible that immigrant parents are less likely to report a disability, even when one exists. In addition, immigrant children are clearly not overreferred to special education, despite concerns expressed among some advocates. There remains the possibility that they are underreferred, a possibility we discuss in more depth in the next section.

Barriers to Immigrant Receipt of Special Education

The US's limited statistics on the underrepresentation of immigrant children among those receiving special educational services are at odds with what is seen in other developed nations around the world. For example, the literature contains reports that immigrant children are overrepresented in special education in Denmark (Kidde, 1986), Finland (Kivirauma, Klemela, & Rinne, 2006), Switzerland (Lanfranchi, 1993), and Germany (Lanfranchi, 1988; Werning, Loser, & Urban, 2008). There are different hypotheses for why such an overrepresentation occurs. For example, it has been observed that Swiss teachers preferentially refer low-SES and immigrant children (often overlapping groups) to special education; which populations, inevitably, often overlap (Lanfranchi, 2007). Along with these statistics, the literature from other developed countries besides the US contains valuable discussions of the problems of addressing the educational needs of immigrant children in general and immigrant children with special educational needs in particular (for a review, see Sideridis, 2007), and range from discussing the development of specific assessment techniques (Haywood & Wingenfeld, 1992) to offering particular intervention programs (e.g., Kozulin, 2006).

Similarly, the US's limited statistics on the underrepresentation of immigrant children among those receiving special educational services are also at odds with US data on racial/ethnic minorities who are overrepresented in special education (Donovan & Cross, 2002; Hosp & Reschly, 2004; Parrish, 2002; Skiba et al., 2008). This pattern of disproportional representation has been consistently in place for the past four decades (Hosp & Reschly, 2004). Two observations are of interest here. First, this overrepresentation appears to be reported for so-called "soft" (i.e., expert-opinion driven) disabilities, such as mental retardation, behavioral and social-emotional disturbances, and learning difficulties, rather than "hard" (i.e., more objectively determined) disabilities, such as visual or hearing impairments (O'Connor & DeLuca Fernandez, 2006). Most children in special education fall into "soft" categories in general and into one of three most prevalent categories in particular (mental retardation, emotional disturbance, or learning disability, see Parrish, 2002). Second, although the term "overrepresentation," as a phenomenon, refers to all minority groups, in reality, there is much minority/ethnicity/race-specific variation (Donovan & Cross, 2002; Hosp & Reschly, 2004; Parrish, 2002; Skiba et al., 2008). To illustrate, overrepresentation, globally, refers to African American and American Indian/Alaska Native students. Specifically, African American students are disproportionally overrepresented in the categories of mental retardation (risk ratio: 2.24) and emotional disturbance (risk ratio: 1.59). American Indian/Alaska Native students are overrepresented in the category of learning disabilities (risk ratio: 1.24). Hispanic students are overrepresented in some localities and underrepresented in others, but, overall, they are represented at about the same rate as White students nationally. At the other extreme, Asian/Pacific Islander students are underrepresented in almost every category.

Here we explore a number of issues that might be relevant to both appraising and contextualizing the empirical observation of underrepresentation of immigrant youth in special education that was presented above.

In the US, the list of challenges to be faced in addressing the needs of immigrant children with various developmental disabilities is rather long on both sides—that of the service seekers and that of the service providers. This list includes stereotyping, the language barrier, getting parents to seek identification and services for their children, and aspects of both the manifestation and how to deal with specific developmental disabilities in groups of immigrants from different ethnic and cultural backgrounds (Carlin, 1990; Wehrly, 1988). As mentioned above, this section reviews the suspected reasons for underrepresentation, including lack of awareness and knowledge of the services available to immigrant children with special needs in the US, cultural and language barriers between schools and immigrant parents, and the lack of proper identification and measurement procedures.

The Information Challenge

One of the obvious challenges is the lack of information possessed by parents of immigrant children with special needs regarding what their children's special needs might be and what they as parents can do about them. Our previous analysis showing that immigrant parents are less likely to report that their child has a disability, lends some support to this hypothesis. The lack of information and awareness has multiple reasons.

First, many cultures from which the US receives immigrants have very different ideas about disabilities, especially innate developmental disabilities. Cultural interpretations of developmental disabilities (Akamatsu & Cole, 2000), particularly by cultures in which these disabilities are viewed as punishments or curse to the families determine the parental attempts to hide the special needs of their children rather than seek services for them. Thus, it is also important to consider the attitudes toward special educational services that immigrant parents bring with them from their source cultures. Conflicts between attitudes toward disabilities and other aspects of life in their old and new cultures (Snyder, May, Zulcic, & Gabbard, 2005) might, at least partially, be accountable for the apparent underidentification of immigrant children with special needs in the US. For example, in Vietnam, special education, as an educational approach, was introduced only in the early 1990s, with minimal training available to its providers (Huer, Saenz, & Doan, 2001). Correspondingly, the concept of special education as reported by Vietnamese immigrant parents is very different from the reality of special education in the US, the Vietnamese concept being more punitive and isolationist than remediating and inclusive. The mismatch between the feelings of shame for having a child with a disability that is characteristic of the attitudes toward disabilities in Vietnam and the constructive approaches to special needs in the US often result in the inability of Vietnamese immigrant parents to capitalize on what is available to their children with special needs in the US, or even the outright refusal of services (Huer et al., 2001). Lack of understanding of developmental disabilities by immigrant parents has been reported to result in blaming the child for a lack of effort or motivation rather than appreciating his/her difficulties (Zhou & Bankston, 1998).

Second, given that the majority of immigrants to the US are from developing countries, where the tradition of special services for children with developmental disabilities is either absent or not well-developed, many immigrant parents do not know and cannot even imagine the services that their children may be eligible for in the US. There is evidence, for example, that immigrant Latino families tend to lack insurance more often than families of individuals born in the US and that, when they have health insurance, they tend to underutilize it (Brown, Ojeda, Wyn, & Levan, 2002), misunderstand services (Earner, 2007), or report difficulties with accessing services (Arcia, Skinner, Bailey, & Correa, 2001; Heller, Markwardt, Rowitz, & Farber, 1994; Miranda & Matheny, 2000). There is also evidence that immigrant parents of children with developmental disabilities are particularly likely to report difficulty obtaining relevant information, understanding and accessing services, and experience dissatisfaction with the quality of services, they report these events at heightened frequency with respect to services provided to children and adolescents with developmental disabilities (Bailey, Skinner, Correa et al., 1999; Bailey, Skinner, Rodriguez, Gut, & Correa, 1999; Zetlin, Padron, & Wilson, 1996). These difficulties seem to magnify when the parents of children with disabilities are undocumented immigrants (Alvarado, 2004).

Third, immigrant parents seem to have particular difficulty accessing information on psychological and educational services as compared to physical health and somatic complaints (Bailey, Skinner, Rodriguez et al., 1999).

The Cultural Challenge

The literature on the provision of services to immigrant families in the US is replete with statements pertaining to the importance of taking into account the country of origin of US immigrants (Lanfranchi, 1988). For example, the social-work literature stresses the importance of the concept of *cultural competence*, which is defined by the Child Welfare League of America as the

> ability of individuals and systems to respond respectfully and effectively to people of all cultures, classes, races, ethnic backgrounds, sexual orientations, and faiths or religions, in a manner that recognizes, affirms, and values the worth of individuals, families, tribes, and communities, and preserves the dignity of each.
>
> (Ingram, 2008, p. 1)

Further, the literature (Lum, 2003) identifies four components for cultural competence (cultural awareness, knowledge acquisition, skill development, and inductive learning) and explicitly stresses the particular importance of cultural competence in providing services to children (Hancock, 2005). Yet, although these issues are being discussed in the literature, the US system of addressing the needs of immigrant children with developmental disabilities is still rather monocultural (Grossman, 2002).

Several issues with regard to the role of cultural competence in providing services (e.g., special accommodations for children with disabilities) to immigrant families have been mentioned in the literature.

First, regarding general recommendations for service delivery, the literature stresses the importance of the client's active participation in the delivery and reception of services (Abramovitz, 1998). Parental involvement in seeking and receiving educational services for children with disabilities is mandated by law (The Individual with Disabilities Education Act, 1997). Yet, such an active position might be difficult to take for immigrant parents. For example, parents themselves might be experiencing complex feelings about leaving their old cultures and their placement in the new society; these feelings might interfere with their ability to recognize the need for their children to be diagnosed and serviced (Koplow & Messinger, 1990), viewing, possibly, their child's disability as yet another negative consequence of their decision to immigrate. In addition, the desire to assimilate might interfere with an objective appreciation of their children's needs, with special services and special placements being viewed as marks of dissimilation and separation from the "mainstream US culture." These complex feelings about belonging and being singled out might interfere with parental attitudes toward obtaining special educational services for their children.

Second, the literature reports clashes between different views on the standards and expectations of care for young children driven by the cultural differences between immigrant consumers and the US practitioners providing this care (Imperatore Blanche, 1996; Larson, 1996, 2000).

Third, immigrant children with special educational needs often require not only educational but also psychological accommodations and services (Ayalan, Fischer, & Naske, 1993; Lanfranchi & Molinari, 1995). Yet, there are quite a few countries—sources of immigrants to the US—in which seeking psychological help is stigmatized (Mooren & Kleber, 1999). Moreover, the literature contains accounts of situations in which children have been diagnosed with neuropsychiatric disorders and their parents have refused to acknowledge these diagnoses and make their children available for treatment (Weine & Laub, 1995).

Fourth, for school-aged immigrant children, the pressure of the new schooling system is often so heavy (Bates et al., 2005; Mayadas & Segal, 2000) that parents are reluctant to stress their children even more with additional changes and challenges, such as pull-out and resource room experiences. The literature contains accounts of difficult experiences of immigrant children with disabilities in US schools (Books, 2007) and these experiences might form the foundation for why immigrant parents are reluctant to expose their children to special accommodations. It is suspected (although not documented), that schooling experiences are particularly difficult for immigrant children with special needs in rural areas of the US (Monk, 2007), where seasonal migrant workers, the least-educated group of immigrants, reside. Furthermore, immigrant parents of children with disabilities have been reported to maintain different, compared to non-immigrant families, attitudes toward the independence and self-determination of their children (Zhang, 2005). Their general attitude toward their children's difficulties appears to be more fatalistic and less active than that of native US parents.

Another layer of complexity is related to the fact that, given the difficulties of acquiring English experienced by immigrant adults, often their children's mastery of English is more advanced than their own (Potocky, 1996), even their children with special educational needs. Often, children of immigrants act as the primary translators of US culture to their parents, challenging or even undermining their parents' authority (Carlin, 1990; Deepak, 2005; Drachman, 1992; Quinones-Mayo & Dempsey, 2005), and it is possible that they communicate negative attitudes toward special education and, thus, "self-isolate" themselves from special accommodations.

Sixth, although there is no specific data on immigrant parents of children with special needs, it has been noted that, overall, the participation of minority parents in Planning and Placement Team (PPT) meetings for their children is much lower than that of their native-majority counterparts (Harry, 1992; Huang & Gibbs, 1992). The literature (Chan, 1986; Constantino, Cui, & Faltis, 1995; Harry, 1992; Harry & Kalyanput, 1994; Huang & Gibbs, 1992; Voltz, 1994) identifies the following reasons for such underparticipation: (a) limited proficiency in English; (b) lack of familiarity with the school system; (c) discomfort or hesitancy in interacting with teachers or other personnel, attributable to both (a) and (b) as well as to different cultural traditions in the home country; (d) belief and trust that teachers are doing their best; (e) a respect for teachers as the experts, especially in dealing with immigrant children; (f) unfamiliarity with the concept and lack of the cultural tradition of parental participation in schools; (g) an insufficient number of teachers from ethnic-minority backgrounds in North America; and (h) different ethnic belief systems pertaining to the role of parent and teacher in the education of a child. Although these factors have been acknowledged in the work examining minority parents in the US, the literature suggests that they are also relevant to immigrant parents (Lai & Ishiyama, 2004).

The Identification and Service Delivery Challenge

Yet another possible explanation for what appears to be the underrepresentation of immigrant children among those receiving special educational services pertains to details of identification (i.e., meeting eligibility criteria) and procedures for receiving these services.

The 1997 amendment and reauthorization of the Individuals with Disabilities Education Act (IDEA) states that students who are referred for special education evaluations and services should be assessed and remediated, when appropriate, in their native languages. These provisions are legally in keeping with Title VI of the Civil Rights Act of 1964, which requires removing the language barrier in the service delivery process (Suleiman, 2003). However, although these provisions were reinforced in 2004, at the subsequent reinstallation of the IDEA, the reality is that there is a tremendous shortage of both assessment devices and multilingual personnel who can deliver on this provision in the law. While a number of assessment devices exist in Spanish and qualified personnel can deliver these assessments, these often do not account for a great variability of usage of the language and cultural peculiarities of great many Spanish-speaking source countries of immigrants to the US. The lack of the availability of assessments and personnel is even more pronounced in the other-than-Spanish languages of immigrants to the US.

We find the following anecdote from the literature to be illustrative (Baugh, 1995). A suburban school district in California used Chapter 1 funds (i.e., funds allocated by the US federal government to support the education of children living in poverty, see Fix & Zimmerman, 1993) to support minority students who attended the local high school as part of an ethnic/low SES desegregation plan. While conducting research on outcomes of this desegregation, a linguist at the school site noticed a Spanish-speaking student whose writing showed signs of specific reading difficulties. This was brought to the attention of school officials who claimed that no program was available to either assess or serve the student. As an ESL (English as Second Language) student, she qualified for bilingual education, but assessment tests and remediation programs for students with specific reading impairment were unavailable in this district in Spanish. Thus, in this district, this student was unlikely to achieve academic success, and such a result would be in opposition to the goals embodied in the system's reform (for a broader discussion, see Fuhrman & Massell, 1992; Smith & O'Day, 1991). Yet, such contradictions between local efforts and national programs are frequent and capture the lack of a systematic allocation of resources in implementing US national policies.

Moreover, it has been stated that assessment for eligibility for special educational services, when carried out with immigrant families, should include not only "assessments proper" for specific deficits, but also "assessment broadly defined" (Segal & Mayadas, 2005), aimed at evaluating not only the child's level of functioning, but also evaluating other relevant functions (e.g., adaptive and family functioning) that might determine the full constellation of services needed by the child. Although the literature calls for the "creativity" of assessors when they work with culturally and linguistically diverse immigrant children (Lee, 1989), it, unfortunately, does not contain specific and explicit recommendations in this regard. Moreover, although, as mentioned above, there are some assessment devices available in languages other than English (e.g., Spanish), these devices are very few and often their psychometric properties are not adequate.

The situation is also quite "trying" with respect to the proper development, evaluation, and application of remedial and accommodation programs. Even though general information regarding educating children with limited English proficiency and who are facing special challenges in the form of special needs is present in the literature (e.g., Genesee, Lindholm-Leary, Saunders, & Christian, 2006; Goldstein, 2004; Menyuk & Brisk, 2005), specifics are lacking with regard to the evaluation and dissemination of evidence-based practices for working with immigrant children with special needs. Often, the bilingual educational programs developed under Title VII and the remedial programs developed under IDEA "do not talk to each other," limiting the possibilities for immigrant children with special needs to receive appropriate and adequate education.

Another important factor to be considered here is the cost, both human and financial, of services for children with special needs. Traditionally in the US, parents of children with special needs tend to be their children's best advocates. Frequently this role takes a tremendous toll on the family, consuming time and financial and emotional resources. Immigrant parents often simply do not have such resources. While the literature contains sporadic examples of successful advocacy for immigrant children with special needs through other-than-parent agents (e.g., *Child Find* programs, see Lee, 1989), these examples are limited. Similarly, although there are examples of the utilization of culture-competent practices in dealing with immigrant families (Carten & Goodman, 2005; Chahine & van Straaten, 2005; Williams et al., 2005) such examples are quite sparse for families of children with disabilities.

Finally, there is a certain lack of guidance and confusion surrounding immigration status and federal, state, and local education agencies' policies concerning immigrants' eligibility for and entitlement to special educational services (Chahine & van Straaten, 2005). This uncertainty is particularly pertinent to children who are undocumented immigrants. Specifically, it has been estimated that in 2004, ~1.6 million children under the age of 18 in the US were undocumented immigrants (AB 1895 Assembly Bill, 2004). Although specific statistics on this group are unknown, given that there were 5,000 immigrant unaccompanied minors in federal custody only in 2004 (~50% increase compared to 1997 (Seugling, 2004) and that 9,900 unaccompanied minors were returned to Mexico in 2002 (Thompson, 2003), there is reason to believe that many of these undocumented unaccompanied minors might need special educational services and do not receive them.

Implications for Policy and Practice

Our exploration of available data suggests that immigrant parents are less or equally likely (depending upon the racial/ethnic group) to report that their child has a disability or uses special education than native-born parents. School system records in New York City also verify that foreign-born children are less likely to participate in special education programs. Our review of the literature highlights some explanations. Most importantly, immigrant parents face a number of barriers, including stereotypes about their children's disabilities, not knowing how to get their children diagnosed, and not knowing how to access special education services.

First, it is very important to involve immigrant parents in the process of advocating for the right of their children with special needs to receive adequate and appropriate education, to accurately represent the home culture of these children (Harry & Kalyanput, 1994), and to make informed interpretations of students' culturally loaded behaviors and attitudes in classrooms. Policies and practices in the US are generally driven by the "best interests of the child," which includes the material, intellectual, and moral welfare of the child (Downs, Moore, McFadden, Michaud, & Costin, 2004). An open and informed discussion, conducted, perhaps, in the context of action research in immigrant communities and/or with immigrant families, might bring together the points of view of both service providers and service recipients on what is the best for immigrant children.

Second, we need better data and better understanding of the disability rates and special needs of our growing immigrant population. It is very important to replicate, support, and extend our empirical findings in other datasets. Direct measures of disability rates among immigrant children would help us better determine whether immigrant parents underreport the needs of their children, how this varies by ethnic group, and how the underrepresentation of immigrant children with special needs in the US can be explained in the context of the data from other developed countries and the minority disproportional representation data from the US. Such a careful reconciliation of the representation in special education among immigrant children, children of immigrants, and minority groups in the US. might inform our general understanding of educational trajectories of various subgroups of children in the US and the characteristics of the special education population. Public school systems may be the best setting to collect such data but they currently vary tremendously in the quality and extent of their record keeping, do not encounter children until they reach school age, and do not capture children in private schools. School systems also do not currently collect information on the legal status of immigrant children or the birthplace of their parents for understandable reasons. Despite these limitations, schools systems provide a useful starting point and may be the most efficient vehicle for gaining more information. Further discussions of how to expand and improve school system records, while maintaining and respecting the privacy of families, would move us closer to understanding the needs of immigrant children. With better data on these children and their families, we can further investigate the dynamics and causes of the apparent underrepresentation of immigrant children among children receiving special educational services in the US.

Acknowledgments

Both authors are grateful to the Foundation for Child Development Young Scholar Program for supporting their work on immigrant children. Dr. Grigorenko is also grateful to Ms. Alex Holod for her bringing to Dr. Grigorenko's attention a number of references regarding the overrepresentation of minority in special education in Ms. Hood's final paper for the HUDK5040 course at Columbia taught by Dr. Grigorenko and to Ms. Mei Tan and Ms. Cheri Stahl for their editorial assistance.

Notes

1. We are grateful to Elizabeth Baker for providing all figures using the ECLS-K.
2. Approximately 25% of the native-born children in the NSAF are missing data for either paternal or maternal nativity status, which prevents reliable comparisons between the children of immigrants and the children of native-born individuals.

References

AB 1895 Assembly Bill. (2004).

Abramovitz, M. (1998). Social work and social reform: An arena of struggle. *Social Work, 43*, 512–526.

Advocates for Children (AFC). (2000).

Akamatsu, C.T., & Cole, E. (2000). Meeting the psychoeducational needs of deaf immigrant and refugee children. *Canadian Journal of School Psychology, 15*, 1–18.

Alvarado, M.I. (2004). Mucho camino: The experiences of two undocumented Mexican mothers participating in their child's early intervention program. *American Journal of Occupational Therapy, 58*, 521–530.

Arcia, E., Skinner, M., Bailey, D., & Correa, V. (2001). Models of acculturation and health behaviors among Latino immigrants to the U.S. *Social Science & Medicine, 53*, 41–53.

Ayalan, S., Fischer, P., & Naske, R. (1993). Behavior problems in Turkish immigrant children. *Zeitschrift fur Kinder- und Jugendpsychiatrie und Psychotherapie, 21*, 226–232.

Bailey, D.B., Skinner, D., Correa, V., Arcia, E., Reyes-Blanes, M.E., Rodriguez, P., et al. (1999). Needs and supports reported by Latino families of young children with developmental disabilities. *American Journal of Mental Retardation, 104*, 437–451.

Bailey, D.B., Skinner, D., Rodriguez, P., Gut, D., & Correa, V. (1999). Awareness, use and satisfaction with services for Latino parents of young children with disabilities. *Exceptional Children, 65*, 367–381.

Bates, L., Baird, D., Johnson, D.J., Lee, R.E., Luster, T., & Rehagen, C. (2005). Sudanese refugee youth in foster care: The "lost boys" in America. *Child Welfare Journal, 84*, 631–648.

Baugh, J. (1995). The law, linguistics, and education: Educational reform for African American language minority students. *Linguistics and Education, 7*, 87–105.

Books, S. (2007). *Invisible children in the society and its schools* (3rd ed.). Mahwah, NJ: Lawrence Erlbaum Associates Publishers.

Brown, E.R., Ojeda, V.D., Wyn, R., & Levan, R. (2002). *Racial and ethnic disparities in access to health insurance and health care.* Los Angeles, CA: University of Los Angeles Center for Health Policy Research and The Henry J. Kaiser Family Foundation.

Capps, R., Fix, M., Ost, J., Reardon-Anderson, J., & Passel, J.E. (2004). *The health and well-being of young children of immigrants.* Washington, DC: Urban Institute Press.

Capps, R., Ku, L., & Fix, M. (2004). *How are immigrants faring after welfare reform? Preliminary evidence from Los Angeles and New York City.* Washington, DC: The Urban Institute.

Carlin, J.E. (1990). Refugee and immigrant populations at special risk: Women, children and the elderly. In W.H. Holtzman & T.H. Bornemann (Eds.), *Mental health of immigrants and refugees* (pp. 224–233). Austin, TX: Hogg Foundation for Mental Health.

Carten, A., & Goodman, H. (2005). An educational model for child welfare practice with English-speaking Caribbean families. *Child Welfare Journal, 84*, 771–789.

Chahine, Z., & van Straaten, J. (2005). Serving immigrant families and children in New York City's child welfare system. *Child Welfare Journal, 84*, 713–724.

Chan, K.S. (1986). Parents of exceptional Asian children. In M.K. Kitano & P.C. Chinn (Eds.), *Exceptional Asian children and youth* (pp. 36–58). Reston, VA: Council of Exceptional Children.

Conger, D., Schwartz, A., & Stiefel, L. (2007). Immigrant and native-born differences in school stability and special education: evidence from New York City. *International Migration Review, 41*(2), 402–431.

Conger, D., Schwartz, A.E., & Stiefel, L. (2003). *Who are our students? A statistical portrait of immigrant students in New York City elementary and middle schools.* New York: New York University, Institute of Education and Social Policy.

Constantino, R., Cui, L., & Faltis, C. (1995). Chinese parental involvement: Reaching new levels. *Equity and Excellence in Education, 28*, 46–50.

Deepak, A.C. (2005). Parenting and the process of migration: Possibilities within South Asian families. *Child Welfare Journal, 84*, 585–606.

Donovan, M.S., & Cross, C.T. (Eds.). (2002). *Minority students in special and gifted education.* Washington, DC: National Academies Press.

Downs, S.W., Moore, E., McFadden, E.J., Michaud, S.M., & Costin, L.B. (2004). *Child welfare and family services: Policies and practice.* Boston, MA: Allyn and Bacon.

Drachman, D. (1992). A stage-of-immigration framework for service to immigrant populations. *Social Work, 37*, 68–72.

Earner, I. (2007). Immigrant families and public child welfare: Barriers to services and approaches for change. *Child Welfare Journal, 86*, 63–91.

Feliciano, C. (2005). Educational selectivity in U.S. immigration: How do immigrants compare to those left behind? *Demography, 42*, 131–152.

Fix, M., & Zimmerman, W. (1993). *Educating immigrant children: Chapter I in the changing city.* Washington, DC: Urban Institute.

Fuhrman, S., & Massell, D. (1992). *Issues and strategies in systemic reform.* New Brunswick, NJ: Rutgers University, Consortium for Policy Research in Education.

Genesee, F., Lindholm-Leary, K., Saunders, W.M., & Christian, D. (2006). *Educating English language learners: A synthesis of research evidence.* New York: Cambridge University Press.

Gershberg, A.I. (2002). *New immigrants and the new school governance in New York: Defining the issues.* Working paper. New York: Community Development Research Center New School University.

Goldstein, B. (Ed.). (2004). *Bilingual language development and disorders in Spanish-English speakers.* Baltimore, MD: Paul H. Brookes Publishing Co.

Grossman, H. (2002). *Ending discrimination in special education* (2nd ed.). Springfield, IL: Charles C. Thomas Publisher.

Guillory, B.R. (2000). *The Hispanic immigration experience: Literature for special education Latino/ Latina students.* Retrieved August 17, 2008, from http://hti.math.uh.edu/curriculum/ units/2000/04/00.04.03.php.

Hancock, T.U. (2005). Cultural competence in the assessment of poor Mexican families in the rural southeastern United States. *Child Welfare Journal, 84,* 689–711.

Harker, K. (2001). Immigrant generation, assimilation, and adolescent psychological well-being. *Social Forces, 79,* 969–1004.

Harris, K.M. (1999). The health status and risk behaviors of adolescents in immigrant families. In D.J. Hernandez (Ed.), *Children of immigrants: Health, adjustment, and public assistance* (pp. 286–347). Washington, DC: National Academy Press.

Harry, B. (1992). *Cultural diversity, families, and the special education system: Communication and empowerment.* New York: Teachers College Press.

Harry, B., & Kalyanput, M. (1994). Cultural underpinning of special education: Implications for professional interactions with culturally diverse families. *Disability & Society, 9,* 145–165.

Haywood, H.C., & Wingenfeld, S.A. (1992). Interactive assessment as a research tool. *The Journal of Special Education, 26,* 253–268.

Heller, T., Markwardt, R., Rowitz, L., & Farber, B. (1994). Adaptation of Hispanic families to a member with mental retardation. *American Journal of Mental Retardation, 99,* 289–300.

Hernandez, D.J. (2004). Demographic change and the life circumstances of immigrant families. *The Future of Children, 14,* 17–47.

Hernandez, D.J., & Charney, E. (1998). *From generation to generation: The health and well-being of children in immigrant families.* Washington, DC: National Academy Press.

Hosp, J.L., & Reschly, D.J. (2004). Disproportionate representation of minority students in special education: Academic, demographic, and economic predictors. *Exceptional Children, 70,* 185–199.

Huang, L.N., & Gibbs, J.T. (1992). Partners or adversaries? Home-school collaboration across culture, race, and ethnicity. In S.L. Christenson & J. Close Conoly (Eds.), *Home-school collaboration: Enhancing children's academic and social competence* (pp. 81–109). Silver Spring, MD: The National Association of School Psychologists.

Huer, M.B., Saenz, T.I., & Doan, J.H.D. (2001). Understanding the Vietnamese American community. *Communication Disorders Quarterly, 23,* 27–39.

Imperatore Blanche, E. (1996). Alma: Coping with culture, poverty, and disability. *American Journal of Occupational Therapy, 50,* 265–276.

Ingram, C. (2008). *Cultural competence: About the program.* Retrieved August 25, 2008, from www.cwla.org/programs/culturalcompetence/culturalabout.htm.

Kao, G., & Tienda, M. (1995). Optimism and achievement: The educational performance of immigrant youth. *Social Science Quarterly, 76,* 1–19.

Kidde, A.M. (1986). The school psychological service and the immigrant children. *Skolepsykologi, 23,* 280–291.

Kivirauma, J., Klemela, K., & Rinne, R. (2006). Segregation, integration, inclusion: The ideology and reality in Finland. *European Journal of Special Needs Education, 21,* 117–133.

Koplow, L., & Messinger, E. (1990). Developmental dilemmas of young children of immigrant parents. *Child & Adolescent Social Work Journal, 7,* 121–134.

Kozulin, A. (2006). Integration of culturally different students in mainstream classes. *Erdelyi Pszichologiai Szemle, 2S,* 99–105.

Lai, Y., & Ishiyama, F.I. (2004). Involvement of immigrant Chinese Canadian mothers of children with disabilities. *Exceptional Children, 71*, 97–108.

Lanfranchi, A. (1988). Immigrant families from Mediterranean countries: Systematic thoughts on the relationship between family of origin and nuclear family. *Praxis der Kinderpsychologie und Kinderpsychiatrie, 37*, 124–131.

Lanfranchi, A. (1993). "…at least in my village it's a custom…": From stagnation to transformation in immigrant family "reality constructs." *Praxis der Kinderpsychologie und Kinderpsychiatrie, 42*, 188–198.

Lanfranchi, A. (2007). Transfer of pupils to special classes or integrative schooling: Do teachers think and act in a culturally neutral way? *Vierteljahresschrift fur Heilpadagogik und ihre Nachbargebiete, 76*, 128–141.

Lanfranchi, A., & Molinari, D. (1995). Is it possible to perform psychotherapy with behaviorally disturbed migrant children of resistant parents? Interdisciplinary cooperation between systems-oriented school psychology and psychoanalytically oriented therapy. *Praxis der Kinderpsychologie und Kinderpsychiatrie, 44*, 260–270.

Larson, E. (1996). The story of Maricela and Miguel: A narrative analysis of dimensions of adaptation. *American Journal of Occupational Therapy, 50*, 286–298.

Larson, E. (2000). The orchestration of occupation: The dance of mothers. *American Journal of Occupational Therapy, 54*, 269–280.

Lee, A. (1989). A socio-cultural framework for the assessment of Chinese children with special needs. *Topics in Language Disorders, 9*, 39–44.

Lum, D. (2003). *Culturally competent practice: A framework for understanding diverse groups and justice issues*. Pacific Grove, CA: Brooks/Cole Publishing Company.

Mayadas, N., & Segal, U. (2000). Refugees in the 1990s: A U.S. perspective. In P. Balgopal (Ed.), *Social work practice with immigrants and refugees* (pp. 198–227). New York: Columbia University Press.

Menyuk, P., & Brisk, M.E. (2005). *Language development and education: Children with varying language experience*. New York: Palgrave Macmillan.

Miranda, A.O., & Matheny, K.B. (2000). Socio-psychological predictors of acculturative stress among Latino adults. *Journal of Mental Health Counseling, 22*, 306–317.

Monk, D.H. (2007). Recruiting and retaining high-quality teachers in rural areas. *The Future of Children, 17*, 155–174.

Mooren, G.T.M., & Kleber, R.J. (1999). War, trauma, and society: Consequences of the disintegration of former Yugoslavia. In K. Nader, N. Dubrow, & B. Hudnall Stamm (Eds.), *Honoring Differences: Cultural issues in the treatment of trauma and loss* (pp. 178–209). Philadelphia, PA: Brunner/Mazel.

O'Connor, C., & DeLuca Fernandez, S. (2006). Race, class, and disproportionality: Reevaluating the relationship between poverty and special education placement. *Educational Researcher, 35*, 6–11.

Parrish, T. (2002). Racial disparities in the identification, funding, and provision of special education. In D.J. Losen & G. Orfield (Eds.), *Racial inequity in special education* (pp. 15–37). Cambridge, MA: Harvard Education Press.

Potocky, M. (1996). Refugee children: How are they faring economically as adults? *Social Work, 41*, 364–373.

Quinones-Mayo, Y., & Dempsey, P. (2005). Finding the bicultural balance: Immigrant Latino mothers raising "American" adolescents. *Child Welfare Journal, 84*, 649–668.

Schemo, D.J. (1992, May 7). Huntington schools accused of bias in special ed programs. *New York Times*.

Segal, U.A., & Mayadas, N.S. (2005). Assessment of issues facing immigrant and refugee families. *Child Welfare Journal, 84*, 563–584.

Seugling, C.J. (2004). Toward a comprehensive response to the transnational migration of unaccompanied minors in the United States. *Vanderbilt Journal of Transnational Law, 37*, 861.

Sideridis, G.D. (2007). International approaches to learning disabilities: More alike or more different? *Learning Disabilities Research & Practice, 22*, 210–215.

Skiba, R.J., Simmons, A.B., Ritter, S., Gibb, A., Rausch, M.K., Cuadrado, J., et al. (2008). Achieving equity in special education: History, status, and current challenges. *Exceptional Children, 74*, 264–288.

Smith, M.S., & O'Day, J. (1991). Systemic school reform. In S. Fuhrman & B. Malen (Eds.), *The politics of curriculum and testing* (pp. 233–267). New York: Falmer Press.

Snyder, C.S., May, J.D., Zulcic, N.N., & Gabbard, W.J. (2005). Social work with Bosnian Muslim refugee children and families: A review of the literature. *Child Welfare Journal, 84*, 607–630.

Suleiman, L.P. (2003). Beyond cultural competence: Language access and Latino civil rights. *Child Welfare, 82*, 185–201.

Thomas, W.B. (1986). Mental testing and tracking for the social adjustment of an urban underclass, 1920–1930. *Journal of Education, 168*, 9–30.

Thompson, G. (2003, November 3). Littlest immigrants, left in hands of smugglers. *New York Times*, p. A1.

Voltz, D.L. (1994). Developing collaborative parent teacher relationships with culturally diverse parents. *Intervention in School & Clinic, 29*, 288–291.

Wehrly, B. (1988). Cultural diversity from an international perspective: II. *Journal of Multicultural Counseling and Development, 16*, 3–15.

Weine, S., & Laub, D. (1995). Narrative constructions of historical realities in testimony with Bosnian survivors of "ethnic cleansing." *Psychiatry, 58*, 246–260.

Werning, R., Loser, J.M., & Urban, M. (2008). Cultural and social diversity: An analysis of minority groups in German schools. *The Journal of Special Education, 42*, 47–54.

Williams, M., Bradshaw, C., Fournier, B., Tachble, A., Bray, R., & Hodson, F. (2005). The Call-Centre: A child welfare liaison program with immigrant serving agencies. *Child Welfare Journal, 84*, 725–746.

Zetlin, A.G., Padron, M., & Wilson, S. (1996). The experience of five Latin American families with the special education system. *Education & Training in Mental Retardation & Developmental Disabilities, 31*, 22–28.

Zhang, D. (2005). Parent practices of facilitating self-determination skills: the influences of culture, socioeconomic status, and children's special education status. *Research & Practice for Persons with Severe Disabilities, 30*, 154–162.

Zhou, M., & Bankston, C. (1998). *Growing up American: How Vietnamese children adapt to life in the United States*. New York: Russell Sage Foundation.

10 Two Generations of Educational Progress in Latin American Immigrant Families in the US

A Conceptual Framework for a New Policy Context

Ariel Kalil and Robert Crosnoe

In 2006, millions flooded the streets of the major cities of the US in pro- and anti-immigration demonstrations sparked by congressional efforts to reform federal immigration laws. Throughout 2007 and 2008, the specter of immigration reform has continued to be a focal issue in the presidential campaign. As the rhetoric on both sides has grown more heated and the debate has become more contentious, immigration from Latin America into the US looks more and more like it will replace other historical race/ethnic conflicts to become—to borrow a term from W.E.B. DuBois—the new problem of the century.

In the eye of this raging storm is the growing population of Latin American immigrants in the US. Migrating north in search of the fabled American Dream, they now constitute a large under-class, experiencing high rates of social and economic disadvantage and facing limited prospects for social mobility. The young children of these Latin American immigrants—millions and counting—symbolize the risks of this great socioeconomic disadvantage but also represent the best long-term hopes for improving the socioeconomic prospects of this growing population. One charge for the partnership between social science and social policy, then, is to figure out how to help translate these hopes into reality. Doing so will serve the interests of these young children and the larger Latin American immigrant population while also promoting the social cohesion and economic productivity of the nation as a whole.

In this chapter, we argue that education is the key to such policy efforts—not just the education of children but the education of their parents too. In this spirit, we put forward a conceptual model that we have developed during our research on young immigrant children over the last several years. The purpose of this conceptual model is to serve as a template for organizing social and behavioral research that supports policy and intervention targeting the growing Latin American population.

Latin American Immigrants' Educational Attainment in a Two Generational Perspective

The children of immigrants from Mexico and other Latin American countries represent two-thirds of the rapidly increasing population of children in the US with at least one foreign-born parent (Hernandez, 2004). The social mobility of these children is a microcosm of our long-term economic prospects as a nation, and, more than in virtually any other child population, their social mobility is linked to the educational system. As stressed by the Suárez-Orozcos (2001), education is the one ticket these children have for "a better tomorrow." Indeed, this better tomorrow was undoubtedly a driving force behind their parents' immigration in the first place.

Historically, the manufacturing sector of the American economy provided a large pool of secure, steady, well-paying jobs with benefits and advancement that allowed social mobility without extensive educational credentials. As this sector has declined over the last several decades, the economy has been transformed into an information and service phase, in which access to the strata of the labor market facilitating social mobility is predicated on educational attainment, especially higher education in specialized areas like science, technology, and business. As a result, economic returns to higher education have reached an all-time high, a trend that has dramatically increased societal inequality (Bernhardt, Morris, Handcock, & Scott, 2001; Fischer & Hout, 2006; Goldin & Katz, 2007; Lemieux, 2006). Traditionally disadvantaged populations—and Latin American immigrants are certainly counted as one by most observers—have been hit especially hard by this economic restructuring, making educational progress that much more crucial.

Unfortunately, the children of Latin American immigrants are widely viewed as academically at-risk in the American educational system. Substantial empirical evidence has documented their low rates of academic progress and performance at all levels of schooling, in terms of school readiness and early elementary achievement, graded and tested achievement in secondary school, high school completion, and college matriculation and completion (Crosnoe, 2006; Driscoll, 1999; Feliciano, 2005; Fry, 2007; Glick & Hohmann-Marriott, 2007; Glick & White, 2003; Hirschman, 2001; Hao and Bornstead-Bruns, 1998; Kao, 1999; Kao & Tienda, 1995; Kao & Thompson, 2003). A good deal of this risk is a function of language barriers, with Limited English Proficient (LEP) designations as high as 30% at the start of school (National Task Force on Early Childhood Education for Hispanics, 2006). These language barriers, which are rarely adequately addressed in formal curricula, interfere with classroom learning in math, reading, and other subjects (Gandara, Rumberger, Maxwell-Jolly, & Callahan, 2003; Reardon & Galindo, 2007).

Beyond the obvious language barriers, these extremely consequential academic struggles also occur because Latin American immigrant parents often have trouble navigating their children through school. The reasons for this trouble are many, including precarious finances, their own language proficiency, and the obstruction of schools themselves. One barrier that we believe should be highlighted is the human capital of Latin American immigrant parents. For example, a clear majority of Latin American immigrant mothers—who typically have primary responsibility for children's education—have not graduated from high school, compared to 18% of all mothers nationally. Moreover, 29% have less than 9 years of schooling, and 9% have less than 5 years of schooling. The corresponding statistics for the subpopulation of Mexican immigrant mothers of young children are even more alarming: 64% have not graduated from high school, 36% have less than 9 years of schooling, and 11% have less than 5 years of schooling (see Hernandez, this volume). Clearly, these numbers capture deep human-capital disadvantages in the parent generation with consequences in the child generation.

Worth noting is that these generational trends occur at the nexus of the receiving and sending contexts of immigration. As illustrated in the work of Bean and colleagues (see Bean & Stevens, 2003, for an overview), Latin American women come into the US from largely poor, rural areas in which girls typically do not advance far in school. As illustrated in segmented assimilation research (see Portes & Zhou, 1993), these women then enter into disadvantaged segments of the race/ethnic hierarchy and class system in the US. Their children are largely absent from the formal pre-school market and then segregated into disadvantaged sectors of the educational system in which their competencies (e.g., potential bilingualism) are devalued and their parents often lack the information, contacts, and status to manage their educational pathways in ways that American schools demand (Crosnoe, 2006; Magnuson, Lahaie, & Waldfogel, 2006; Matthews & Ewen, 2006). Thus, the immigration flow between Latin American and the US often—although not inevitably—sets up a situation in which mothers are isolated from major institutions of American society and their children are less able to take advantage of public education in ways that they need to get ahead. The end result is two generations on the margins of public life (Feliciano, 2005).

With this two-generation process in mind, one potentially valuable policy objective is to develop the human capital of Latin American immigrant mothers in order to promote the long-term educational trajectories of their children. Such a strategy may be especially important for immigrant mothers of *young* children, given research in economics, neuroscience, and developmental psychology that early childhood is the foundational period for the development of competencies and skills that carry young people into adulthood (Knudsen, Heckman, Cameron, & Shonkoff, 2006). Research in sociology and education adopts a similar stance that schooling in the US takes a highly cumulative form that translates small initial differences in academic skills and preparation into large ending differences in attainment (Entwisle & Alexander, 2002; Barnett & Belfield, 2006).

A Conceptual Model

Figure 10.1 depicts a conceptual model guiding our thinking about the long-term prospects for educational success in the Latin American immigrant population. Each of the blocks (and the constructs listed within them) represented in the conceptual model is included based on the existence of at least some empirical evidence in the literature on the relevance of those specific constructs. The studies that produced this evidence will be described below. It should be noted, however, that much of the existing evidence is not based on our population of interest here (Latin American immigrants). For this reason, the model remains a "conceptual" one. Moreover, because our model is based upon existing empirical evidence, it is necessarily limited by the data used to generate those findings. As new studies on this topic emerge, and as these studies galvanize new data-collection efforts, the model can be refined and elaborated upon.

To begin, our model recognizes that the American education system has long been a powerful agent of socialization and incorporation, especially for immigrants (Dee, 2004; Milligan, Moretti, & Oreopoulos, 2004; Sawhill, 2006; Sherrod, Flanagan, &

Youniss, 2002; Tyack, 1974). We argue, therefore, that this system must be central to efforts to achieve the full incorporation of Latin American immigrants and their children in the US. By incorporation we mean such important activities as actively participating in the political process and societal institutions, being recognized by other groups as "equal" members of American society, and absorbing American cultural traditions even as immigrants contribute new customs, values, and practices to those traditions.

This model has four distinctive features. First, we focus on the immigrant portion of this population, which is its fastest-growing, most disadvantaged, and most isolated segment (Bean & Stevens, 2003; Hernandez, 2004). Second, among immigrants, we focus on mothers, who typically hold the primary responsibility for raising the second generation and, compared to the general US population, are more likely to be outside the paid labor force (Suárez-Orozco & Suárez-Orozco, 1995). Third, we focus on the young children of these Latina immigrants, who, unlike their adolescent counterparts who have received substantial attention from social scientists (Fuligni & Yoshikawa, 2004; Hirschman, 2001; Portes & Rumbaut, 2001; Kao, 1999; Kao & Thompson, 2003; Kao & Tienda, 1995), have not yet been pushed to the margins of a system of schooling that is highly cumulative. Fourth, and most importantly, we view the education system as having the power to foster achievement in *both* the first and second generation of Latin American immigrants *simultaneously*.

As depicted in Figure 10.1, our conceptual model posits that the entry of Latina immigrants into American high schools, vocational schools, junior colleges, and colleges—the probability of which is a function of their background and current circumstances—will cultivate important skills, knowledge, and insights (Dee, 2004; Milligan et al., 2004). These new resources will empower them to partner with teachers, counselors, and administrators at their children's elementary schools at just the time when such participation has the greatest potential to facilitate the academic progress of their children. With a better start to the early school career eventually translating into greater human capital (Entwisle & Alexander, 2002; Knudsen et al., 2006), these second-generation children will enter adulthood better positioned to actively engage their civic responsibilities and privileges and contribute to economic productivity.

Like many conceptual models, this one is, of course, oversimplified, depicted as a linear, additive pathway. In reality, the different pieces of this model interact with and condition each other, and feedback goes in both directions. As one example, children's experiences in schools can elicit more participation from parents in their schools. As another example, an increase in parents' informational resources does not just facilitate parents' engagement in partnerships with schools, but likely increases the impact of those partnerships on children. We propose this conceptual model simply as a starting point for what we argue should be a new line of research. The structure and content of the model can be refined and reorganized as work on this topic proceeds.

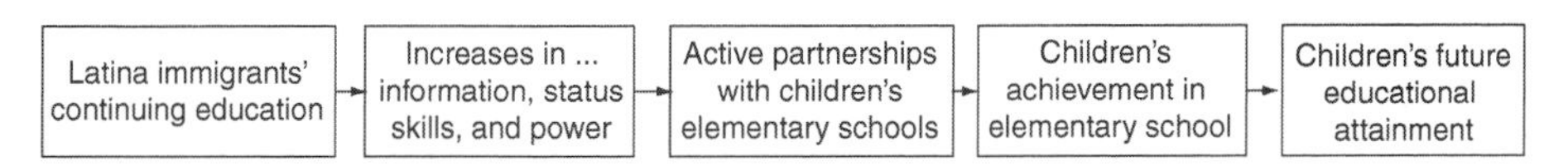

Figure 10.1 Educational Attainment in a Two Generational Perspective.

Evidence Linking Maternal Education to Child Outcomes

The heart of this conceptual model is the link between mothers' experiences in the educational system and their children's progress through the same system, which is presumably mediated by two-way exchanges between mothers and their children's schools. This hypothesized linkage is empirically justified.

The positive association between parent education (particularly maternal education) and child health and well-being has been demonstrated in numerous studies focusing on native populations. Not surprisingly, therefore, many have argued that policies to increase parental education represent one of the most effective means of improving child well-being and the stock of human capital (Deaton, 2002). A primary channel of the intergenerational transfer of human capital is parents' management of children's academic progress. Educated and economically advantaged parents have the means and motivation to create stimulating environments for their children, plan their children's curricular pathways, and successfully advocate for their children at school. Not surprisingly, then, observational and experimental research has shown that improvements in economically disadvantaged, native-born parents' educational statuses and incomes affect child outcomes, in part through concomitant changes in parenting (Duncan, Huston, & Weisner, 2007; Magnuson, 2003).

Recent evidence suggests that this pattern could apply to Latin American immigrants. In this important population, children's academic risks are closely tied to financial and human capital disadvantages that reduce their parents' involvement efforts and the receptivity of schools to these efforts (Crosnoe, 2006; Lopez, 2001; Suárez-Orozco & Suárez-Orozco, 2001). Thus, improved socioeconomic circumstances—by, for example, increased educational attainment—could give Latin American immigrants more opportunities and ability to work with schools to promote their children's interests, especially in light of the added obstacles they face (e.g., language barriers, unfamiliarity with American schools) compared to native-born parents.

Clearly, observed associations between parental (maternal) education and child outcomes are rife with selection problems. For example, women who pursue more education likely differ from other women in many ways that could affect how they raise their children and what their children do. Economic research has made important contributions to solving this problem by adopting a variety of methodological techniques to better isolate causal effects. A number of studies use quasi-experimental variation to estimate the association between maternal educational attainment and various measures of child well-being (e.g., Black, Devereux, & Salvanes, 2005; Currie & Moretti, 2003; Oreopolous, Page, & Stevens, 2006). Many of these studies, especially in development economics, have focused on children's health, which itself is an important determinant of children's education. Several studies take advantage of quasi-experimental variation in compulsory schooling or the availability of schools to link higher maternal education to children's birthweight and gestational age (Chou, Liu, Grossman, & Joyce, 2003; Currie & Moretti, 2003).

In relation to children's educational outcomes, Oreopolous and colleagues (2006) rely on random variation in compulsory schooling laws to link maternal education to the likelihood that children will be held back a grade in school or will drop out of high school. For example, they find that a one-year increase in the education of either parent reduces the probability that a child repeats a grade by between 2 and 7 percentage points. Carneiro, Meghir, and Parey (2007) study the intergenerational effects of maternal education on children's cognitive achievement, behavioral problems, grade repetition, and obesity, also using advanced methodological techniques to deal with selection-bias problems. Their results show substantial intergenerational returns to education. For children aged 7–8, for example, the results indicate that an additional year of mother's schooling increases the child's performance on a standardized math test by almost 0.1 of a standard deviation, increases reading performance by a similar amount, and reduces the incidence of behavioral problems. A one-year increase in mothers' education also reduces the likelihood of children's grade repetition by 2.8 percentage points. Carneiro et al. provide some evidence that these impacts may arise from the higher educational expectations and better-quality home-learning environments that characterize mothers with more years of education.

For the most part, these studies have focused on the level of education that women have attained prior to their children's birth rather than postfertility changes in their educational statuses. This omission is noteworthy because evidence suggests that educational credentials are increasingly acquired in a discontinuous fashion and also that many economically disadvantaged mothers pursue education following the birth of their children (Astone, Schoen, Ensminger & Rothert, 2000; Magnuson, 2007). But, almost no studies on this particular topic have focused on low-income mothers with young children or on immigrant populations.

Magnuson (2007) is one of few studies to address this issue using advanced methods to account for selection bias. She found significant positive associations between increases in mothers' completed schooling and concurrent improvements in the growth of children's reading recognition and reading comprehension for children between the ages of 6 and 8 as well as 8 and 10. For example, between ages 8 and 10, an additional year of maternal educational attainment was associated with a 0.16 standard deviation increase in reading recognition and a 0.21 standard deviation increase in reading comprehension. Associations between improved math skills and mothers' additional education were only apparent between ages 6 and 8 (effect size of 0.30). Interestingly, these strong linkages existed only among children of young mothers with low educational achievement. A key question for future research is to understand the impact of changes in maternal education among Latin American immigrant mothers with very limited education. This question motivated the formulation of our conceptual model.

How Might Maternal Education Affect Child Outcomes?

Establishing the link between maternal education and child academic outcomes is one piece of the puzzle. Identifying the mechanisms underlying this link is another. At least three plausible pathways exist (Currie & Moretti, 2003; Magnuson, 2007; Thomas, Strauss, & Henriques, 1991).

First, improved literacy or numeracy among mothers might translate into higher economic resources (e.g., income) with which to invest in children, such as by purchasing books, selecting children into higher-quality childcare or schools, and/or enrolling children in community and extracurricular activities. Improved language or math abilities might also provide mothers with the skills or confidence they need to make better investments in their children's education.

Second, increased educational attainment among mothers might improve "academic socialization," or cognitively stimulating and academically preparatory parent–child interactions in the home environment, such as through shared book-reading, time spent on education-focused activities, parenting behavior to foster children's independent thinking, and parents' educational aspirations and expectations for their children.

Third, increased educational attainment might strengthen bonds between parents and their children's schools—that is, increase the frequency and quality of interactions of parents with teachers and other school personnel—by providing more information to mothers about how schools work and by making schools more open to their input and attempts at involvement. Our conceptual model focuses on the latter two of these pathways—broadly characterized as family–school partnerships—as a first step in establishing the potential impact of increases in maternal education on children's own educational attainment.

The Role of Family–School Partnerships

Why should we prioritize family–school partnerships in our conceptual model of two generations of education in the Latin American immigrant population? For decades, such partnerships have been a reflexive piece of educational policies, including No Child Left Behind (Epstein, 2005). Certainly, this focus is not misguided. Empirical research from multiple disciplines has documented that, even controlling for the obvious selection factors, students do better in school when their parents forge direct and/or supportive ties with their teachers and other school personnel (Entwisle, Alexander, & Olson, 1997; Coleman, 1988; Hill, 2001; Okagaki & Frensch, 1998; Raver, Gershoff, & Aber, 2007).

Two broad dimensions of family–school partnerships are generally studied by social and behavioral scientists. First, direct partnerships involve interactions between parents and school personnel (e.g., parents participating in school activities, school personnel contacting parents). These partnerships empower parents by increasing their understanding of what goes on at school, their ability to convey their own values and circumstances to school personnel, and their power to advocate for their children. Second, supportive partnerships involve parents' efforts to build learning environments at home that complement what goes on in the classroom (e.g., parents supplementing schoolwork with cognitively stimulating activities). They allow the lessons learned at school to be embraced and reinforced at home. The latter dimension of this family–school partnership is important because children cannot succeed in school unless the lessons that are learned there are also practiced at home. Thus, parents who cannot understand the purpose or intent of their children's schoolwork and who cannot supplement schoolwork with enriching or cognitively stimulating activities, such as reading, will have children who fare less well.

In direct and supportive partnerships, children benefit academically, especially in the earliest stages of schooling. Yet, these kinds of partnerships are not just important to academic achievement and learning during this stage but also to demographic disparities in educational outcomes. They are thought to build protective scaffolding around at-risk children—where risk is defined in terms of membership in historically disenfranchised and disadvantaged segments of the population defined by race, ethnicity, and social class—that keeps them from falling through the cracks of the educational system. Reducing risk reduces disparities (Eccles & Harold, 1993; Epstein, 2005; Hoover-Dempsey & Sandler, 1997; Pianta & Walsh, 1996).

Unfortunately, family–school partnerships are affected by racial and economic stratification. Despite evidence that socioeconomically disadvantaged children, especially those from race/ethnic minority groups, benefit more from such partnerships, they are also less likely to have them, due to a mixture of dismissal and devaluation on the part of schools and of distrust, lack of knowledge, and lack of social standing on the part of parents (Entwisle et al., 1997; Lareau, 1989). As illustrated by Crosnoe (2006), this problem is writ large in the Latin American immigrant population. As a product of their ethnic status, low human capital, English-language difficulties, and certain cultural norms, Latina immigrant mothers rarely have strong connections to their children's schools. For example, Spanish-speaking parents of all economic statuses report receiving fewer communications from their children's schools than other parents and are less likely to be aware of events and opportunities at these schools. They are also less likely to engage in shared reading or other home-learning activities with their children (National Center for Education Statistics, 2006; Quezada, Diaz, & Sanchez, 2003).

Thus, the children most in need of strong family–school partnerships early in their educational careers are least likely to have them, a phenomenon that is a product of both supply and demand forces. Again, we argue that low rates of maternal education in the Latin American immigrant population underlie this important social problem. Low educational attainment interferes with the building of family–school partnerships through seven factors (Bean & Stevens, 2003; Crosnoe, 2006; Lopez, 2001; Reese, Balzano, Gallimore, & Goldberg, 1995; Suárez-Orozco & Suárez-Orozco, 2001):

- *Economic stresses*, including being incapacitated from participating by lack of resources, such as transportation and childcare, material resources, and the worries and fears inherent in economic insecurity.
- *Time constraints*, such as work and family demands.
- *Reduced personal efficacy*, such as not believing that actions will make a difference for children's prospects.
- *Unfamiliarity with schools and other social institutions*, such as not knowing what is valued or how to work the system.
- *Lack of standing in schools*, such as being devalued or ignored by school personnel.
- *Limited social networks*, including having few contacts to provide inside information or advocacy.
- *Communication barriers*, such as mothers' low English skills and a lack of bilingual speakers at school.

Increasing the educational attainment of Latin American mothers, therefore, will likely help them interact more effectively with schools by providing opportunities to reduce economic stresses (e.g., new jobs), easing time constraints (e.g., allowing women to purchase help or services), cultivating feelings of personal control (a well-documented side effect of education), providing inside information about how schools work, elevating social status in the eyes of school personnel, expanding the size and diversity of the pool of social contacts and information sources, and enhancing English-language proficiency.

The Larger Context

The Policy Context

The No Child Left Behind Act (NCLB) of 2002 is the most extensive federal initiative targeting the American education system. Charged with boosting national performance rates and closing demographic performance gaps, it has a broad system of goals and strategies (Epstein, 2005; Karen, 2005). One central, if underpublicized, element of this legislation (Section 1118) is its emphasis on building family–school partnerships to improve performance in high-risk segments of the student population. Another is its focus on English-language learners—predominantly the children of immigrants from Latin America—as one such high-risk segment.

Although NCLB represents the most important recent shift in US education policy, it was preceded by dramatic changes in US social welfare policy that were ushered in only a few years earlier under the Welfare Reform Act of 1996. Known formally as the Personal Responsibility and Work Opportunity Reconciliation Act (PRWORA), welfare reform has reshaped the opportunities and supports for the disadvantaged mothers of young children. Among its many provisions, it sharply reduced opportunities for education and training, especially for parents with limited English skills. For example, under PRWORA, the number of hours in educational activities that states can count toward hours of work for a welfare client has shrunk dramatically. Under the Workforce Investment Act of 1998 (or WIA, which is the country's primary workforce development program for unemployed workers), access to post-secondary education has also diminished, and, where training is still available, it is generally limited to short-term training courses rather than those that count toward a degree. Moreover, educational service providers (e.g., community colleges) are increasingly reluctant to offer services to disadvantaged WIA clients due to WIA's strict new accountability policies (Goldrick-Rab & Shaw, 2005; Shaw & Goldrick-Rab, 2006). At the same time, PRWORA dramatically restricted immigrants' access to welfare and other social programs, which has exacerbated their already-precarious financial position (Fix & Passel, 1999).

The coupling of these various NCLB and welfare-reform initiatives positions our conceptual model as quite relevant to extant policy goals and how these goals work in support of and in opposition to each other. Indeed, we argue that the disconnect between NCLB, welfare reform, and the circumstances and needs of the Latin American immigrant population has obscured the important issue of how policies in both realms (education and social welfare) will ultimately affect the development and achievement of the current generation of immigrant children from Latin America. Our conceptual model, then, is designed to promote research on the potential ramifications of this disconnect. The future research generated by this model will seek to identify which avenues offer the most promising route to meeting the twin goals of achieving economic self-sufficiency (the stated aim of PRWORA) and bridging the distance between families and schools in the Latino/a immigrant population (a mandate of NCLB). Going forward, it will be critical for studies of parental education and the early educational experiences of Latin American immigrant children in the US to keep this policy backdrop in mind. In other words, research aiming to inform the parental involvement and English-language learner provisions of NCLB needs to remember the socioeconomic obstacles that, if left unaddressed, will likely undermine any action on this provision, while research aiming to understand welfare reform needs to recognize the qualifying role of human capital in efforts to raise financial capital in economically disadvantaged populations.

Life Course Dynamics and the Isolation of Educational Attainment Effects

The redesign of welfare reform and the substantial body of social and behavioral research that it has generated over the last decade (see Blank, 2002; Duncan et al., 2007) clearly demonstrates how the educational attainment of women—the driving force of our conceptual model—is intricately entangled with other life-course trajectories. Employment histories and marital histories are two prominent examples. Importantly, these two other life-course trajectories have also been clearly and convincingly implicated in the prevalence of and disparities in family–school partnerships. Consequently, carefully considering how these other life circumstances overlap with increased maternal educational attainment is absolutely vital to assessing the value of our conceptual model.

First, as maternal educational attainment was deprioritized by welfare reform, maternal employment was prioritized. Reflecting an ideology that low-income mothers can best achieve economic self-sufficiency through committed attachments to the paid labor force, PRWORA requires that low-income mothers work as a condition of receiving cash assistance (Blank, 2002). To help boost their employment prospects, new work-support programs were developed, including large expansions of the Earned Income Tax Credit, transitional Medicaid and new State Children's Health Insurance Programs, and Child Care Block Grants so that working mothers can better secure childcare (Blank, 2002). Similarly, WIA followed its "philosophical cousin" PRWORA by promoting a work-first approach (Goldrick-Rab & Shaw, 2005).

Presumably, maternal employment could both increase and decrease mothers' propensity to partner with their young children's schools. On one hand, working increases constraints on how mothers can invest their time. On the other, working also increases access to social capital and expands world views, both of which motivate more effective maternal investments in children (Muller, 1995; Waldfogel, 2006). Some evidence suggests that the latter change outweighs the former, especially for part-time workers. Yet, this evidence is based on samples drawn from the general population and may or may not hold for Latin American immigrants. These women have low rates of paid employment relative to the overall female labor-force participation rate and, when they do work, are typically segregated in the unstable low-wage labor market (Capps, Fix, Passel, Ost, & Perez-Lopez, 2003).

If increased work effort translates into relatively few material rewards and potentially more time constraints and stress for low-income Latina immigrant mothers, the potential for this human-capital development strategy to lead to their increased involvement with schools and in educational activities at home is questionable. This potential stumbling block heightens the relevance of the link between maternal education change and employment changes. Educational attainment can improve the type of employment a woman secures, in terms of stability, control of time, cognitive stimulation, and exposure to social networks. Thus, with increased educational attainment, the positives of maternal employment—for family–school partnerships at least—might counterbalance or exceed the negatives.

Second, in tandem with the rise in the work-first philosophy at the expense of educational investments, welfare reform has also increasingly emphasized marriage. For example, it provides states with bonuses if they raise marriage rates among their welfare populations (Parke, 2004). The second Bush administration's "Healthy Marriage Initiative" expands on these ideas by additionally providing funding of $150 million each year to states for healthy marriage promotion and fatherhood programs (Administration for Children and Families, 2006). A guiding principle is that marriage can improve the economic prospects and psychological health of men and women and the children they might eventually parent together (Administration for Children and Families, 2006). Again, the philosophy behind this initiative is relevant to family–school partnerships but that relevance is weaker in the Latin American population.

Marital transitions are strongly related to income and economic stress, and they also could affect a mother's opportunities to invest in and manage children's education (McLanahan, 2004). Marriage has the potential to improve economic security due to its economies of scale and the possibility of increasing the number of earners in a household. Presumably, the number of participating parents also increases, possibly easing the parenting burden of women. Little is known, as yet, about how mothers' transitions to marriage will affect parental behavior (including education-focused behavior) and child outcomes (e.g., achievement and learning), in part because existing studies of the populations targeted by the reforms have registered little change in marriage patterns of single mothers in the post-welfare-reform period (Gibson-Davis, Edin, & McLanahan, 2006).

In theory, then, married mothers should face fewer constraints on and enjoy more opportunities to build family–school partnerships. Yet, in the Latin American immigrant population, marriage rates (both legal and common-law) are already quite high and stable (Phillips & Sweeney, 2005; Wildsmith & Raley, 2005). Moreover, many dual-parent families in this population adopt more "traditional" arrangements whereby mothers have full responsibility for childcare. At the same time, Latino men (the largest pool of potential partners for these women) are also segregated in the unstable low-wage labor market (Hernandez, 2004; Hernandez & Darke, 1999). As a result, the relation between marriage and family–school partnerships is likely dependent on the co-occurring educational experiences of women.

Thus, employment and marital statuses of Latin American immigrant mothers are likely both cause and consequence of their educational attainment. Moreover, employment and marital changes that result from increased educational attainment likely play the biggest role in mothers' abilities to build family–school partnerships. As a result, disentangling the interconnected threads of education, work, and marriage is a must for testing the validity of our conceptual model.

A Note of Caution

As noted earlier, mothers who are motivated to advance their own education are conceivably also more inclined and able to invest in their children's education (Behrman & Wolfe, 1987). This possibility is even stronger for Latin American immigrant mothers, whose overall experiences in the education system tend to be limited. This selection (or endogeneity) problem represents a major vulnerability in all research with observational data, even longitudinal data, that interferes with researchers' ability to make causal inferences (Duncan, Magnuson, & Ludwig, 2004). Without sound causal inference, the potential for social research to inform policy is limited. Thus, any serious attempt to assess our conceptual model must address these selection issues.

The best tools for addressing selection in our conceptual model and promoting causal inference necessary for linking this model to policy goals are data from experiments and/or natural experiments. Examples of the former include random assignment demonstrations. Examples of the latter include exogenously determined increases in education (Shadish, Cook, & Campbell, 2002). At the moment, we know of no such data sources for studying Latin American immigrants and their children. Until such data sources are available, other methods must be utilized. One option is the use of propensity scores, in which the variables that index the probability of being in some state (e.g., increasing educational attainment) according to a host of factors are entered into regression models as covariates or instead are used to weight such models (Morgan, 2001). Another option, common in economic research, is instrumental variable analysis, a strategy in which a researcher must identify a factor that affects a child outcome only through its effect on the predictor variable of interest (here, increased maternal education) and does not have a direct effect on that child outcome (Gennetian, Morris, & Magnuson, 2008). Currie and Morretti (2003) demonstrated how a measure of the opening of colleges in women's geographic areas can be used as an instrumental variable to promote causal inference about the developmental significance of increased maternal education.

In the absence of experimental or quasi-experimental data, no easy solution exists for establishing causal inference in our conceptual model. Various alternatives have pros and cons. Triangulating these alternatives might be the best solution for now. Whatever the case, the selection problem is large enough that it cannot be ignored.

Conclusion

Our goal in this chapter has been to introduce a two-generation approach to social mobility—investing in education in the first generation to realize gains in the second—for social and behavioral scientists to pursue. A focus on maternal education is especially relevant to the plight of Latina immigrants and their young children. Incorporating these mothers into the education system as *students* will likely empower them to engage the system as *parents* at a time when their children's educational trajectories are at their most malleable and educational investments have the biggest long-term payoff.

At the same time, it will also be important for social scientists testing this approach to give thought to cost–benefit considerations. Many have argued recently that the best value per dollar invested is in early education (Heckman, 2006). Some might argue that investing in mothers, therefore, is potentially time consuming and ineffective. In response to this concern, we turn to Holzer and Lerman (2007), who present compelling new evidence that workforce development (which includes education and training) can be an effective antipoverty strategy for disadvantaged individuals. Specifically, these authors analyze data on recent employment and wage trends to assess the likely future demand for workers in "middle-skill" jobs—i.e., those requiring more than secondary school but less than a bachelor's degree. They find that demand for such jobs will remain quite robust and that growth in supply of workers with these skills will likely shrink. Thus, they argue, education and training programs that help less-educated workers gain these skills remain a worthwhile investment. Moreover, LaLonde (1995) points out that the one group of less-skilled workers who benefits from public-sector-sponsored training programs is disadvantaged women.

It is also instructive to compare the results in Carneiro et al. (2007) on the impact of maternal years of education on children's outcomes to the impacts of other types of interventions (recall the impacts in Carneiro et al. were such that a one-year increase in maternal education translated into a 0.10 standard deviation increase in children's test scores). In comparison, the large class-size reductions (from 22 to 15 students per class) in the Tennessee STAR experiment (Krueger, 1999) yielded test score gains of 0.20 standard deviations, or two years of maternal schooling; Dahl and Locher (2006) found that a $1,000 increase in family income increases children's math test scores by 0.026 of a standard deviation (0.036 for reading). Looked at this way, policies to increase mothers' education are serious competitors to other types of interventions.

The policy relevance of this line of work we are proposing is clear. It also addresses many of the issues fueling the public and political debate over immigration. Finally, it reflects the valued role of the education system as a tool for social change. We encourage social and behavioral scientists, therefore, to test this conceptual model, assess variability in the model by developmental status, type of educational experience, and other kinds of parenting behavior, and then extend the model to other types of child outcomes and other segments of the immigrant population.

Acknowledgment

This research was supported by two young scholar awards, one to each of the authors, from the Changing Faces of America's Children program at the Foundation for Child Development. It was also supported by a center grant (R24 HD042849) from the National Institute of Child Health and Human Development to the Population Research Center at the University of Texas at Austin. Opinions are those of the authors and not necessarily those of the funders.

References

Administration for Children and Families. (2006). *Healthy marriage initiative.* www.acf.dhhs.gov/healthymarriage/index.html.

Astone, N., Schoen, R., Ensminger, M., & Rothert, K. (2000). School re-entry in early adulthood: The case of inner city African Americans. *Sociology of Education, 73*, 133–154.

Barnett, W.S., & Belfield, C. (2006). Early childhood development and social mobility. *The Future of Children, 16*, 73–98.

Bean, F., & Stevens, G. (2003). *America's newcomers and the dynamics of diversity.* New York: Russell Sage.

Bean, F.D., Brown, S.K., & Rumbaut, R.G. (2006). Mexican immigrant political and economic incorporation. *Perspectives on Politics, 4*, 309–313.

Behrman, J., & Wolfe, B. (1987). How does mothers' schooling affect family health, nutrition, medical care usage, and household sanitation? *Journal of Econometrics, 36*, 185–104.

Bernhardt, A., Morris, M., Handcock, M.S., & Scott, M.A. (2001). *Divergent paths: Economic mobility in the new American labor market.* New York: Russell Sage.

Black, S., Devereux, P., & Salvanes, K. (2005). *The more the merrier? The effect of family size and birth order on children's education.* Centre for the Economics of Education Discussion Paper 0050.

Blank, R. (2002). Evaluating welfare reform in the United States. *Journal of Economic Literature*, 1105–1166.

Capps, R. (2001). *Hardship among children of immigrants: Findings from the 1999 National Survey of America's Families, Series B, No. B-29.* Washington, DC: Urban Institute.

Capps, R., Fix, M., Passel, J., Ost, J., & Perez-Lopez, D. (2003). *A profile of the low-wage immigrant workforce.* Washington, DC: Urban Institute.

Carneiro, P., Meghir, C., & Parey, M. (2007). *Maternal education, home environments and the development of children and adolescents.* Institute for the Study of Labor (IZA) Discussion Paper 3072.

Chou, S.Y., Liu, J.T., Grossman, M., & Joyce, T. (2003). *Parental education and child health: Evidence from a natural experiment in Taiwan.* National Bureau of Economic Research Working Paper 13466.

Coleman, J.S. (1988). Social capital and the creation of human capital. *American Journal of Sociology, 94*, S95–120.

Crosnoe, R. (2006). *Mexican roots, American schools: Helping Mexican immigrant children succeed.* Palo Alto, CA: Stanford University Press.

Crosnoe, R. (2007). Child care and the early educational experiences of children from Mexican immigrant families. *International Migration Review, 41*, 152–181.

Currie, J., & Moretti, E. (2002). *Mothers' education and the intergenerational transmission of human capital: Evidence from college openings and longitudinal data.* National Bureau of Economic Research Working Paper W9360.

Dahl, G., & Lochner, L. (2006). *The impact of family income on child achievement.* Unpublished manuscript.

Deaton, A. (2002). Policy implications of the gradient of health and wealth. *Health Affairs, 21*, 13–30.

Dee, T. (2004). Are there civic returns to education? *Journal of Public Economics, 88*, 1697–1720.

Driscoll, A.K. (1999). Risk of high school dropout among immigrant and native Hispanic youth. *International Migration Review, 33*, 857–876.

Duncan, G.J., Huston, A.C., & Weisner, T.S. (2007). *Higher ground: New hope for the working poor and their children.* New York: Russell Sage.

Duncan, G.J., Magnuson, K., & Ludwig, J. (2004). The endogeneity problem in developmental studies. *Research in Human Development, 1*, 59–80.

Eccles, J.S., & Harold, R.D. (1993). Parent-school involvement during the early adolescent years. *Teachers College Record, 94*, 568–587.

Entwisle, D.R., & Alexander, K.L. (2002). The first grade transition in life course perspective. In J. Mortimer & M. Shanahan (Eds.), *Handbook of the life course* (pp. 229–250). New York: Kluwer Academic/Plenum.

Entwisle, D., Alexander, K.L., & Olson, L.S. (1997). *Children, schools and inequality.* Boulder, CO: Westview Press.

Epstein, J.L. (2005). Attainable goals? The spirit and letter of the No Child Left Behind Act on parental involvement. *Sociology of Education, 78,* 179–182.

Feliciano, C. (2005). Does selective migration matter? Explaining ethnic disparities in educational attainment among immigrants' children. *International Migration Review, 39*(4), 841–871.

Fischer, C.S., & Hout, M. (2006). *Century of difference: How America changed in the last one hundred years.* New York: Russell Sage.

Fix, M., & Passel, J. (1999, March). *Trends in noncitizens' and citizens' use of public benefits following welfare reform.* Urban Institute Research Report. Washington, DC: The Urban Institute.

Fry, R. (2007). Are immigrant youth faring better in American schools? *International Migration Review, 41,* 579–601.

Fuligni, A., & Yoshikawa, H. (2004). Parental investments in children in immigrant families. In A. Kalil & T. DeLeire (Eds.), *Family investments in children: Resources and parenting behaviors that promote success* (pp. 139–161). Mahwah, NJ: Erlbaum.

Gandara, P., Rumberger, R., Maxwell-Jolly, J., & Callahan, R. (2003). English learners in California schools: Unequal resources, unequal outcomes. *Education Policy Analysis Archives, 11*(36). Retrieved April 5, 2009, from http://epaa.asu.edu/epaa/v11n36.

Gennetian, L., Magnuson, K., & Morris, P. (2008). From statistical associations to causation: What developmentalists can learn from instrumental variables techniques coupled with experimental data. *Developmental Psychology, 44*(2), 381–394.

Gibson-Davis, C., Edin, K., & McLanahan, S. (2006). High hopes but even higher expectations: The retreat from marriage of low-income couples. *Journal of Marriage and Family, 67,* 1301–1312.

Glick, J.E., & Hohmann Marriott, B. (2007). Academic performance of young children in immigrant families: The significance of race, ethnicity, and national origin. *International Migration Review, 41,* 371–402.

Glick, J.E., & White, M.J. (2003). The academic trajectories of immigrant youths: Analysis within and across cohorts. *Demography, 40,* 589–603.

Goldin, C., & Katz, L. (2007). *Long-run changes in the U.S. wage structure: Narrowing, widening, polarizing.* National Bureau of Economic Research working paper series 13568.

Goldrick-Rab, S., & Shaw, K. (2005). Racial and ethnic differences in the impact of Work-First reforms on access to postsecondary education. *Educational Evaluation and Policy Analysis, 27,* 291–307.

Grieco, E., & Ray, B. (2004). *Mexican immigrants in the US labor force.* Washington, DC: Migration Policy Institute.

Heckman, J. (2006). Skill formation and the economics of investing in disadvantaged children. *Science, 312*(5782), 1900–1902.

Hernandez, D.J. (2004). Demographic change and the life circumstances of immigrant families. *The Future of Children, 14,* 17–48.

Hernandez, D. (2006). Young Hispanic children in the U.S.: A demographic portrait based on Census 2000. *Report to the National Task Force on Early Childhood Education for Hispanics.* Tempe, AZ: Arizona State University.

Hernandez, D.J., & Darke, K. (1999). Socioeconomic and demographic risk factors and resources among children in immigrant and native-born families: 1910, 1960, and 1990. In D.J. Hernandez (Ed.), *Children of immigrants: Health, adjustment, and public assistance* (pp. 19–125). Washington, DC: National Academy Press.

Hill, N.E. (2001). Parenting and academic socialization as they relate to school readiness: The role of ethnicity and family income. *Journal of Educational Psychology, 93,* 686–697.

Hirschman, C. (2001). The educational enrollment of immigrant youth: A test of the segmented-assimilation hypothesis. *Demography, 38*, 317–336.

Holzer, H., & Lerman, R. (2007). *America's forgotten middle-skill jobs.* Washington, DC: Urban Institute.

Hoover-Dempsey, K., & Sandler, H.M. (1997). Why do parents become involved in their children's education? *Review of Educational Research, 67*, 3–42.

Kao, G., & Thompson, J. (2003). Race and ethnic stratification in educational achievement and attainment. *Annual Review of Sociology, 29*, 417–442.

Kao, G., & Tienda, M. (1995). Optimism and achievement: The educational performance of immigrant youth. *Social Science Quarterly, 76*, 1–19.

Kao, G. (1999). Psychological well-being and educational achievement among immigrant youth. In D.J. Hernandez (Ed.), *Children of immigrants: Health, adjustment, and public assistance* (pp. 410–477). Washington, DC: National Academy.

Karen, D. (2005). No Child Left Behind? Sociology ignored! *Sociology of Education, 78*, 165–182.

Kasinitz, P., Mollenkopf, J., & Waters, M. (Eds.). (2004). *Becoming New Yorkers: Ethnographies of the new second generation.* New York: Russell Sage.

Knudsen, E., Heckman, J., Cameron, J., & Shonkoff, J. (2006). Economic, neurobiological, and behavioral perspectives on building America's future workforce. *Proceedings of the National Academy of Sciences, 103*, 10155–10162.

Krueger, A. (1999). Experimental estimates of education production functions. *Quarterly Journal of Economics, 114*, 497–532.

LaLonde, R. (1995). The promise of public sector-sponsored training programs. *Journal of Economic Perspectives, 9*, 149–168.

Lareau, A. (1989). *Home advantage: Social class and parental intervention in elementary education.* London: Falmer Press.

Lemieux, T. (2006). Postsecondary education and increased wage inequality. *American Economic Review, 96*, 195–199.

Lopez, G. (2001). The value of hard work: Lessons on parent involvement from an (im)migrant household. *Harvard Educational Review, 71*, 416–437.

Magnuson, K. (2003). *The effect of increases in welfare mothers' education on their young children's academic and behavioral outcomes.* University of Wisconsin, Institute for Research on Poverty Discussion Paper, 1274-03.

Magnuson, K. (2006). *Maternal education and children's academic trajectories during middle childhood.* Mimeograph, University of Wisconsin.

Magnuson, K., Lahaie, C., & Waldfogel, J. (2006). Preschool and school readiness of children of immigrants. *Social Science Quarterly, 87*, 1241–1262.

Matthews, H., & Ewen, D. (2006). *Reaching all children? Understanding early care and education participation among immigrant families.* Washington, DC: Center for Law and Social Policy.

McLanahan, S. (2004). Children and the second demographic transition. *Demography, 41*, 607–628.

Milligan, K., Moretti, E., & Oreopoulos, P. (2004). Does education improve citizenship? Evidence from the United States and the United Kingdom. *Journal of Public Economics, 88*, 1667–1695.

Morgan, S.L. (2001). Counterfactuals, causal effect heterogeneity, and the Catholic school effect on learning. *Sociology of Education, 74*, 341–374.

Muller, C. (1995). Maternal employment, parent involvement, and mathematics achievement among adolescents. *Journal of Marriage and the Family, 57*, 85–100.

National Center for Education Statistics. (2006). *School and parent interaction by household language and poverty status: 2002–03.* US Department of Education: NCES Report 2006-086.

National Task Force on Early Childhood Education for Hispanics. (2006). *A demographic portrait of young Hispanic children in the United States.* Retrieved April 5, 2009, from www.ecehispanic.org.

Okagaki, L., & Frensch, P.A. (1998). Parenting and children's school achievement: A multi-ethnic perspective. *American Educational Research Journal, 35*, 123–144.

Oreopolous, P., Page, M., & Stevens, A. (2006). The intergenerational effects of compulsory schooling. *Journal of Labor Economics, 24*, 729–760.

Parke, M. (2004). *Marriage-related provisions in recent welfare reauthorization proposals: A summary.* Washington, DC: Center for Law and Social Policy.

Phillips, J.A., & Sweeney, M.M. (2005). Premarital cohabitation and the risk of marital disruption among white, black, and Mexican American women. *Journal of Marriage and Family, 67*, 296–314.

Pianta, R.C., & Walsh, D.J. (1996). *High-risk children in schools: Constructing sustaining relationships.* New York: Routledge.

Portes, A., & Rumbaut, R.G. (2001). *Legacies: The story of the immigrant second generation.* Berkeley, CA: University of California.

Portes, A., & Zhou, M. (1993). The new second generation: Segmented assimilation and its variants among post-1965 immigrant youth. *Annals of the American Academy of Political and Social Science, 530*, 740–798.

Quezada, R., Diaz, D., & Sanchez, M. (2003). Involving Latino parents. *Leadership, 33*, 32–34.

Raver, C.C., Gershoff, E., & Aber, L. (2007). Testing equivalence of mediating models of income, parenting, and school readiness for White, Black, and Hispanic children in a national sample. *Child Development, 78*, 96–115.

Reardon, S., & Galindo, C. (2007). Patterns of Hispanic students' math skill proficiency in the early elementary grades. *Journal of Latinos and Education, 6*(3), 229–251.

Reese, L., Balzano, S. Gallimore, R., & Goldberg, C. (1995). The concept of educacion: Latino family values and American schooling. *International Journal of Educational Research, 23*, 57–61.

Sawhill, I. (2006). Opportunity in America: The role of education. *The Future of Children Policy Brief.* Retrieved April 5, 2009, from www.futureofchildren.org.

Shadish, W.R., Cook, T.D., & Campbell, D.T. (2002). *Experimental and quasi-experimental designs for causal inference.* New York: Houghton Mifflin.

Shaw, K., & Goldrick-Rab, S. (2006). The effect of work-first federal policies on access to community colleges for Latinos. *New Directions in Community Colleges, 133*, 61–70.

Sherrod, L.R., Flanagan, C., & Youniss, J. (2002). Dimensions of citizenship and opportunities for youth development: The what, why, when, where and who of citizenship development. *Applied Developmental Science, 6*, 264–272.

Suárez-Orozco, C., & Suárez-Orozco, M. (1995). *Transformations: Immigration, family life, and achievement motivation among Latino adolescents.* Stanford, CA: Stanford University Press.

Suárez-Orozco, C., & Suárez-Orozco, M. (2001). *Children of immigration.* Cambridge, MA: Harvard University Press.

Thomas, D., Strauss, J., & Henriques, M.H. (1991). How does mother's education affect child height? *Journal of Human Resources, 26*, 183–211.

Tyack, D.B. (1974). *The one best system: A history of American urban education.* Cambridge, MA: Harvard University Press.

Waldfogel, J. (2006). *What children need.* Cambridge, MA: Harvard University Press.

Wildsmith, E., & Raley, R.K. (2005). Race/ethnic differences in non-marital fertility: A focus on Mexican American women. *Journal of Marriage and the Family, 68*, 491–508.

Wojtkiewicz, R.A., & Donato, K.M. (1995). Hispanic educational attainment and the effects of family background and nativity. *Social Forces, 74*, 559–574.

11 Does It Begin at School or Home?

Institutional Origins of Overweight Among Young Children in Immigrant Families

Jennifer Van Hook, Elizabeth Baker, and Claire Altman

Introduction

Children of immigrants and their families face unique challenges as they adjust to life in the US. These challenges are not only related to the multiple and often difficult adjustments they must make with respect to schooling, language learning, and their social lives, but also concern possible threats to their health. Children of immigrants may be particularly vulnerable to health risks because more than half of the children of immigrants in the US are living in families with low incomes (i.e., incomes lower than twice the official poverty level) (Reardon-Anderson, Capps, & Fix, 2002). In addition, as children of immigrants and their families attempt to navigate their new environments, they may find it more difficult to avoid health hazards than others who may be more familiar with the US environment (primarily schools, neighborhoods, businesses, and cities) and US healthcare systems. In this chapter, we focus on one potential threat to health among children of immigrants: overweight among children. Following the recommendations of the Centers for Disease Control, we use the term "overweight" rather than "obesity" when referring to adiposity among children. The two terms are distinct in that "obesity" refers to an excess of body fat while "overweight" is a measure of weight relative to height, and it is not well-established how to measure excess body fat in children, particularly on the basis of height and weight. We specifically examine the degree to which children of immigrants vs. children of natives encounter hazards or unique challenges in their environments that could lead to overweight, and further seek to explain differences in overweight in terms of factors associated with the home environment versus those factors associated with neighborhoods and schools.

In the past 25 years in the US, the prevalence of overweight and at-risk for overweight children quadrupled, increasing from roughly 4% to 16% (National Center for Health Statistics, 2004). Using the guidelines provided by the Center for Disease Control, we define the term "overweight" as having a body mass index (BMI) at or exceeding the 95th percentile within age- and gender-specific groupings (of a standard population of children taken from the 1970s and 1980s), and "at-risk for overweight" as between the 85th and 95th percentiles. Percentile BMI is the most widely used measure of adiposity in children because it is strongly related to health outcomes in children. Overweight among children has been linked to a number of health problems including hypertension, elevated blood pressure, and diabetes that track into adulthood (Deckelbaum & Williams, 2001a; Dietz, 1998; Strauss & Pollack, 2003), and is related to difficulties in social adjustment, poor mental health, and lower academic achievement (Datar, 2004; Strauss & Pollack, 2003).

Children of immigrants may face particularly high risks for developing overweight. A common finding emerging from research on immigrant health is that health outcomes of immigrants are better than natives when they first arrive in the US, but are likely to deteriorate with increased time and generations in the US (Hummer, Rogers, Nam, & LeClere, 1999; Landale, Oropesa, Llanes, & Gorman, 1999; Rumbaut & Weeks, 1989). Although selective migration may account in part for immigrants' initial healthy outcomes (Palloni & Arias, 2004), the dominant hypothesis is that exposure to the American environment (e.g., fast food industry and advertising, availability of cheap, prepackaged food, reliance on cars) leads to the "Americanization" of health behaviors involving diet, exercise, and smoking, which in turn leads to overweight and obesity (Blumenthal, 2002; Carter, 2002; Fried & Nestle, 2002). Immigrant families may be particularly vulnerable to health risks involving diet and exercise for a number of reasons related to their unfamiliarity with American food, language barriers, and inability to purchase ingredients to make foods from their countries of origin.

The Early Childhood Longitudinal Survey

To gain some insight about the health behaviors and weight status of children of immigrants as well as the relative influence of home vs. school environments on these outcomes, we draw upon a unique survey conducted by the National Center for Education Statistics: the Early Childhood Longitudinal Survey—Kindergarten Class of 1998–1999 (ECLS-K). The ECLS-K followed a nationally representative sample of roughly 21,000 children from kindergarten through fifth grade. The ECLS-K is currently the only nationally representative sample that both provides a wide breadth of measures about the health and well-being of children in middle childhood and includes an oversample of Asian and Hispanic children. The ECLS-K thus enables us to examine the development of US children of immigrants in greater detail than has ever been possible before. Like many longitudinal data collections, the ECLS-K was unable to collect data from all subjects for all time periods. In particular, 22% of the respondents were missing information on parent's nativity status. To address this issue, we used multiple imputation to fill in the missing values.[1] The final analytic sample for the results we present here includes 10,995 children: 2,300 children of immigrants and 8,695 children of natives.

The children were weighed and measured during the spring and fall of kindergarten and first grade, and during the fall of third and fifth grades. We rely primarily on the fifth-grade data because the ECLS-K asked children information about their diet and physical activity only in fifth grade. Much of the prior research on child obesity has established body-mass index (weight/height^2) as the most suitable adiposity index for children (Poskitt, 2000). BMI is also a preferred measure because height and weight are easy to obtain with a reasonable degree of accuracy across different settings. Here, we rely on two BMI-based indicators that were especially designed to measure children's weight status. Percentile BMI provides the BMI ranking of a child compared against age- and sex-specific Center for Disease Control growth charts (Kuczmarski, Ogden, & Guo, 2002) and the percentage overweight or at-risk for overweight is the percentage of children with BMIs above the 85th percentile. Percentile BMI compares children today against a standard population of children taken from US surveys and vital statistics from the 1970s and 1980s (Kuczmarski et al., 2002), a time period prior to the rapid increase in overweight among children. Thus the measure does not change or "recalibrate" over time as overweight becomes more prevalent. One potential problem with the measure, however, is that body shapes and children's growth patterns may vary across race/ethnic and national origin groups, so the same standard may not be validly applied to all groups uniformly (Cole, Bellizzi, Flegal, & Dietz, 2000). These types of variations may affect comparisons across groups (such as between Hispanics and non-Hispanic Whites), but are unlikely to affect comparisons within groups (such as between children of immigrants vs. children of natives within the same national origin or race/ethnic group). For this reason, and because the CDC standards are widely used in the US context, we opted to continue to use the CDC standards here, although we recognize that further research on this topic is warranted.

In addition to possible differences in height and weight growth patterns, immigrant groups vary widely with respect to the timing and motivations for migration, their legal status, the reception they have once they arrive in the country, socioeconomic status, and level of community- and family-level support available to them (Bean & Stevens, 2003). Therefore, we distinguish among broad race/ethnic groupings: non-Hispanic Whites, non-Hispanic Blacks, Mexicans, other Hispanics, and Asians. These groupings are subdivided into the children of immigrants (i.e., having at least one parent born outside the US) and children of natives (i.e., having both parents born in the US). Although Puerto Ricans living in the US are US citizens by birth and not immigrants, we treat island-born parents as immigrants here because the process of migration and incorporation for them is similar in many respects to those of immigrants. Unfortunately, the ECSL-K sample does not include enough Asian children of natives to produce reliable estimates, so we excluded them from the sample. Throughout the remainder of the chapter, we refer to non-Hispanic Whites and non-Hispanic Blacks simply as "whites" and "blacks," and we refer to children of immigrants and children of natives simply as "immigrant children" and "native children."

Weight Status Among Children of Immigrants

The existing research literature is consistent with the idea that young children in immigrant families may be at higher risk of developing overweight and obesity. First, Hispanic children, many of whom are the children of immigrants, have been disproportionately affected by the obesity epidemic. Among children aged 6–11 in 2003/2004, 22.5% of Mexican Americans vs. 17.7% of non-Hispanic Whites were classified as overweight (Ogden et al., 2006), and 42.9% of Mexican American children compared with roughly one-third (36.9%) of non-Hispanic White children were overweight or at risk for overweight. Second, Hispanic children of immigrants appear to be even more likely to be overweight than Hispanic children of natives (Baker, Balistreri, & Van Hook, 2007).

As we show in Table 11.1, immigrant children in the ECLS-K are more likely to be overweight or at risk for overweight than native children, but this is much more apparent among boys than girls. Among native fifth-grade boys, 53% of Hispanics, 36% of Blacks, and 40% of Whites were overweight or at risk. Although these figures are high

Table 11.1 At-Risk for overweight among Fifth Grade Children by Race/ethnicity, Generation, and Gender

% at risk for overweight	*Children of natives*			*Children of immigrants*				
	Hispanic	*Black*	*White*	*Mexican*	*Other Hispanic*	*Asian*	*Black*	*White*
Boys	53.4*	36.0	39.3	57.0***	51.3*	41.6	48.6	53.5
Girls	47.3**	48.4***	33.9	44.2*	32.7**	27.6	26.7*	25.0*

Source: Early Childhood Longitudinal Study – Kindergarten Class of 1998–1999.

Notes
t-tests were used to assess the significance of differences from native non-Hispanic white children.
$^{***}p < 0.001$, $^{**}p < 0.01$, $^{*}p < 0.05$, and $^{\dagger}p < 0.10$.

(relative to the past), they are even higher for immigrant boys, particularly among Hispanics. For example, 57% of Mexican immigrant boys were overweight or at risk (17 points higher than White native boys). In addition, immigrant boys tended to weigh more than native boys *within each racial/ethnic grouping*. For example, 57% of Mexican immigrant boys were overweight or at risk compared to 53% of Hispanic native boys. Similarly, 49% and 53% of Black and White immigrant boys were overweight or at risk compared with 36% and 39% of Black and White native boys, respectively.

Among girls, immigrants tend to weigh less than natives. Among White children, 27% of immigrant girls vs. 34% of native girls were overweight or at risk for overweight. The immigrant advantage was even greater among Black girls. One-quarter (25%) of Black immigrant girls were overweight or at risk compared with nearly half (48.4%) of Black native girls. Finally, Mexican and other Hispanic immigrant girls tended to be less likely to be overweight or at risk than Hispanic native girls, although the difference between Mexican immigrant girls and Hispanic native girls is small (44.2% vs. 47.3%).

Diet and Physical Activity Among Children of Immigrants

These patterns in children's weight status may be linked to health behaviors. The ECSL-K data asked children a limited set of questions about the types and amounts of foods they ate during the previous week. Two items—soda and juice—are known to be associated with child obesity (Cullen, Ash, Warneke, & de Moor, 2002). As shown in Table 11.2, Mexican immigrant boys drank on average more servings of soda per week than did native children, while Asian and Black immigrant boys drank less. This corresponds with the finding that Mexican immigrant boys were the most likely to be overweight or at risk for overweight. On the other hand, among girls, Black immigrants drank more soda than White natives but there were few other differences in soda or juice consumption. Two other food items—fruit and vegetables—are known to be negatively associated with child obesity (although some fruits have more calories than others). Here, the immigrant children were more advantaged than native children. Among both boys and girls, immigrant children tended to eat more servings of fruit than native Whites, but we found no significant differences in the tendency to eat vegetables.

Table 11.2 Diet and Physical Activity Among Fifth Grade Children by Race/ethnicity, Generation, and Gender

	Children of natives			*Children of immigrants*				
	Hispanic	*Black*	*White*	*Mexican*	*Other Hispanic*	*Asian*	*Black*	*White*
Diet								
Boys								
Soda (servings/wk)	3.1	3.1	3.0	3.3*	3.0	2.8†	2.4*	3.1
Juice (servings/wk)	2.7	2.7	2.6	2.7	2.9	2.7	3.1	3.0
Fruit (servings/wk)	3.3	3.2	3.1	3.8***	3.3†	3.8***	3.6	3.4
Vegetables (servings/wk)	6.6	7.0	6.8	6.5	6.6	6.6	7.1	7.3
Girls								
Soda (servings/wk)	3.1†	3.2*	2.8	3.0	2.8	2.8	3.5†	2.9
Juice (servings/wk)	3.0	2.6	2.8	2.6	2.6	2.6	2.3	3.0
Fruit (servings/wk)	3.2	3.6	3.3	3.8*	3.4	3.6†	3.5	3.7*
Vegetables (servings/wk)	7.4	6.4	6.7	56.9	6.4	6.9	7.0	6.7
Physical Activity								
Boys								
Exercise (days/weeks)	4.1	4.2	4.1	3.8*	3.9	3.4***	3.7	3.8†
% in group sport	78.8*	61.1**	73.4	59.0***	66.8	62.1*	53.5*	70.4
% in individual sport	38.0†	45.7	48.7	42.3	42.8	42.8	52.2	54.5
% in rec/outdoor sport	69.7	64.4*	75.7	57.2***	64.8*	53.9***	66.1	74.7
% in martial arts	8.1	5.7	8.5	7.6	10.5	14.4*	3.1	16.5*
% in dance	2.2	10.5***	3.6	3.6*	7.5	5.7	2.0	11.3*
% general calistatics	36.7	33.3*	44.5	30.3***	34.3*	34.6†	33.7	33.2†
% playground activities	77.2	65.5†	73.0	50.2***	64.1*	56.7***	66.5	68.2
Girls								
Exercise (days/weeks)	3.9	3.3	3.5	3.4	3.1 c	3.2*	3.0	3.5
% in group sport	59.6	58.5**	71.5	43.9***	41.2***	49.5***	69.6	67.5
% in individual sport	47.7	39.2*	49.8	33.5**	37.8*	42.7	49.0	56.8
% in rec/outdoor sport	67.4	54.1***	71.1	44.7***	39.6***	46.8***	57.8	69.7
% in martial arts	6.6	4.2	4.6	3.0	7.8	8.0	1.8	4.9
% in dance	16.5	26.1	20.4	13.2†	17.0	16.4	41.6*	32.6*
% general calistatics	37.5*	33.1*	43.1	23.2***	25.4**	31.5*	25.3†	45.1
% playground activities	61.6	60.3†	69.9	39.2***	46.0***	48.5***	66.2	67.0

Source: Early Childhood Longitudinal Survey Kindergarten Class of 1998–1999.

Notes
t-tests were used to assess the significance of differences from native non-Hispanic white children.
$^{***}p < 0.001$, $^{**}p < 0.01$, $^{*}p < 0.05$, and $^{\dagger}p < 0.10$.

Lower levels of physical activity may also contribute to the risk of overweight among children of immigrants. As shown in the lower panel of Table 11.2, immigrant boys and girls (particularly Asian boys and other Hispanic, Asian, and Black girls) on average exercised fewer days per week than native White boys and girls. In addition, Hispanic, Asian, and Black immigrant boys and girls were less likely to be engaged in special activities (such as group sports, outdoor sports, general calistatics, and playground activities) than White natives. For example, 59% of Mexican immigrant boys vs. 73% of White native boys were involved in group sports. Physical activity levels were particularly low among immigrant girls. For example, only 43% of Mexican, 41% of other Hispanic, and 50% of Asian immigrants were involved in group sports compared with 72% of White natives. A similar pattern can be seen for other activities except martial arts (Asian and White immigrant boys were more likely to be in martial arts than native boys).

Overall, these results suggest that immigrant boys—particularly Mexican boys—are at greater risk of developing overweight than native boys, and that this difference may be linked to higher levels of soda consumption and lower levels of physical activity. In addition, even though immigrant girls do not weigh more than native White girls in the fifth grade, their lower levels of physical activity may place them at risk for overweight in the future. However, these findings do not reveal much if anything about the environments that contribute to overweight among the young children of immigrants. Schools, neighborhoods, and families all may shape children's eating and physical activity patterns in ways that contribute to childhood obesity. For example, children of immigrants are more likely to live in poor neighborhoods and attend inner-city, low-income schools (Pong & Hao, 2007). If assimilation to American lifestyles is associated with overweight, children may pick up poor health habits and behaviors at school and among peers in their neighborhood. To this end, immigrant families themselves may buffer children from harmful influences beyond the home. On the other hand, immigrant parents may find it challenging to provide healthy meals and opportunities for exercise for their children, so children's obesity may originate from factors related to the home environment. We therefore turn our attention next to the broader contexts within which immigrant families and children live their lives.

School and Neighborhood Effects

The research literature is generally mixed concerning the relative importance of home versus school or neighborhood effects on children's health. Perhaps because it is easier for policy makers to change schools than parenting styles, prior research has focused heavily on school and neighborhood effects. Children spend roughly one-third of their waking hours in school (Hofferth & Sandberg, 2001) and half of American children receive either breakfast or lunch in school and one in ten receive both (Dwyer, 1995). Therefore, schools are in a unique position to positively influence the health and nutrition of children. Prior research has demonstrated that schools may be an effective tool to help counteract the increasing obesity epidemic. Datar and Strum (2004) demonstrate that increases in physical education are associated with decreased probabilities of overweight among school-aged girls. Similarly other research has found that offering nutritious breakfasts to low-income school children may be an effective way to combat child obesity (O'Dea & Wilson, 2006).

Despite the obviously prime position that schools have to influence health, many schools have been criticized for accepting offers from snack-food and soda companies to establish vending machines in their buildings (Anderson & Butcher, 2005; Wechsler, Brener, Kuester, & Miller, 2001). Soda and other sugar-sweetened drinks have consistently been found to increase odds of overweight among children and adolescents and significantly contribute to the amount of calories they consume (Cullen et al., 2002). While research has consistently shown that soda has adverse effects on children's health, access to vending machines in schools has increased rapidly. In 2000, 27% of elementary schools, 67% of middle schools, and 96% of high schools had vending machines and there were also increases in schools offering brand-name fast food and soda advertising on school grounds (Anderson, 2003).

Financial hardship seems to contribute to schools allowing vending machines on campus. Anderson and Butcher (2005) found that schools that received less of their revenues from the state or had tax and expenditure limits are more likely to have contracts with soda or snack-food companies. This finding is particularly troubling because low-income students are more likely to be overrepresented at these schools and low-income children are more at risk for becoming obese or overweight compared to their middle- or high-income counterparts (O'Malley, Johnston, Delva, Bachman, & Schulenberg, 2007). Indeed, Anderson and Butcher (2005) find a positive relationship between access to junk food at school and students' BMI. A 10% increase in access to junk food is associated with a 1% increase in student's BMI and children who have at least one obese parent appear to be especially susceptible to weight gain in schools that offer junk food. This suggests that environment and genetic propensity may interact to produce a higher risk of obesity and overweight among certain children.

Though interest of neighborhood-level correlates and obesity has continued to increase, very little empirical research has examined this association. Among adults, Robert and Reither (2004), found that community-level disadvantage and income inequality is positively associated with BMI, even after controlling for individual-level factors. In children, neighborhood influences appear to indirectly affect weight status through their effect on physical activity and television viewing. Molnar, Gortmaker, Bull, and Buka (2004) found that parental perceptions of neighborhood safety and neighborhood social disorder are negatively associated with physical activity among adolescents. Similarly, Burdette and Whitaker (2005) found that among preschool-aged children, neighborhood safety was negatively associated with outdoor play and positively associated with television viewing (Burdette & Whitaker, 2005; Molnar et al., 2004).

On the basis of this research, many scholars argue that the school environment with vending machines, shortened physical education and recess requirements, and high-fat lunches deserve blame for the childhood-obesity surge in recent decades. The idea that schools and neighborhoods pose significant risks to poor children resonates strongly with the major theoretical perspectives currently used to understand the assimilation of immigrants. Segmented assimilation theory in particular stresses the importance of the context of reception for shaping the incorporation patterns of immigrants (Bean & Stevens, 2003; Portes, 1998; Portes & Rumbaut, 2001; Portes & Zhou, 1993). A central theme is that schools and neighborhoods constitute important settings within which children of immigrants are introduced to the social hierarchies and racial barriers within American society (Bankston & Caldas, 1996; Fernandez-Kelly, 1995; Fernandez-Kelly & Schauffler, 1996; Portes, 1998; Portes & Zhou, 1993; Stanton-Salazar & Dornbusch, 1995). It is well-known that children of immigrants, particularly Hispanic children of immigrants, are more likely to attend high-poverty schools than other children (Crosnoe, 2005; Van Hook & Balistreri, 2002; Van Hook & Snyder, 2007) and live in high-poverty neighborhoods (Pong & Hao, 2007). Given the association between the affluence of neighborhoods and schools and health behaviors, diet, and weight status,

Table 11.3 School and Neighborhood Characteristics Among Fifth Grade Children by Race/ethnicity, Generation, and Gender

School and neighborhood characteristics	*Children of natives*			*Children of immigrants*				
	Hispanic	*Black*	*White*	*Mexican*	*Other Hispanic*	*Asian*	*Black*	*White*
Boys								
PE (min/wk)	81.9	75.1	78.5	91.5	66.5*	70.1	78.7	69.2
Recess (min/day)	18.4	14.0***	20.0	17.1*	17.3†	21.1	15.7	21.2
Sweets sold in school (%)	58.9	56.8	53.5	55.1	53.3	46.3	46.8	53.0
Snacks sold in school (%)	55.3	53.5	48.2	53.2	50.7	42.9	43.2	51.3
Soda sold in school (%)	41.6	40.6	40.7	41.6	41.5	39.0	25.8 c	45.6
Unsafe neighborhood (%)	37.8***	47.0***	11.4	50.8***	37.0***	29.5***	23.7*	23.2**
Girls								
PE (min/wk)	86.6	72.4	73.6	85.1	74.6	72.8	64.5	65.3*
Recess (min/day)	18.7	14.8***	20.2	16.2**	14.9***	19.6	12.4***	21.5
Sweets sold in school (%)	49.1	52.2	51.8	54.1	47.4	53.1	39.9	51.7
Snacks sold in school (%)	48.8	51.7	50.6	58.9	44.3	43.5	38.9	41.7
Soda sold in school (%)	37.3	38.1	40.0	43.0	31.9†	38.0	40.1	40.7
Unsafe neighborhood (%)	31.1***	46.7***	15.0	55.9***	48.9***	28.7***	42.9***	22.6*

Source: Early Childhood Longitudinal Survey – Kindergarten Class of 1998–1999.

Notes

t-tests were used to assess the significance of differences from native non-Hispanic White children.
***$p < 0.001$, **$p < 0.01$, *$p < 0.05$, and †$p < 0.10$.

children of immigrants are likely to face greater risks of overweight and obesity on account of the characteristics of their neighborhoods and the schools they attend.

Evidence from the ECLS-K also suggests that children of immigrants attend schools and live in neighborhoods that put them at greater risk for overweight and obesity. As shown in Table 11.3, Hispanic and Black immigrant boys and girls had fewer minutes of recess per day than did White natives, which may contribute to lower levels of physical activity. Lack of exercise may also be associated with living in an unsafe neighborhood. Immigrant children, particularly Hispanics, are more likely to live in "unsafe" neighborhoods than native White children. For example, among boys, over half of Mexican immigrant parents reported living in an "unsafe" neighborhood compared with only 11.4% of native White parents, and 38% among native Hispanic parents. Surprisingly however, immigrant children were no more likely to attend schools that sold foods of low nutritional quality (sweets, snacks, or soda) than were White native children.

Home and Family Effects

Despite the emphasis of school and neighborhood characteristics in both theoretical and policy discussions, it is important to emphasize that school and neighborhood effects on young children's health tend to be weak. In a recent study of children, von Hippel, Powell, Downey, and Rowland (2007) compared BMI for children from kindergarten through first grade during the school year and during summer vacation. They found that the growth in BMI was twice as fast during summer vacation as during either the kindergarten or first-grade school year. Additionally, Hispanic and Black kindergartners on average began the school year with higher BMI than White children; however, the BMI gap for these ethnic groups increased only over summer vacation, not during the school year (von Hippel et al., 2007). This suggests that schools may actually help reduce health differentials in young children while home environments widen them.

Various family and home environment characteristics are related to overweight status in children. Parents may exert control over the type of food made available in the home for snacks and mealtime, the physical activities their children participate in, and the amount of television or video games a child plays. Parents play a critical role teaching their children healthy eating habits (Gable & Lutz, 2000). For example, family meals often serve as an opportunity for parents to model eating habits and positive food choices. When families eat together, the meals are usually of higher nutritional value including increased consumption of fruits, vegetables, key nutrients, and fewer soft drinks, and the pattern of family meals established in adolescence predicts the meal pattern and nutritional quality of diet in early adulthood (Larson, Neumark-Sztainer, Hannan, & Story, 2007).

Parenting styles also appear to be associated with children's food consumption and weight status. Parenting styles may range from controlling (or authoritarian) to monitoring and reinforcing (authoritative), and to permissive (or even neglectful) and may vary across ethnic groups (Baumrind, 1971). When parents are overly controlling or overly lax regarding dietary guidelines, children tend to have difficulties establishing healthy caloric limits for themselves. Rhee, Lumeng, Appugliese, Kaciroti, and Bradley (2006) show that children of authoritative parents have the lowest odds of overweight status, while children whose parents are authoritarian have the highest odds of overweight status. Children with permissive and neglectful parents had twice the odds of overweight status compared to children with authoritative parents.

In addition to diet, parents may exert control over children's free-time activities. Sedentary activities such as television and video-game use are often thought to contribute to the increasing pervasiveness of childhood obesity. About one-quarter of American youth watch four or more hours of television per day, but non-Hispanic Blacks and Mexican Americans report higher prevalence rates. Some 43% of non-Hispanic Black boys and girls watch four or more hours of television per day while 33% of Mexican American boys and 28% of Mexican American girls watch four or more hours of television per day (Andersen et al. 1998).

Despite the sedentary activity associated with watching television, Vandewater, Shim, and Caplovitz (2004) found no clear evidence for television's contribution to obesity in youth. However, they did find that video game use "is strongly related to children's weight status" especially for children under 8 years old. Another important factor is whether children have a TV set in their bedrooms. Hispanic children are more likely to have television in their room than other groups, and children with a TV set in their bedroom watch 4.6 hours more per week and are significantly more likely to be at risk of overweight (BMI > 85th percentile) (Dennison, Erb, & Jenkins, 2002).

How do immigrant and native families differ with respect to these factors? When we examined home environments of children in the ECLS-K, we found very few differences between immigrant and White native families, and in some cases, we found immigrant advantages (Table 11.4). For example, Mexican immigrant boys watched significantly less TV per week than White, Black, or Hispanic native boys, and Asian, Black, and White immigrant girls watched less than White native girls. In addition, although immigrant families were less likely than White native families to eat breakfast together or regularly (particularly among Hispanics), they were more likely to eat dinner regularly, and did not differ from White native families with respect to care arrangements for children after school. Overall, these results suggest that immigrant parents, even with the added stress associated with adjustment to their new homes, are just as, if not more, involved in their children's daily lives at home as native parents. On the face of things, then, it appears that overweight among children of immigrants is unlikely to be related to their family or home environments.

Table 11.4 Home/Family Environment Among Fifth Grade Children by Race/ethnicity, Generation, and Gender

Home and family environment	*Children of natives*			*Children of immigrants*				
	Hispanic	*Black*	*White*	*Mexican*	*Other Hispanic*	*Asian*	*Black*	*White*
Boys								
TV (minutes/weekday)	138.2	146.1*	122.6	109.5*	118.0	110.9	123.7	127.0
Breakfast together (times/wk)	3.0**	2.6***	3.7	3.0***	3.6	3.6	3.2	3.7
Breakfast regularly (times/wk)	4.9†	4.4***	5.3	5.0*	5.2	5.1	4.8†	5.0
Dinner together (times/wk)	5.3	5.1*	5.5	5.5	5.4	5.4	4.6†	5.4
Dinner regularly (times/wk)	4.6	4.5	4.8	5.1†	5.1	5.5***	4.7	5.2†
Adult supervision after school (%)								
Self care	7.9	15.1	11.1	11.3	9.0	11.6	5.4	8.6
Parental care	52.1	60.6	51.8	51.3	53.4	51.7	68.2	61.9
Relative care	23.8	12.1 c	19.6	18.9	23.7	18.5	10.6	14.6
Non-relative of center care	16.2	12.2	17.5	18.5	13.9	18.2	15.7	14.9
Girls								
TV (minutes/weekday)	112.5	140.1***	113.9	116.6	111.9	93.7***	83.7**	100.1*
Breakfast together (times/wk)	2.9***	2.7***	3.7	3.3*	3.4	3.6	3.3	4.0
Breakfast regularly (times/wk)	5.0†	4.7*	5.3	5.0*	4.9*	4.8*	4.7	5.3
Dinner together (times/wk)	5.5	5.4	5.5	5.5	5.3	5.8	5.0	5.3
Dinner regularly (times/wk)	4.9	4.8	4.9	5.2†	5.2	5.5**	5.0	5.1
Adult supervision after school (%)								
Self care	12.2	13.6	11.7	9.6	10.7	10.1	3.9	6.5*
Parental care	49.7	45.5	49.1	51.9	49.9	50.2	74.6	77.2
Relative care	20.5	23.2	20.1	22.8	19.3	23.7	14.1	1.9
Non-relative of center care	17.6	17.8	19.1	15.7	20.1	16.0	7.5	14.4

Source: Early Childhood Longitudinal Survey – Kindergarten Class of 1998–1999.

Notes

t-tests were used to assess the significance of differences from native non-Hispanic White children.

$^{***}p < 0.001$, $^{**}p < 0.01$, $^{*}p < 0.05$, and $^{\dagger}p < 0.10$.

Institutional Origins of Overweight Among Children of Immigrants

Can differences in home, neighborhood, and school characteristics help explain why some groups (e.g., Hispanic immigrant boys) tend to be heavier than others? To shed light on this question, we estimated multivariate regression models. These models relate variations in children's diet, physical activity, school, neighborhood, and home characteristics to variations in their percentile BMI in fifth grade. Our strategy was to first examine the association between nativity/race/ethnicity and BMI while controlling only for the child's socioeconomic status (Model 1). These results then provided a baseline with which we made further comparisons with models that control for other characteristics of the child's environment. School characteristics were added in Model 2, neighborhood characteristics and participation in group activities in Model 3, and home characteristics and health behaviors in Model 4. If the associations between nativity/race/ethnicity and BMI decreased or disappeared when these factors were added, this would suggest that the group differences can be attributed to school, neighborhood, or home environments. Finally, we recognize that group differences may not emerge in middle childhood while children are attending school, but may pre-date entry into the school system. Therefore, as a final step, we controlled for children's percentile BMI from kindergarten in Model 5. If group differences diminished or disappeared in Model 5, this would suggest that overweight among certain groups of children is linked to preschool experiences. The results are presented for boys in Table 11.5 and girls in Table 11.6.

Even after controlling for SES, immigrant boys for all groups except Asians tended to weigh more than White native children (Table 11.5, Model 1). Among girls, only Mexican immigrants weighed more than White natives (Table 11.6, Model 1). Furthermore, these differences were not explained by school or neighborhood characteristics. Children who attended schools that sold sweets tended to be heavier (particularly boys) (Model 2). In addition, boys in individual or group sports and girls in recreational sports tended to weigh less than other children. But when we added school characteristics in Model 2 and neighborhood characteristics (along with participation in group activities, which may also be related to opportunities in neighborhoods and schools) in Model 3, the coefficients for children of immigrants did not change. In fact, for Mexican and other Hispanic immigrants and natives, the effects increased between Models 2 and 3 (especially for girls). This may be related to some puzzling effects we observed among girls. Girls who participated in group sports tended to be heavier (perhaps reflecting interventions designed to increase physical activity for heavy girls). Also, girls who lived in unsafe neighborhoods tended to weigh less than other girls, and among boys, living in an unsafe neighborhood had no effect on weight status. It is important to keep in mind, however, that our measure of neighborhood safety comes from parental reports, and groups may differ in their perceptions of safety even for identical neighborhoods. In addition, it is possible that children living in unsafe neighborhoods may be more likely to live in cities where people walk more than in suburbs or rural areas. Thus, even though immigrant children are more likely to live in unsafe neighborhoods and less likely to participate in physical activities, these disadvantages do not appear to pose additional risks to their weight status in fifth grade.

The observed group differences were not explained by home environments or health

Table 11.5 Models of Fifth Grade Percentile BMI Among Boys

	Model 1	*Model 2*	*Model 3*	*Model 4*	*Model 5*
Intercept	66.88***	64.32***	67.14***	68.77***	33.35***
Children of natives	–	–	–	–	–
Hispanic	6.80*	6.78*	7.19*	7.06*	3.81†
Black	0.08	0.17	0.30	0.19	–2.10
Children of immigrants					
Mexican	6.90***	6.82***	7.18***	7.94***	4.33*
Other Hispanic	5.24†	5.66†	5.81†	6.43*	2.09
Asian	1.43	1.73	1.61	1.81	3.63†
Black	12.09***	12.19***	11.89***	12.33***	9.74***
White	6.47*	6.68*	6.72*	6.66*	3.43
SES	–3.75***	–3.60***	–3.32***	–2.62*	–2.54**
Sweets sold in school (y/n)	–	3.88*	3.89*	3.77*	2.53
Snacks sold in school (y/n)	–	–1.75	–1.74	–1.67	–1.82
Soda sold in school (y/n)	–	–0.76	–0.68	–0.76	–0.35
PE (min/wk)	–	0.02	0.02	0.02	0.01
Recess (min/wk)	–	0.01	0.01	0.00	0.00
Unsafe neighborhood	–	–	–1.15	–1.25	–1.84
Group sport	–	–	–3.65†	–3.26	–1.99
Individual sport	–	–	–2.79*	–2.54†	–2.23†
Recreational/outdoor sport	–	–	0.34	0.53	0.43
Martial arts	–	–	2.39	2.51	–0.57
Dance	–	–	2.39	2.51	–0.57
General calistatics	–	–	1.13	1.27	0.44
Playground activities	–	–	0.62	0.58	1.29
Exercise (dy/wk)	–	–	–	–0.16	–0.21
Television (min/day)	–	–	–	0.02	0.01
Soda	–	–	–	–0.41	–0.18
Juice	–	–	–	1.53	–0.59†
Fruit	–	–	–	3.19	–0.21
Vegetables	–	–	–	1.31	0.20
Breakfast together	–	–	–	–0.27	–0.23
Breakfast regularly	–	–	–	–0.68	–0.41
Dinner regularly	–	–	–	0.20	0.28
Dinner together	–	–	–	0.49	0.23
Self care	–	–	–	–0.41	–1.57
Relative care	–	–	–	1.31	0.81
Non-relative care	–	–	–	1.53	1.42
Center-based child care	–	–	–	3.19	0.45
Baseline Percentile BMI	–	–	–	–	0.58***

Notes
***$p < 0.005$, **$p < 0.001$, *$p < 0.005$.

behaviors either. None of the home/family-related factors had significant effects on BMI among boys, and only juice consumption and TV viewing were associated with BMI among girls. When these factors were added in Model 4, the coefficients for the various race/ethnic/nativity groups retained their size and significance levels. It is important to recognize, however, that many of the factors associated with schools, neighborhoods, and the home were measured during children's school years, and that

Table 11.6 Models of Fifth Grade Percentile BMI Among Girls

	Model 1	*Model 2*	*Model 3*	*Model 4*	*Model 5*
Intercept	63.81***	62.79***	62.20***	60.49***	22.45***
Children of natives	–	–	–	–	–
Hispanic	5.52*	5.10†	6.56*	7.07**	3.30
Black	5.48†	4.99†	6.87*	6.85**	3.53†
Children of immigrants					
Mexican	5.18*	4.47†	6.74**	7.36**	0.68
Other Hispanic	2.60	2.29	4.42†	4.85†	2.36
Asian	–4.07	–4.32	–3.28	–3.10	–1.58
Black	–5.83	–5.77	–4.09	–3.38	1.83
White	–1.66	–1.79	–0.62	–0.82	–0.97
SES	–3.32*	–3.57**	–3.88**	–3.23*	–3.78***
Sweets sold in school (y/n)	–	0.80	0.35	0.43	0.00
Snacks sold in school (y/n)	–	1.82	1.79	2.92	2.35
Soda sold in school (y/n)	–	–0.72	–0.47	–0.44	1.01
PE (min/wk)	–	0.00	0.00	0.00	0.00
Recess (min/wk)	–	0.01	0.04	0.03	0.04
Unsafe neighborhood	–	–	–4.09*	–4.05*	–3.42*
Group sport	–	–	6.66**	5.81**	3.40†
Individual sport	–	–	0.46	0.73	–0.54
Recreational/outdoor sport	–	–	–4.81*	–4.65*	–2.95
Martial arts	–	–	0.79	1.09	–0.27
Dance	–	–	–2.78	–2.92	–2.46
General calistatics	–	–	0.63	0.43	–0.45
Playground activities	–	–	–0.52	–0.39	1.12
Exercise (dy/wk)	–	–	–	–0.59	–0.66†
Television (min/day)	–	–	–	0.02*	0.02*
Soda	–	–	–	–0.28	–0.46
Juice	–	–	–	1.09*	0.93*
Fruit	–	–	–	0.06	0.25
Vegetables	–	–	–	–0.11	–0.23
Breakfast together	–	–	–	0.12	–0.04
Breakfast regularly	–	–	–	–0.63	–0.31
Dinner regularly	–	–	–	0.08	0.17
Dinner together	–	–	–	0.37	0.38
(Parental care)	–	–	–	–	–
Self care	–	–	–	–3.32	–2.13
Relative care	–	–	–	1.25	0.53
Non-relative care	–	–	–	–4.47	–2.78
Center-based child care	–	–	–	–1.82	–0.80
Baseline percentile BMI	–	–	–	–	0.643***

Notes
***$p < 0.05$, **$p < 0.01$, *$p < 0.001$.

many of the measures (particularly those related to physical activity, diet, and home and family) were crudely measured. When we added children's BMI from when they were in kindergarten (Model 5), the coefficients for race/ethnicity and nativity declined significantly. Among Mexican immigrant boys, for example, the average percentile BMI was nearly 8 points higher than White native boys in Model 4, but this difference was nearly cut in half (down to 4.3 points) when kindergarten BMI was added. The disadvantage for Mexican immigrant girls (7.4 points in Model 4) was reduced to nearly zero (0.7 points and insignificant) once differences in kindergarten weight were taken into account. The only group not following this pattern was Asian boys. When kindergarten BMI was taken into account, the coefficient for Asian immigrant boys increased from 1.8 to 3.6. These results therefore suggest that the higher levels of overweight observed in fifth grade among some children of immigrants (particularly Mexicans) originated prior to starting school and may be associated with the home or daycare environments. For Asian boys, on the other hand, exposure to school appears to be associated with faster growth in BMI than native White boys. Since Asian boys weighed about the same as White native boys on average in fifth grade, this means that they were catching up to native White boys between kindergarten and fifth grade.

Conclusions

The Early Childhood Longitudinal Survey provides a unique and valuable picture of both the health risks confronted by the children of immigrants (particularly Mexican immigrant boys), and the environments that may contribute to these risks. Immigrant boys tend to weigh more than native boys in fifth grade, and Mexican immigrant children are less likely to be engaged in exercise (particularly group activities) both after school and in school (in that they have fewer minutes of recess per day on average). In addition, immigrant children of all groups are more likely to live in an unsafe neighborhood than are native White children. Although the factors children encounter at school and in their neighborhoods do not appear to directly contribute to their higher risk of overweight in fifth grade, these conditions may negatively impact their health in the future as they grow up. It will be important to continue to follow these children as they enter adolescence.

The results also suggest that it would be highly productive to examine children's preschool experiences and environments. The preliminary evidence presented here suggests that group differences in overweight in fifth grade actually emerged prior to kindergarten. Among Mexican immigrant boys, nearly half of the difference in BMI from native Whites pre-dates entry into kindergarten, and for Mexican girls, nearly all of the difference can be traced back to kindergarten. This suggests that the health problems we see among children of immigrants (particularly Mexican boys and girls) are rooted in the environments they encounter at home or perhaps are genetically based. Additional research that would examine shared patterns of diet, exercise, and overweight among family members (parents, siblings, twins) could further help separate the effects of genetic influences from factors originating from shared experiences in the home.

More research on preschool children with better measures of parenting and home characteristics is necessary to confirm these ideas. The family/home measures we used in this chapter fail to capture parenting goals or the actual messages parents send to children, so the effects of parental involvement or supervision could vary across groups. For example, parental supervision at mealtimes and after school may be associated with smaller portions for some groups but larger portions for others. Indeed, recently published research suggests that less-acculturated immigrant families themselves may operate in ways that promote a "food culture" that leads to obesity. One study found that less-acculturated Latino parents in the US were more likely to encourage their children to eat more or "clean their plates" (Arredondo et al., 2006), and these parenting behaviors were associated with unhealthier diets among girls. Another study examining rural Mexican children in Mexico found that children were largely responsible for structuring and choosing the foods they ate (Garcia, Kaiser, & Dewey, 1990). Similar findings are also found among Mexican American preschool-aged children living in the US where child-led snacking was common (Kaiser, Melgar-Quinonez, Lamp, Johns, & Harwood, 2001). Also, less-acculturated Mexican American mothers with preschool children are more likely to offer their children alternative foods if they refused to eat, with children more likely to prefer more Americanized foods over traditional foods (Kaiser et al., 2001), and low-income Mexican American mothers of preschool-aged children often allowed their children to drink juice as a snack, which is associated with overweight (Melgar-Quinonez & Kaiser, 2004). This evidence on parental feeding practices is further supported by research showing that obesity in kindergarten is positively associated with family income among Hispanic children of immigrants (Balistreri & Van Hook, under review). This suggests that higher income and higher levels of consumption (possibly associated with eating out, fast food, and prepackaged food at home), rather than economic disadvantage, may be associated with overweight among children of immigrants.

Given that overweight among immigrant children appears to be linked to preschool environments, what can be done about it? As noted earlier, it is often more challenging to develop interventions for families than to work through schools to try to change children's health behaviors. Yet prior research indicates that the family and home environments are an important context for interventions that aim to reduce overweight (Deckelbaum & Williams, 2001b; Flynn et al., 2006; Golan & Crow, 2004; von Hippel et al., 2007). Golan, Fainaru, and Weizm (1998) found that parent-only interventions, where the parent received classes and training in regards to weight management, were more effective in reducing overweight compared to child-only interventions and this difference was still evident 7 years later (Golan & Crow, 2004). On the other hand, school-based interventions tend to be disappointing, resulting in healthier eating habits or greater physical activity (depending on whether the intervention targeted one or both) than controls, but not having significant effects on overweight, BMI, or other measures of adiposity (Summerbell et al., 2005). In addition, school-based interventions may have benefits that are short-lived if parents are not involved. One study found that the treatment group ate better and had greater physical activity levels compared to the control group while in school, but that the treatment group was less active and ate less-healthy foods outside school (Donnelly et al., 1996).

Unfortunately, very few interventions have been developed specifically for children of immigrants (Flynn et al., 2006), though the Calgary Health Region is currently conducting a study to identify effective prevention programs for reducing overweight in immigrant children (not yet published). Reaching immigrant parents and communicating with them about diet and physical activity in culturally appropriate ways is likely to be challenging. Simply connecting with parents of children of immigrants—particularly those with preschool children—may be difficult as this population is less likely to be involved in formal institutions (e.g., they are less likely to place their children in child-care or preschool (Hernandez & Charney, 1998)). It may be important to work through intermediaries such as clergy, employers, or influential people within the community to reach parents. For example, one health-promotion study ("Secretos de la Buena Vida," conducted by Ayala et al., 2001) targeted Hispanic girls and their families through the use of "promotoras," Spanish-speaking volunteers from within the community who had received special training on how to give "neighborly" nutrition counseling. Promotoras made in-home visits and provided advice, encouragement, and print materials to clients. With respect to dietary counseling, it is important that counselors take into account where a client is in the process of dietary acculturation (Satia-Abouta, Patterson, Neuhouser, & Elder, 2002), and then help them select the healthiest choices from among the foods they prefer. Many foods from immigrants' countries of origin are healthier than American foods but it may be difficult for immigrants to purchase and prepare them. On the other hand, some cultural foods (such as lard in some Mexican foods) may not necessarily be healthier than some American choices, which is a different kind of problem requiring a different approach. As our study suggests, it may also be important that interventions take into account the gender of children. Very few interventions have been developed separately for boys vs. girls (Flynn et al., 2006). Yet boys in immigrant families may be particularly at high risk for overweight, and this may be due to differences in parenting and feeding practices for boys vs. girls. Although more research is necessary to confirm this idea, it would suggest that special care (in a non-offensive way) must be made to help parents recognize and adjust how they treat sons vs. daughters.

In conclusion, the idea that immigrant families, rather than US schools and neighborhoods, contribute to child overweight is at odds with the major theoretical perspectives currently used to understand the adaptation and assimilation of immigrants. But it is important to keep in mind that assimilation theories make an implicit assumption that there exist large differences between immigrant-sending (i.e., less-developed countries) and immigrant-receiving countries (i.e., more-developed countries). In fact, obesity is no longer restricted to the US or even to more-developed countries (Popkin, 1994, 2002). For example, according to the World Health Organization (World Health Organization, 2008), the US ranks 13th among 148 countries in the percentage of obese women (with BMIs $\geq$ 30), ranking lower than Egypt and Kuwait, and Mexico—the country that sends more immigrants to the US than any other country—ranks in the top 25. A careful reading of the empirical evidence—including the evidence shown here—supports a more nuanced story in which the cultural patterns brought by immigrants to the US interact with the environments they encounter once they arrive in ways that can increase children's BMIs. For example, higher SES is associated with greater levels of overweight in less-developed countries (Sobal & Stunkard, 1989), and studies of children in Latin America suggest that middle-class parents are likely to indulge their children with food, especially the boys. This practice may not immediately result in obesity, particularly in some countries where there may less high-fat, high-sugar food readily and cheaply available. But if parents bring these cultural patterns with them when they move to the US, as appears to be the case (Van Hook & Balistreri, 2007), the combination of these parenting behaviors together with the US food environment could lead to higher levels of obesity in children than even among native families.

Acknowledgment

This research was supported by a grant to the first author from the Foundation for Child Development.

Note

1. We used sequential regression multivariate imputation adopted by the imputation software IVEware. We estimated five distinct values for each missing data point, and then substituted those values for the missing data to form five different datasets, all of which were used to generate five sets of multivariate results. We combined the results into one set of regression coefficients and standard errors. In this analysis we did not impute the dependent variable (BMI).

References

Anderson, P.M. (2003). Economic perspectives on childhood obesity. *Economic Perspectives, 27*(3), 30–48.

Anderson, P.M., & Butcher, K.F. (2005). *Reading, writing, and raisinets: are school finances contributing to children's obesity?* National Bureau of Economic Research (working paper no. 11177).

Arredondo, E.M., Elder, J.P., Ayala, G.X., Campbell, N., Baquero, B., & Duerksen, S. (2006). Is parenting style related to children's healthy eating and physical activity in Latino families? *Health Education Research, 21*(6), 862–871.

Ayala, G., Elder, J., Campbell, N., Engelberg, M., Olson, S., Moreno, C., et al. (2001). Nutrition communication for a Latino community: Formative research foundations. *Family Community Health, 24*(3), 72–87.

Baker, E., Balistreri, K.S., & Van Hook, J. (2007). Maternal employment and overweight among Hispanic children of immigrants and children of natives. *Journal of Immigrant and Minority Health*, 1157–1912.

Bankston, C.L., & Caldas, S.J. (1996). Majority black schools and the perpetuation of social injustice: The influence of de facto segregation on academic achievement. *Social Forces, 75*, 535–555.

Baumrind, D. (1971). Current patterns of parental authority. *Developmental Psychology Monograph, Part 2, 4*(1), 1–103.

Bean, F.D., & Stevens, G. (2003). *America's newcomers and the dynamics of diversity.* New York: Russell Sage Foundation.

Blumenthal, S.J. (2002). A public health approach to decreasing obesity. *Journal of the American Medical Association, 288*(17), 2178.

Burdette, H.L., & Whitaker, R.C. (2005). A national study of neighborhood safety, outdoor play, television viewing, and obesity in preschool children. *Pediatrics, 116*(3), 657–662.

Carter, R. (2002). The impact of public schools on childhood obesity. *Journal of the American Medical Association, 288*(17), 2180.

Cole, T.J., Bellizzi, M.C., Flegal, K.M., & Dietz, W.H. (2000). Establishing a standard definition for child overweight and obesity worldwide: International survey. *British Medical Journal, 320*, 1–6.

Crosnoe, R. (2005). Double disadvantage or signs of resilience? The elementary school contexts of children from Mexican immigrant families. *American Educational Research Journal, 42*(2), 269–303.

Cullen, K.W., Ash, D.M., Warneke, C., & de Moor, C. (2002). Intake of soft drinks, fruit-flavored beverages, and fruits and vegetables by children in grades 4 through 6. *American Journal of Public Health, 92*(9), 1475–1478.

Datar, A. (2004). Childhood overweight and academic performance: National study of kindergarteners and first-graders. *Obesity Research, 12*(1), 58–68.
Datar, A., & Strum, R. (2004). Physical education in elementary school and body mass index: Evidence from the early childhood longitudinal study. *American Journal of Public Health, 94*(4), 1501–1506.
Deckelbaum, R.J., & Williams, C.L. (2001). Childhood obesity: The health issue. *Obesity Research, 9*, S239–S243.
Dennison, B.A., Erb, T.A., & Jenkins, P.L. (2002). Television viewing and television in bedroom associated with overweight risk among low-income preschool children. *Pediatrics, 109*(6), 1028–1035.
Dietz, W. (1998). Health consequences of obesity in youth: Childhood predictors of adult disease. *Pediatrics, 101*(3), 518–525.
Donnelly, J.E., Jacobsen, D.J., Whatley, J.E., Hill, J.O., Swift, L.L., Cherrington, A., et al. (1996). Nutrition and physical activity program to attenuate obesity and promote physical and metabolic fitness in elementary school children. *Obesity Research, 4*(3), 229–243.
Dwyer, J. (1995). The school nutrition dietary assessment study. *American Journal of Clinical Nutrition, 61*(supplement 1), 173S–177S.
Fernandez-Kelly, M.P. (1995). Social and cultural capital in the urban ghetto: Implications for the economic sociology of immigration. In A. Portes (Ed.), *The economic sociology of immigration* (pp. 213–247). New York: Russell Sage Foundation.
Fernandez-Kelly, M.P., & Schauffler, R. (1996). Divided fates: Immigrant children and the new assimilation. In A. Portes (Ed.), *The new second generation* (pp. 30–53). New York: Russell Sage Foundation.
Flynn, M.A., McNeil, D.M., Tough, S.C., Maloff, B., Ford, C., Mutasingwa, D., et al. (2006). Reducing obesity and related chronic disease risk in children and youth: A synthesis of evidence with best practice recommendations. *Obesity Reviews, 7* (Supplement 1), 7–66.
Fried, E.J., & Nestle, M. (2002). The growing political movement against soft drinks in schools. *Journal of the American Medical Association, 288*(17), 2181.
Gable, S., & Lutz, S. (2000). Household, parent, and child contributions to childhood obesity. *Family Relations, 49*(3), 293–300.
Garcia, S.E., Kaiser, L.L., & Dewey, K.G. (1990). Self-regulation of food intake among rural Mexican preschool children. *European Journal of Clinical Nutrition, 44*, 371–380.
Golan, M., & Crow, S. (2004). Targeting parents exclusively in the treatment of childhood obesity: Long-term results. *Obesity Research, 12*, 357–361.
Golan, M., Fainaru, M., & Weizm, A. (1998). Role of behaviour modification in the treatment of childhood obesity with parents as the exclusive agents of change. *International Journal of Obesity, 22*, 1217–1224.
Hernandez, D., & Charney, E. (1998). *From generation to generation: The health and well-being of children in immigrant families.* Washington, DC: National Academy Press.
Hofferth, S.L., & Sandberg, J.F. (2001). How American children spend their time. *Journal of Marriage and Family, 63*(2), 295–308.
Hummer, R.A., Rogers, R.G., Nam, C.B., & LeClere, F.B. (1999). Race/ethnicity, nativity, and US adult mortality. *Social Science Quarterly, 80*, 136–153.
Kaiser, L.L., Melgar-Quinonez, H.R., Lamp, C.L., Johns, M.C., & Harwood, J.O. (2001). Acculturation of Mexican-American mothers influences child feeding strategies. *Journal of the American Dietic Association, 101*(5), 542–547.
Kuczmarski, R.J., Ogden, C.L., & Guo, S.S. (2002). *2000 CDC growth charts for the United States: Methods and development.* Hyattsville, MD: National Center for Health Statistics.
Landale, N.S., Oropesa, R.S., Llanes, D., & Gorman, B.K. (1999). Does Americanization have adverse effects on health?: Stress, health habits, and infant health outcomes among Puerto Ricans. *Social Forces, 78*, 613–642.

Larson, N.I., Neumark-Sztainer, D.D., Hannan, P.J., & Story, M.M. (2007). Family meals during adolescence are associated with higher diet quality and healthful meal patterns during young adulthood. *Journal of the American Dietetic Association, 107*(9), 1502–1510.

Melgar-Quinonez, H.R., & Kaiser, L.L. (2004). Relationships of child-feeding practices to overweight in low-income Mexican-American preschool-aged children. *Journal of the American Dietetic Association, 104*(7), 1110–1119.

Molnar, B.E., Gortmaker, S.L., Bull, F.C., & Buka, S.L. (2004). Unsafe to play? Neighborhood disorder and lack of safety predict reduced physical activity among urban children and adolescents. *American Journal of Health Promotion, 18*(5), 378–386.

National Center for Health Statistics. (2004). *Prevalence of overweight among children and adolescents: United States, 1999–2002.* Retrieved April 5, 2009, from www.cdc.gov/nchs/products/pubs/pubd/hestats/overwght99.htm.

O'Dea, J.A., & Wilson, R. (2006). Socio-cognitive and nutritional factors associated with body mass index in children and adolescents: Possibilities for childhood obesity prevention. *Health Education Research, 21*(6), 796–805.

O'Malley, P., Johnston, L., Delva, J., Bachman, J., & Schulenberg, J.E. (2007). Variation in obesity among American secondary school students by school and school characteristics. *American Journal of Preventive Medicine, 33*(4), S187–S194.

Ogden, C.L., Carroll, M.D., Curtin, L.R., McDowell, M.A., Tabak, C.J., & Flegal, K.M. (2006). Prevalence of overweight and obesity in the United States, 1999–2004. *Journal of the American Medical Association, 295*, 1549–1555.

Palloni, A., & Arias, E. (2004). Paradox lost: Explaining the Hispanic adult mortality advantage. *Demography, 41*(3), 385–415.

Pong, S.-L., & Hao, L. (2007). Neighborhood and school factors in the school performance of immigrants' children. *International Migration Review, 41*(1), 206–241.

Popkin, B.M. (1994). The nutrition transition in low-income countries: An emerging crisis. *Nutrition Reviews, 52*(9), 285–298.

Popkin, B.M. (2002). The nutrition transition and obesity in the developing world. *Journal of Nutrition, 131*, 871S–973S.

Portes, A. (1998). Social capital: Its origins and applications in modern sociology. *Annual Review of Sociology, 24*, 1–24.

Portes, A., & Rumbaut, R.G. (2001). *Legacies: The story of the immigrant second generation.* New York: Russell Sage Foundation.

Portes, A., & Zhou, M. (1993). The new second generation: Segmented assimilation and its variants. *The Annals of the American Academy of Political and Social Science, 530*, 74–96.

Poskitt, E.M.E. (2000). Body mass index and childhood obesity: Are we nearing a solution? *Acta Paediatrica, 89*, 507–509.

Reardon-Anderson, J., Capps, R., & Fix, M.E. (2002). *The health and well-being of children in immigrant families.* Washington, DC: The Urban Institute.

Rhee, K.E., Lumeng, J.C., Appugliese, D.P., Kaciroti, N., & Bradley, R.H. (2006). Parenting styles and overweight status in first grade. *Pediatrics, 117*(6), 2047–2054.

Robert, S.A., & Reither, E.N. (2004). A multilevel analysis of race, community disadvantage, and body mass index among adults in the US. *Social Science & Medicine, 59*(12), 2421–2434.

Rumbaut, R.G., & Weeks, J.R. (1989). Infant health among Indochinese refugees: Patterns of infant mortality, birthweight, and prenatal care in comparative perspective. *Research in the Sociology of Health Care, 8*, 137–196.

Satia-Abouta, J., Patterson, R.E., Neuhouser, M.L., & Elder, J. (2002). Dietary acculturation: Applications to nutrition research and dietetics. *Journal of the American Dietetic Association, 102*, 1105–1118.

Sobal, J., & Stunkard, A.J. (1989). Socioeconomic-status and obesity: A review of the literature. *Psychological Bulletin, 105*, 260–275.

Stanton-Salazar, R., & Dornbusch, S. (1995). Social capital and the reproduction of inequality: Information networks among Mexican-origin high school students. *Sociology of Education, 68*(2), 116–135.

Strauss, R.S., & Pollack, H.A. (2003). Social marginalization of overweight children. *Archives of Pediatrics and Adolescent Medicine, 157*(8), 52.

Summerbell, C.D., Waters, E., Edmunds, L.D., Kelly, S., Brown, T., & Campbell, K.J. (2005). Interventions for preventing obesity in children. *Cochrane Database of Systematic Reviews, 3*, 1–70.

Van Hook, J., & Balistreri, K. (2002). Diversity and change in the institutional context of immigrant adaptation: California schools 1985–2000. *Demography, 39*, 639–654.

Van Hook, J., & Balistreri, K.S. (2007). Immigrant generation, socioeconomic status, and economic development of countries of origin: A longitudinal study of body mass index among children. *Social Science Medicine, 65*, 976–989.

Van Hook, J., & Snyder, J. (2007). Immigration, ethnicity, and the loss of white students from California public schools, 1990–2000. *Population Research and Policy Review, 26*(3), 259–277.

Vandewater, E.A., Shim, M.S., & Caplovitz, A.G. (2004). Linking obesity and activity level with children's television and video game use. *Journal of Adolescence, 27*(1), 71–85.

von Hippel, P.T., Powell, B.B., Downey, D.B., & Rowland, N.J. (2007). The effect of school on overweight in childhood: Gain in body mass index during the school year and during summer vacation. *American Journal of Public Health, 97*(4), 696–702.

Wechsler, H., Brener, N.D., Kuester, S., & Miller, C. (2001). Food service and foods and beverages available at school: Results from the school health policies and programs study 2000. *Journal of School Health, 71*(7), 313–324.

World Health Organization. (2008). *Global database on body mass index.* Retrieved April 5, 2009, from www.who.int/bmi/index.jsp.

12 Parenting of Young Immigrant Chinese Children

Challenges Facing Their Social-Emotional and Intellectual Development

Charissa S.L. Cheah and Jin Li

Introduction

Immigration is one of the major factors contributing to the rapid increase in minority population, predicted to account for half the US population by the year 2050 (García Coll, 2001), as discussed by Hernandez, Denton, and Macartney in this volume. Among the diverse immigrant population, Asians are one of the fastest-growing ethnic groups in the US (Harwood, Leyendecker, & Carlson, 2002). The term "Asian" refers to any of the original peoples of the Far East, Southeast Asia, or the Indian subcontinent; for example, China, India, Japan, Korea, Malaysia (Barnes & Bennett, 2002). Compared to an increase of 13.2% for the total population between 1990 and 2000, the Asian population grew by 48% (3.3 million) from 6.9 million to 10.2 million. As of 2000, 3.6% of the total US population was Asian. According to the 2000 census, Chinese was the largest Asian ethnic group in the US (Barnes & Bennett, 2002). The terms "Chinese" may be represented by people mainly from three different geographic designations, including the People's Republic of China (P.R.C.), Hong Kong, and Taiwan (Chao, 2002). Many Chinese immigrants also came from other geographic destinations such as Malaysia, Singapore, and Vietnam. Of the 8.2 million foreign-born Asian Americans, 1.5 million were from China, making China the leading source of foreign-born Asians in the US (Malone, Baluja, Costanzo, & Davis, 2003).

Not only is there rapid increase in this immigrant population, but this population is also generally younger than the European American population (García Coll, 2001). The Census Bureau Reports cited an increase in the school-age population (ages 5–17 yrs) in the past few years, due to the increasing number of children of new immigrants. Chinese immigrant children also reflect this trend (Jamieson, 2001).

However, the dramatic increase in this child population stands in sharp contrast with little research on these children. The limited research, mostly on older children, indicates a peculiar picture: higher socioemotional challenges and difficulties despite their general good achievement in school. How do Chinese immigrant children develop? What are familial and larger contextual factors that influence their adaptation to a new culture? What enables them to fare better and what makes them particularly vulnerable in this new environment? There is a pressing need to address these and other issues that impact this large Asian American population.

In this chapter, we examine an important topic of Chinese immigrant (ChI) children's development: the parental socialization practices by families with young children. We focus on the two essential areas of socioemotional development and academic achievement. We review the available scholarly work and empirical research on Chinese culturally based socialization practice in these two developmental domains in order to provide the frameworks for this needed research. We then discuss the specific gaps in research pertaining to ChI children and families. Next, we turn our attention to the ongoing research of each of the authors that addresses the specific issues raised in the review. We conclude the chapter with the potential applications of the new research.

Chinese Parental Socialization

The historical roots of childhood and child-rearing emphasized in China have often been traced to Confucian sources and Buddhist influences that spread throughout many regions of Asia. According to D.Y.H. Wu (1996), Chinese scholars and political authorities have maintained a relatively clear idea about the concept of the child, the meaning of childhood, and the function of the family in educating young children. According to the Confucian view, the biological birth alone does not make a person fully human; instead, an emphasis is placed both on parental responsibility for guiding, instructing, and disciplining the child consistently. At the same time, the child is believed to be in need and capable of effortful learning to become a socially and morally mature human being. This process is commonly referred to as *zuoren*. In other words, *zuoren* is a lifelong process for one to become harmonized with one's world (Yang, 2006). This process begins with one being first nurtured by one's family but then learning to reciprocate others with like nurture and ultimately contributing to the commonwealth of the community (Rosemont & Ames, in press). Because this process requires consistent learning, self-examination and self-improving, this is also the very process that underlies Chinese learning, including academic learning. Much of Chinese parental socialization is directed toward achieving these social, moral, and intellectual goals.

Parental Obligation and Filial Piety

Chinese child-rearing practice rests on two basic, mutually constitutive obligations that are espoused by Confucianism: (1) parents' total commitment to children's welfare and (2) children's reciprocal commitment to their parents known as *filial piety*. With regard to basic care and social/moral guidance, parents are expected to extend their utmost dedication to their children, also known as parental sacrifice. This means that parents work constantly to provide and care for their children. In expressing their filial piety, children show respect to their parents and follow parents' guidance. In addition, grown-up children are expected to provide for the material and mental well-being of their aged parents, to perform ceremonial duties of ancestral worship, to avoid harm to one's own body, to ensure the continuity of the family line, and in general, to conduct oneself so as to bring honor and not disgrace to the family name (Li, Holloway, Bempechat, & Loh, in press).

Because ensuring good learning of their children is an essential part of parental obligation, parents need to instill in children what is known as good learning virtues of diligence, endurance of hardship, perseverance, concentration, and humility (Li, 2003). Parents instruct children by embodying these virtues of hard work and by engaging in daily monitoring and supervision of children's school learning. In observing filial piety, children demonstrate their great effort to learn and to achieve well in school (Yao, 1985). Children's academic achievement is testimony of good parenting and brings honor and respect to the family from the community.

In the long Chinese history, filial piety as practiced in these specific forms demanded absolutistic parental authority over children (Ho, 1996). However, since the turn of last century, this level of parental authority has lessened substantially, becoming increasingly egalitarian. Although the external form and ancient style of filial piety for the most part have disappeared, the substance of filial piety is still alive and flourishing. For example, returning one's indebtedness to parents and bringing high achievement to honor one's parents continue to be affirmed, while absolute obedience and subjugation of individual needs and interests to those of parents and kin is decreasing (Ho, 1986; Kuo-Shu, 1998).

Children's Nature and Parents' Role

Chinese parenting is strongly shaped by one of the most basic assumptions held by Confucians that children are born good with all capabilities germinating and developing from birth. Although children can be led astray by varying environments, their good nature is never really lost (Mencius, 1970). Even when children are misguided, it is believed that they can recover their good nature if they are corrected. Due to this traditional belief, parents are expected to exercise control and monitor/guide their children daily toward the desired behavior and to correct any deviations. The process of training begins early and continues throughout childhood and adolescence. Children are trained for proper conduct, compliance, impulse control, respect for authority, and the acceptance of social obligations. There is a relative lack of emphasis on children's independence, assertiveness, and creativity (Ho, 1986). Research indeed shows that Chinese mothers report that they must provide guidance leading the child toward desired behavior to set a lifelong foundation for the child (Cheah & Rubin, 2003). In research comparing European American or Canadian parents with Chinese parents, Chinese parents were found to be more controlling, protective, directive, and authoritarian, in child-rearing (e.g., Lin & Fu, 1990; Chao, 1994).

Socializing for Emotional/Behavioral Restraint and Discouragement of Pride

In accordance with social harmony, Chinese parenting emphasizes sensitivity to others in the family, guiding children to attend to the needs, emotions, and views of others more than to their own individuality. Also due to the strong concerns about social harmony, Chinese parents may regard both positive and negative (particularly negative) emotions as potentially disruptive, even dangerous to social relations (Klineberg, 1938). They value moderation over excessive and uncontrolled expression of emotions (Kleinman, 1986). This cultural tendency may motivate Chinese parents to socialize their children to view emotions in less-dramatic terms, choose less-extreme forms of expressions and behavior, even suppress certain emotions altogether. Instead, parents are expected to instill solemnity and self-control early on in their children (Bond & Wang, 1983).

One specific way of self-restraint is discouragement of pride. Chinese culture stresses the personal need to self-improve throughout life as noted earlier. Parents are strongly motivated to guide their children in this direction. When their children behave or achieve well in school, they rarely praise their children in any form. They are particularly reluctant to praise their children verbally in front of others in an attempt to discourage too much pride in their children. Parents are concerned that praising children for expected good behavior and expected achievement may lead children to arrogance and hubris, which can impede their children's effort to self-improve continuously (Li & Wang, 2004). This is especially true of academic learning. Praising children in front of others, especially their peers, may make others feel bad about themselves, consequently jeopardizing their children's harmonious social relationships. Recent research shows that, unlike Western people who experience pride as mostly a positive emotion, Chinese people experience pride as a double-valenced emotion, both positive and negative (Eid & Diener, 2001; Ross, Heine, Wilson, & Sugimori, 2005; Scollon, Diener, Oishi, & Biswas-Diener, 2005). The positive valence is experienced when the cause of achievement involves significant others of oneself such as one's siblings, children, peers, and the collective (e.g., school sports team). The negativity is directed at the self wanting to express self-achievement in front of others (in fear of being viewed as boastful) and viewing others' boastful behavior. As a result, parents tend to downplay their children's achievement and alert their children to remain humble all the time (Stipek, 1998).

Is Chinese Parenting More Authoritarian?

Authoritarian parenting style is one that is associated with children's adjustment problems and poor school achievement due to its harshness, demands, and rejection instead of warmth, reasoning, and acceptance characteristic of the authoritative parenting style as studied among European Americans (Baumrind, 1971). Over the years, Chinese parents have been shown to be more controlling and power-assertive in child-rearing, compared to their European American counterparts (e.g., Ho, 1989, 1994; Jose, Huntsinger, Huntsinger, & Liaw, 2000; Lin, 1990; Kelley, 1992; Wolf, 1970). However, Chinese children's relative high academic achievement contradicts the general finding with regard to the authoritarian parenting style. The applicability of Baumrind's original parenting typology to Chinese parenting has been questioned because important dimensions such as training and governing (e.g., Chao, 1994) were not part of the original research and theory.

An increasing number of recent studies demonstrate that authoritarian parenting (harsh, power-assertive) in mainland China is associated with children's externalizing (aggressive/disruptive) behaviors (Chang, Schwartz, Dodge, & McBride-Chang, 2003; Chang, Lansford, Schwartz, & Farver, 2004; Chen, 1997; Chen, Wu, Chen, Wang, & Cen, 2001; Chen, Wang, & Chen, & Liu, 2002; Yang et al., 2004). Research focusing on parental psychological control (that reduces children's emotional experience and expression) has been found to be linked to aggression in Chinese preschool girls whereas parental physical coercion was associated with aggressive behavior in boys. Moreover, maternal directiveness, overprotection, and coercion and shaming were found to be associated with withdrawn behaviors in Chinese preschool children (Nelson, Hart, & Yang, 2006; Nelson, L. et al., 2006). Despite this cross-cultural support for the maladaptive child outcomes resulting from these particular parenting practices, research remains unclear about whether Chinese parents are predominantly authoritarian as defined in the West. A related challenge to the research cited above is that overall, Asian Americans tend to have less mental illness compared to European Americans (Takeuchi, Chung, Lin et al., 1998), particularly among the first-generation immigrants (Takeuchi et al., 2007), a finding that does not point to the expected consequence of the so-called "authoritarian parenting" of Asians. Much research is needed to clarify this important parenting topic.

New Challenges: Parental Socialization Among Chinese Immigrants

Immigration presents tremendous and multifaceted challenges to individuals and families of any cultural origin (Suárez-Orozco & Suárez-Orozco, 2001; Suárez-Orozco, Suárez-Orozco, & Todorova, 2008). One key issue for immigrant parents is the process of reconciling the cultural differences between their cultural origin and their adopted culture with regard to socialization. This reconciliation, often involving discrepant beliefs, practices, behaviors, and values, has been conceptualized as the process of *acculturation*, by which an individual changes as a result of contact and interaction with another distinct culture (Berry, Trimble, & Olmedo, 1986). The process and extent of acculturation differ among individuals (Roysircar-Sodowsky & Maestas, 2000; Sue, Mak, & Sue, 1998). New immigrants often experience acculturative stress due to language, employment, and social problems (see Dion & Dion, 1996). The degree to which immigrants can retain their cultural heritage but at the same time integrate to the host culture may predict how well they fare in the new environment (Lu, 2001; Ryder, Alden, & Paulhus, 2000; Berry, Kim, Minde, & Mok, 1987; Berry, Kim, Power, Young, & Bujaki, 1989; Phinney, 1995).

However, raising children in the midst of this acculturation can intensify the difficulties. Acculturation for parents and children proceeds at different rates. Children acquire English and American culture much more quickly and deeply than their parents. When this kind of dissimilar levels of acculturation occurs, parents' ethnic traditions are at odds with children's experiences in the new culture (Kwak, 2003). It is common for immigrant parents to feel confusion, disorientation, and sometimes despair in their role as parents (Suárez-Orozco et al., 2008).

Although this process is common among any immigrant groups, there may be culture-specific patterns for Chinese immigrants in experiencing these difficulties. As indicated previously, little research exists on ChI parental socialization. The limited research that exists focuses mostly on adolescence (Chao & Tseng, 2002), addressing generally parent–child relationships and related socioemotional difficulties on the one hand and socialization of academic learning on the other.

Socioemotional Difficulties in Distanced Parent–Children Relationships

Available research indicates that Chinese American youth experience greater psychological and social emotional difficulties, particularly internalized problems, including depression and suicidal risk, than their Euro-American counterparts (e.g., Stewart et al., 1999; Sue & Sue, 2003; Zhou, Peverly, Xin, Huang, & Wang, 2003). Asian American adolescent girls had the highest rates of depressive symptoms of all racial/ethnic and gender groups (National Council for Health Statistics, 1997). Recent research documents increased parent–child conflict due to the cross-language use with parents initiating conversations in Chinese but children responding in English (Tseng & Fuligni, 2000). Chinese adolescents also tend to think that their parents show them less warmth, and they desire more parental love to a much larger extent than their European American peers. Moreover, Chinese adolescents' perceived gap between their actual and desired parental warmth predicted their internalized difficulties (Wu & Chao, 2005). Most recently, Qin (2006) documented increasing difficulties in new immigrant families of adolescents over a period of 5 years: the longer these families resided in the US, the less time they spent together, the less they communicated, the more conflict they had, and the less emotional bonding they experienced.

However, research on the socioemotional domain has paid little attention to a number of key areas. First, virtually no research documents the developmental origin of these later problems. Second, few researchers have studied the dynamic processes at home, particularly the acculturative experiences of both parents and children, and the specific ways in which these experiences shape family life and child-rearing practices. Third, virtually no research exists on factors that, although lying outside the immediate family setting, affect immigrant children nevertheless. For example, we know little of how ChI families build and use social networks as social capital (Li et al., in press) and how community elements such as neighborhood, daycare, school, and church influence families.

Socialization for Academic Achievement

Research generally shows consistently that ChI children achieve well in school relative to other groups (Sue & Okazaki, 1990). Compared to other groups, Asian American families invest the largest amount of family resources to their children's education (Hsia & Hirano-Nakanishi, 1989; Kao & Tienda, 1996). Research indicates that because of the dominant value of education, Chinese immigrants continue to endorse their basic cultural orientation toward learning and education. Parents are still strongly motivated to do their utmost in order to ensure their children's learning (Li et al., in press; Zhou & Kim, 2006). Within the family, parents spend more time than other groups on monitoring their children's schoolwork (Yao, 1985). They also routinely enroll them in afternoon and weekend academic-enrichment programs. In the larger community such as Chinatown and suburban areas with higher concentration of Chinese population, it is commonplace to read in the Chinese-language newspapers and other print materials about educational information, exemplary students, and opportunities for achieving academic excellence. Due to the high demand of such supplementary educational need, Chinese schools have mushroomed in North American in recent decades. Such schools do not only offer Chinese language, but everything parents deem desirable for their children's enrichment, ranging from extra math and science classes to Chinese dance (Zhou & Kim, 2006).

Despite these intriguing facts, there are also clear gaps in the research. First, as in the socioemotional domain, very little research documents the process of how families socialize their children in developing their basic learning beliefs. Lacking are detailed analyses of daily routines and interactions between parents and children. Second, recent research shows that in spite of some ChI children's impressive academic achievement, they are not well-adjusted. The acculturative process may contribute to this paradoxical phenomenon (Qin, 2008). The very value of self-perfection through learning that the Chinese have held for millennia may not serve ChI children well because the US has very different cultural values and social norms. For the first time, learning well in school may not be seen as admirable from the perspective of peers (Li & Wang, 2004). Instead, ChI children, like their other Asian-immigrant peers, are common targets of pejorative name-calling such as nerds and geeks. Research indeed found Chinese adolescents report most peer discrimination among ethnic groups (Greene, Way, & Pahl, 2006). Because Chinese children tend to be quiet in school, peer harshness can further exacerbate these children's social development, particularly friendship making (Huang, 1997). Many children are caught between the forces that often are in conflict, that is, parental pressure to achieve well in school on the one hand and peer rejection on the other. This general home–school incongruence can seriously undermine ChI parents' effort to socialize their children's academic learning, and consequently produce unprecedented distress and conflict between parents and children.

New Research

In this section, we describe the ongoing research that the present authors are conducting in order to address the research gaps as outline previously. We discuss parenting in the domain of socioemotional development first followed by the domain of socialization of children's learning beliefs.

Documenting Parenting in Immigrant Children's Socioemotional Development

The first author is conducting a 3-year longitudinal project examining the interaction between child, family, and sociocultural characteristics in the development of ChI children's social skills. As mentioned previously, most of the studies regarding Chinese immigrants were conducted in cities with large Chinese populations already residing there. Thus, the generalizability of these findings to Chinese immigrants residing in smaller Chinese centers is unknown. Our participants will include 200 children between the ages of 3 and 5 years old and their parents residing in areas with relatively low concentrations of other Chinese (co-ethnics) in the Mid-Atlantic region. Moreover, the vast majority of existing studies regarding children of Chinese immigrants have targeted the adolescent developmental period (Chao & Tseng, 2002) but much less is known about the social and emotional development of young children over time. Specifically, we focus on the development of various subtypes of aggressive, socially withdrawn, sociable, and prosocial behaviors, and the emotion-regulation abilities of young ChI children.

The interactive contribution of individual, relationship, and contextual variables as families acculturate and develop over time is of interest. Another overall aim of this project is to evaluate acculturation changes over time and whether any change relates to a subsequent change in approaches to parenting. As parents negotiate the child-rearing beliefs and practices of their traditional culture and the host culture, some changes in parenting are expected with implications for their children's social-skill development. Thus, the changes and consistency of acculturation, parenting, and children's social skills over time will be examined. The families are visited at home four times during this period and both quantitative and qualitative methods of assessment in their language and dialect of choice are utilized.

Besides extensive demographic, childcare, and neighborhood information about these families, parents were interviewed regarding their immigration and acculturative experiences, and their parenting goals and beliefs. Both parents' and children's social networks were assessed. We are also interested in how their parenting practices and goals may have changed as a result of acculturation. Information regarding parents' behavioral and psychological acculturation, self-esteem, psychological well-being, and ethnic identity are assessed, in addition to their parent–child and marital relationship quality, family functioning, and their experienced stress (including racism) and social support. Parents also provide their perception of their child's temperamental characteristics. Children are interviewed regarding their social cognitive problem-solving skills, and their academic-readiness skills are assessed at the last time point. We also obtain teacher assessments of the children's social skills and behavioral difficulties in the classroom. Very few longitudinal studies exist that examine parenting and its role in the social-skill development of immigrant Chinese children using naturalistic observations. Thus, we are conducting observations of mother–child interactions during a series of structured tasks (a free-play, teaching, and clean-up task), and at the last time point, the children's emotional-regulation ability and their mothers' socialization of emotion regulation is observed.

Next, we present preliminary analyses on the parenting styles of a subgroup of participants to address several issues. First, as we expected, the families in our sample reside in areas with low concentration of co-ethnics, with 11% residing in neighborhoods with no co-ethnics, and 65% reporting less than 25% of co-ethnics.

Our first goal was to assess authoritative parenting style in Chinese immigrant mothers of young children residing in areas of low co-ethnic populations. Our second goal was to examine the association between authoritative parenting style and immigrant Chinese children's outcomes; specifically, we wanted to investigate the potential mediating role of the child's behavioral and attentional self-regulation. Thus, authoritative parenting was predicted to increase behavioral and attention-regulation abilities (lower hyperactivity/inattention) in children, resulting in decreased children's difficulties as rated by teachers. Our third goal is to present data from our interviews regarding mothers' conceptions of warmth and strictness.

Authoritative Parenting

In order to address our first goal, mothers' ratings on warmth, reasoning induction, autonomy granting, and the overall authoritative score were examined. In support of our hypothesis, mothers endorsed high levels of warmth ($M=4.30$, $SD=0.47$), reasoning induction ($M=4.12$, $SD=0.58$), autonomy granting ($M=3.69$, $SD=0.62$), and overall authoritative parenting style ($M=4.04$, $SD=0.48$), with ratings of 4 indicating that mothers engaged in these behaviors "very often."

Child Outcomes and Authoritative Parenting

In order to examine the mediating role of the child's behavioral and attentional self-regulation as indexed by their maternal ratings of hyperactivity/inattention on the SDQ in the relation between authoritative parenting style and teacher rating of the child's overall difficulties, the mediation effect was tested by a series of regression analyses (Baron & Kenny, 1986; Judd & Kenny, 1981). Mediation regression analyses revealed that authoritative parenting style *negatively* predicted children's difficulties, $\beta = -2.61$, $t(71) = -2.28$, $p < 0.05$, $f^2 = 0.07$ and *negatively* predicted children's hyperactivity/inattention, $\beta = -0.40$, $t(81) = -3.88$, $p < 0.001$, $f^2 = 0.19$. Moreover, children's hyperactivity/inattention *positively* predicted children's difficulties above and beyond authoritative parenting style, $\beta = 0.31$, $t(69) = 2.62$, $p < 0.05$, $f^2 = 0.10$. When controlling for children's hyperactivity/inattention, the effect of authoritative parenting style on children's difficulties decreased and became insignificant, $\beta = -0.15$, $t(69) = -1.31$, $p > 0.05$. Sobel test (1982) indicated a significant full mediation effect of authoritative parenting style on teacher report of children's difficulties through children's hyperactivity/inattention, $t(69) = -2.17$, $p < 0.5$, $f^2 = 0.07$.

Consistent with our expectations and in support of a growing body of research (e.g., Chen et al., 1997a, b; Chang et al., 2003, 2004), authoritative parenting was associated negatively with children's adjustment problems in the Chinese culture. Moreover, the influence of parenting style on children's behavioral adjustment was mediated by their behavioral and attentional regulation abilities. Highly authoritative mothers emphasize demands for action and future-oriented controls within a harmonious social context of early self-regulation, leading to fewer child behavior problems (Kuczynski & Kochanska, 1995).

In addition, the authoritative model of discipline which emphasizes the use of reasoning and induction directs children's attention to the consequences of their misdemeanors on others. Children's internalization of family and social rules about regulating behavior is more likely to be fostered (Grusec & Goodnow, 1994; Hoffman, 2000). Moreover, authoritative parents tend to encourage their child's autonomy, and thus provide opportunities for their child to develop self-regulatory abilities (Zhou, Eisenberg, Wang, & Reiser, 2004). These children's ability to regulate behavior and attention was related to lower levels of children's difficulties including emotional symptoms, conduct problems, hyperactivity, and peer problems, as rated by their preschool or daycare teachers.

These findings are particularly important given that Chinese American children have been found to experience greater school adjustment difficulties (Zhou, 2003). Importantly, our results suggest that not only are parenting techniques which are proactive, democratic, and nonpunitive highly endorsed by immigrant Chinese parents, these techniques also foster greater abilities to self-regulate, which reduce difficulties in the preschool and daycare setting, thus improving immigrant Chinese children's adaptation.

Parents' Conceptions of Warmth and Strictness

Our qualitative interviews shed more light on the dimensions of parental warmth and control in this sample. Parents expressed the importance of showing their child that they are loved and cared for, and doing so was more important than being strict with their children because their young child had to be nurtured. This developmental understanding among Chinese parents (known in the traditional literature as the "age of understanding") has been used to describe Chinese parents' indulgence in their young children before these children are thought to have reached an age when they can understand their actions. When interviewed about the importance of showing love and care, they cited reasons including its importance for the child's emotional development, but also to set the foundation for learning. Parents also talked about how love and care will protect their child from the culturally different outside world. Being strict with their child was thought to be important for the establishment of good morals and behaviors to ensure family and larger group harmony.

Our ChI parents said that they demonstrate love and care for their child through the following ways: spending time with their child (23.66%); providing basic care like warm clothing, food, and shelter (16.1%); making sure that the child had educational opportunities (11.98%); physical displays of love (9.68%); disciplining their child and being stern with him/her (8.63%); making their child's favorite foods (8.62%); sacrificing parents' own needs and comforts for their child (7.53%); buying things that the child liked (6.45%); and finally telling the child "I love you" (4.30%); and praising and rewarding their child (3.23%).

Interestingly, outright spoken forms of expressing affection and praising their child were the least popular ways of showing love and care whereas other more indirect and functional means of investing in the child's future were cited more frequently. Thus, although the importance of love and care was unanimously supported by parents, the ways in which they reported expressing them had cultural undertones. These initial findings indicate the importance of examining specific aspects of parenting in addition to overall parenting styles and utilizing a more emic approach to identify more culturally unique parenting practices and more fully capture the dynamic nature of Chinese immigrant parenting. These results can contribute to advance contextualized and culturally sensitive models of community planning of services (including parenting classes) targeted toward the healthy adaptation of immigrant children and their parents.

Documenting Socialization of Immigrant Children's Learning Beliefs

Currently, the second author is conducting a 3-year comparative longitudinal research project on how European American (EA) and ChI preschool children develop learning beliefs and how they are socialized at home. The sample consists of 300 children and their families, with 100 from middle-class EA, 100 from middle-class ChI, and 100 from low-income ChI families. The EA sample was included as a baseline, representing the US cultural norm toward which immigrant children are socialized. The two SES ChI groups were included because there is very little research involving low-income ChI families. Our goal is to document the kind of learning beliefs that these children develop, related parental socialization, and the relationship between children's learning beliefs and their actual learning and achievement. Data collection starts with children at 4 years of age and continues for 3 consecutive years. We focus on this age group because our previous cross-sectional research showed that 4 is the youngest age children of both cultural groups begin to express some consistent BLs beyond chance.

Both qualitative and quantitative methods are used to collect data. Specifically, we collect data from children themselves, the caregivers, caregiver–child interactions, and teachers/schools for each family. From ChI children themselves, we first screen their English proficiency in order to determine what language to use with children. Subsequently, we assess both EA and ChI children's literacy and numeracy achievement and collect their stories about learning scenarios. From caregivers, we collect basic demographic data, daily family activities, childcare routines, social networks, child-rearing goals, beliefs, and practices, parent–child relationships, and parental views of learning and school. From the ChI parents, we collect data on their ethnic identity, ethnic socialization, and acculturative process and stress. From caregiver–child interactions, we record the caregiver–child conversations about learning. In addition, we videotape the caregiver teaching the child math skills. Finally, from schools, we collected teacher's independent assessment of children's learning engagement and school records. Thus far, we have recruited 70 EA and 145 ChI families with a total of 215. We have collected the first wave of data from the majority of these children and families, and the second wave of data collection is underway.

Here, we discuss two preliminary sets of analyses from some of our first wave of data: (1) intellectual activities that parents provide to their children outside school and their associated outcomes and (2) mother–child conversations about learning. With regard to the first analysis, we tallied the average intellectual activities from the 7-day Mother Diary where the mother detailed what she or other household members did with the child outside school. The activities included reading books, teaching numbers and simple math, drawing pictures, telling stories, asking the child to recount the day, reciting poems, playing music instruments, and taking the child to a library.

We randomly selected 22 families from half middle-class and half low-income backgrounds. The results pointed to the anticipated direction (slightly short of the conventional significant probability level) that low-income families provided fewer such activities to their children than middle-class families ($t=-1.82$, $p=0.08$). Total time spent on intellectual activities tended to be correlated with children's total achievement consisting of oral expression, basic reading, and quantitative skills, $r=0.36$, $p=0.09$, as measured with the Woodcock-Johnson batteries. More specifically, time spent on home intellectual activities was highly correlated with children's math achievement, $r=0.55$, $p<0.01$, regardless of SES.

However, noteworthy is the finding that, despite the possible differential home intellectual stimulation by SES, both middle-class and low-income children showed no difference in their relatively low score on English oral expression (90 for both groups, compared to 119 vs. 112 for reading and 121 vs. 112 for math, respectively, with 100 as the national mean). Although their children performed above the national average at 4 years of age in reading and math, their oral expressivity was below the national average. The disparity is quite striking. This finding may be a result of Chinese immigrant families speaking predominantly Chinese at home. Bilingual development is a complex process, and it is not the primary aim of the present study; nevertheless, we wonder if the early display of low oral expressivity may predict the well-documented phenomenon of Chinese children's quietness or the more negatively perceived reticence in later years. As noted previously, this could present difficulties in their socioemotional adjustment. The large disparity between their below-national mean of oral expressivity and significant above-national mean reading and math achievement may pose further challenges to Chinese immigrant children among peers when they enter school. This early detection urges us to attend to the *types* of home activities. As we collect and analyze more data from different waves, we will endeavor to explore the possible factors that contribute to this disparity.

The second data set is on caregiver–child conversations about learning, again addressing the topic of parenting in real time. The preliminary findings are qualitative in nature since we have looked at only a few dyads. We asked each caregiver, frequently the mother but sometimes the father and grandmother, to recall two specific incidents where she or he believed that the child showed either good or not-perfect learning attitudes/behaviors about which to talk with the child. We then left the caregiver and child alone to converse about the situation for unlimited time. These conversations typically lasted between 10–15 minutes. We transcribed the conversations verbatim.

These conversations revealed rich and detailed information of parental socialization processes. With regard to two main structural elements, turns and length of responses, EA pairs showed more turns and longer child-responses. ChI middle-class pairs were in the middle, that is, having more turns and child responses than the low-income pairs but fewer than the EA pairs. For stylistic elements, EA caregivers tended to co-recall the events with the children more and leave more space for children to fill in their perspectives. Middle-class ChI caregivers appeared to be more like the EA caregivers whereas the low-income ChI caregivers used more instructional talking style where the caregiver talked more and the child listened attentively and responded less verbally. EA caregivers were mostly reluctant to address their children's less-perfect learning; however, the low-income ChI caregivers were most ready to point out their children's imperfections and their need to self-improve. Middle-class ChI caregivers were in the middle again. Moreover, EA and middle-class ChI caregivers shared similarly soft and gentle emotional tone in their talking. Finally, for content of the conversations, EA caregivers elaborated most on their children's positive learning and promoted positive emotions (e.g., "You must be proud of yourself!"). However, in talking about their not-perfect learning, caregivers separated the imperfect behavior from the goodness of the whole child, with the goal to comfort the child. Middle-class ChI caregivers acknowledged their children's good learning as do the low-income caregivers. However, they seldom focused on emotional responses to either good or inadequate learning attitude/behavior. Instead, they stressed their children's need to continue to self-improve. For less-perfect learning, they did not discuss the difference between behavior and the whole child. Rather, their focus was on strategies for how to improve. Low-income ChI were most forthcoming in pointing out their children's inadequacies. They were clear about what they expected of their children and talked directly about how to learn better accordingly.

As stated earlier, due to the preliminary nature of our analysis, these patterns needed to be taken with caution. As we analyze more data, more accurate findings will emerge. Nevertheless, it is still useful to offer some summary remarks about what we have been able to glean. Accordingly, the two ChI groups may display different patterns of adaptation and maintenance of their cultural values in their child-rearing practice. Middle-class ChI parents may adapt to the host cultural norms at a deeper level due to their greater exposure to American life with higher education and higher SES level. However, it is erroneous to assume that they wholly embrace the cultural norms of the host culture at the expense of their own. Their adaptation appears to be more selective. Guiding children's learning may still be viewed as an essential parental obligation, but their style may be somewhat altered to adjust to the demand of the host culture. Low-income families may have less access and exposure to American cultural norms and styles. They may therefore rely more heavily on the parenting model from their own culture they know well. The developmental outcomes may be two-fold. On the one hand, their effort to uphold Confucian values regarding learning may serve their children well in their education. On the other hand, parents may be less cognizant that certain elements of their socialization may result in developmental outcomes that may pose socioemotional challenges to their children in later years.

Implications and Conclusion

The authors' ongoing research documents some emerging trends of ChI families and child development. In light of our introduction of Chinese cultural norms regarding socioemotional functioning and intellectual development, the ChI parents appear to continue to endorse the basic values of Chinese culture, particularly the Confucian tradition and use that to guide their practice. They are also displaying expected acculturation and adjustment. However, the authors have also documented hitherto not well understood challenges in both domains that may be quite specific to the Chinese immigrant families

Although preliminary, the findings have implications for families as well as education policy. For families, there is a great need to provide research findings to this increasing population in the US. Many parents, particularly better-educated parents, are aware that raising children in a vastly different culture is bound to face challenges. Yet, few are clear about how such challenges arise in their family, and what to expect, and how to respond to them. Research findings that present the developmental paths of differences in parenting styles, particularly the specific communicative forms of love and care, between the mainstream culture and Chinese culture can guide parents in choosing a style that suits their needs. Likewise, it is the type of intellectual activities, not a general category of intellectual stimulation that may be more predictive of specific child outcomes. It is important for parents to know what types of intellectual activities are linked to which specific child outcomes before they can make informed decisions about their interactions with children. Such dissemination of research findings is even more acute to low-income parents due to their much greater life hardship and reduced access to research information.

Similarly and toward greater impact of research, schools that serve immigrant children also have a great need for research-based guidance. Yet, currently there is little such advice because research is generally lacking. Our preliminary and more conclusive findings in the near future can inform daycare centers that what happens inside the daycare center may not suffice to promote successful adaptation for these children's socioemotional needs. Daycare centers may offer programs to address issues regarding parenting style and child outcomes and to support parental effort much more extensively than has been customarily done in the past.

In trying to promote Chinese immigrant children's intellectual development, schools stand to benefit from understanding parenting factors at home that contribute to the success of children's learning as well as factors that result in uneven development such as the disparity noted in our findings. Understanding ethnic strengths promotes positive development of children's ethnic identity and pride. Understanding the nature of challenges can enable schools to develop specific ways to communicate with parents, particularly low-income parents, about these issues in order to help their children reach their full intellectual potential.

Both authors are collecting a large amount of data pertaining to many other related areas of Chinese immigrant families and children. This research, we hope, will document many more specific developmental processes and outcomes that will enlighten our scientific theories of child development. At the same time, we also strive to promote the well-being of not only Chinese but all immigrant children, in the US and throughout the world.

References

Barnes, J.S., & Bennett, C.E. (2002). *The Asian population: 2000. Census 2000 brief.* Retrieved January 7, 2005, from www.census.gov/prod/2002pubs/c2kbr01-16.pdf.

Baumrind, D. (1971). Current patterns of parental authority. *Developmental Psychology Monograph, 4*(1, Part 2), 1–103.

Berry, J.W., Kim, U., Minde, T., & Mok, D. (1987). Comparative studies of acculturative stress. *International Migration Review, 21*, 491–511.

Berry, J.W., Kim, U., Power, S., Young, M., & Bujaki, M. (1989). Acculturation attitudes in plural societies. *Applied Psychology: An International Review, 38*, 185–206.

Berry, J.W., Trimble, J.E., & Olmedo, E.L. (1986). Assessment of acculturation. In W.J. Lonner & J.W. Berry (Eds.), *Field methods in cross-cultural research* (pp. 291–324). Beverly Hills, CA: Sage.

Bond, M.H., & Wang, S.H. (1983). Aggression behavior in Chinese society: The problem of maintaining order and harmony. In A.P. Goldstein & M. Segall (Eds.), *Global perspectives on aggression* (pp. 58–74). New York: Pergamon.

Chang, L., Lansford, J., Schwartz, D., & Farver, J.M. (2004). Marital quality, maternal depressed affect, harsh parenting, and child externalising in Hong Kong Chinese families. *International Journal of Behavioral Development, 28*, 311–318.

Chang, L., Schwartz, D., Dodge, K.A., & McBride-Chang, C. (2003). Harsh parenting in relation to child emotion regulation and aggression. *Journal of Family Psychology, 17*, 598–606.

Chao, R.K. (1994). Beyond parental control and authoritarian parenting style: Understanding Chinese parenting through the cultural notion of training. *Child Development, 65*, 1111–1119.

Chao, R., & Tseng, V. (2002). Parenting of Asians. In M.H. Bornstein (Ed.), *Handbook of parenting, Vol. 4* (2nd ed., pp. 59–93). Hillsdale, NJ: Lawrence Erlbaum Associates.

Cheah, C.S.L., & Rubin, K.H. (2003). European American and Mainland Chinese mothers' socialization beliefs regarding preschoolers' social skills. *Parenting: Science and Practice, 3*, 1–22.

Chen, X. (1997). *Chinese children acculturation scale* [Unpublished questionnaire]. University of Western Ontario, Canada.

Chen, X., Wang, L., Chen, H., & Liu, M. (2002). Noncompliance and child-rearing attitudes as predictors of aggressive behaviour: A longitudinal study in Chinese children. *International Journal of Behavioral Development, 26*, 225–233.

Chen, X., Wu, H., Chen, H., Wang, L., & Cen, G. (2001). Parenting practices and aggressive behavior in Chinese children. *Parenting: Science and Practice, 1*(3), 159–184.

Dion, K.L., & Dion, K.K. (1996). Chinese adaptation to foreign cultures. In M.H. Bond (Ed.), *Chinese psychology* (pp. 190–201). Hong Kong: Oxford University Press.

Eid, M., & Diener, E. (2001). Norms for experiencing emotions in different cultures: Inter- and intranational differences. *Journal of Personality and Social Psychology, 81*(5), 869–885.

García Coll, C., & Pachter, L. (2001). Ethnic and minority parenting. In M.H. Bornstein (Ed.), *Handbook of parenting, Vol. 4* (2nd ed., pp. 1–20). Hillsdale, NJ: Lawrence Erlbaum Associates.

Greene, M.L., Way, N., & Pahl, K. (2006). Trajectories of perceived adult and peer discrimination among Black, Latino, and Asian American adolescents: Patterns and psychological correlates. *Developmental Psychology, 42*(2), 218–238.

Harwood, R., Leyendecker, B., & Carlson, V. (2002). Parenting among Latino families in the U.S. In M.H. Bornstein (Ed.), *Handbook of parenting: Vol. 4: Social conditions and applied parenting* (2nd ed., pp. 21–46). Mahwah, NJ: Lawrence Erlbaum Associates.

Ho, D.Y.F. (1996). Filial piety and its psychological consequences. In M.H. Bond (Ed.), *The handbook of Chinese psychology* (pp. 155–165). Hong Kong: Oxford University Press.

Ho, D.Y.F. (1994). Filial piety, authoritarian moralism, and cognitive conservation. *Genetic, Social, and General Psychology Monographs, 120*, 347–365.

Ho, D.Y.F. (1989). Continuity and variation in Chinese patterns of socialization. *Journal of Marriage and the Family, 51*, 149–163.

Ho, D.Y.F. (1986). Chinese patterns of socialization: A critical review. In M.H. Bond (Ed.), *The psychology of the Chinese people* (pp. 1–37). Hong Kong: Oxford University Press.

Hsia, J., & Hirano-Nakanishi, M. (1989). The demographics of diversity: Asian Americans and higher education. *Change*, 20–27.

Huang, S. (1997). Social adjustment of Chinese immigrant children in the US educational system. *Education and Society, 15*, 77–81.

Jamieson, A. (2001). Children of "baby boomers" and immigrants boost school enrollment to equal all-time high. *Census Bureau Reports.* Retrieved January 7, 2005, from www.census.gov/Press-Release/www/2001/cb01–52.html.

Jose, P.E., Huntsinger, C.S., Huntsinger, P.R., & Liaw, F. (2000). Parental values and practices relevant to young children's social development in Taiwan and the United States. *Journal of Cross-Cultural Psychology, 31*(6), 677–702.

Kao, G., & Tienda, M. (1998). Educational aspirations of minority youth. *American Journal of Education, 106*(3), 349–384.

Kelley, M.L., & Tseng, H.M. (1992). Cultural differences in child-rearing: A comparison of immigrant Chinese and Caucasian American mothers. *Journal of Cross-Cultural Psychology, 23*, 444–455.

Kleinman, A. (1986). *Social origins in distress and disease.* New Haven, CT: Yale University Press.

Klineberg, O. (1938). Emotional experience in Chinese literature. *Journal of Abnormal and Social Psychology, 33*, 517–520.

Kuo-Shu, Y. (1998). Chinese responses to modernization: A psychological analysis. *Asian Journal of Social Psychology, 1*(1), 75–97.

Kwak, K. (2003). Adolescents and their parents: A review of intergenerational family relations for immigrant and non-immigrant families. *Human Development, 46*(2–3), 15–136.

Li, J. (2003). U.S. and Chinese cultural beliefs about learning. *Journal of Educational Psychology, 95*(2), 258–267.

Li, J., Holloway, S.D., Bempechat, J., & Loh, E. (in press). Building and using a social network: Nurture for low-income Chinese American adolescents' learning. In H. Yoshikawa & N. Way (Eds.), *Beyond families and schools: How broader social contexts shape the adjustment of children and youth in immigrant families.* San Francisco, CA: Jossey-Bass.

Li, J., & Wang, Q. (2004). Perceptions of achievement and achieving peers in U.S. and Chinese kindergartners. *Social Development, 13*(3), 413–436.

Lin, C.Y.C., & Fu, V.R. (1990). A Comparison of child-rearing practices among Chinese, immigrant Chinese, and Caucasian-American parents. *Child Development, 61*(2), 429–433.

Lu, X. (2001). Bicultural identity development and Chinese community formation: An ethnographic study of Chinese schools in Chicago. *Howard Journal of Communications, 12*(4), 203–220.

Malone, N., Baluja, K.F., Costanzo, J.M., & Davis, C.J. (2003). The foreign-born population: 2000. *Census 2000 brief.* Retrieved January 7, 2005, from www.census.gov/prod/2003pubs/c2kbr-34.pdf.

Mencius. (1970). *Mencius.* D.C. Lao, trans. Harmondsworth: Penguin Books.

National Council for Health Statistics/Center for Disease Control, Prevention. (1997). *Monthly Vital Statistics Report, 46*(1). Hyattsville, MD: US Public Health Service.

Nelson, D.A., Hart, C.H., & Yang, C. (2006). Aversive parenting in China: Associations with child physical and relational aggression. *Child Development, 77*, 554–572.

Nelson, L.J., Hart, C.H., Wu, B., Yang, C., Olsen Roper, S., & Jin, S. (2006). Relations between Chinese mothers' parenting practices and social withdrawal in early childhood. *International Journal of Behavioral Development, 30*, 261–271.

Olson, S.L., Kashiwagi, K., & Crystal, D. (2001). Concepts of adaptive and maladaptive child behaviors: A comparison of U.S. and Japanese mothers of preschool-age children. *Journal of Cross-Cultural Psychology, 32*, 43–57.

Phinney, J. (1995). Ethnic identity and self-esteem: A review and integration. In A. Padilla (Ed.), *Hispanic psychology* (pp. 57–70). Thousand Oaks, CA: Sage.

Qin, D.B.-L. (2006). "Our child doesn't talk to us anymore": Alienation in immigrant Chinese families. *Anthropology and Education Quarterly, 37*(2), 162–179.

Qin, D.B.-L. (2008). Doing well vs. feeling well: Understanding family dynamics and the psychological adjustment of Chinese immigrant adolescent. *Journal of Youth and Adolescence, 37*(1), 22–35.

Rosemont, H., Jr., & Ames, R.T. (in press). *The classic of family reverence: A philosophical translation.*

Ross, M., Heine, S.J., Wilson, A.E., & Sugimori, S. (2005). Cross-cultural discrepancies in self-appraisals. *Personality and Social Psychology Bulletin, 31*(9), 1175–1188.

Roysircar-Sodowsky, G., & Maestas, M.V. (2000). Acculturation, ethnic identity, and acculturative stress: Evidence and measurement. In R.H. Dana (Ed.), *Handbook of cross-cultural and multicultural personality assessment* (pp. 131–172). Mahwah, NJ: Erlbaum.

Ryder, A.G., Alden, L.E., & Paulhus, D. (2000). Is acculturation unidimensional or bidimensional? A16. Iwamasa, G.Y. (1996). Acculturation of Asian American university students. *Assessment, 3*, 99–102.

Scollon, C.N., Diener, E., Oishi, S., & Biswas-Diener, R. (2005). An experience sampling and cross-cultural investigation of the relation between pleasant and unpleasant effect. *Cognition and Emotion, 19*(1), 27–52.

Short, K.H., & Johnston, C. (1997). Stress, maternal distress, and children's adjustment following immigration: The buffering role of social support. *Journal of Consulting and Clinical Psychology, 65*(3), 494–503.

Slote, W.H., & De Vos, G.A. (1998). *Confucianism and the family.* New York: State University of New York Press.

Stewart, S.M., Betson, C.L., Lam, T.H., Chung, S.F., Ho, H.H., & Chung, T.C.F. (1999). The correlates of depressed mood in adolescents in Hong Kong. *Journal of Adolescent Health, 25*(1), 27–34.

Stipek, D. (1998). Differences between Americans and Chinese in the circumstances evoking pride, shame, and guilt. *Journal of Cross-Cultural Psychology, 29*(5), 616–629.

Suárez-Orozco, C., & Suárez-Orozco, M. (2001). *Children of immigration: The developing child.* Cambridge, MA: Harvard University Press.

Suárez-Orozco, C., Suárez-Orozco, M., & Todorova, I. (2008). *Learning a new land: Immigrant students in American society.* New York: Belknap.

Sue, D., Mak, W.S., & Sue, D.W. (1998). Ethnic identity. In L.C. Lee & N.W.S. Zane (Eds.), *Handbook of Asian American psychology* (pp. 289–323). Thousand Oaks, CA: Sage.

Sue, S., & Okazaki, S. (1990). Asian-American educational achievements: A phenomenon in search of an explanation. *American Psychologist, 45*, 913–920.

Sue, D.W., & Sue, D. (2003). *Counseling the culturally diverse: Theory and practice* (4th ed.). New York: Wiley & Sons, Inc.

Takeuchi, D.T., Chung, R.C.Y., Lin, K.M., et al. (1998). Lifetime and twelve-month prevalence rates of major depressive episodes and dysthymia among Chinese Americans in Los Angeles. *American Journal of Psychiatry, 155*, 1407–1414.

Takeuchi, D.T., Zane, N., Hong, S., Chae, D.H., Gong, F., Gee, G., et al. (2007). Immigration-related factors and mental disorders among Asian Americans. *American Journal of Public Health, 97*(1), 84–90.

Tseng, V., & Fuligni, A.J. (2000). Parent-adolescent language use and relationships among immigrant families with east Asian, Filipino and Latin American backgrounds. *Journal of Marriage & the Family, 62*(2), 465–476.

Wolf, M. (1970). Child training and the Chinese family. In M. Freedman (Ed.), *Family and kinship in Chinese societies* (pp. 221–246). Palo Alto, CA: Stanford University Press.

Wu, C.-X., & Chao, R.K. (2005). Intergenerational cultural conflicts in norms of parental warmth among Chinese American immigrants. *International Journal of Behavioral Development, 29*(6), 516–523.

Wu, D.Y.H. (1996). Chinese childhood socialization. In M.H. Bond (Ed.), *The handbook of Chinese psychology* (pp. 155–165). Hong Kong: Oxford University Press.

Yang, C.F. (2006). The Chinese conception of the self: Toward a person-making (做人) perspective. In U. Kim, K.S. Yang, & K.G. Hwang (Eds.), *Indigenous and cultural psychology: Understanding people in context* (pp. 327–356). New York: Springer.

Yang, C., Hart, C.H., Nelson, D.A., Porter, C.L., Olsen, S.F., & Robinson, C.C. (2004). Fathering in a Beijing, Chinese sample: Associations with boys' and girls' negative emotionality and aggression. In R.D. Day & M.C. Lamb (Eds.), *Conceptualizing and measuring father involvement* (pp. 185–215) Mahwah, NJ: Lawrence Erlbaum Associates.

Yao, E. (1985). A comparison of family characteristics of Asian-American and Anglo-American high achievers. *International Journal of Comparative Sociology, 26*(34), 198–208.

Zhou, M., & Kim, S.S. (2006). Community forces, social capital, and educational achievement: The case of supplementary education in the Chinese and Korean immigrant communities. *Harvard Educational Review, 76*, 1–29.

Zhou, Z., Peverly, S.T., Xin, T., Huang, A.S., & Wang, W. (2003). School adjustment of first-generation Chinese-American adolescents. *Psychology in the Schools, 40*(1), 71–84.

13 More than the A-B-Cs and 1-2-3s

The Importance of Family Cultural Socialization and Ethnic Identity Development for Children of Immigrants' Early School Success

Amy Kerivan Marks, Flannery Patton, and Cynthia García Coll

Introduction

Children of immigrants[1] are a rapidly growing subset of the US population. Today, one in five school children are from immigrant families, while approximately 25% of the US population under the age of 10 is first or second-generation youth (Hernandez, Denton, Macartney, this volume). Moreover, children of immigrants come from families of increasingly diverse ethnic, linguistic, and socioeconomic backgrounds (see Hernandez et al., this volume). With this diversification of our nation's population and schools also have come mixed academic achievement patterns and outcomes by immigrant generation, ethnicity, and acculturation. For example, some immigrants appear to be doing *worse* in school (in achievement as well as academic attitudes and behaviors) as they acculturate to the US. Alternately stated, it is often the most recent arrivals and the first generation of immigrants who fare best across a broad array of education outcomes (Fuligni, 1997; Crosnoe, 2005b; Kao, 2004; Crosnoe & Lopez-Gonzalez, 2005; Conger, Schwartz, & Stiefel, 2003; Pong, Hao, & Gardner, 2005; Portes & Rumbaut, 2001). Because acculturation typically comes with an increase in family wealth, education opportunities, and social capital, these counterintuitive patterns are puzzling, referred to by some researchers as an "immigrant paradox" in education (see Patton, Yang, Marks, & García Coll, in preparation).

Further, these achievement patterns appear to vary somewhat by ethnicity. There is strong evidence of the paradox for some Asian groups, who typically exhibit overall high academic achievement, with mixed findings among Latinos depending on type of academic outcome (Crosnoe, 2005a; Fuligni, 1997; Glick & Hohmann-Marriott, 2007; Han, 2006; Hao & Bonstead-Bruns, 1998; Pong, 2003). In addition, achievement patterns change throughout development from childhood to adolescence where achievement gaps and school-related problems are most pronounced (Alspaugh, 1998; Gutman & Midgley, 2000; Seidman, Allen, Aber, Mitchell, & Feinman, 1994). But understanding achievement is only one component of understanding immigrant children's academic success. In their work with adolescents, Bankston and Zhou have pointed out that there is often a distinction for immigrant youth between "doing well versus being well" in school, emphasizing the importance of looking beyond grades to understand immigrant youth's school adjustment (2002). Psychological studies independent of research on academic achievement have shown that children and adolescents in immigrant families have higher levels of depression, angst, and alienation, as well as lower amounts of self-reported positive well-being and locus of control than children in native families (e.g. Bankston & Zhou, 2002; Kao, 1999; Portes & Rumbaut, 2001). As such, psychological aspects of children's experiences in school are increasingly recognized as an important component of immigrant youth school adjustment.

Although research examining education and psychological adaptation to school among young children of immigrants has been sparse compared to research on adolescence or adulthood, it is generally accepted that the education trajectories of childhood lay the foundation for students' future successes (Stipek, 2005; Entwisle, Alexander, Pallas, & Cadigan, 1987). These early education processes are therefore particularly important to examine among immigrant groups who not only exhibit increased risk for academic problems as acculturation proceeds, but also must make their transitions into the US education system across home–school cultural contexts that may differ dramatically (Delgado-Gaitan & Trueba, 1991; García Coll & Marks, in press; Suárez-Orozco & Suárez-Orozco, 1995, 2001; Suárez-Orozco, Suárez-Orozco, & Todrava, 2008). In addition, the complexities of political, social, and economic situations among the US's immigrant student populations challenge our understanding of how best to serve families as they acculturate; for instance, immigrant families are more likely to live in poverty, and are less likely to seek health and education services than non-immigrant families (see Takanishi, 2004). Increasingly, across many states and cities in this nation, immigrant families are seen as a source of economic demand leading to resource depletions. Yet as this fastest-growing subset of the US population enters school at increasingly high rates, evidence-based approaches for understanding and supporting positive immigrant youth school adjustment are sorely needed. How best to support the early academic attainment of these children is therefore a complex question that demands our consideration.

A fundamental question therefore is: what is it about the acculturation process in the US that might put immigrant children at risk for unhealthy school adjustment and poor academic success? Numerous studies have documented the strong motivation and commitment immigrant families have for promoting their children's education (Fuligni, 1997; Glick & White, 2004; Kao & Tienda, 1995; Hao & Bonstead-Burns, 1998). It is therefore *not* likely that the decline in achievement across acculturation is due to a lack of family values in children's education. Although research has yet to establish the mechanisms by which settings such as families, schools, and peers may promote or hinder the immigrant paradox in education, clues from research of family cultural socialization processes may provide a basis for exploration of this important topic. For example, recent research findings demonstrate that as families acculturate to the US, children's attitudes toward school become less aligned with parents' (Fuligni, 1997; Goyette & Xie, 1999; Rosenbaum & Rochford, 2008; Suárez-Orozco & Suárez-Orozco, 2001). Other research highlights the bi-directionality of parent educational expectations and children's academic performance, whereby Latino immigrant parents' education beliefs are influenced both by their original cultural beliefs, and by their children's experiences in elementary school (Goldenberg, Gallimore, Reese, & Garnier, 2001). Further, children of immigrants in the elementary school years are not only forming their identities as students, but also as members of ethnic and racial social groups; how these early student-ethnic identity processes align (or do not align) may have strong implications for children's future academic success and psychological well-being. Unfortunately, the processes of family cultural socialization and early ethnic-identity development among children of immigrants are rarely studied with respect to school adjustment prior to adolescence. These topics are addressed in the current chapter in hopes of drawing out new avenues for early-childhood education research and identifying points of education intervention on behalf of immigrant children and their families.

In this chapter, we review theoretical perspectives and research related to immigrant families' cultural socialization regarding their children's educations, focusing on some of the unique developmental experiences of children of immigrants as they adjust to their early years in school. In doing so, we wish to highlight the importance of understanding the family immigration context as well as cultural beliefs and practices for supporting children's transitions to school. Next, we make use of research on emerging ethnic identity development and early peer social processes to highlight the necessity of establishing positive student-ethnic identities early on in schooling for later academic success. Lastly, we consider how schools and teachers may support immigrant children and their families with these psychological adjustments to school in early childhood.

Immigrant Children's Cultural Socialization and School Adjustment

The notion of "school adjustment" has appeared for decades in education-related literature, with varied meanings. Oftentimes, studies of school adjustment have documented students' success according to commonly examined academic outcomes (e.g., how well students perform on tests of cognitive skill development or earn good grades), while other studies document classroom behavior (e.g., attention, self-regulation) and social competencies (Birch & Ladd, 1996; Perry & Weinstein, 1998). More recently, the idea of school adjustment has taken on additional psychological meanings to include students' abilities to make positive emotional adaptations to the school context in and of itself (see Huffman, Mehlinger, & Kerivan, 2000). In fact, it is increasingly recognized that healthy psychological (or socioemotional) school adjustment in kindergarten is at least as important—if not more important—as making early gains in quantitative reasoning and reading skills for establishing children's future academic success (Huffman et al., 2000; Marks & García Coll, 2007).

Though under-studied in quantitative research, psychological aspects of adjustment to school among children of immigrants might be best considered alongside the psychological processes that tend to occur during acculturation. "Acculturation" denotes a social process of change that occurs upon an encounter between two cultures. Such encounters precipitate a series of psychological adaptations (e.g., changes in behaviors, beliefs, values and customs) that must be made by the newcomer in order to thrive in the new host cultural environment (Berry, 1997). The psychological experiences that occur during acculturation are therefore typically thought to stem from changes in practice with both the culture of origin (e.g., the "home" culture, or original culture of immigrant children's parents), and the new host culture (e.g., the dominant culture, or the culture of school). As immigrant children's first transitions to school (entry at preschool and/or kindergarten) often occur in a school context that differs culturally from their family, the traditional ideas of school adjustment take on new psychological meanings and acculturation challenges for both children of immigrants and their families (e.g., Delgado-Gaitan & Trueba, 1991). Indeed, the notion of socioemotional "readiness" for kindergarten itself changes when applied to children of immigrant families, as parents must learn to socialize (i.e., "ready") their children in ways that are compatible with their children's new school cultural environments. For parents that have had very little formal education (or education that has taken place in another country), these tasks might seem daunting. Given the increasing diversity within immigration contexts in the US today, it is therefore no surprise that children's psychological adjustment at the transition to school varies greatly by family ethnicity, cultural socialization processes, as well as by school climate and resources.

Nevertheless, there are some common processes of adjustment to school that should be considered in the context of immigrant youth, regardless of parents' specific cultural orientations. These universal processes are ones that are faced by all immigrant children who must make particular adaptations to the new cultural context of school, thereby overcoming "cultural discontinuities" between home and school. One helpful framework for understanding the specific school adaptations required of immigrant families was proposed by Ogbu, who presents three types of cultural discontinuities to capture these processes (Ogbu, 1982). In the "universal" type of cultural discontinuity, *all* children must learn to adjust to the unique environment of school, adapting to classroom organization, new social norms, and novel daily routines. In the "primary" discontinuity, immigrant children must adapt to new cultural concepts (e.g., American conceptualizations of "liberty" and "rights"), learning styles, language use, and even basic mathematical principles such as length and time. Finally, in "secondary" discontinuity, populations who are stratified to low social statuses based on historical subjugation (e.g., racial minorities) must learn to adapt psychologically to a host of caste-based "collective struggles" related to religious, political, and legal rights. For the majority of today's immigrant children, both primary *and* secondary adjustments must be made upon entry to school. Today's immigrant families are therefore in the unique position of preparing their children for novel, often unforeseen social and cultural challenges in school.

What are some of the unique ways in which immigrant parents might influence their children's adjustment to school? One such mechanism may be through parents' direct and indirect messages to children regarding their roles and goals as students—or their education socialization. Such socialization, for children of immigrants, is couched in parents' cultural perspectives and orientations. For recent immigrants, socialization may reflect parents' traditional notions of schooling and education expectations based on their culture of origin, whereas for more highly acculturated immigrant parents, education socialization is likely to be based on more traditional American education expectations (García Coll & Marks, in press). For example, in an ethnographic study of six Mexican American families' education socialization practices, immigrant parents—like most parents, regardless of immigration status—expressed high academic aspirations for their children, and gave numerous structural and social supports to their children to increase their children's chances of academic success. Nevertheless, as low-educated, relatively recent immigrants (less than 10 years' residence in the US), these parents' limited cultural knowledge of the US schools their children were attending hampered their abilities to help with their children's homework, often misleading the child on their assignments and causing confusion in the family when the children's grades did not reflect their high levels of effort (Delgado-Gaitan, 1992). These findings demonstrate the intricacies and importance of understanding parents' immigration contexts (e.g., Did the parents attend school in their country of origin? How long have the parents lived in the US? What US community resources are available to help support immigrant parents in their education socialization efforts?). Such immigration-context considerations can be made regardless of parents' cultures of origin; much more research is needed with ethnically and socially diverse samples to fully pull together a working model of how early education socialization typically unfolds among immigrant families.

Though we are unaware of an empirically derived theoretical framework specifically designed for understanding education socialization among children of immigrants, related theory in cultural socialization may help provide a basis for understanding some of these processes. In a recent literature review examining parents' ethnic socialization practices, Hughes and colleagues proposed a framework for understanding many of the ways in which parents socialize their children to understand their ethnic and racial heritages, and prepare them for both positive and negative encounters with others (i.e., ethnic or racial "out-group" members) about their ethnicity and race (Hughes, Rodrigues, Smith, Johnson, & Stevenson, 2006). A recent surge in interest in this topic directly reflects the changing demographics of the US—parents must prepare their children to live in increasingly diverse ethnic and racial communities and schools, thus rendering these socialization processes increasingly important to understand. For families of color in particular, ethnic and racial socialization serves many purposes, including bolstering children's ethnic pride, promoting children's self-esteem, and preparing children for negative encounters of bias or prejudice. Importantly, in studies of African American families, research has shown that parents' messages are often received by children, regardless of whether their parents are aware of (or report) sending them (Caughy, Ocampo, Randolph, & Nickerson, 2002; Marshall, 1995). Further, messages promoting pride in children's culture are associated with greater academic achievement, whereas messages regarding racial barriers are associated with lower academic achievement (Smith, Atkins, & Connell, 2003), demonstrating a link between the quality of parents' cultural socialization messages and children's grades. The implications of cultural socialization messages for children's education have yet to be fully explored, and warrant further investigation. It may be that, for instance, parents' education and cultural socialization messages are most potent for facilitating academic achievement across the earliest years of schooling, prior to adolescence. New research is needed to document such processes.

Although the majority of research conducted in this area has focused on African American parents' approaches to ethnically or racially socializing their children, the idea of *cultural socialization*, or the "parental practices that teach children about their racial or ethnic heritage and history; that promote cultural customs and traditions; and that promote children's cultural, racial, and ethnic pride, either deliberately or implicitly" (Hughes et al., 2006, p. 749) is one readily applicable to early education processes in immigrant families. As acculturation proceeds, the frequency of parents' traditional cultural socialization messages to their children decrease; earlier generations routinely engage in traditional customs of parents' cultures of origins, while later generations must actively seek opportunities to do so (see Suárez-Orozco & Suárez-Orozco, 1995, 2001). In addition, the nature of parents' understanding of race and ethnicity in the US changes as acculturation proceeds: the longer a family resides in the US, the more American their perspectives become (Portes & Zhou, 1993; Rumbaut, 1994; Waters, 1990).

Despite a lack of research specifically examining cultural socialization practices in the context of immigrant children's psychological adjustment to school, we might expect the nature of messages from parents to children regarding appropriate classroom behaviors, education goals and values, as well as suitable social practices with peers to vary as acculturation proceeds. Though not directly observed as socialization behaviors, these messages may be reflected in research regarding parents' own reported education values and beliefs. For example, in a study examining the quality of parental beliefs about children's academic skill development at the start of elementary school, notable differences between immigrant and non-immigrant parents were observed (Okagaki & Sternberg, 1993). Immigrant parents (primarily of Cambodian, Filipino, and Vietnamese origin) were more likely to endorse conforming to "external standards" as more important than autonomous behaviors for children's early development, than Anglo-American parents. In addition, in contrast to Anglo-American parents, immigrant parents emphasized social and emotional development as more important than cognitive skills (e.g., problem solving) in their conception of an intelligent child. Importantly, immigrant parents' conceptualizations about their children's conformity behaviors was negatively associated with academic skill development—the greater the parents' endorsement of conformity, the lower their children's academic skills across kindergarten, first, and second grades. Although it seems that parents' cultural socialization of their children regarding conformity and ideas of what it means to be "intelligent" might be one possible mechanism behind the patterns revealed by studies such as these, this research is based on parental reports and therefore specific socialization behaviors of immigrant patterns around early education socialization have yet to be documented. Given a vast literature documenting linkages among parents' education beliefs and academic achievement in adolescence (e.g., Fan & Chen, 2001; Okagaki & Frensch, 1998), this area is one worthy of further exploration in early childhood.

Early Ethnic Identity Processes and Education

If immigrant parents can influence their children's adjustment to school in part through their socialization practices, then immigrant children will likely internalize and act upon those socialization practices in part through their *ethnic-identity* development. Although ethnic-identity development is not a psychological process specific to immigrant youth, it is influenced by acculturation and the accompanying adaptations children must make across new cultural contexts (i.e., from home to school), making it an important component of psychological adjustment to school for immigrant youth. In essence, ethnic-identity development among children of immigrants is in part an essential self-defining process for discovering how (and how well) a child "fits in" socially and academically to their school environment. Acculturation processes such as language acquisition and changes in cultural values and practices from home to school all influence the development of ethnic identities among immigrant children, which in turn shape the qualities of their school adjustment.

Broadly speaking, ethnic identities encompass a broad array of feelings and attitudes regarding one's membership in an ethnic and/or racial group, based on family, peer, and community socialization (see reviews by Marks, Powell, & García Coll, in press; Phinney, 1990). Developing positive feelings toward one's ethnic identity as well as ethnic identity centrality (i.e., understanding ethnic identity as important to the sense of self), protects youth from perceptions of discrimination (Verkuyten, 1998, 2002; Wong, Eccles, & Sameroff, 2003), which can be detrimental to school belonging and engagement, academic motivation, positive well-being and self-esteem (Liebkind, Jasinskaja-Lahti, & Solheim, 2004; Szalacha et al., 2003; Wong et al., 2003). Though identity development is typically thought to be a psychological process unique to adolescence, its emergent developmental processes (including those pertaining to culture and ethnicity) occur much earlier in childhood. Interestingly, Erik Erikson (often credited with placing identity development at the forefront of the adolescent developmental experience) writes in his book *Childhood and Society* that,

> The emerging identity bridges the stages of childhood when the bodily self and the parental images are given their cultural connotations … The growing child must, at every step, derive a vitalizing sense of actuality from the awareness that his individual way of mastering experience is a successful variant of a group identity and is in accord with its space-time and life plan.
>
> (Erikson, 1963, p. 235)

Despite ample past research documenting the importance of developing a positive, healthy ethnic identity for academic success and overall psychological well-being in adolescence (Phinney, 1990; Phinney, Cantu, & Kurtz, 1997; Phinney & Chavira, 1992; Fuligni, Witkow, & Garcia, 2005), very few studies have examined the nascence of these important social and psychological processes during the preschool and elementary years among immigrants.

Nevertheless, recent research suggests that early ethnic identities not only are robustly explored by immigrant youth, but also are influenced by parents' cultural socialization practices. For example, in research with African American third–fifth-grade children, early ethnic-identity exploration (e.g., how often the child thinks of himself or herself as being part of a particular ethnic or racial group) was directly related to the frequency of parents' messages to children regarding discrimination (Hughes & Johnson, 2001). New research also suggests that immigrant children as early as 6 years old indeed explore their ethnic identities in ways that show multifaceted understanding of what it means to be a member of their parents' culture as well as to be American (Aboud & Doyle, 1993; Ocampo, Knight, & Bernal, 1997; Marks, Szalacha, Lamarre, Boyd, & García Coll, 2007). In a study of immigrant children in first and third grade (García Coll & Marks, in press), children were able to clearly articulate why their identity was rooted in both cultures; one child stated, "[I am] Portuguese-American" because "when I grow up I'll know both things and both languages." Another stated they are, "Dominican-American" because "I have my mom's blood and she was born in the Dominican Republic and I was born here." Or as one Cambodian third grader told us "[I am] Asian American [because] ... I look Asian and I know how to talk American." Importantly, differing levels of acculturation among first- and second-generation youth may predict differing types of early ethnic-identity development. While children in the first generation may be more apt to identify strongly with a national label (i.e., Mexican) corresponding to their parents' nativity, children from the second generation may face a struggle between equally strong but substantially different identifications with their US ethnic (i.e., Latino, American) and parents' national identities (Rumbaut, 1994). The successful integration of these multiple identities (e.g., resulting in high ethnic pride and centrality) is particularly important for the psychological school adjustment of second-generation youth (Phinney, Berry, Sam, & Vedder, 2006).

These early identity processes directly bear on immigrant students' school-based social practices, as well as their early academic achievement. For example, in a longitudinal study of Cambodian, Dominican, and Portuguese second-generation children in first–sixth grades, immigrant children's reports of ethnic pride and ethnic-identity centrality were positively associated with academic achievement over time (García Coll & Marks, in press). In other words, the greater the immigrant child's identification with their parents' cultural heritage, and the greater their pride in that heritage, the better the child performed academically across the elementary school years. This was particularly true of the Cambodian group, for whom being proud of being Cambodian often was synonymous with being proud of being a student. Both Cambodian boys and girls reported greater happiness with being a student if also satisfied with being Cambodian. This was not necessarily the case, however, for the Dominican group. These youth also showed early evidence of exploration and pride in their ethnic identities; however, this aspect of their identity was not tied as tightly to their student identities as was observed for the Cambodians. Moreover, these differing patterns of student-ethnic identity alignment (or lack of alignment) reflected the children's academic achievement: the Cambodian children (despite having less social and economic resources at home) were far more successful in school (based on grades and teacher classroom-behavior reports) than their Dominican peers.

If children generally are expected to forge their student identities during their early education years to facilitate their roles as students as they adjust to the school environment (Perry & Weinstein, 1998), it is not surprising that immigrant children who do so in congruence with their developing ethnic identities may have more optimal academic outcomes. During the early academic years, children of immigrants are not only developing their ethnic identities but their identities as students and learners. These identities will be central to their experiences in school and will be influenced by the nature and valence of their ethnic identities. The task of developing positive ethnic identities in conjunction with positive student identities may be further complicated for immigrant youth whose ethnic labels may be—based on social stereotypes—associated with devaluing academics or poor academic performance. For example, having an African American identity has been linked (especially in urban centers) with devaluing academics. Ogbu noted in several studies that African American children who were academically oriented were deemed as "acting white" by peers and thus estranged from a collective African American identity (Ogbu, 2004). Youth whose ethnic or racial labels can be linked by stereotype with academic failure may distance themselves from their ethnic identities in order to develop and preserve a positive student identity. This may be true for some immigrant groups as well, particularly for those who may be developing identities in ascribed social categories that are associated with school failure. For example, as noted above we find that for Dominican youth (who also are members of larger urban Hispanic/Latino population with high school dropout rates), high ethnic centrality is associated with lower levels of academic achievement. In this way, some immigrant youth may face additional obstacles in developing a positive ethnic identity in conjunction with a positive student identity as a result of the sociohistorical context of their ethnic or racial group membership in the US.

Ethnic-identity development is not only important to a child's developing sense of self-efficacy in school, but may also predict the types of relationships they develop within the school context (Phinney, Ferguson, & Tate, 1997). Peer and teacher relationships will be built within the framework of developing conceptions of culturally based social in-groups and out-groups, and these conceptualizations will be evidenced in the social preferences made by children. For example, in a study of second-generation youth, children who reported greater ethnic-identity exploration also tended to be more social with peers of *both* similar and other ethnic-group orientations (Marks et al., 2007). As such, developing positive early ethnic identities may promote prosocial peer behavior in school—an important domain for psychological adaptation to the school environment. In sum, the experience with "multiple worlds" created by moving among differing family and school cultures heightens immigrant children's awareness of race and ethnicity well before the adolescent years (Cooper, Jackson, Azmitia, & Lopez, 1998; Suárez-Orozco & Suárez-Orozco, 2001), making early ethnic-identity development an important part of immigrant children's school adjustment.

How Schools and Teachers Can Support Healthy School Adjustment and Identities Among Children of Immigrants

Throughout much of the research perspectives presented in this chapter, the ideas of cultural continuity and discontinuity between home and school are central to understanding immigrant youth school adjustment. We noted above that immigrant youth must make additional "primary" and "secondary" adjustments to the school context as they cross home–school cultural discontinuities and navigate school systems subject to sociohistorical hierarchies. However, despite their proximal influences on early children's academic outcomes, parents' socialization practices and education beliefs do not occur in a social vacuum—rather they are shaped by larger contexts of schools and neighborhoods. Although there is much yet to be learned about how immigrant parents socialize their children to attain their education and how immigrant children learn to form positive student-ethnic identities, the best-made efforts of immigrant families may not be able to overcome the negative qualities of schools attended by their children. For example, disproportionately high numbers of Mexican American immigrant children attend low-achieving schools in kindergarten. Furthermore, attending these schools places these students at significant risk for problems both in academic achievement (e.g., mathematics skill development) as well as social and emotional development in the classroom (Crosnoe, 2005a). But we can not blame poor academic achievement outcomes among immigrant children on structural and financial school deficits alone. In order to effectively close immigration and ethnic/racial achievement gaps, socioemotional characteristics of the school environment may be equally—if not more—important to target than structural school supports (see Becker & Luthar, 2002). It is therefore vital that we take a close look at the qualities of social processes occurring in schools to identify areas for supporting immigrant families' adjustment to school.

Because of its emphasis on social contexts, Perry and Weinstein's (1998) general framework for understanding children's school adjustment may be of particular relevance for understanding socioemotional readiness and psychological adjustment to school among young children of immigrants. According to this framework, classroom, teacher, and school environment characteristics interact with children and families to influence children's psychological adjustment to school. Importantly, their model of school adjustment includes a focus on the quality of peer and adult relationships with the child in the school setting using indicators such as children's sense of belonging, acceptance by peers, qualities of friendships, and social goals. Such perspectives have been empirically supported in past research; in a recent study of over 250 children in first grade, students of teachers who offered greater social and emotional support—including supports for creating positive social relationships—made greater gains in both academic and behavioral domains across the academic year (Perry, Donohue, & Weinstein, 2007).

What characteristics specific to immigrant families' school contexts are not covered by this existing model? The importance of understanding schools for immigrant children's academic success can be seen, in part, in the ways immigrant families interact with them. On one hand, there is strong evidence that parents are responsive to their children's experiences at school and engage with schools by adopting these practices into their home routines. For example, research with Mexican American immigrant families has demonstrated the intricate ways in which parents adopt new perspectives and behaviors based on their children's experiences in schools, while children's cultural practices are shaped by the games, stories, and social encounters experienced in the classroom (Delgado-Gaitan & Trueba, 1991). On the other hand, a strong, direct relationship between schools and parents for some immigrant groups may be lacking. Instead this relationship may exist only through the child, acting as a mediator and/or broker between the home and school contexts. Immigrant parents are met with many obstacles to developing a direct relationship with teachers and schools; parent language barriers and lack of knowledge of what American schools may expect of the parent in a child's educational experience are just a few of the many obstacles they face. While these obstacles can be overcome, a risk is that schools may misinterpret parental hesitancy to be involved in their children's school as disinterest in their children's education—a perception that is far from the truth. Schools and teachers may therefore not take the necessary steps to develop and maintain the strong relationships needed with these parents. Recognizing, understanding, and supportively responding to immigrant parents facing such barriers to school involvement is just one of the many ways schools and teachers may support children of immigrant families' education socialization.

When children are left to navigate home and school worlds on their own, teachers can play an important mentorship role in allowing immigrant youth to find belonging and guidance in their schools. While there is little research on the effect of teacher relationships specifically on early-childhood immigrant children's school adjustment, there is strong evidence in the literature that a positive relationship with teachers can be a life raft for some children's academic achievement. Suárez-Orozco et al. (2008) find that the most academically successful immigrant children often have strong relationships with adult mentors (oftentimes a teacher) in the school, while those who fall behind often lack these crucial in-school adult supports. In particular, teachers demonstrating cultural awareness may be especially supportive. For example, research indicates that among Chinese American adolescents teachers' pedagogy and cultural awareness plays an important role in promoting students' trust in teachers and positive attitudes in school (Zhou, Peverly, Xin, Huang, & Wang, 2003). Ethnic similarity of teachers may also facilitate these student–teacher bonds. For ethnic-minority students, same-race teacher and student pairing (Dee, 2004) as well as greater representation of minority teachers in schools (Bali & Alvarez, 2003; Meier, Wrinkle, & Polinard, 1999) also are related to more positive education outcomes. The support of culturally sensitive teachers may also be a vital part of fostering positive student-ethnic identity development.

Lastly, the social processes occurring in classrooms among peers are also important for promoting immigrant children's academic successes. Peer acceptance and social competence are related not only to perceptions of school quality but also directly to student academic performance (Chen, Rubin, & Li, 1997; Ladd, 1990; Wentzel, 1991; Wentzel & Caldwell, 1997; Welsh, Parke, Widaman, & O'Neil, 2001). For example, Ladd (1990) found in non-immigrant families that peer rejection in kindergarten increased school avoidance and decreased academic successes. Given the importance of maintaining positive peer relations, particular consideration should be given by teachers and school staff to promote positive ethnic in- and out-group social dynamics in schools with immigrant children. One way to do this may be by fostering immigrant children's positive ethnic identities and in-group perceptions, which have been shown to contribute to higher levels of out-group preferences as well (Marks & García Coll, in press).

Conclusion

This chapter presents two key psychological processes important to supporting immigrant children's early education. Family *cultural socialization* regarding their children's education, and children's early *ethnic identity development* are both distinctive psychological processes important to most immigrant children's early school experiences regardless of race, ethnicity and social status. In addition, both of these psychological tasks of early childhood are influenced by the larger immigration acculturation context. As acculturation proceeds, educational and cultural socialization in families continually changes as parents learn more about American education systems through their children, and through increasing contact with the school. Cultural socialization may occur both explicitly and implicitly as part of their parenting, stressing cultural values and identities to children as they navigate between their different home and school cultural contexts. Further, acculturation acts on children as well through the development of their ethnic identities. These identities shape a child's sense of self as students as well as ethnic/racial group members, and influence the social preferences and practices immigrant children have with peers at school. It is likely that parents' cultural socialization and children's early ethnic-identity development therefore work together to promote children of immigrants' psychological well-being in school. New research is needed to fully document these processes. Future research may, for example, wish to explore the ways in which family educational and socialization processes change over time and how such change may aid or hinder children's academic progress and socio-emotional school adjustment. It is likely that change in these processes, related to acculturation, will have both positive and negative effects on children. For example, while parents' increased English-language proficiency and understanding of their children's academic curriculum could allow them to deliver stronger guidance on homework, decreased cultural socialization and cultural routines in the home could diminish children's ethnic-identity pride and centrality, which might in turn have a negative impact on children's academic outcomes. The intricacies of the home–school and parent–child associations discussed throughout this chapter require greater research attention if we are to better understand the "immigrant paradox" in education, and find effective strategies for its early education intervention.

Despite the early stage of our study in this area, the research findings presented in this chapter suggest numerous ways in which schools and teachers may support immigrant families during their children's early education. In particular, the research and theory reviewed here reveals several relational mechanisms that may promote greater connectedness between immigrant families and their schools. By focusing early on immigrant children's adjustment to the school context, we may pre-empt some of the more pronounced academic and social problems encountered by immigrant youth in adolescence. So how do we support immigrant families and children to both "do well" and "be well" in school? First, we might train teachers to understand some of the commonly encountered education socialization difficulties facing immigrant families, and to act as advocates on behalf of immigrant children. Teachers (and school administrators) can act as cultural mediators for immigrant children by understanding the importance of early schooling for immigrant child identity formation through a willingness to act on students' behalf. For example, well-informed teachers may act on behalf of language-minority students in the classroom to facilitate peer connectedness, and may facilitate positive ethnic identities among students who may feel marginalized for being "different." Feelings of school connection are vital for any child, but immigrant children who feel alienated or feel disconnected from their school may be at particular risk for dropping out or academic disengagement. Connection with peers, teachers, and school personnel will help immigrant youth navigate the school environment and help overcome the additional home–school discontinuities and sociohistorical obstacles that they may face as a result of their immigrant status.

Lastly, we might foster more effective parent involvement in children's educations by bridging cultural gaps between families and schools. Immigrant families highly value their children's educations, but their involvement may vary widely for a variety of reasons (e.g., differing cultural orientation, little experience with their own education, language barriers, time/work involvement barriers). Without the help of school staff to engage and educate immigrant families about their children's in-school academic processes and milestones, children's adjustment to school (and their ultimate academic success) may be in jeopardy. Connecting parents and teachers will not only help parents understand and connect with their child's academic journey more fully and effectively, but will give teachers a much-needed insight into parents' perspectives, concerns, and strong aspirations and expectations for their children. Clearing misunderstandings and creating lines of communication between teachers, parents, and immigrant children will enable adults to support immigrant children in the complex navigation of home and school responsibilities, no longer placing them in the tenuous position of acting alone.

Note

1. In this chapter, the phrases "children of immigrants" and "immigrant youth" broadly refer to children of first- (parent and child born in country of origin) or second-generation immigrant status (parents are immigrants but children are born here).

References

Aboud, F.E., & Doyle, A.B. (1993). The early development of ethnic identity and attitudes. In M.E. Bernal (Ed.), *Ethnic identity: Formation and transmission among Hispanics and other minorities. SUNY series, United States Hispanic studies* (pp. 47–59). Albany, NY: State University of New York Press.

Alspaugh, J.W. (1998). Achievement loss associated with the transition to middle school and high school. *Journal of Educational Research, 92*, 20–25.

Bali, V.A., & Alvarez, R.M. (2003). Schools and educational outcomes: What causes the "race gap" in student test sources? *Social Science Quarterly, 84*, 485.

Bankston, C.L., & Zhou, M. (2002). Being well vs. doing well: Self esteem and school performance among immigrant and nonimmigrant race and ethnic groups. *International Migration Review, 36*, 389–415.

Becker, B.E., & Luthar, S.S. (2002). Social-emotional factors affecting achievement outcomes among disadvantaged students: Closing the achievement gap. *Educational Psychologist, 37*(4), 197–214.

Berry, J.W. (1997). Immigration, acculturation, and adaptation. *Applied Psychology: An International Review, 46*, 62–68.

Caughy, M.O., Ocampo, P.J., Randolph, S.M., & Nickerson, K. (2002). The influence of racial socialization practices on the cognitive and behavioral competence of African American preschoolers. *Child Development, 73*, 1611–1625.

Conger, R.D., Schwartz, A.E., & Stiefel, L. (2003). *Who are our students? A statistical portrait of immigrant students in New York City elementary and middle schools.* New York: Taub Urban Research Center.

Cooper, C.R., Jackson, J.F., Azmitia, M., & Lopez, E.M. (1998). Multiple selves, multiple worlds: Three useful strategies for research with ethnic minority youth on identity, relationships, and opportunity structures. In V. McLoyd & L. Steinberg (Eds.), *Studying minority adolescents: Conceptual, methodological, and theoretical issues* (pp. 111–125). Mahwah, NJ: Lawrence Erlbaum Associates.

Crosnoe, R. (2005a). Double disadvantage or signs of resilience? The elementary school contexts of children from Mexican immigrant families. *American Educational Research Journal, 42*(2), 269–303.

Crosnoe, R. (2005b). The diverse experiences of Hispanic students in the American educational system. *Sociological Forum, 20*(4), 561–588.

Crosnoe, R., & Lopez-Gonzalez, L. (2005). Immigration from Mexico, school composition, and adolescent functioning. *Sociological Perspectives, 48*(1), 1–24.

Dee, T.S. (2004). Teachers, race and student achievement in a randomized experiment. *Review of Economics and Statistics, 86*(1), 195–210.

Delgado-Gaitan, C. (1992). School matters in the Mexican-American home: Socializing children to education. *American Educational Research Journal, 29*(3), 495–513.

Delgado-Gaitan, C., & Trueba, H. (1991). *Crossing cultural borders: Education for immigrant families in America.* Bristol, PA: Falmer Press, Taylor & Francis Inc.

Entwisle, D.R., Alexander, K.L., Pallas, A.M., & Cadigan, D. (1987). The emergent academic self-image of first graders: Its response to social structure. *Child Development, 58*(5), 1190–1206.

Erikson, E.H. (1963). *Childhood and society.* New York: W.W. Norton & Company.

Fan, X., & Chen, M. (2001). Parental involvement and students' academic achievement: A meta-analysis. *Educational Psychology Review, 13*(1), 1–22.

Fuligni, A.J. (1997). The academic achievement of adolescents from immigrant families: The roles of family background, attitudes, and behavior. *Child Development, 68*(2), 351–363.

Fuligni, A., Wikow, M., & Garcia, C. (2005). Ethnic identity and the academic adjustment of adolescents from Mexican, Chinese, and European backgrounds. *Developmental Psychology, 41*(5), 799–811.

García Coll, C., & Marks, A.K. (in press). *Immigrant stories: Identity and academic pathways during middle childhood.* New York: Oxford University Press.

Glick, J.E., & Hohmann-Marriott. (2007). Academic performance of young children in immigrant families: The significance of race, ethnicity, and national origins. *International Migration Review, 41*(2), 371–402.

Glick, J.E., & White, M.J. (2004). Post-secondary school participation of immigrant and native youth: The role of familial resources and educational expectations. *Social Science Research, 33,* 272–299.

Goldenberg, C., Gallimore, R., Reese, L., & Garnier, H. (2001). Cause or effect? A longitudinal study of immigrant Latino parents' aspirations and expectations, and their children's school performance. *American Educational Research Journal, 38*(3), 547–582.

Goyette, K., & Xie, Y. (1999). Educational expectations of Asian American youths: Determinants and ethnic differences. *Sociology of Education, 72,* 22–36.

Gutman, L.M., & Midgley, C. (2000). The role of protective factors in supporting the academic achievement of poor African American students during middle school transition. *Journal of Youth and Adolescence, 29*(2), 223–249.

Han, W.-J. (2006). Academic achievements of children in immigrant families. *Educational Research and Review, 1*(8), 286–318.

Hao, L., & Bonstead-Bruns, M. (1998). Parent–child differences in educational expectations and academic achievement of immigrant and native students. *Sociology of Education, 71*(3), 175–198.

Huffman, L.C., Mehlinger, S.L., & Kerivan, A.S. (2000). *Risk factors for academic and behavioral problems at the beginning of school.* Chapel Hill, NC: University of North Carolina.

Hughes, D., & Johnson, D. (2001). Correlates in children's experiences of parents' racial socialization behaviors. *Journal of Marriage and the Family, 63*(4), 981–995.

Hughes, D., Rodrigues, J., Smith, E., Johnson, D., & Stevenson, H. (2006). Parents' ethnic-racial socialization practices: A review of research and directions for future study. *Developmental Psychology, 42*(5), 747–770.

Kao, G. (1999). Psychological well-being and educational achievement among immigrant youth. In D.J. Hernandez (Ed.), *Children of immigrants: Health, adjustment, and public assistance* (pp. 410–477). Washington, DC: National Academy Press.

Kao, G. (2004). Parental influences on the educational outcomes of immigrant youth. *International Migration Review, 38*(2), 427–449.

Kao, G., & Tienda, M. (1995). Optimism and achievement: The educational performance of immigrant youth. *Social Science Quarterly, 76*(1), 1.

Ladd, G.W. (1990). Having friends, keeping friends, making friends, and being liked by peers in the classroom: Predictors of children's early school adjustment? *Child Development, 61*(4), 1081–1100.

Liebkind, K., Jasinskaja Lahti, I., & Solheim, E. (2004). Cultural identity, perceived discrimination, and parental support as determinants of immigrants' school adjustments: Vietnamese youth in Finland. *Journal of Adolescent Research, 19*(6), 635–656.

Marks, A.K., & García Coll, C. (2007). Psychological and demographic correlates of early academic skill development among American Indian and Alaska Native youth: A growth modeling study. *Developmental Psychology, 43*(3), 663–674.

Marks, A.K., Powell, K., & García Coll, C. (in press). Ethnic identity. In *The Chicago companion to the child.* Chicago, IL: University of Chicago Press.

Marks, A.K., Szalacha, L.S., Lamarre, M., Boyd, M.J., & García Coll, C. (2007). Emerging ethnic identity and interethnic group social preferences in middle childhood: Findings from the Children of Immigrants Development in Context (CIDC) study. *International Journal of Behavioral Development, 31*(5), 501–513.

Marshall, S. (1995). Ethnic socialization of African American children: Implications for parenting, identity development, and academic achievement. *Journal of Youth and Adolescence, 24,* 377–396.

Meier, K.J., Wrinkle, R.D., & Polinard, J.L. (1999). Representative bureaucracy and distributional equity: Addressing the hard question. *Journal of Politics, 61*(4), 1025–1041.

Nettles, S.M., Caughy, M.O., & Ocampo, P.J. (2008). School adjustment in the early grades: Toward an integrated model of neighborhood, parental, and child processes. *Review of Educational Research, 78*(1), 3–32.

Ocampo, K.A., Knight, G.P., & Bernal, M.E. (1997). The development of cognitive abilities and social identities in children: The case of ethnic identity. *International Journal of Behavioral Development, 21*(3), 479–500.

Ogbu, J. (2004). Collective identity and the burden "acting white" in Black history, community, and education. *Urban Review, 36*(1), 1–35.

Ogbu, J.U. (1982). Cultural discontinuities and schooling. *Anthropology & Education Quarterly, 13*(4), 290–307.

Okagaki, L., & Frensch, P.A. (1998). Parenting and children's school achievement: A multiethnic approach. *American Educational Research Journal, 35*(1), 123–144.

Okagaki, L., & Sternberg, R.J. (1993). Parental beliefs and children's school performance. *Child Development, 64*(1), 36–56.

Palacios, N., Guttmannova, K., & Chase-Lansdale, L. (2008). Early reading achievement of children in immigrant families: Is there an immigrant paradox? *Developmental Psychology, 44*(5), 1381–1395.

Patton, F., Yang, H., Marks, A.K., & García Coll, C. (in preparation). The immigrant paradox in child development.

Perry, K.E., Donohue, K.M., & Weinstein, R.S. (2007). Teaching practices and the promotion of achievement and adjustment in first grade. *Journal of School Psychology, 45,* 269–292.

Perry, K.E., & Weinstein, R.S. (1998). The social context of early schooling and children's school adjustment. *Educational Psychologist, 33*(4), 177–194.

Phinney, J.S. (1990). Ethnic identity in adolescents and adults: Review of research. *Psychological Bulletin, 10,* 499–514.

Phinney, J., Berry, J.W., Sam, D.L., & Vedder, P. (2006). Understanding immigrant youth: Conclusions and implications. In J.W. Berry, J. Phinney, D.L. Sam, & P. Vedder (Eds.), *Immigrant youth in cultural transition: Acculturation, identity, and adaptation across national contexts* (pp. 211–235). Mahwah, NJ: Lawrence Erlbaum Associates.

Phinney, J.S., Cantu, C.L., & Kurtz, D.A. (1997). Ethnic and American identity as predictors of

self-esteem among African American, Latino and White adolescents. *Journal of Youth and Adolescence, 26*, 167–185.
Phinney, J.S., & Chavira, V. (1992). Ethnic identity and self-esteem: An exploratory longitudinal study. *Journal of Adolescence, 15*(3), 271–281.
Phinney, J.S., Ferguson, D.L., & Tate, J.D. (1997). Intergroup attitudes among ethnic minority adolescents: A causal model. *Child Development, 68*(5), 955–969.
Phinney, J.S., Horenczyk, G., Liebkind, K., & Vedder, P. (2001). Ethnic identity, immigration, and well-being: An interactional perspective. *Journal of Social Issues, 57*(3), 493–510.
Pong, S.-L. (2003). *Immigrant children's school performance.* Atlanta, GA: American Sociological Association.
Pong, S.-L., Hao, L., & Gardner, E. (2005). The roles of parenting styles and social capital in the school performance of immigrant Asian and Hispanic adolescents. *Social Science Quarterly, 86*(4), 928–950.
Portes, A., & Rumbaut, R.G. (2001). *Legacies: The story of the immigrant second generation.* Berkeley, CA: University of California Press.
Portes, A., & Zhou, M. (1993). The new second generation: Segmented assimilation and its variants. *Annals of the American Academy of Political and Social Sciences, 530*, 74–96.
Rosenbaum, E., & Rochford, J.A. (2008). Generational patterns in academic performance: The variable effects of attitudes and social capital. *Social Science Research, 37*, 350–372.
Rumbaut, R.G. (1994). The crucible within: Ethnic identity, self-esteem, and segmented assimilation among children of immigrants. *International Migration Review, 28*(4), 748–781.
Seidman, Allen, Aber, Mitchell & Feinman. (1994). The impact of school transitions in early adolescence on the self-system and perceived social context of poor urban youth. *Child Development, 65*, 507–522.
Smith, E.P., Atkins, J., & Connell, C.M. (2003). Family, school, and community factors and relationships to racial-ethnic attitudes and academic achievement. *American Journal of Community Psychology, 32*, 159–173.
Stipek, D. (2005). Children as unwitting agents in their developmental pathways. In C.R. Copper, C. García Coll, T. Bartko, H.M. Davis, & C. Chatman (Eds.), *Developmental pathways through middle childhood* (pp. 99–120). London: Lawrence Erlbaum Associates.
Suárez-Orozco, C., & Suárez-Orozco, M.M. (1995). *Transformations: Migration, family life, and achievement motivation among Latino adolescents.* Stanford, CA: Stanford University Press.
Suárez-Orozco, C., & Suárez-Orozco, M.M. (2001). *Children of immigration.* Cambridge, MA: Harvard University Press.
Suárez-Orozco, C., Suárez-Orozco, M., & Todorova, I. (2008). *Learning a new land: Immigrant students in American society.* Cambridge, MA: Belknap Press of Harvard University Press.
Szalacha, L.A., Erkut, S., García Coll, C., Fields, J.P., Alarcon, O., & Ceder, I. (2003). Perceived discrimination and resilience. In S.S. Luthar (Ed.), *Resilience and vulnerability: Adaptation in the context of childhood adversities* (pp. 414–435). New York: Cambridge University Press.
Takanishi, R. (2004). Leveling the playing field: Supporting immigrant children from birth to eight. *The Future of Children, 14*(2), 61–79.
Verkuyten, M. (1998). Perceived discrimination and self-esteem among ethnic minority adolescents. *The Journal of Social Psychology, 138*(4), 479–493.
Verkuyten, M. (2002). Perceptions of ethnic discrimination by minority and majority early adolescents in the Netherlands. *International Journal of Psychology, 37*(6), 321–332.
Waters, M. (1990). *Ethnic options.* Berkeley, CA: University of California Press.
Wentzel, K.R. (1991). Relations between social competence and academic achievement in early adolescence. *Child Development, 62*(5), 1066–1078.
Wentzel, K.R., & Caldwell, C. (1997). Friendships, peer acceptance, and group membership: Relations to academic achievement in middle school. *Child Development, 68*(6), 1198–1209.

Welsh, M., Parke, R.D., Widaman, K., & O'Neil, R. (2001). Linkages between children's social and academic competence: A longitudinal analysis. *Journal of School Psychology, 39*(6), 463–481.

Wong, C.A., Eccles, J.S., & Sameroff, A. (2003). The influence of ethnic discrimination and ethnic identification on African American adolescents' school and socioemotional adjustment. *J Personality, 71*(6), 1197–1232.

Zhou, Z., Peverly, S.T., Xin, T., Huang, A.S., & Wang, W. (2003). School adjustment of first-generation Chinese American adolescents. *Psychology in the Schools, 40*(1), 71–84.

14 Emergent Literacy in Immigrant Children

Home and School Environment Interface

Iliana Reyes and Yuuko Uchikoshi

Introduction

> We are trying to teach them as much English as possible, but at the same time we want to respect their culture, we want them to be proud of their culture.
>
> (Ms. Vásquez, teacher, personal interview, February 2, 2005)

These comments shared by a preschool teacher during an interview with the first author reflect the ongoing challenges many teachers and educators face in their classrooms when their multicultural student population reflects the changing demographics of the general population; to meet these students' educational needs, they feel they need to be prepared to teach them English while honoring and teaching them about their home culture. Although we focus our discussion on immigrant groups in the US, many of the challenges discussed in this chapter are faced by other immigrant communities around the world, wherever families from foreign places decide to make their home in a new community (Takanishi, this volume).

In what Halcón (2001) and others call "mainstream ideology," immigrants to the US are judged successful if their beliefs and practices embrace the ideals of the dominant American society, including understanding and becoming fluent speakers of English. Numerous studies have documented that for immigrant families, gaining English proficiency is one of their main goals (Delgado-Gaitan, 2001); however, because of the many other transitions they are undergoing (e.g., relocating to a new place, searching for a job) many of them have difficulty doing so (Tse, 2001). Despite these challenges, immigrant parents are committed to having their children learn English, because they know this is one of the keys to success and to pursuing the American dream (Santa Ana, 2004; Tse, 2001).

Research on young English-language learners has typically focused on how children develop language and literacy skills and transfer them from one language to the other within the classroom context. We acknowledge that this is a very important context and that a smooth transition from their home language to English is critical for eventual success in US society. Yet we also emphasize that the other contexts and "social configurations" (Moll, 2003), such as home and community, in which the child is developing and acquiring multiple competencies and literacies are equally important and deserve attention. Our work with immigrant families has focused on home and community contexts, providing us with important tools and resources that we share in this chapter.

In this chapter we review and describe the current state of research with regard to the language and literacy development of young immigrant English-language learners (pre-K–grade 3), in particular those whose first language is Spanish as much of the past literature has focused on this population. First, we describe who these immigrant children are and how they may benefit from maintaining their bilingualism. Second, we review the existing research on acquisition of specific language and literacy competencies; and then we review some of the recent literature on home literacy practices with immigrant families (Schecter & Bayley, 2002; Zentella, 2005). We then draw specific examples from the work we both have been conducting in recent years with Latino immigrant families in the US that shed light on the significance of home literacy practices. Finally, we discuss the impact of family literacy practices on immigrant children's language and literacy development in the dominant language, English, and their home language. We will also consider how our findings may generalize to other immigrant populations.

Immigrant English Language Learners

Immigrant children come to the US from all parts of the world, but in recent years, large percentages have arrived from Latin America and Asia (Tse, 2001). Suárez-Orozco and Suárez-Orozco (2002) distinguish between "immigrant children" and "children of immigrants." Immigrant children are foreign-born whereas the latter are born in the host country to parents who are immigrants. Although these definitions and others available in the literature can be useful, the distinctions are not always black and white, and a complicating factor is that within one immigrant family you may find some siblings born in the country of origin and others born in the host country (thus, some children are first-generation and others second-generation immigrants). Another layer of complexity is that not all immigrant children share the same linguistic and literacy backgrounds, despite the fact that educational policy often treats them as if that were the case. For example, many children of immigrants who are second- or third-generation only speak English and have lost their family's heritage language, while immigrant children often speak a language other than English as their first language. One aspect that Reyes (2006) has discussed is the significant role family interactions play in promoting the literacy development of preschool children who are learning two languages at an early age and are developing literacy in two languages simultaneously. Another important aspect influencing the learning of the second language is the linguistic environment, including the geographic area of the community (e.g., Southwest vs. Midwest, given the percentage differential of immigrant students who speak the same language) and the school context (whether there is support for bilingual programs or not), both of which impact the opportunities children may have to develop English and maintain their native language. A case in point is provided by a study of Swedish speakers in Finland that yielded data that could be interpreted as consistent with the hypothesis that language practices and policies in a community that recognizes the value of bilingualism can minimize the negative effects of language-minority status on student literacy outcomes (Brunell & Linnakylä, 1994).

The current US Department of Education label for children whose first language is other than English is *English-Language Learners* (ELLs). This label is based on a subtractive perspective that these children are "lacking" English-language competencies and skills rather than having strengths in their home language. On this criterion, most first-generation immigrants are considered ELLs. We prefer other terms such as "emergent bilingual" which acknowledge that competencies in two languages can be an asset. In this chapter we use the terms *ELL* and *bilingual* interchangeably to refer to first- or second-generation immigrant children whose first language is other than English.

We view literacy development from a broad perspective that considers the impact of multiple social interactions rather than examining only the acquisition of discrete skills, such as letter recognition. Moreover, an assumption in our research approach is that typically *all* children have the potential to develop fluency and literacy in English if they and their families are given the necessary support. Based on the literature we recognize that there are many *ways* and *means* to develop language and literacy, and we support a holistic perspective and approach to defining and describing ELLs (Gregory, Long, & Volk, 2004).

The literature in the fields of bilingual education and second-language learning has focused on how children acquire their second language and transfer linguistic or literacy skills from one language to the other. In this regard, Grosjean (1982) argues that a child's total linguistic ability is greater than the sum of the two separate languages because the two languages interact to increase the functionality of each. The ideal for young immigrant children attending preschool through early elementary grades (4–7 years old) would be to acquire *balanced* bilingual competence in speaking, thinking, reading, and writing, meaning that they have equivalent fluency in the two languages. However, research has shown that balanced bilingualism is very difficult, perhaps impossible, to truly achieve; instead, bilingualism should be understood as a continuum in which language ability changes constantly in relation to the individual's social, educational, and linguistic contexts (Hornberger, 2001; Reyes, forthcoming). Each child follows a unique trajectory in learning a second language, and the linguistic and literacy practices used to support language and literacy development also vary from family to family. Sociocultural, economic, and political factors also influence children's language and literacy development, although many of these have not been well-described in the literature (Goldenberg, Rueda, & August, 2006).

In their landmark longitudinal study of second-generation children in the US, Portes and Rumbaut (2001) report that fluent young adolescent bilinguals accrue substantial social and intellectual advantages, including higher professional aspirations, self-esteem, and academic achievement than non-fluent bilinguals or English monolinguals. Portes and Rumbaut also report that these bilinguals had stronger ties with family and community, leading to a highly beneficial "selective" acculturation into society. Therefore, developing and maintaining fluent bilingualism has significant advantages. However, recent political mandates in states such as Arizona, California, and Massachusetts make it harder for young immigrant children to take advantage of the linguistic resources available at home and in their communities to develop bilingual proficiency (Reyes, Alexandra, & Azuara, 2007).

In the next section we review studies of young ELL children from two different perspectives: the psycholinguistic one that focuses on specific skills and linguistic competencies ELL children develop, and the sociocultural perspective that examines how children develop linguistic competencies during the multiple social interactions in which they participate with adults, siblings, and peers.

Research on the Language and Literacy Development of Young Spanish-Speaking Children

Sulzby (1989) defined emergent literacy as "the reading and writing behaviors of young children that precede and develop into conventional literacy" (p. 24). Some of these behaviors include learning how to hold a book and turn pages, telling a story from a picture book while pretending to read it, and using drawings and scribbled letters to "write" messages to Mom and Dad (Goodman, 1984). It has been recognized that children who are learning to read and write in a language they are not orally proficient in are at high risk for later reading difficulties (Snow, Burns, & Griffin, 1998). Yet only a few studies have examined the development of emergent literacy in young bilingual children and what factors are important for their success (Kenner, Kress, Hayat, Kam, & Tsai, 2004; Reese, Garner, Gallimore, & Goldenberg, 2000; Paez, Tabors, & Lopez, 2007; Reyes, 2006; Schwarzer, 2001). Most of the research has addressed monolingual children (Clay, 1975; Sulzby, 1989). Research with these children has shown that language experiences and early exposure to literacy are the foundations for good language and literacy development (Snow et al., 1998). Specifically, two main groups of preschool literacy-related skills have been identified as important for the development of conventional literacy: (a) early literacy skills, as represented by phonological awareness, letter and word recognition, and spelling and writing; and (b) oral proficiency, as represented by vocabulary and language recall (Dickenson & Snow, 1987; Whitehurst & Lonigan, 1998).

Children's Emergent Literacy

Phonological Awareness

Existing research with Spanish-speaking ELL children shows that stimulation of phonological awareness in either L1 or L2 is likely to transfer to the other language (Dickenson, McCabe, Clark-Chiarelli, & Wolf, 2004; Durgulonoglu, 1998; Lindsey, Manis, & Bailey, 2003). Dickenson and colleagues found strong transfer of phonological awareness skills from L1 to L2 and vice versa in a study of 123 Spanish–English 2- and 4-year-old bilingual children in Head Start. At the end of the school year, the most important predictor of phonological awareness in each language was phonological awareness in the other language. Likewise, Durgulonoglu (1998) found that Spanish–English bilingual first-graders who performed well on Spanish phonological tasks were much more successful in reading English words and English-sounding pseudo-words than were students with low Spanish phonological awareness. Additionally, Durgulonoglu (1998) found that among first-graders enrolled in transitional bilingual programs, Spanish phonological awareness correlated significantly with English phonological awareness, English spelling, and Spanish word recognition. Lindsey and colleagues (2003) suggest that phonological awareness is a general rather than a language-specific cognitive process.

Letter and Word Recognition

Recent studies on letter recognition among ELL children suggest that the language of instruction plays a key role in the development of letter- and word-recognition skills. Paez et al. (2007) report that 4-year-old Spanish-speaking ELL children attending English-language preschools scored lower on English letter identification than monolingual English speakers did; by the end of preschool, these children did better on English than Spanish letter identification. This was partially accounted for by a loss of Spanish-language competence. On the other hand, Lindsey and colleagues (2003) found that English letter- and word-identification skills of 249 Spanish-speaking ELL children attending bilingual programs were within the average range for monolingual students at the end of first grade, even though the ELL children had limited English abilities at the beginning of kindergarten. Their Spanish letter- and word-identification skills were below average at the onset of kindergarten, but moved into the average range by the end of kindergarten, and were well above average by the end of first grade. In sum, these studies show that young emergent bilinguals rapidly advanced to at least "average" letter- and word-recognition abilities in comparison to their monolingual peers. In addition, there is evidence that ELLs frequently score low on tests of letter and word recognition at the beginning of their school careers, and teachers should be cautious about referring them to special education prematurely, as they are able to catch up with their peers when given direct instruction.

Relatively little is known about the English spelling development of Spanish-speaking ELL children. Whereas English has a deep (i.e., unintuitive) orthography, Spanish has a relatively shallow, transparent orthography. Studies have shown that for children who initially learn to read in Spanish, their knowledge of Spanish influences their English spelling (Dressler, 2002; Fashola, Drum, Mayer, & Kang, 1996). This effect is only seen, however, if the students received direct literacy instruction in Spanish and was not found among bilingual students receiving strictly English-language instruction (Rolla San Francisco, Mo, Carlo, August, & Snow, 2006).

Oral Proficiency and Vocabulary

Research with monolingual English children shows vocabulary to be one of the strongest predictors of later reading success (Snow et al., 1998). Recent work suggests that the same may be true for Spanish-speaking ELL children as well (Gottardo, 2002). Past research with monolingual children has shown that the size of their vocabulary is heavily dependent on the amount of language exposure (Huttenlocher, Haight, Bryk, Seltzer, & Lyons, 1991; Hart & Risley, 1995); for bilinguals, their relative vocabulary development in each language depends on the amount of input per language (de Houwer, 1995; Pearson, Fernández, Lewedig, & Oller, 1997; Patterson, 2002). Native English speakers have lexicons of 5,000 to 7,000 English words by the time they reach kindergarten (Hart & Risley, 1995). Because bilingual children must sort out input from two linguistic systems, studies have shown that even when they have higher socioeconomic status than their monolingual peers (normally a predictor of good vocabulary development), Spanish-speaking ELL children score significantly below the mean for monolingual English speakers on measures of English vocabulary (Umbel, Pearson, Fernandez, & Oller, 1992).

There is a relationship between Spanish–English bilingual children's L1 and L2 vocabulary development (e.g., Ordóñez, Carlo, Snow, & McLaughlin, 2002); that is, research has found transfer effects at the lexical level. Specifically, knowledge of cognates between Spanish and English assists them in English vocabulary development and reading comprehension. Ordóñez and colleagues (2002) found that Spanish superordinate performance was a significant predictor of English superordinate performance for Spanish–English bilinguals in fourth and fifth grades. The children's depth of knowledge for high-frequency Spanish nouns was related to their depth of knowledge for similar English nouns. Vocabulary tasks that tapped into metalinguistic skills, such as providing superordinates, tended to transfer from Spanish to English. The authors suggested that there was a direct lexical effect, where students who knew Spanish words such as *animal* and *humano* easily acquired the English cognates *animal* and *human*. More recent research shows that teachers can apply this strategy in the classroom to connect content-area knowledge with vocabulary development (Bravo, Hiebert, & Pearson, 2007).

Although many of the transfer studies on Spanish-speaking ELLs have been conducted on children in grades 4 through 8, Uchikoshi (2006) examined the influence of L1 (Spanish) vocabulary on the development of receptive and expressive vocabulary in the L2 (English) in 150 ELL kindergarteners. Spanish vocabulary data were collected at the beginning of the year (in October), whereas English vocabulary was tested at three time points during the academic year: October, February, and June. Overall these native-Spanish-speaking kindergarteners achieved Spanish receptive vocabulary scores expected for 4.8- to 5.0-year-old Spanish monolinguals residing in Mexico, according to the age norms of the test (Dunn, Padilla, Lugo, & Dunn, 1986). As the children's average age was 5.6 years, their vocabulary levels were slightly lower than those of their monolingual Spanish counterparts. Interestingly, in October the children scored on average at the level of a 3.2-year-old monolingual English-speaking child on receptive English vocabulary; by June they had acquired enough English vocabulary to achieve the level of a 4.5-year-old monolingual English-speaking child. Thus, in 7 months, these ELL children had a vocabulary spurt roughly equivalent to 1.3 years' development for a monolingual English child. On English expressive vocabulary, the children averaged the level of a 3.0-year monolingual English child in October; by June they had achieved an average score of 3.9 years.

Initial Spanish vocabulary is a predictor of English vocabulary acquisition. Children starting kindergarten with higher initial Spanish receptive vocabulary scores tended also to have higher English receptive vocabulary scores than children who had low initial Spanish receptive vocabulary scores, and the gap remained constant throughout their kindergarten year (Uchikoshi, 2006). Thus, there appears to be an association between L1 and L2 receptive lexical knowledge even at school entry. This may be due to the many cognates between Spanish and English, which facilitates reading comprehension for these children.

Interestingly, however, there was no relationship between Spanish receptive vocabulary and English expressive vocabulary (Uchikoshi, 2006). It appears that not all links between L1 and L2 vocabulary are facilitative. This may be due to several factors. First, expressive vocabulary tends to lag behind receptive vocabulary, even in first-language acquisition (deVilliers & deVilliers, 1978). The effects of L1 Spanish receptive vocabulary may not have been evident yet. It would be interesting to examine the growth of Spanish receptive and English expressive vocabulary over longer periods to see if the relationship changes over the years. Second, the relationship may depend on the specific words on the expressive vocabulary test. Many English words on the Picture Vocabulary subtest of the Woodcock Language Proficiency Battery–R do not share cognates with Spanish; the results might have been different had there been more cognates.

Other tools such as media and technology (e.g., computers) are known to influence the development of language and literacy in young children. Specifically, educational television has the potential to facilitate the language acquisition of young Latino children. Uchikoshi (2006) found home viewing of *Arthur* and *Between the Lions* (two educational television shows targeting children aged 3 to 7 years) increased Spanish-speaking ELL kindergarteners' English vocabulary growth. *Arthur* home viewing was associated with higher expressive vocabulary scores, and *Between the Lions* home viewing was associated with higher receptive and expressive vocabulary scores at the start of kindergarten. Home viewing of educational programming may imply an overall family environment supportive of learning, however, so variables in addition to television viewing may be at play here. In this study, the total number of children's books in the home, indicating shared book reading, also had positive associations with children's English expressive vocabulary scores. Further research is needed to determine how specific features of these experiences enable immigrant ELL children to learn the second language and develop literacy.

Sociocultural Influences on Children's Emergent Literacy and Family Literacy Practices

Early literacy development starts long before children enroll in preschool and kindergarten. The impact of family practices before children begin formal schooling must be explored to further our understanding of young children's early literacy development. It is particularly important to understand the early biliteracy development of immigrant children in order to support their learning effectively as they interact with native English speakers in the increasing linguistically and culturally diverse classrooms across the US (Brisk & Harrington, 2000). Language and literacy events at home support immigrant children's reading development. Many also learn to recognize print in two languages (and sometimes more than two), and consequently increase their vocabulary through exposure to environmental print, as well as through storybook reading with family members (Reyes & Azuara, in press). Patterson (2002) found that the frequency of being read to in each language was related to bilingual 2-year-old children's expressive vocabulary size in that language. Yet, how the home literacy environments and family interactions of Spanish–English bilingual preschoolers relate to emergent literacy has received limited research attention.

Early studies in this area tended to compare middle-class Anglo families with immigrant families, finding a "mismatch" between immigrant parents' literacy practices and those expected and emphasized in the classroom (Goldenberg et al., 2006). Anderson and Stokes (1984) observed differences in home literacy practices between middle-class monolingual English-speaking families and Mexican American families. Specifically, the former group spent, on average, four times as much time reading storybooks. In a sample of 43 Spanish–English bilingual children attending Head Start, Hammer, Miccio, and Wagstaff (2003) found that the mothers read to their children several times a week but on average there were fewer than 10 books in the home. This study, however, does not account for other literacy activities in which immigrant parents might engage, such as oral storytelling or reading magazines, religious pamphlets, and books borrowed from the library. In a recent study, Reyes (forthcoming) found that among 40 first-generation immigrant families, the parents did not *own* many books, but the children still had access to many books, with about 85% of the books around the house being borrowed from the local library. In addition, about 55% of the parents reported visiting the local library on a biweekly basis and the remainder reported visiting on a monthly basis to check out new books. These findings indicate that immigrant Latino families do make use of books; however, because of economic and other factors, they borrow rather than purchase them. These findings also warn researchers to be careful in evaluating different communities that may have variant but still beneficial literacy practices.

Recent studies on the kinds of adult–child interactions in Latino families indicates that there is no one *pattern* or *way* in which young Latino children learn and develop language and literacy (Vasquez, 2003; Zentella, 2005). An important finding not often acknowledged by teachers and school staff is that older siblings and extended family members living in the same household play important roles in young children's language and literacy development. The typical young immigrant child has multiple opportunities to interact and learn during interactions not only with parents, but also with grandparents, aunts or uncles, older siblings, cousins, and other peers (Reyes, 2006; Roca, 2005; Rodriguez, 2005). Gregory (1998) studied interactions between older and younger siblings of Bangladeshi origin living in London. She found that older siblings assisted their younger siblings by scaffolding while reading books in English. As the younger children gained confidence in reading English, the siblings gave them the freedom to read what they felt they could attempt on their own. Thus, immigrant children benefit from the knowledge their older siblings acquire in school.

In their literature review, Goldenberg et al. (2006) identify three important findings with regard to parent and family influences on the literacy development of language-minority children and youth. First, parents express their willingness to help their children succeed in school and often actively seek to assist them; however, teachers and school administrators often underestimate parents' interest in contributing to students' educational development and the knowledge that they have (Gonzalez, Moll, & Amanti, 2005). Second, many researchers claim that more home literacy opportunities are generally associated with better literacy outcomes, but in fact, the findings in this area are "not consistent and precise conclusions are difficult to find" (p. 257). Third, the relationship between home language use and children's literacy outcomes is not always straightforward. Some studies point to a modest positive correlation between home experiences with the first language and children's literacy achievement in their first and second languages; other studies however found that promoting English home literacy activities had no effect on English literacy achievement in first grade (Brunell & Saretsalo, 1999; Buriel & Cardoza, 1988; Connor, 1983; Hancock, 2002).

Another important and understudied factor is the relationship between children's linguistic and literacy development and the language ideologies that their parents acquired from their experiences growing up in their home countries. For example, Relaño Pastor (2005) describes through interviews how first-generation Latino mothers from El Salvador, Guatemala, and Mexico and now living in California express their "fears of linguistic, cultural, and consequently moral loss in their children." She specifically describes the impact that the devaluation of Spanish has on children's motivation to continue speaking and learning their native language at home, and worse yet, how current ideologies and prejudice against the Spanish language influence children to distance themselves from their home language, widening the linguistic and moral gap between mother and child (Relaño Pastor, 2005; Tse, 2001).

What We Know About Latino Immigrant Families and Children's Emergent Literacy

As this literature review indicates, there is a dearth of research on the literacy practices in immigrant homes and how they affect Spanish-speaking ELL children's emergent language and literacy development. In order to address this gap, our recent research has examined the influence of home literacy practices on young Spanish-speaking ELL children's language and literacy development. Uchikoshi's data on Mexican immigrant families living in northern California come primarily from parental questionnaires asking about their kindergarten-age children's acquisition of English and their native language, Spanish. In addition, parents were asked about their literacy practices at home and in their community. Reyes draws from her findings and qualitative observations of Mexican immigrant families and their 4-year-old children living in southern Arizona. The data described here come primarily from parent interviews about their attitudes and practices regarding children's language and literacy development in both languages.

Influence of Home Literacy Practices on Children's Language and Emergent Literacy Development

In this study, questionnaires were collected from parents to understand immigrant children's backgrounds and home situations. Data were collected from 67 Spanish-speaking ELL children attending kindergarten in northern California school districts and their parents. The schools were in low-SES neighborhoods, and Spanish was spoken in all homes. Of the 67 children, 41 came from one urban school district, where they attended full-day transitional bilingual Spanish–English kindergarten programs that taught both Spanish and English literacy. The remaining 26 children came from another urban school district, where they attended half-day English-immersion kindergarten programs where Spanish literacy was not taught. The data were collected as part of a larger project examining the development of oral language and literacy in ELLs from kindergarten through second grade.[1]

All children were administered a series of language and literacy tests in both English and Spanish. Background data were collected through parental questionnaires. Questions addressed how long the family had resided in the US, age of English acquisition, mother's education, number of children's books in the home, how often the family visited the home country, and how satisfied the mother was with the child's language skills in L1 and L2.

Descriptive results show that the majority of the children were born in the US, but the mean age of formal English learning was 3 years. The home language tended to be Spanish only for the parents, but many parents reported that the kindergarteners spoke both English and Spanish at home. A third of the children were first-born in the family, and the majority had attended Head Start, preschool, or daycare prior to enrolling in kindergarten.

Correlational results showed the number of English books in the house was strongly associated with English expressive vocabulary and English letter and word recognition. The participating families had 1 to 10 Spanish-language books and 11 to 25 English-language books in the home on average. Library experience was also associated with English receptive vocabulary scores. Parents reported that they took their kindergarteners to the library an average of two or three times each month. Similar to Reyes's (forthcoming) study, although the number of books in the home was limited, the children still had access to a variety of books through library visits. The number of children's books in the home and library exposure both indicates family environments generally supportive of literacy development.

The language of instruction at school also influenced these ELL kindergarteners' emergent literacy in Spanish and English. On average, those attending English-immersion programs had significantly higher scores on English letter and word identification (slightly over one standard deviation), English concepts of print (slightly under three-quarters of a standard deviation), and English receptive vocabulary (slightly over half a standard deviation) than their counterparts who attended bilingual programs. On the other hand, children enrolled in the transitional bilingual programs had significantly higher scores on Spanish expressive vocabulary (slightly over three-quarters of a standard deviation) and Spanish letter and word identification (slightly over one standard deviation) than their peers in English-immersion programs. As expected, the more the children were exposed to a language, the better their scores were in that language.

A Sociocultural Perspective on Children's Language and Emergent Literacy Development

From a critical sociocultural perspective, the different studies presented by Reyes and Halcón (2001) and the special issue on biliteracy by Dworin and Moll (2006) are significant efforts in the area of early literacy development of immigrant Latino ELL children in Spanish-speaking communities. These studies offer evidence that integration of the native language and culture in a supportive learning environment can lead to successful acquisition of biliteracy (Reyes & Halcón, 2001). Moreover, when literacy instruction is integrated and contextualized in the child's background knowledge and daily experiences, learning is increased (Freeman & Freeman, 1999). Understanding the home and community language, literacy, and cultural practices in which children participate, and linking these to school, is the key to better serving Latino immigrant children and their families.

The examples in this section come from longitudinal research[2] on preschool Spanish-speaking ELLs in a predominantly Mexican community in southern Arizona. At the beginning of the longitudinal study, the children were 4 years old and attending an English-dominant preschool program. Reyes (forthcoming) and Reyes et al. (2007) report on the results of parental questionnaires and home observations about how immigrant children are acquiring language and literacy in both their first language, Spanish, and their second language, English, in *natural ways* as they participate with their families and peers in everyday literacy interactions (see also Goodman & Goodman, 1979; Heath, 1983). The theoretical framework and research design are informed by psycholinguistic, sociolinguistic, sociocultural, and developmental perspectives.

During this research, first-generation Mexican immigrant parents were interviewed about their language and literacy practices and their overall attitudes about their preschool children's learning of Spanish and of English, and their perspectives on bilingualism. Forty families participated in these interviews; eight of the families had emigrated from central or southern Mexico (the states of Guanajuato, Jalisco, Oaxaca, and Michoacán), and the remaining families had emigrated from the northern states of Sonora, Sinaloa, and Baja California Norte. In the spring semester, a smaller cohort of 20 families was selected for home and school observations to identify the language experiences and competencies the children have. These families are to be followed for 3 years in order to develop in-depth case studies of their daily literacy practices at home and how these affect the children's development of literacy in their two languages (see Reyes, 2006; Reyes et al., 2007).

Parents and primary caregivers participated in an interview with a bilingual researcher about their children's general early childhood development, and their language and literacy practices at home, Following a Vygotskian perspective, Reyes (2006) analyzed the parents' responses and interactions with their children in terms of how they view their children as learners and how they co-create and re-create language and literacy knowledge within the home.

Some of the general findings from the interviews and ethnographic observations that took place during the first year are as follows:

1. *All* of the Mexican-immigrant parents valued their children's development of literacy and bilingualism.
2. The parents felt confident that their children would develop English fluency and literacy with the support of schoolteachers; however, they also expressed concern over how they would maintain the family heritage language (Spanish) in an English-dominant school context.
3. Although many parents expressed interest in supporting their children's development of Spanish literacy and Spanish–English biliteracy, only a few had taken concrete steps in this direction by, for example, teaching the alphabet in both languages, reading and telling stories in Spanish, or collecting and reading bilingual books and other materials.

From the home observations and parent interviews, it is clear that Spanish-dominant bilingual children develop a variety of emergent literacy abilities in both languages across different tasks, such as producing narratives, reading school materials, or writing cards, often in *cooperation* with adults in their family. These activities contribute to language learning and socialization in their bilingual community. In the following example,

Angel shares his letter to Santa with his mom and sister. (All names are pseudonyms; translations to English are provided in parentheses.)

ANGEL: *Esta es la carta que le escribí a Santa Claus*
(this is the letter that I wrote to Santa)
MOM: *¿Y que le escribiste?*
(What did you write?)
ANGEL: *Pues ya sabes lo que tu me ayudaste y Wendy*
(Well, you know, what you helped me write and Wendy)
WENDY: *Si que quiere un perrito y…*
(He asked for a puppy and…)
MOM TO ANGEL: *A ver léeme que mas le pediste*
(Read it and tell me what else you asked Santa for)
ANGEL: *un puppy y la película de Sponge Bob*
(A puppy and the Sponge Bob movie)

(Reyes, field notes, December 12, 2005)

Of significance in this example is that the mother and sister support and scaffold the child's emergent literacy using various cultural tools, such as verbal and nonverbal language, artifacts, and print and sign symbols. They serve as mediators in the construction of meaning that takes place through dialogue and interactions, supporting Angel in maintaining his native language while naturally acquiring English as a second language (Reyes, 2006; Moll, Saez, & Dworin, 2001).

Conclusions and Implications

The review of the literature on Spanish–English bilingual children indicates that (1) young bilingual children when compared with monolingual children tend to be behind their peers on English-language knowledge on school entry but quickly catch up; (2) there is evidence of transfer of phonological and lexical knowledge between languages, so instruction in Spanish could support and improve English skills; and (3) when literacy instruction is integrated and contextualized in the child's background knowledge and daily experiences, learning is increased (Freeman & Freeman, 1999). The first and third summary points are generalizable to other immigrant populations. How quickly the child catches up or how much the learning is increased may depend on the linguistic environment of the school or even the city. If the teacher understands the child's cultural and linguistic background, the teacher may be better able to advance the child's learning. However, although some classrooms are made up of children from the same home languages, in reality there are many classrooms in the US that are made of children with many different home languages. Nonetheless, even under these circumstances where the teacher does not speak the child's native language, teachers can be supportive of the child's cultural and linguistic backgrounds by recruiting parent volunteers to help out in the classroom or by asking other children with the same home language who may be more fluent in English to facilitate (Pérez, 2004).

To become competent bilingual and biliterate speakers, children need to make complex connections between knowledge they acquire at home and at school, particularly when both languages are not necessarily shared in all their various social contexts. An important area for future research is to document systematically the emergent biliteracy development of young children and their transition into conventional literacy (i.e., understanding print, letter identification, early writing and reading) in two languages (Reyes & Azuara, in press). Non-English-speaking children are expected to develop competence in English quickly in order to move into mainstream classrooms. This pressure means, however, that teachers often undervalue and do not take time to understand families' socialization practices at home, which increases stress on teachers, parents, and students while losing the opportunity to build on the child's existing knowledge in the classroom and their social strengths that are the result of parents' positive socialization practices (Espinosa, 2008).

The National Literacy Panel on Language Minority Children and Youth (August & Shanahan, 2006) reports that (1) there are differences in the "norms and expectations for social interaction between the home and school environments of some language-minority students"; and (2) the impact of these differences on students' literacy attainment and the effects of attempts to accommodate these differences in the classroom are not necessarily clear. Some of the specific discontinuities between home and school cultures cited in the literature are bans on using languages other than English at school, a curricular culture that stresses drill on isolated skills rather than more meaningful and contextual literacy experiences where children are actively supported in constructing their literacy knowledge through social interactions (Goldenberg et al., 2006). Some studies show that a successful interface can be built between children's home literacy practices and those in the classroom by allowing children to develop expertise in a variety of written genres in either or both languages; to use both academic and social content as subject matter for their reading and writing; and to use either or both languages deliberately as a tool for thinking (Moll et al., 2001; Martinez-Roldán & Sayer, 2006).

The literature on English-language learners reveals that becoming literate and fluent in the dominant language, English, is a complex and challenging process. There is still much to learn about how best to support children in this transition, but the potential to enhance the lives of so many children and their families should continue motivating us to do research in this area. One important aspect to highlight as we close this chapter is that *not all* immigrant children—even those who share the same native language—have the same language and literacy learning experiences. Therefore, there is no one correct path to literacy for all children. When provided with supportive learning environments, children can be fast and efficient learners of one, two, or more languages (Genesee, 2001; Dworin & Moll, 2006; M. Reyes, 2001). As teachers and educational researchers, we should adopt *responsive* teaching and learning practices informed by educational research. Such practices can in turn lead to educational policies that are based on *sound* and *scientific* research to promote the acquisition of English by different immigrant communities.

Notes

1. This study is supported by a grant from the Foundation for Child Development.
2. This study is supported by a grant from the Foundation for Child Development.

References

Anderson, A.B., & Stokes, S.J. (1984). Social and institutional influences on the development and practice of literacy. In H. Goelman, A. Oberg, & F. Smith (Eds.), *Awakening to literacy* (pp. 24–37). London: Heinemann.

August, D., & Shanahan, T. (2006). *Developing literacy in second-language learners: Report of the National Literacy Panel on Language-Minority Children and Youth.* Hillsdale, NJ: Lawrence Erlbaum Associates.

Bravo, M., Hiebert, E.H., & Pearson, P.D. (2007). Tapping the linguistic resources of Spanish-English bilinguals: The role of cognates in science. In R. Wagner, A. Muse, & K.R. Tannenbaum (Eds.), *Vocabulary acquisition: Implications for reading comprehension.* Guilford Publications.

Brisk, M.E. & Harrington, M.M. (2000). *Literacy and bilingualism: A handbook for all teachers.* Mahwah, NJ: Lawrence Erlbaum Associates.

Brunell V., & Linnakylä, P. (1994). Swedish speakers' literacy in the Finnish society. *Journal of Reading, 37*(5), 368–375.

Brunell, V., & Saretsalo, L. (1999). Sociocultural diversity and reading literacy in a Finland-Swedish environment. *Scandinavian Journal of Educational Research, 43*(2), 173–190.

Buriel, R., & Cardoza, D. (1988). Sociocultural correlates of achievement among three generations of Mexican American high school seniors. *American Educational Research Journal, 25*(2), 177–192.

Clay, M. (1975). *What did I write?: Beginning writer behavior.* London: Heinemann Educational.

Connor, U. (1983). Predictors of second-language reading performance. *Journal of Multilingual and Multicultural Development, 4*(4), 271–288.

De Houwer, A. (1995). Bilingual language acquisition. In P. Fletcher & B. MacWhinney (Eds.), *The handbook of child language* (pp. 219–250). Oxford: Blackwell.

Delgado-Gaitan, C. (2001). *The power of community: Mobilizing for family and schooling.* Lanham, MD: Rowman and Littlefield Publishers.

deVilliers, J.G., & deVilliers, P.A. (1978). *Language Acquisition.* Cambridge, MA: Harvard University Press.

Dickenson, D.K., McCabe, A., Clark-Chiarelli, N., & Wolf, A. (2004). Cross-language transfer of phonological awareness in low-income Spanish and English bilingual preschool children. *Applied Psycholinguistics, 25*, 323–347.

Dickenson, D.K., & Snow, C.E. (1987). Interrelationships among prereading and oral language skills in kindergarteners from two social classes. *Early Childhood Research Quarterly, 2*, 1–25.

Dickenson, D.K., & Tabors, P. (Eds.). (2001). *Beginning literacy with language: Young children learning at home and school.* Baltimore, MD: Paul H. Brookes Publishing.

Dressler, C. (2002). *Inter- and intra-language influences on the English spelling development of 5th Grade Spanish-speaking English-language learners.* Unpublished doctoral thesis, Harvard University.

Dunn, L.M., Padilla, E.R., Lugo, D.E., & Dunn, L.M. (1986). *Test de Vocabulario en Imágenes Peabody.* Circle Pines, MN: American Guidance Service.

Durgulonoglu, A.Y. (1998). Acquiring literacy in English and Spanish in the United States. In A.Y. Durgulonoglu & L. Verhoeven (Eds.), *Literacy development in a multilingual context: Cross-cultural perspectives* (pp. 135–145). Mahwah, NJ: Erlbaum.

Dworin, J., & Moll, L. (2006). Introduction to special issue on biliteracy. *Journal of Early Childhood Literacy, 6*(3), 293–322.

Espinosa, L.M. (2008). Challenging common myths about young English language learners. *Foundation for Child Development Policy Brief*, No. 8.

Fashola, O.S., Drum, P.A., Mayer, R.E., & Kang, S.J. (1996). A cognitive theory of orthographic transitioning: Predictable errors in how Spanish-speaking children spell English words. *American Educational Research Journal, 4*, 825–843.

Freeman, D., & Freeman, Y. (1999). The California Reading Initiative: A formula for failure for bilingual students? *Language Arts, 76*(3), 241–248.

Genesee, F. (2001). Bilingual first language acquisition: Exploring the limits of the language faculty. *Annual Review of Applied Linguistics: Language and Psychology, 5*(21), 153–168.

Goldenberg, C., Rueda, R., & August, D. (2006). Sociocultural influences on the literacy attainment of language-minority children and youth. In D. August & T. Shanahan (Eds.), *Developing literacy in second-language learners: Report of the National Literacy Panel on Language-Minority Children and Youth* (pp. 269–347). Mahwah, NJ: Lawrence Erlbaum Associates.

González, N., Moll, L., & Amanti, R. (2005). *Theorizing home, school and community practices.* Mahwah, NJ: Lawrence Erlbaum Associates.

Goodman, K., & Goodman, Y. (1979). Learning to read is natural. In L.B. Resnick & P.A. Weaver (Eds.), *Theory and practice of early reading* (pp. 137–155). Hillsdale, NJ: Lawrence Erlbaum Associates.

Goodman, Y. (1984). The development of initial literacy. In H. Goelman, A. Oberg, & F. Smith (Eds.), *Awakening to literacy* (pp. 102–109). Exeter, NH: Heinemann Educational Books.

Gottardo, A. (2002). The relationship between language and reading skills in bilingual Spanish-English speakers. *Topics in Language Disorders, 22*(5), 46–71.

Gregory, E. (1998). Siblings as mediators of literacy in linguistic minority communities. *Language and Education, 12*(1), 33–55.

Gregory, E., Long, S., & Volk, D. (2004). *Many pathways to literacy: Young children learning with siblings, peers, grandparents, and in communities.* New York: Routledge.

Grosjean, F. (1982). *Life with two languages: An introduction to bilingualism.* Cambridge, MA: Harvard University Press.

Halcón, J.J. (2001). Mainstream ideology and literacy instruction for Spanish-speaking children. In M. Reyes & J. J. Halcón (Eds.), *Best for our children: Critical perspectives on literacy for Latino students.* New York: Teachers College Press.

Hammer, C.S., Miccio, A.W., & Wagstaff, D.A. (2003). Home literacy experiences and their relationship to bilingual preschoolers' developing English literacy abilities: an initial investigation. *Language, Speech, and Hearing Services in Schools, 34,* 20–30.

Hancock, D.R. (2002). The effects of native language books on the pre-literacy skill development of language minority kindergartners. *Journal of Research in Childhood Education, 17*(1), 62–68.

Hart, B., & Risley, T. (1995). *Meaningful differences in the everyday experience of young American children.* Baltimore, MD: Brookes Publishing.

Heath, S.B. (1983). *Ways with words: Language, life, and work in communities and classrooms.* New York: Cambridge University Press.

Hornberger, N.H. (2000). Multilingual literacies, literacy practices, and the continua of biliteracy. In M. Martin-Jones & K.E. Jones (Eds.), *Multilingual literacies: Reading and writing different worlds* (pp. 353–367). Amsterdam: John Benjamins.

Huttenlocher, J., Haight, W., Bryk, A., Seltzer, M., & Lyons, T. (1991). Early vocabulary growth: Relation to language input and gender. *Developmental Psychology, 27,* 236–248.

Kenner, C., Kress, G., Hayat, H.A., Kam, R., & Tsai, K. (2004). Finding the keys to biliteracy: How young children interpret different writing systems. *Language and Education, 18*(2), 124–144.

Lindsey, K.A., Manis, F.R., & Bailey, C.E. (2003). Prediction of first-grade reading in Spanish-speaking English language learners. *Journal of Educational Psychology, 95*(3), 482–494.

Martinez-Roldán, C.M., & Sayer, P. (2006). Reading through linguistic borderlands: Latino students' transactions with narrative texts. *Journal of Early Childhood Literacy, 6*(3), 293–322.

Moll, L.C. (2003). *Cultural-historical psychology and education research with US Latinos: An example from a study of biliteracy.* Paper presented at the Symposium on Cognitive Psychology and Education: A Latin-American Perspective, 9th International Conference of the International Association for Cognitive Education and Psychology, University of Washington, Seattle, WA, July 8.

Moll, L.C., Saez, R., & Dworin, J. (2001). Exploring biliteracy: Two student case examples of writing as a social practice. *Elementary School Journal, 100*, 435–450.

Ordóñez, C., Carlo, M., Snow, C., & McLaughlin, B. (2002). Depth and breadth of vocabulary in two languages: Which vocabulary skills transfer? *Journal of Educational Psychology, 94*(4), 719–728.

Paez, M.M., Tabors, P.O., & Lopez, L.M. (2007). Dual language and literacy development of Spanish-speaking preschool children. *Journal of Applied Developmental Psychology, 28*, 85–102.

Patterson, J. (2002). Relationships of expressive vocabulary to frequency of reading and television experience among bilingual toddlers. *Applied Psycholinguistics, 23*, 493–508.

Pearson, B., Fernández, S., Lewedeg, V., & Oller, D.K. (1997). The relation of input factors to lexical learning by bilingual infants. *Applied Psycholinguistics, 23*, 493–508.

Pérez, B. (Ed.). (2004). *Sociocultural contexts of language and literacy.* Mahwah, NJ: Lawrence Erlbaum Associates.

Reese, L., Garnier, H., Gallimore, R., & Goldenberg, C. (2000). Longitudinal analysis of the antecedents of emergent Spanish literacy and middle-school English reading achievement of Spanish-speaking students. *American Educational Research Journal, 37*(3), 633–662.

Relaño Pastor, A.M. (2005). The language socialization experiences of Latina mothers in southern California. In A.C. Zentella (Ed.). *Building on strength: Language and literacy in Latino families and communities.* New York: Teachers College Press; Covina, CA: California Association for Bilingual Education.

Reyes, I. (2006). Exploring connections between emergent biliteracy and bilingualism. *Journal of Early Childhood Literacy, 6*(3), 267–292.

Reyes, I. (in press). Language and cultural literacy practices in Mexican immigrant families living in the Southwest. *Sociolinguistics Studies.*

Reyes, I., Alexandra, D., & Azuara, P. (2007). Home literacy practices in Mexican households. *Journal of Cultura y Educación, 19*(4) 395–407.

Reyes, I., & Azuara, P. (in press). Emergent biliteracy in young Mexican immigrant children. *Reading Research Quarterly.*

Reyes, M. (2001). Unleashing possibilities: Biliteracy in the primary grades. In M. Reyes de la Luz & J.J. Halcón (Eds.), *Best for our children: Critical perspectives on literacy for Latino students.* New York: Teachers College Press.

Reyes, M., & Halcón, J.J. (Eds.). (2001). *Best for our children: Critical perspectives on literacy for Latino students.* New York: Teachers College Press.

Roca, A. (2005). Raising a bilingual child in Miami: Reflections on language and culture. In A.C. Zentella (Ed.), *Building on strength: Language and literacy in Latino families and communities.* New York: Teachers College Press; Covina, CA: California Association for Bilingual Education.

Rodriguez, M.V. (2005). Dominican children with special needs in New York City: Language and literacy practices. In A.C. Zentella (Ed.), *Building on strength: Language and literacy in Latino families and communities.* New York: Teachers College Press; Covina, CA: California Association for Bilingual Education.

Rolla San Francisco, A., Mo, E., Carlo, M., August, D., & Snow, C. (2006). The influences of language, of literacy instruction and vocabulary on the spelling of Spanish-English bilinguals. *Reading and Writing, 19*, 627–642.

Santa Ana, O. (2004). *Tongue tied: The lives of multilingual children in public education.* Oxford: Rowman & Littlefield.

Schecter, S.R., & Bayley, R. (2002). *Language as cultural practice: Mexicanos en el Norte.* Hillsdale, NJ: Lawrence Erlbaum Associates.

Schwarzer, D. (2001). *Noa's Ark: One child's voyage into multiliteracy.* Portsmouth, NJ: Heinemann.

Snow, C., Burns, M., & Griffin, P. (Eds.). (1998). *Preventing reading difficulties in young children.* Washington, DC: National Academy Press.

Suárez-Orozco, C., & Suárez-Orozco, M. (2002). *Children of immigration.* Cambridge, MA: Harvard University Press.

Sulzby, E. (1989). Assessment of writing and children's language while writing. In L. Morrow & J. Smith (Eds.), *The role of assessment and measurement in early literacy instruction* (pp. 83–109). Englewood Cliffs, NJ: Prentice-Hall.

Tse, L. (2001). *Why don't they learn English?* New York: Teachers College Press.

Uchikoshi, Y. (2006). English vocabulary development in bilingual kindergartners: What are the best predictors? *Bilingualism: Language and Cognition, 9*(1), 33–49.

Umbel, V.M., Pearson, B.Z., Fernandez, M.C., & Oller, D.K. (1992). Measuring bilingual children's receptive vocabularies. *Child Development, 63*(4), 1012–1020.

Vasquez, O. (2003). *La Clase Mágica: Imagining optimal possibilities in a bilingual community of learners.* Hillsdale, NJ: Lawrence Erlbaum Associates.

Whitehurst, G.J., & Lonigan, C.J. (1998). Child development and early literacy. *Child Development, 69*(3), 848–872.

Zentella, A. (2005). *Building on strength: Language and literacy in Latino families and communities.* New York: Teachers College Press; Covina, CA: California Association for Bilingual Education.

15 Development of Tolerance and Respect for Diversity in Children in the Context of Immigration

Oscar Barbarin, Micaela Mercado, and Dari Jigjidsuren

I Introduction

America has a long history as a nation of immigrants. It has been a haven for immigrants seeking a more prosperous life. Immigration is an issue that often surfaces in public debates especially those surrounding electoral politics during periods of economic downturns. This discussion is often exacerbated by political demagoguery, which plays on citizens' suspicion, hostility, and fear of encroachment by newcomers. The social divisions reflected in public commentary are strong and the debates are partisan and shrill. Unfortunately these debates legitimize and encourage expressions of pejorative views about immigrants who are seen as a source of terror and a social threat to national culture and way of life. At many different points in our modern history, the discourse on immigration ignores the important contributions made by immigrants and inflames emotions against those who are different.

Discrimination Against Immigrants

In the case of the US, the dream of prosperity and freedom which motivates new arrivals to American shores is often supplanted by the harsh reality of stinging poverty, economic exploitation, social isolation, and ethnic/racial prejudices. This process of social denigration is becoming more pronounced as the waves of white immigrants from Europe gives way to successive waves of brown, black, and yellow immigrants from Latin America, Africa, and Asia. The fact that these immigrants are not WASPs (White Anglo-Saxon Protestants) makes them even more vulnerable to negative stereotyping. Because recent waves of immigrants also differ in ethnicity, culture, and religion, they may be viewed as soldiers in the cultural wars, which are viewed by some as a threat to national unity and the cultural legacy of the US as an Anglo-Saxon Christian English-speaking society. Such an outcome is not necessary. Differences need not be responded to with stereotyping but they often are. In truth, diversity does present challenges but it can also enrich. Peaceful coexistence is possible if divergent groups can come to understand and respect differences and even more so if cultural diversity is viewed as a source of strength and not division. What can be done to increase the likelihood that the people who make up this country will be more likely to view diversity as an asset than a liability?

Respect for Diversity in Young Children

To reach a more optimal state in which diversity strengthens rather than divides a society, it is necessary to foster tolerance and nurture respect for diversity. In building respect for diversity, as in many things, starting early in life may be advantageous. Subtle forms of intolerance and lack of respect for diversity that occur early in life take many forms. In the relationships between immigrant and non-immigrant children there may occur a vigorous trading of disparaging comments, social rejection, exclusion from play, and prejudiced attitudes about those who are different. At any age allaying fears of, reducing conflict with, and nurturing acceptance of those who are different is easier said than done. These are arguably more likely to be achieved if we lay a foundation of mutual respect among children before attitudes become hardened and behavior habitual and intractable. The early manifestations of intolerance may present opportunities for parents, teachers, and caregivers to intervene in ways that plant the seeds of tolerance, open children to more positive attitudes toward those who are different and create a climate in which stigmatizing behavior is less likely to occur. To do this effectively requires an understanding of the processes underlying the development of tolerance on one hand and of the conditions that give rise to negative attitudes, stigmatizing behavior, and social rejection on the other hand. These are complex processes and for that reason it may be helpful to seek guidance from developmental theory empirical research about promising theories and empirical research that illuminate how children develop attitudes and behaviors that reflect tolerance for those who are different and respect for cultural diversity.

Research specifically on development of a non-stigmatizing approach to social difference *and a valuing of cultural diversity* is limited. However, these notions fit conceptually within a larger class of pro-social behaviors on which there is a considerable body of research from which insights might be gleaned. Because this work explores the developmental processes involved in the acquisition of prosocial attitudes and behavior, it can illuminate the processes of and the factors that can be useful to parents and teachers in nurturing prosocial behavior in their offspring and students. Even though not much empirical work has been done directly on development of tolerance and respect for diversity it is possible to extend conclusions from research on the broader class of prosocial behaviors to which it belongs. The evolution of tolerance and respect for diversity is best illuminated by drawing on insights about the formation of prosocial attitudes and behaviors. Figure 15.1 illustrates how DTRD is positioned within a larger framework of social development. It arranges the relevant constructs in a series of three bands surrounding the core constructs of interest, DTRD. The three bands, (1) general cognitive and moral development; (2) specific social developmental processes; and (3) social awareness, identity, and cultural competence are arranged in the order of their conceptual proximity to the core construct of DTRD. The inner or closest band surrounding the core constructs includes the closely related processes of social awareness (e.g., see Selman, 2003; Turiel, 2002), social identity (e.g., see Bem, 1983; Hughes, 2003) and cultural competence (e.g., Rogoff, 2003). Cultural competence is an outcome of children's experiences with diversity and their abilities to negotiate differences. For our purposes identity incorporates ethnic, family, cultural, religious, gender, sexual, and class identity. These are all important features used in defining the self and determining our primary associations. Development of personal identity and social awareness are closely aligned with the development of tolerance and respect for diversity and are best understood as analogues. The content of the view of self, the affiliations that one makes, the allegiances that one develops to an in-group have implications for how one regards and treats the out-groups. This band captures cognitive and social processes implicated in how self and others are perceived, experienced, evaluated, and responded to, especially those who are different. It includes opposing processes, some of which are positively related to diversity and tolerance (e.g. cultural competence) and others are inversely related (e.g. bias, stigma, stereotyping, discrimination). Although less directly related to respect for diversity and tolerance, the two outer rings are nonetheless implicated in their development. The second or middle band includes constructs, which can be grouped under the rubric of *specific* social-developmental *processes.* These are related, but not as closely to the core constructs.

These specific social processes include dispositions toward altruism, empathy, and non-aggressive conflict management. For example, by encouraging prosocial and moral reasoning, children are better able to consider issues of fairness and understand how

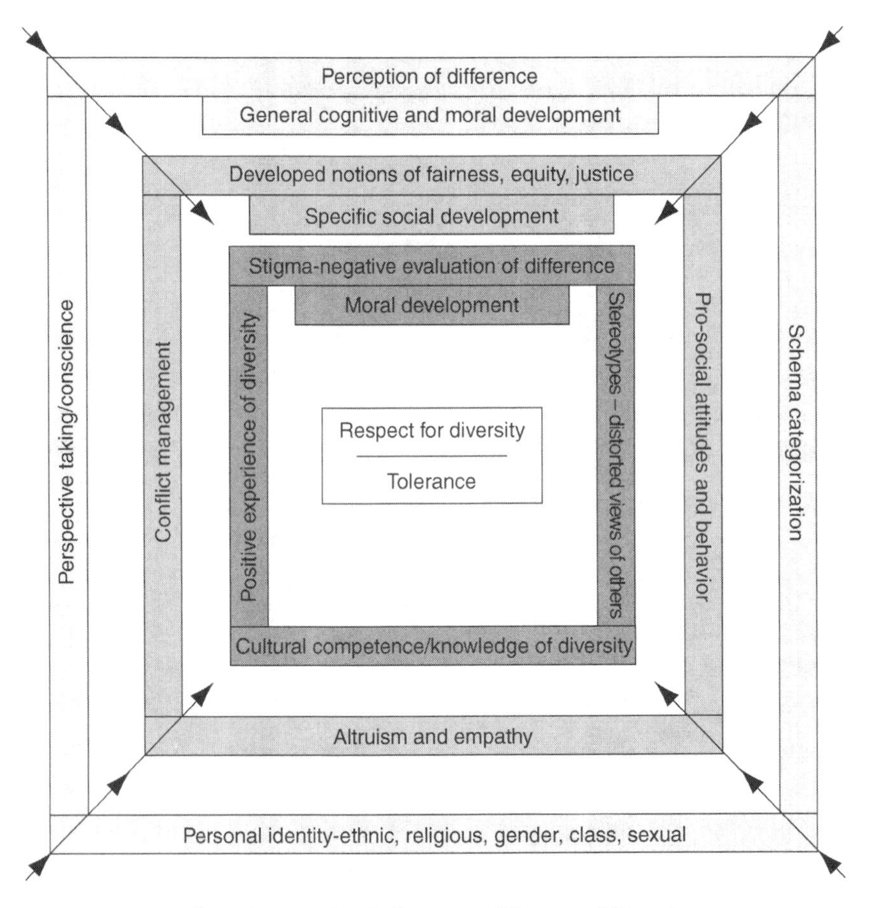

Figure 15.1 Nomological Network of Tolerance and Respect of Diversity.

social systems contribute to inequities (Spears-Brown & Bigler, 2005). These exemplify generally humane approaches to life that may under-gird or serve as a foundation for tolerance and respect but is not co-terminus with them. When one occurs or develops the other is usually present. The third or outer band represents basic cognitive and social developmental processes, which serve as a foundation for processes represented in the two inner bands. This includes research on basic developmental processes such as the development of schema, the capacity for categorization and discrimination, perspective taking, conscience and moral reasoning.

By positioning DTRD conceptually within a broad class of prosocial behaviors it is possible to benefit from an extensive body of theory and empirical work to understand the developmental processes which give rise to tolerance and respect for diversity. Using this body of work, we can explore questions about children's capacity to discern social differences, their proclivity to interpret those differences positively or negatively, and the ability of adults to influence those attitudes. Answers to the core questions we have about parent and teacher socialization of tolerance and respect for diversity in preschool children can be mined from the body of work identified as analogues of diversity and tolerance, on the humanistic behaviors that underlie diversity and tolerance, on identity formation, and on basic processes involved in moral and social development. A review of this literature provides at least partial answers to the following questions:

- To what extent can children detect, perceive and understand differences that exist between groups such as those stemming from culture, religion, race, ethnicity, gender, sexual orientation, socioeconomic status and national origin?
- What is the prevalence and valence of children's attitudes about those who are different, and how do they change over time?
- What factors shape how young children evaluate and respond to those differences?
- Can adult caregivers, particularly parents and teachers, influence the valence of children's attitudes and responses to differences?

II Development of Tolerance and Respect for Diversity in Early Childhood

Capacity to Detect Differences

The ability to detect or notice difference is fundamental to the formation of social attitudes about others. The research literature offers an unambiguous answer to questions about young children's ability to discern social differences. For example, awareness of gender differences emerges early in life. By the age of two most children are able to make gender distinctions and accurately label male and female (Campbell, Shirley, & Caygill, 2002). The ability of a child to make these distinctions appears to be based on body type, hair (Intons-Peterson, 1988), and facial features (Quinn, Yahr, Kuhn, Slater, & Pascalis, 2000). By preschool age, children perceive and are well aware of a range of other differences such as those based on skin color, ethnicity, race, language, religion, etc. Using habituation tasks, Katz (2003) found that even at preverbal stages children will attend to novel race cues after seeing same-race faces. Additionally, at 6 months of age, gender cues are salient within same-race faces. Detection of race and gender has been observed in young children's self-identification and is reflected in their social interactions. From 18–30 months there is a linear increase in children's ability to self-label and sort dolls and pictures based on race and gender when prompted. At 36–72 months, White children begin to show same-race peer preference while Black children are more likely to make more cross-race friendships (Katz, 2003). Thus this study suggests the development of racial bias at even very young ages, at least for White children.

It is not a far stretch to suggest that this bias may appear in the interaction of immigrant and non-immigrant children. When immigrant and non-immigrant preschool children are placed in close proximity and where repeated social interactions are possible children come to note ways in which they are similar and different from one another. These differences may take the form of dress, language, physical features, behavioral habits, and preferred foods. At the outset it should be noted that discrimination and perception of differences are not inherently bad and to the contrary may be ethologically adaptive and functionally necessary especially in risky environments. The ability to detect differences and discriminate between those who are similar and familiar from those who are different and strange is harmless *in se.* However, much is determined by the meaning attributed to these differences. Similarity and familiarity may be linked to a higher probability of nurture and safety, just as difference and unfamiliarity may be associated with the higher probability of harm such as from predators. In this way recognizing difference is part of a biologically driven developmental pathway that may be linked to species survival.

Children's Evaluation of Differences

When the ability to detect differences is combined with growing personal identity, interesting consequences emerge. In many cases, children show an explicit preference for the familiar, for characteristics associated with self and the persons the child cares about, especially family. Although even male children show a preference for female faces (arguably because of greater familiarity and attachment to female caregivers), young children often display a preference for and have more favorable attitudes toward persons who are like them on some salient dimension. This proclivity to the familiar establishes a fertile ground for negative evaluations of those who are different. Thus, early stages of childhood have great potentials for ethnocentrism and strong preferences for in-groups (persons like themselves) versus out-groups (persons different in some way from themselves). The possible link between strong identity with one's own group and intolerance of other groups, poses a significant problem for adults who must care for mixed groups that consist for example of immigrant and non-immigrant children.

How much should caregivers nurture and encourage in young children a strong identification with their own ethnic, racial, national or religious groups if it means that non-immigrant children will develop negative views of immigrant children or that immigrant children will be conflicted about assimilating into their new setting? With the significant pressures among immigrants to assimilate, there may be ambivalence about how much to retain an affiliation with the country from which the family emigrated and its people. Among first-generation immigrants the pressure from immigrant parents to assimilate may be great. The age of the immigrant child may impact the nature of those strains. The push to assimilate may be especially strong in the absence of a critical mass of persons with the same language and background. Young children who have not yet mastered their parents' native language and who must learn English may face stiff pressure to forsake the home language and thereby lose an important tie to the parent's culture. Those who choose to promote affiliation and group loyalty, that is a fierce attachment in line with their own group, exploit the natural proclivity and preference children have for their own group over others. This process for same group identification arises from instincts for self protection and need for affiliation. As a consequence of good experiences such as affection, attachment to a maternal figure, as well as likeness to ethnic, cultural and racial characteristics, the child associates their group with safety, comfort and support. Disdain, dislike, and avoidance of strangers, specifically those who are different from the child's in-group, are a parallel process because it is associated with the absence of succor. This reaction may be a reflex, that it is truly unnecessary for survival. One can exist without the other. Viewing one's own group favorably does not necessarily have to trigger avoidance or hatred. It should be possible to nurture attachment to familiar figures without the need to foster suspicion or denigration of out-group members. Fortunately, extreme ethnocentrism and preference for the in-group over the out-group wanes as children mature and gain experience and familiarity with those who are different. Positive experiences with diverse populations may facilitate the decline of ethnocentrism. Although many families and early care environments espouse a color-blind approach to child socialization, research evidence suggests that children become aware of differences and develop negative attitudes toward those who are different far earlier than many adults recognize or acknowledge. Understanding how tolerance and respect for diversity evolve and develop in children is particularly important as America becomes racially, ethnically, and socially diverse.

DTRD and Social Development

Some theorists have proffered a natural human propensity to categorize people, to discriminate and to join groups based on similarity (Katz, 2003). If this position is correct, there is a need to understand more about how these attitudes are formed and how parents and teachers might explicitly socialize children to be prosocial in attitudes and behaviors. Specifically, we need a better understanding of the specific behaviors and processes between children and adults that promote tolerance and respect for diversity.

Since children are able to discriminate among categories of people earlier than once believed and given that differences based on race, gender, and ethnicity at some point become salient and attached to negative valences, the implications for how parents encourage tolerance and respect for diversity should be explored. Although there are many psychological theories that indicate how attitudes develop and how adults come to be biased, very few address how some children develop racist attitudes and others do not.

By extending research of prosocial development and applying them to DTRD, a discernible developmental progression from infancy to adolescence may be explored. In infancy, representations of secure attachment, as an internalized state, are associated with prosocial attitudes and behaviors. By inference, children are more likely to exhibit tolerance and respect diversity. However, it is unlikely that secure attachments by themselves guarantee tolerance. It is in toddlerhood where children's development of a sense of empathy and concern for others provides a less egoistic and firmer foundation on which to build attitudes of tolerance and respect for diversity. This underscores the importance of the need for caregivers to emphasize moments (i.e., behaviors displayed by the child) that may occur within the home or in the context of early childhood programs. Later in middle childhood, children have better defined consciences and a surer moral compass. This established conscience and refined sense of justice provide a durable and resilient basis for tolerance. As sociocognitive competencies related to perspective taking, empathy, and conscience develop and strengthen, the child's capacity to exhibit tolerance and respect for diversity inevitably strengthens.

The relationship between child and adult caregiver is important to the ability to redirect the child's stereotypical thinking or discriminatory behavior. Attachment literature indicates that only when the attachment relationship reflects a secure and responsive one, will children be open to moral socialization messages. Current research assumes that children are motivated to adopt and internalize messages of anti-bias from teachers. However, research indicates that children may actively form racial stereotypes that are opposite that of their authority figures (Bigler, 1999). Second, researchers may also want to include environmental influences such as the media and neighborhood factors (i.e., role models) in future models of the development of anti-biased (or biased) behaviors. Current research assumes that children are passive absorbers of information (Bigler, 1999). However, because of research from the friendship literature, we have indications that children assume some of the stereotypes of society, as reflected in their gendered and racial nature in choice of friendships. Highly biased children are more likely to have same race and same gender peers as friends (Katz, 2003). Finally, future research should include more data on the transactional nature of notions of discrimination and prejudice among child only groupings. Some talk about race and gender occurs outside of the classroom among peer groups. In a study of third- and fourth-grade students' conversations about race, it was found that when low-prejudiced peers were matched with high-prejudiced peers, high-prejudiced peers were less likely to make biased statements. The decrease in bias was significantly related to low-prejudiced peers' positive statements and examples about Blacks and references to cross-race (Black and White) similarities (Aboud & Fenwick, 1999). As a consequence, it is important to understand the mechanisms of how activist children may be used to revise the stereotypes of their peers.

Summary of the Research

The principles extracted from research on prosocial development that may be applicable to the development of prosocial attitudes and respect for diversity include the following:

1. Emotions play a central role in children's prosocial behavior and development.
2. Children who are more easily aroused and who form empathic responses to the emotional distress of others are more likely to display prosocial behavior. By extension these children are more likely to show tolerance and respect for diversity.
3. Relationships are important in the early development of prosocial behavior.

Children who have stronger and more secure attachments to adult caretakers are more likely to exhibit prosocial behavior.

4. The social-cognitive processing skills that are critical to prosocial behavior develop and increase with age. These social cognitive skills include the ability to detect differences and empathy.
5. Motivations for prosocial behavior change with age. In infancy and toddlerhood, prosocial behavior is motivated by concern for self and personal distress. Self-oriented hedonism as a motivation for prosocial behavior is manifested in compliance with social norms to help, tolerate, or respect diversity mostly to gain rewards, avoid punishment, or personal distress experienced when someone else is hurt. This is not true during early childhood. In preschool the child moves away from self-oriented hedonism. At this stage the child does not feel distress over the suffering of another and is not motivated to help as a way of relieving personal distress. Instead the child is able to anticipate that one day he might be in the same situation and need help. Thus, a child's empathic behavior is motivated by the need for social approval and by the expectation of reciprocity. Beyond early and middle childhood, children internalize abstract norms and come to view help, tolerance, and respect for diversity as values.
6. Motivation for prosocial behavior parallels and perhaps is driven by social cognitive development. This involves increases of social cognitive skills in the following domains:
    - detecting or *discriminating differences* among people;
    - forming and maintaining securely *attached relationships*;
    - understanding and decoding others' *emotions*;
    - evaluating others behaviors against some *moral code or standard.*

It is the social norms established early in childhood that are predictive of prosocial behavior and willingness to help others. Secure attachment representations, notions of fairness and equity, the development of empathic and guilt responses, and the development of a moral conscience are indicative of altruistic responses. It may be assumed that the social norms regarding how children are taught to respond favorably to racial, gender, ethnic, social, and religious differences include similar variables.

Adult Contributions to DTRD in Children

Figure 15.2 models the different modalities through which adults influence children's development of tolerance and respect for diversity. These modalities include attached relationships, open-minded attitudes, nurturing practices and prosocial modeling.

Our current understanding of parent and teacher contribution to DTRD arises from the quality of the adult–child relationship. Strong attachments, social support, emotional closeness, and adult sensitivity and responsiveness to children's needs promote positive behaviors. When adults display emotionally supportive relationships and respond sensitively to children, children reciprocate the behaviors. For this reason the efficacy of adult practices and implicit adult modeling is contingent on the quality of the adult–child relationship. Accordingly, adult practices such as intentional instruction, use of conversations and literature for socialization of identity and promotion of

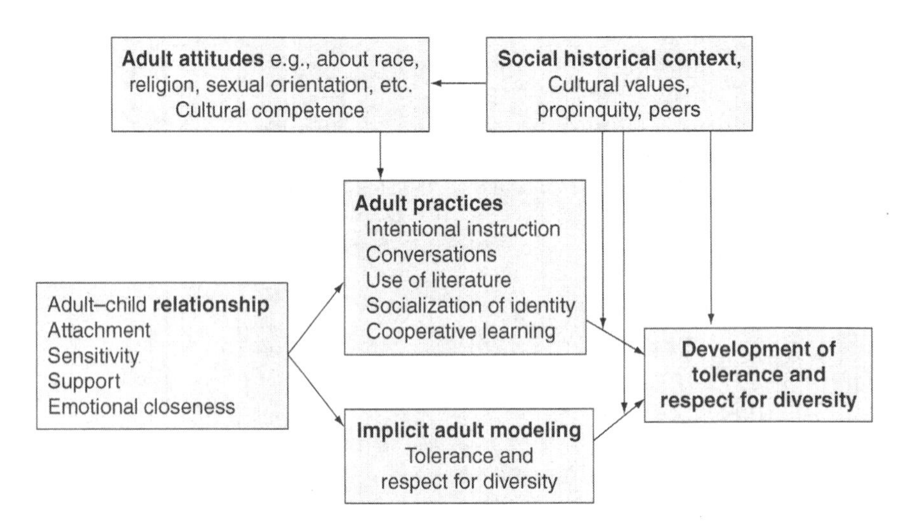

Figure 15.2 Parent and Teacher Influences on the Development of Tolerance and Respect for Diversity.

cooperative learning are all more effective when the adult and child have a strong emotional bond. A similar relation has been demonstrated for the effectiveness of adults as models. To the extent that adults are esteemed and liked by children, their behavior and attitudes are more likely to be emulated by children. And this way, adult practices and modeling can shape and encourage DTRD. Adult behavior and attitudes are likely to be moderated by historical context, attitudes and values that parents have developed about identity, race, religion, sexual orientation, and personal experiences with diversity. To the extent that adults develop open attitudes, judge experiences with diverse populations as positive, and hold cultural values that favor acceptance of difference, the social context can be a positive influence on adult practices and modeling and in turn provides a propitious spawning ground for DTRD.

Promotion of DTRD by Adult Caregivers

- Adults display a variety of behaviors that children learn to internalize as they develop and build relationships. Parents who display high levels of sensitivity, display relaxed firmness, engage in mutual negotiation of conflict with their child, and make efforts to be emotional available and responsive are closely linked to a child's ability to resolve conflict without aggression.
- Adults who converse and practice scaffolding discourse styles contribute to better language-skill development in children.
- Adults who reason, demonstrate warmth, provide guidance, positive reinforcement, model prosocial behavior, and give their child a chance to perform prosocial behaviors are more likely to have altruistic children.
- Adults may help children establish social norms that are predictive of altruistic behavior such as turn-taking, sharing, cooperating, and helping others in visible distress.

- Adults may impart prosocial behavior such as positive conflict management through modeling as well as promoting discussion and conversation.
- Adults should focus children's judgment of others on internal rather than external attributes.
- In schools, adults may provide children with empathy training activities to increase supportive behavior, helpfulness, cooperativeness, and concern for others and decrease aggressive behavior.

As suggested above, research on moral and prosocial development provides a rich base of knowledge on which to draw inferences about DTRD. This body of work has pointed to the important care giving roles of parents and teachers; relationship interactions such as secure attachment behaviors; the child's cognitive development and ability to detect differences; the critical role of emotional arousal and responses; the shifting basis of prosocial motivation from egoistic of avoidance of punishment to reciprocity and justice; and the development of a range of socio-cognitive competencies such as empathy, social comparisons, conscience and altruism.

III Programs to Promote DTRD in Schools and Community Settings

Several curricula and model programs have been developed to promote tolerance and respect for diversity. *Anti-Bias Education* (ABE) (Derman-Sparks, 1989) promulgated by the National Association for the Education of Young Children is one of several anti-bias curricula developed to promote acceptance of diversity. Another example of ABE can be found in the work of Kinderwelt, an organization based in Berlin, Germany. It has developed outreach training projects that seek to address discrimination and bias that immigrant children often face in German preschools. As a group, anti-bias curricula and programs are committed to the educational equality of a diversity of children, and they tend to be more comprehensive in nature by addressing cultural diversity, gender differences, and differences in physical ability (Derman-Sparks, 1989). The principal goal of the Derman-Sparks ABE program is to foster in young children the following outcomes: (1) a firm and positive self concept and group identity, (2) empathy for others, and (3) critical thinking about and the courage to confront bias wherever they see it.

Implementation of anti-bias education (ABE) requires that every aspect of the child's experience at school be rethought and possibly changed from the material aspects and resources of the environment (toys, books, art materials, and center options), to events, stories, and social relations (Derman-Sparks, 1993). By design, ABE is committed to thoughtful and responsive answers to children's questions about difference. To do this well teachers must be involved in a reflective process about the past and current impact of discrimination in society, how personal biases are acted out, how to adjust teaching styles to accommodated differences, and how to address cultural conflict when it arises in the classroom (Derman-Sparks, 1993). Because, self-awareness is a critical first step in the recognition of and positive response to difference, ABE aims to help children recognize that their thoughts, beliefs, characteristics and needs are not the same as others. Because the capacity for self-categorization as belonging to a social group can lead to invidious in-group versus out-group comparisons, nurturance of positive self-concept and group identity must also be balanced by the notions that no child or group is superior to or has the right to be privileged over another (Derman-Sparks, 1993). Such positive self-awareness is not surprisingly associated with peer acceptance (Ramsey & Myers, 1990).

Empathic concern for others is essential to the development of prosocial behavior in young children. Empathy is important because it engenders an appreciation of similarities and differences among people. Even in infancy children will respond empathetically to the cries of other infants. Comparisons of classrooms using ABE and classrooms that did not implement any type of multicultural curriculum revealed that children in ABE classrooms were able to identify more positive attributes about racial minorities than were children in classrooms devoid of a multicultural agenda (Perkins & Mebert, 2005). Moreover, children who acquire multiple classification skills (ability to classify people along multiple characteristics i.e., gender, race, occupation) through teacher implementation of anti-bias curriculum, have better memory for counter-stereotypic information (Bigler & Liben, 1992).

Biases, disparaging attitudes and stigmatizing behavior arise from errors in perception and information reprocessing. ABE curricula often cover historical facts and cultural practices to demonstrate what is common in a group but at the same time underscores the existence of within group differences (Sardo-Brown & Hershey, 1995). When children learn about group differences they are helped to question the negative connotations society attaches to some differences. Fostering critical-thinking skills about bias may help children to see the subtle nuances in social situations and help them to internalize moral standards. In classrooms that use teachable moments to discuss racial and gender biases and that employ curricula devoted that address and counter ethnic biases, children are more likely to classify individuals on characteristics other than race (Bernstein Zimmerman, Schindler, Werner-Wilson, & Vosburg, 2000). However, children's encoding of non-stereotyped information has to be monitored and activities must be continual in order to enhance their development of counter-stereotypic information (Bigler & Liben, 1993). Finally, although the goal of interventions is the elimination of racially biased responding, however, to date most interventions only report very small reductions in children's racial bias (Bigler, 1999).

The Morningside Center for Teaching Social Responsibility (www.MorningsideCenter.Org) in New York City has developed an approach to DTRD to give emphasis to conflict resolution and intercultural understanding. These approaches are embodied in two programs: "Resolving Conflict Creatively" and the "4 Rs" (reading, writing, respect, and resolution). Both programs have at their core the teaching of children skills in resolving conflicts without resorting to violence, valuing diversity, especially cultural differences, countering bias and confronting prejudice. The program involves classroom coaching for teachers, peer mediation of conflict as well as training for school administrators and parents. The 4 Rs program integrates conflict resolution into the classroom curriculum for language arts in kindergarten through fifth grade. For example, high-quality children's literature is selected and used to raise issues that may be potentially divisive, and discussed among students. As a part of the program students are engaged in talking, writing and role-playing on universal themes of relationships, community, identity, and conflict. The goal of the discussion is to build skills and understanding in areas such as listening, community building, cooperation, negotiation, celebrating differences, and countering bias.

Another example is the *Al-Bustan Seeds of Culture* (www.albustanseeds.org) a non-profit organization based in Philadelphia, Pennsylvania. Like ABE and the Morningside Center it attempts to promote DTRD but is more narrowly focused on issues that intersect with Arab American populations. Specifically it attempts to promote understanding of language and culture of the Arab world and respect within the diverse community of Arab-Americans. The program offers children and youth an opportunity to develop new language skills and appreciate Arabic culture. Al-Bustan encourages dialogue, tolerance, and a celebration of diversity.

In contrast to the Al-Bustan Seeds of Culture is the *Early Childhood Equity Initiative* (www.teachingforchange.org/DC_Projects/ECEI/ecei.html). This is a more broadly focused effort of Teaching for Change to develop leaders in early childhood education, in the metro DC area and nationwide, with an understanding of the theory and practice that helps create culturally responsive environments for young children. By working with teachers, daycare providers and parents of preschool aged children can collaborate to identify and promote anti-bias education goals for young children.

IV Concluding Remarks

Researchers have come to recognize the integral role of the early childhood experience for children's social and cognitive development. Over the past few decades, as more women have entered the workforce, more children have entered childcare at even earlier ages. These children come from families that represent a diverse array of ethnic, cultural, socioeconomic, and religious backgrounds. As a result, today's childcare environment may represent a diversity that may not have existed at any time point in history. Childcare classrooms reflect the diversity of American families and represent an important microcosm to be studied.

Even in early childhood, children must learn to negotiate difference reflected in larger society. Although young children's expressions may not have the same deliberate, affective tenor of adults', it is important to reduce these biases to foster positive self-identities for all children (Banks, 1995). Social and emotional competencies have been linked to positive academic outcomes for children. Thus, the study of curriculum that helps to promote a positive, anti-biased classroom environment is integral to an equal and just education for all children. Parents also play an important role for their children through guidance and modeling behaviors. As children exit childhood and enter the world of adolescence and adulthood, it is inevitable that their new relationships and interactions with others will be highly dependent on their ability to accept norms, values, and standards different from their own.

References

Aboud, F., & Fenwick, V. (1999). Exploring and evaluating school-based interventions to reduce prejudice. *Journal of Social Issues, 55*(4), 767–785.

Aksan, N., & Kochanska, G. (2004). Links between systems of inhibition from infancy to preschool years. *Child Development, 75*(5), 1477–1490.

Banks, C., & Banks, J. (1995). Equity pedagogy: An essential component of multicultural education. *Theory into Practice, 34*(3), 152–158.

Berlin, L.J., & Cassidy, J. (1999). Relations among relationships: Contributions from attachment theory and research. In J. Cassidy & P.R. Shaver (Eds.), *Handbook of attachment: Theory, research and clinical applications* (pp. 688–712). New York: Guilford Press.

Bernstein, J., Zimmerman, Schindler, T., Werner-Wilson, Ronald, J. & Vosburg, J. (2000). Preschool children's classification skills and a multicultural education intervention to promote acceptance of ethnic diversity. *Journal of Research in Childhood Education, 14*(2), 181–192.

Bigler, R. (1999). The use of multicultural curricula and materials to counter racism in children. *Journal of Social Issues, 55*(4), 687–705.

Bigler, R., & Liben, L. (1992). Cognitive mechanisms in children's gender stereotyping: Theoretical and educational implications of a cognitive-based intervention. *Child Development, 63*(6), 1351–1363.

Bigler, R., & Liben, L. (1993). A cognitive-developmental approach to racial stereotyping and reconstructive memory in Euro-American children. *Child Development, 64*(5), 1507–1518.

Campbell, A., Shirley, L., & Caygill, L. (2002). Sex-typed preferences in three domains: Do 2-year-olds need cognitive variables? *British Journal of Developmental Psychology, 18*, 479–498.

Charlesworth, R. (1998). Developmentally appropriate practice is for everyone. *Childhood Education, 74*(5), 274–282.

Derman-Sparks, L. (1989). *The antibias curriculum*. Washington, DC: National Association for the Education of Young Children.

Derman-Sparks, L. (1993). Empowering children to create a caring culture in a world of differences. *Childhood Education, 70*(2), 66–71.

Intons-Peterson, M. (1988). *Children's concepts of gender*. Norwood, NJ: Ablex.

Jones, E., & Derman-Sparks, L. (1992). Meeting the challenge of diversity. *Young Children, 47*(2), 12–18.

Katz, P.A. (2003) Racists or tolerant multiculturalists? How do they begin? *American Psychologist, 58*(11), 897–909.

Maccoby, E. (1992). The role of parents in the socialization of children: A historical overview. *Developmental Psychology, 28*(6), 1006–1017.

Perkins, D., & Mebert, C. (2005). Efficacy of multicultural education for preschool children. *Journal of Cross-Cultural Psychology, 36*(4), 497–512.

Quinn, P.C., Yahr, J., Kuhn, A., Slater, A., & Pascalis, O. (2000). Representation of the gender of human faces by infants: A preference for female. *Perception, 31*, 1109–1121.

Ramsey, P., & Myers, L. (1990). Salience of race in young children's cognitive, affective, and behavioral responses to social environments. *Journal of Applied Developmental Psychology, 11*(1), 49–67.

Sardo-Brown, D., & Hershey, M. (1995). Training of intermediate level teachers on how to develop and implement integrated multi-cultural lesson plan: Assessment of attitudes. *Journal of Instructional Psychology, 22*(3), 259–277.

Spears-Brown, C., & Bigler, R. (2005). Children's perceptions of discrimination: A developmental model. *Child Development, 76*(3), 533–553.

Steelman, L., Assel, M., Swank, P., Smith, K., & Landry, S. (2002). Early maternal warm responsiveness as a predictor of child social skills: Direct and indirect paths of influence over time. *Journal of Applied Developmental Psychology, 23*(2), 135–156.

Stephan, W., & Finlay, K. (1999). The role of empathy in improving intergroup relations. *Journal of Social Issues, 55*(4), 729–743.

Thompson, R. (1999). Early attachment and later development. In J. Cassidy & P.R. Shaver (Eds.), *Handbook of attachment: Theory, research and clinical applications* (pp. 265–286). New York: Guilford Press.

Walker, L., & Taylor, J. (1991). Family interactions and the development of moral reasoning. *Child Development, 62*(2), 264–283.

Zahn-Waxler, C., Radke-Yarrow, M., Wagner, E., & Chapman, M. (1992). Development of concern for others. *Developmental Psychology, 28*(1), 126–136.

Conclusion

Commenting on What We Know and What We Need to Learn

Elena L. Grigorenko

Not a single week goes by without one of the major mass media sources, whether in the US or in other developed countries, publishing an article or more on immigration. Even in these times of financial meltdown, issues of immigration are central, whether discussed in passing or intentionally avoided, due to their complexity, and to the platforms of the 2008 US presidential candidates, Barack Obama and John McCain.

This edited volume, explicitly and implicitly, touches on a number of issues of immigration—a complex dynamic that is charged with feelings and is so central to the history and identity of the United States of America. But the book's main focus is on children. Whether handled by comprehensive reform or not, whether sorted out now or later, immigration is happening on a large scale, changing the landscape of many child-related policy topics and formulating new challenges to policy makers. It is estimated that nearly 20% of all US children live in immigrant households. The majority of them are citizens, although their parents might not be, but there are also many undocumented or illegal immigrant children. Although the research on long-term outcomes for immigrants is still young, there is evidence that predicts that the majority of these children will stay in the US, growing up to contribute substantially to the US labor force and economy, as well as to the nation's Social Security and Medicare programs. Thus, immigrant children should be considered, proactively, in US economic and social policies. But what about now, what about the current considerations?

Enough research exists today to indicate that, as a group, immigrant children in the US are considerably behind native-born children in a number of developmental domains. Given the importance of these children in the future of the US, policy questions arising with regard to addressing these developmental issues should not be asking if something should be done but when.

It is of note that critical issues concerning immigrant children are, of course, not limited to the US. The "immigration question" is a question of importance for many developed countries, as acknowledged by, in particular, the Organisation for Economic Cooperation and Development (OECD). OECD carries out a number of international activities, including its Programme for International Student Assessment (PISA), which tested 15-year-old students in 41 countries in mathematics, reading, comprehension, science, and problem-solving skills. PISA's 2006 data provide a number of opportunities to quantify educational outcomes of immigrant children in a number of developed countries and compare these outcomes with those of native-born adolescents. Specifically, PISA 2006 samples from 17 territories with large immigrant populations: Australia, Austria, Belgium, Canada, Denmark, France, Germany, Luxembourg, the Netherlands, New Zealand, Norway, Sweden, Switzerland, and the US, and three non-OECD PISA participants, the Russian Federation, Hong Kong, and Macau. They also track immigrant children according to their countries of origin. Specifically, enough families of the former Soviet Union, the former Yugoslavia, Turkey, and China left their home countries and spread through enough other countries to draw conclusions about the quality of schooling in their home countries and levels of performance of their children. The OECD released its new report on these 2006 data in September of 2008; the data and their interpretations are interesting and diverse and, no doubt, will stimulate multiple discussions, but one message from this report is of particular importance here. Unlike the US, where children of immigrants appear to underperform academically as a group, this is not the case across a number of developed countries. Even more interestingly, children who have immigrated from the same country do very differently depending on the country they have immigrated into; they might underperform in many countries, but shine intensely in a country with no gap between academic performance among native-born and immigrant children. Interpreting these findings, *The Economist* suggests that

> any country that figures out how to let incomers shine will reap big benefits ... Their varying fates—helped to the top in some places, consigned to the scrapheap in others—show that although what happens outside the school gates is important, what happens in classrooms is too.
> (*The Economist*, 2008, p. 69)

And this quotation captures the essence of this volume because all of its contributors share the same sentiment. The quality and quantity of schooling could and should make a difference for immigrant children, and if it does not, then something is wrong with it. In communicating this message, the authors of this volume consider the state of immigrant children in the US from multiple perspectives and advocate changes in the policies and practices currently in place for educating these children.

The emotional tone of the volume is set by the Introduction by Ruby Takanishi. Takanishi's references to the 2007–2008 raids on workplaces by the Immigration and Customs Enforcement (ICE) agency both stresses the vulnerability of the people labeled "illegal immigrants" in the US and underscores the importance of this problem given the estimated numbers of "illegal" and legal immigrants. Yet, the focus of this volume is on children, and Takanishi brings this issue to the fore in a very powerful manner, stating that inhospitable policies toward immigrants first and foremost affect immigrant children. She supports her argument with references to findings that indicate that well-thought-out and rational national policies can make a difference in the health, education, and labor-force outcomes for immigrants and their children. Takanishi then introduces, in brief, the main themes of the book. Specifically, she comments on the changing demographic profile of the US, discusses the issue of cultural and ethnic diversity, and exemplifies this issue with illustrations from studies on school readiness, early schooling, life style, and health practices. Takanishi concludes with the remark that the field of studies of immigrant families and children is relatively new and that this volume offers a unique opportunity to grasp the state of the field at a glance.

The general parameters of the field are defined in the first chapter of the volume by authors Donald Hernandez, Nancy Denton, and Suzanne Macartney. These authors provide a clear description of the current social demography of America's children. Using data from Census 2000, they offer a new set of analyses and provide both a set of interpretations to their results and direct access to the data used in these analyses (through a reference to the corresponding website). This chapter sets the stage for all of the subsequent chapters. During the last 40 years, the number of immigrant children has increased dramatically, not only in the US but also around the world. The US's figures are particularly stunning: "less than 25 years from now, a new American majority will emerge among children (ages 0–17), a majority consisting of the current minorities." This very sentence encompasses a number of the major themes of this chapter. First, there is no single minority that will replace the current majority; there are multiple minorities, and these minorities are very diverse. This diversity encompasses about 100 different languages and hundreds of different cultures. These languages and cultures might or might not be congruent with English and mainstream American culture. Thus, this diversity needs to be carefully considered and investigated, and Hernandez and colleagues provide the reader with a description of this diversity. Second, the minority-into-majority transformation is not going to happen overnight; we still have about 25 years to influence the policies that need to be in place during this transformation. Hernandez and colleagues share with the reader what is known about current living arrangements, residential stability and clustering, educational attainments, employment status and history, earnings, and health insurance coverage for immigrants, focusing specifically on immigrant children and children of immigrants in the US. The authors conclude:

> America cannot afford to ignore children of immigrants, or to let them fall behind as they seek to integrate and succeed in school and in life. It is in the self-interest of all Americans that we make the public investment in education, health, and other services that the children of the new American majority require to thrive and succeed.

This chapter is the gateway into the book because all that follows unfolds these general observations made by Hernandez and his colleagues, and exemplifies these observations in particular settings using data from particular studies.

The observation made by Hernandez and his colleagues that the number of immigrant children has increased not only in the US, but also in many other developed countries around the world is substantiated in the following chapter by Timothy Smeeding, Coady Wing, and Karen Robson. These authors contextualize the issue of immigration by considering it as one of the characteristics of a globalized world. And in this context, immigrants, their families, and their children are viewed as particularly vulnerable to poverty, inequality, and diminished opportunities. Taking a cross-national perspective and working with data from the Luxemburg Income Study, these authors investigate the relationships between poverty and various national incentives and policies in the US, Australia, Canada, and Europe. This chapter's investigation is not only rich with data, but is also plentiful with comments on terminology (e.g., the definition of "immigrants"), remarks on measurement (e.g., quantifications of "poverty"), and descriptions of various international "best practices" for addressing issues of immigration. Smeeding and his colleagues close their chapter with policy recommendations stating clearly that the US could and should do much more to reduce poverty in general and child poverty in particular. But the question remains "Will it?" And the authors conclude: "at least until the 2008 election, it is our guess that helping immigrant kids will be an even harder sell than helping native and majority children, especially in the US."

The majority of the chapters in the book address the kinds of help immigrant kids need. In general terms, the chapters sample the experiences of immigrant children in school and home settings in the US, discussing the main co-acting, counteracting, and interacting effects of American mainstream and immigrant-specific cultural influences on the development of immigrant children and children of immigrants.

This string of chapters begins with a contribution by Jessica Johnson De Feyter and Adam Winsler. They start by reviewing a list of skills that are considered the basic foundation needed for young children at entry into a formal schooling system and provide a review of the literature on the school readiness of immigrant children in the US. In doing so, they constantly make reference to the diversity of immigrants and stratify their observations by referring to the variability in school readiness among immigrants depending on their countries of origin. They further exemplify this differentiation by referring to older immigrant youth. They conclude their data presentation and discussion by placing their findings within the literature on the *immigrant paradox*—a phenomenon that is referred to in the literature as the discrepancy between the drive and desire to succeed characteristic of the first generation of immigrants that tends to fade away with subsequent generations and assimilation into the mainstream society.

The theme of school readiness is further explored in the chapter by Krista Perreira, Linda Beeber, Todd Schwartz, Diane Holditch-Davis, India Ornelas, and Lauren Maxwell. Perreira and her colleagues take the reader to North Carolina and provide a very detailed discussion of new Latino settlement communities in this state. During the 1990s, the Latino population in North Carolina increased by 394%, and this growth brought with it new opportunities and new challenges, both for the Latino immigrants and for the state of North Carolina. One of the programs that experienced this influx was the Early Head Start Program. In particular, Perreira and her colleagues investigate the reported heightened rates of depression among young Latino mothers and the effects of emotional dysregulation on immigrant infants and toddlers.

This accent on Latino families and early education remains central in the contribution from Eugene Carcía, Kent Scribner, and Delis Cuéllar. These authors examine the diversity of Latino families, focusing on the variability of educational outcomes among individual children. Although, as a group, Latino children lag behind other ethnic groups, there is a huge dispersion in their outcomes, which, as described in this chapter, can be linked to characteristics of the families and/or characteristics of the early education programs that are attended (if attended) by these children.

Jennifer E. Glick and Littisha Bates continue the flow of the volume by further unfolding the theme of differentiation in educational outcomes of immigrant children. These authors quantify academic performance using math test scores and link time-based changes in these scores to a combination of family background characteristics, variation in parental school involvement and the variation in the school context. Once again, the data presented in this chapter indicate that immigrant status alone does not predict a single trajectory for children's achievement. Moreover, there exists an interesting dynamic of various factors such that some of them (e.g., non-English-speaking family background) are associated with the initial performance gap, but do not predict the rate of growth in the academic skills after that gap is closed, whereas others (e.g., low socioeconomic status) are predictive of smaller gains, demonstrating negative cumulative effects for children's progress through school. This chapter also points out some directions for interventions: parental attendance at school open-house events is linked to initial math scores, but it is also associated with positive growth in math scores. Thus, programs aimed at bringing parents of immigrant children to school have a potential to reduce the initial achievement gap and accelerate the subsequent growth of immigrant children.

The exploration of "things that work" for the differentiation of educational pathways for immigrant children continues in the context of looking at math achievement in the chapter by Marta Civil and Núria Planas. This contribution provides qualitative analyses of these pathways and is grounded in a phenomenological perspective. The data and their interpretation emphasize the importance of establishing a dialogue between teachers and Latino/a immigrant parents about mathematical education. Civil and Planas argue that such a dialogue would result in the acceptance of shared responsibilities for educating immigrant children in their new home culture, and a more successful negotiation of the similarities and differences between old and new cultures, traditions, and ideas of success. Thus, these two chapters, using different methodologies and different approaches, arrive essentially at the same conclusion—that parental participation in the education of immigrant children is a strong enhancing factor for academic growth and that policy should take this observation into account.

However, such positive parental participation might not be easy to obtain. In the following chapter, Selcuk R. Sirin and Patrice Ryce suggest that one of the reasons for the lack of parental engagement by immigrant parents with mainstream US education has to do with the mismatch between an increasingly heterogeneous student body and a continuously homogeneous teaching profession. This diversity (various cultures and ethnicities and primarily low SES) in students and lack of such (primarily White and middle class) in teachers results in multiple divides in values and interpretations of schooling. These divides exist not only between students and teachers, but also between parents and teachers. Such a shortage of "cultural congruency," as Sirin and Ryce refer to it, is quite costly for immigrant children and might manifest itself in lowered teacher expectations, disproportionate special education referrals, and placement in lower educational tracks.

The issue of disproportional overrepresentation of children of immigrants in special education is closely investigated in the following chapter by Dylan Conger and Elena L. Grigorenko. This chapter provides an overview of what is known at this point about the rates of disability and special education among immigrant youths compared to native-born children. The authors conclude that, although native minority children are repeatedly reported, as a group, to be overrepresented in special education programs, immigrant youths are less likely to participate in such programs. Conger and Grigorenko review the existing, although limited, literature on issues of special education for immigrant children, offer some hypotheses for why such underrepresentation occurs, and suggest some relevant applications for policy and practice that might be put in place.

In their chapter, Ariel Kalil and Robert Crosnoe bring us back to the work with Latin American immigrants. The authors do so in a conceptual summary of their research of the past few years, putting forward a model that was conceived as a means for structuring the social and behavioral research that could potentially be translated into applied programs and interventions for the growing Latin American population. The "heart" of this conceptual model is the connection between parents' (especially mothers') views of and encounters with the school system in which their/her immigrant child is being educated. Correspondingly, the "vessels" structure that supports this "heart" necessarily incorporates parents (especially mothers) into the educational network of their children. And, it is not only the inclusion that matters. According to Kalil and Crosnoe, what is most important is educating parents. Therefore they refer to their model as "a two-generation approach to social mobility—investing in education in the first generation to realize gains in the second."

The importance of taking parents into account is a central theme in the four following chapters of the book. These chapters put the issue of academic achievement and education somewhat aside and concentrate on issues of health and well-being, and social-emotional and cognitive development.

Jennifer Van Hook, Elizabeth Baker, and Claire Altman offer the reader an additional angle in their consideration of the lives of immigrant children in the US—that of their health. These authors present data on health risks confronted by children of immigrants, focusing primarily on issues of weight and being overweight. Specifically, they present evidence that immigrant boys (especially children from Mexico or of Mexican descent) tend to weigh more, and the authors attempt to explain this observation by analyzing factors such as after-school exercise, quality of neighborhoods, and preschool experiences and environments. Van Hook, Baker, and Altman conclude by stating that "the health problems we see among children of immigrants (particularly Mexican boys and girls) are rooted in the environments they encounter at home."

The relevance of home environment for the development of immigrant Chinese children is also discussed in the chapter by Charissa S.L. Cheah and Jin Lin. These authors share with the reader their intimate knowledge of Chinese family life and indicate the junctions at which some of these familial traditions can interfere with and/or enhance the acculturation of Chinese immigrant children into mainstream American culture. Cheah and Lin examine these junctions by discussing facets of the social-emotional development of these immigrant children. They also connect their discourse to the main theme of this volume, the education of immigrant children.

Amy Kerivian Marks, Flannery Patton, and Cynthia García Coll continue the discussion of social-emotional development by addressing ethnic identity development. In their chapter, these authors review theoretical perspectives and the status of research on aspects of immigrant families' cultural socialization (e.g., cultural beliefs and practices), of early peer social processes in schooling, and the role of schools and teachers in balancing the external and internal cultural forces influencing the development of immigrant children.

The discussion of home environment, too, is central to the contribution by Iliana Reyes and Yuuko Uchikoshi. Focusing on emergent literacy, these authors bring the flow of the volume's discussion back to the issue of academic success. They review the current state of knowledge with regard to issues of bilingualism and language and literacy development of young immigrant English-language learners (pre-K–grade 3), focusing primarily on children whose native language is Spanish and stressing the importance of home literacy practices for the current and future academic success of these and other immigrant children. Concluding their chapter, Reyes and Uchikoshi circle back to the issue of the diversity and heterogeneity of immigrant children:

> *Not all* immigrant children—even those who share the same native language—have the same language and literacy learning experiences. Therefore, there is no one correct path to literacy for all children ... As teachers and educational researchers, we should adopt *responsive* teaching and learning practices informed by educational research.

Oscar Barbarin, Micaela Mercado, and Dari Jigjidsuren shaped their contribution to the volume around this issue of diversity, respect, and responsiveness. In the opening of their chapter, they briefly review the history and the current state of immigration in the US, using this information to set up the discussion for their primary focus, the respect for diversity in young children. Stressing the unequivocal acceptance that early stages of social-emotional and intellectual development deeply influence subsequent life characteristics and accomplishments, these authors argue for the penetration of this recognition through all practices at all stages of serving, dealing with, or encountering young immigrant children. If adults respect, respond to, and value diversity in young immigrant children, these children, when exiting childhood and entering the world of adolescence and adulthood, will demonstrate respectful and responsive attitudes to "norms, values, and standards different from their own."

The volume closes with this thought. But, of course, the end of a book, any book, is often only the beginning of something new. In this case, the volume gives the reader a taste of the field, but by no means does it answer all (or even a major part!) of the existing questions, or address all (or even a major part!) of the existing issues. Nor does it offer all there is to offer in the way of policy advice. Yet, the book constructs a platform of cohesive points of view supported by empirical research to survey where the field is and what is known and what is not known in the field.

The volume is based primarily on studies carried out in North America. However, it is contextualized within a larger framework of patterns of migration around the world, which have many things in common with those in North America. And, although the authors of the book readily acknowledge the limitations of their knowledge, they are adamant about one main message of this volume. That the world is changing. That diversity is a given of the future. Patterns of migration intensify in the globalization of the world. These patterns are not only characteristic of the US and North America; they reshape demographic profiles of the world. The world, then, had better be ready to embrace, deal with, and accommodate this diversity so as to maximize every individual's potential to develop and succeed, regardless of their native language, culture, country of origin, and religion. And finding these points of convergence so that the resulting society has a place for everyone and can function in a way that magnifies and embraces positive human potential is a true challenge. Realizing that this challenge exists is the first step to finding ways to meet it successfully. Hopefully, this volume contributes to that realization.

Reference

The Economist. (2008, September 13). Huddled classes. *The Economist, 388,* 68–69.

List of Contributors

Claire Altman, The Pennsylvania State University

Elizabeth Baker, The Pennsylvania State University

Oscar Barbarin, PhD, University of North Carolina, Chapel Hill

Littisha Bates, School of Social and Family Dynamics, Arizona State University

Linda Beeber, PhD, University of North Carolina

Charissa S.L. Cheah, PhD, University of Maryland, Baltimore County

Marta Civil, PhD, University of Arizona

Cynthia García Coll, PhD, Brown University

Dylan Conger, PhD, The George Washington University

Robert Crosnoe, PhD, Department of Sociology and Population Research Center, University of Texas at Austin

Delis Cuéllar, Arizona State University

Jessica Johnson De Feyter, George Mason University

Nancy A. Denton, PhD, University at Albany, State University of New York

Eugene E. García, Arizona State University

Jennifer E. Glick, PhD, School of Social and Family Dynamics, Arizona State University

Elena L. Grigorenko, PhD, Yale University

Donald J. Hernandez, PhD, University at Albany, State University of New York

Diane Holditch-Davis, PhD., R.N. FAAN, Duke University

Dari Jigjidsuren, School of Social Work, University of North Carolina, Chapel Hill

Ariel Kalil, PhD, Harris School of Public Policy Studies and Population Research Center, University of Chicago

Jin Li, PhD, Brown University

Suzanne E. Macartney, University at Albany, State University of New York

Amy Kerivan Marks, PhD, Suffolk University

Lauren Maxwell, University of North Carolina

Micaela Mercado, University of North Carolina, Chapel Hill

India Ornelas, University of North Carolina

Flannery Patton, Brown University

Krista M. Perreira, PhD, University of North Carolina

Núria Planas, Universitat Autonoma de Barcelona

Iliana Reyes, PhD, University of Arizona

Karen Robson, The Geary Institute, University College Dublin

Patrice Ryce, New York University

Todd Schwartz, PhD, University of North Carolina

Kent Scribner, Phoenix Union High School District

Selcuk R. Sirin, PhD, New York University

Timothy Smeeding, PhD, Center for Policy Research, Maxwell School, Syracuse University; Russell Sage Foundation

Ruby Takanishi, PhD, Foundation for Child Development

Yuuko Uchikoshi, PhD, University of California, Davis

Jennifer Van Hook, PhD, The Pennsylvania State University

Coady Wing, Center for Policy Research, Maxwell School, Syracuse University

Adam Winsler, PhD, George Mason University

Index